THE Newark EAGLES TAKE FLIGHT:

THE STORY OF THE 1946 NEGRO LEAGUE CHAMPIONS

EDITED BY FREDERICK C. BUSH AND BILL NOWLIN • ASSOCIATE EDITORS RICH APPLEGATE AND LEN LEVIN

Saociety for American Baseball Research, Inc.
Phoenix, AZ

THE EAGLES TAKE FLIGHT: THE STORY OF THE 1946 NEGRO LEAGUE CHAMPIONS
Edited by Frederick C. Bush and Bill Nowlin
Associate editors Rich Applegate and Len Levin

Society for American Baseball Research, Inc.
Phoenix, AZ

ISBN:
978-1-970159-06-6   Newark Eagles ebook
978-1-970159-07-3   Newark Eagles paper

Book design: Rachael Sullivan
Society for American Baseball Research
Cronkite School at ASU
555 N. Central Ave. #416
Phoenix, AZ 85004
Phone: (602) 496-1460
Web: www.sabr.org
Facebook: Society for American Baseball Research
Twitter: @SABR

Cover photography:
Front cover: Larry Doby slides into home plate on Opening Day – May 5, 1946 (photograph courtesy of the National Baseball Hall of Fame)
Back cover: Larry Doby statue in Paterson, NJ/1947 Newark Eagles logo celebrating the previous season's championship/Monte Irvin statue in Orange, NJ (Photos courtesy of John T. Saccoman/Logo from Black Baseball before Integration, courtesy of St. Johann Press, Haworth, NJ)

CONTENTS

PREFACE AND ACKNOWLEDGMENTS

Team Photo of the 1946 Newark Eagles. Front: Benny Felder, Charles Parks, Clarence Isreal, Biz Mackey, Bob Harvey, Leon Day. Middle: Leon Ruffin, Warren Peace, Jim Wilkes, Bobby Williams, bat boy Ron Murphy. Back: Monte Irvin, Johnny Davis, Lennie Pearson, Len Hooker, Max Manning, Cecil Cole, Rufus Lewis, Larry Doby. *(Courtesy of Hakes Auctions)*

In 2010, the leadership of SABR's Elysian Fields (New Jersey) chapter conceived of the idea to write a book about the 1946 Newark Eagles that would include biographies of the team's players and co-owners. The project was initiated, but, as is often the case in human endeavors, different circumstances converged that put the book on hold. After the July 2017 publication of the SABR book *Bittersweet Goodbye* about the 1948 Birmingham Black Barons and Homestead Grays, a proposal was made to revive the dormant Newark book venture. Rich Puerzer, a member of the Elysian Fields chapter's leadership, provided pertinent information about the genesis and early progress of the project. Members who had previously submitted player biographies were contacted, new authors were solicited for the remaining articles, and things were off and running once again.

One of the primary reasons why the Elysian Fields chapter chose the Newark Eagles as their subject was the team's connection to the chapter's home state of New Jersey. However, the 1946 Negro League champion Eagles were a team for the ages, and to state that they are still of interest to baseball fans all over the globe is no exaggeration. Player-manager Biz Mackey was well-known in Japan for being a member of Negro League teams which toured that Pacific nation prior to World War II. Pitcher Max Manning plied his trade in Mexico, Venezuela, and also Cuba, where he earned the nickname "Profesor." Additionally, there are five Hall of Famers who were members of the franchise in 1946. Leon Day, Larry Doby, Monte Irvin, and Mackey are the players who have joined of the ranks of the immortals. Doby is best known, of course, as the player who integrated the American League with the Cleveland Indians in 1947. The fifth member of this elite club is co-owner Effa Manley, who also holds the distinction of being the only woman enshrined in the National Baseball Hall of Fame in Cooperstown, New York.

This book presents not only the famous individuals, but also tells the tales of the other stars and the lesser-known players insofar as history allows them to be revealed. In addition to biographies of the players, co-owners, and P.A. announcer, there are also articles about Ruppert Stadium, Leon Day's Opening Day no-hitter and a sensational mid-season game, the season's two East-West All-Star games, and the 1946 Negro League World Series between the Eagles and the renowned Kansas City Monarchs. A season timeline and a history of the Eagles' years in Newark help to present the entire context of the team and its lone championship season.

It must be mentioned, however, that researching Negro League teams and players is a difficult endeavor that sometimes results in dead ends. Two players have had to be omitted from this book because their names most likely were reported incorrectly, a not uncommon occurrence in newspapers of the mid-twentieth century. The *New York Amsterdam News* named "George Dusphy" as a Newark player in the team's July 25 game against the Cleveland Buckeyes. The accompanying box score shows that he went 0-for-1 at the plate and played first base, but his name is there spelled "Dusphyn." No player by either name, or by any close approximation – such as "Dunphy" – has been identified. Similarly, the *Philadelphia Inquirer* printed the box score of the Eagles' May 24 game against the Philadelphia Stars in which is found a catcher by the last name of "Fox," who played briefly for Newark that day. "Fox's" identity also remains a mystery and neither he nor "Dusphy" were mentioned in any other game articles or box scores.

That the team, its personnel, and the games could be covered in as great as depth as has been accomplished is a tribute to all the people who have contributed their efforts to this book. Thanks are due to all of the authors who researched and wrote the articles that have been published in this volume. Our editorial staff has also been first-rate. Len Levin is well-known as SABR's copy editor and continues to excel at improving every single article that comes his way. Rich Applegate served as the fact-checker for all articles. He was new to this task and received a baptism of fire by taking on a Negro League project as his first such assignment, but he showed the keen eye for detail that is necessary for the job.

There were numerous other individuals who contributed to the success of this book. First and foremost among this group is Bob Golon, who made several trips to the Newark Public Library to scan all of the documents in the Effa Manley collection and to find articles from Newark-area newspapers that covered the 1946 Eagles. The fruits of his labor were made available to every author who worked on this book. Bob later agreed to write the franchise history article, which was only fitting in light of all the research he had done. James Overmyer, author of the Effa Manley biography titled *Queen of the Negro Leagues*, was generous in providing transcripts of interviews he conducted in the course of researching his own book more than 20 years ago. Jay-Dell Mah, who maintains the Western Canada Baseball website, once again graciously provided us with several player photos for the book.

Additionally, thanks are due to the following individuals: SABR Negro League Committee Chair Larry Lester for the many excellent photographs he contributed via his company Noir-Tech Research, Inc.; Kathryn Irvin, widow of Cal Irvin, for the picture of her late husband and Bryan Steverson for contacting Mrs. Irvin; SABR members John T. Saccoman and Bill Hickman for taking the time to go to historical sites in New Jersey and Maryland to photograph memorials dedicated to 1946 Newark Eagles players; Robert Fitts for his insights into Negro League players' influence on Japanese baseball; Natasha Walker at Jersey City's Lincoln High School for providing Vernon Harrison's high school yearbook photo; Leslie Willis-Lowry, Archivist of the Charles L. Blockson Afro-American Collection at Temple University Libraries for providing several photographs; John Horne of the National Baseball Hall of Fame for providing a large number of the images we have used; Gary Ashwill and Mike Lynch of Seamheads; and thanks as well to Dave Biesel, Rich Bogovich, Ronnie Bolton, Mike Cooney, Robert Cvornyek, Ray Doswell, Peggy Gripshover, Larry Hogan, Ted Knorr, David Lippman, Jacob Pomrenke, Bob Richardson, Harry Snyder, Jeb Stewart, Mark Stewart, Skip Watkins, and John Zinn for help or encouragement along the way.

If anyone who rendered assistance has been omitted, please accept our apologies here. The process was long and our memories are sometimes too short, though unintentionally so.

Each editor would also like to make individual expressions of gratitude:

Frederick: I would like to thank Bill Nowlin for the friendly relationship we have developed over the course of our two Negro League book projects. The third book is already in the works, and I hope there will be more to follow. Lastly, I want to thank my wife, Michelle, for her support of my research and writing activities as well as my three young sons – Michael, Andrew, and Daniel – for catching baseball fever and regularly playing sandlot ball with their friends in the small field beside our house. Sometimes I go outside and play with them. At other times, I take occasional glances at their games from the upstairs window of my home office while I write and am reminded of the reasons why I love the game of baseball and its history so much.

Sez Bill: It has been a great working relationship, Rick. We seem to always be on the same page and it seems like we both enjoy digging in and rooting stuff out – baseball research. We're already underway pursuing your idea of a book on the 1935 Pittsburgh Crawfords. It will be a worthy addition to this growing series. It will be a success, I know, as was this book on the 1946 Newark Eagles, because of all the dedicated work put in by SABR researchers, and all the others who have helped out along the way – public librarians and others to whom we have reached out for help. The spirit in SABR is excellent and I never hesitate to reach into the online SABR directory to try to find someone in a town or city where we might be looking for information on a player, a game, or an event.

Frederick C. Bush

Bill Nowlin

March 2019

JAMES BOYD

BY FREDERICK C. BUSH

The 1946 Newark Eagles pitching staff was filled with front-line hurlers like Leon Day, Max Manning, Rufus Lewis, and Len Hooker. However, the team's roster also lists Jimmy Boyd, who fashioned a 1-0 record with three strikeouts, two walks, and a 1.29 ERA over seven innings in two appearances (one start). Boyd signed a contract with Newark on May 25, 1946, but he was informed by co-owner Effa Manley on July 4 that he was being reassigned to the Asheville Blues and that he should report to his new team on July 8. At that point, Boyd's tenure with the Eagles was at an end after little more than a month. Documents exist to show that he refused to go gently into that good night, although his ultimate baseball fate remains unknown.

James Edward Boyd was born on March 31, 1918, in Winnsboro, South Carolina. He was the second child of farmer Dennis Boyd and his wife, Minnie; the couple eventually had nine children — eight boys and one girl. The 1940 census shows that James Boyd worked as a granite crusher. Presumably he found time to ply his trade as a baseball player during parts of the year, perhaps as a member of a company team.

Any prospective pitching career in the Negro major leagues was put on hold as Boyd served in the US Army from February 17, 1942 to October 18, 1945, during World War II. Seven months after his military discharge, he signed with the Newark Eagles to play for $225 per month.[1]

As Boyd's statistics show, he was seldom used. His lone relief appearance came in a game against the New York Cubans, Newark's bitter rival, on June 10 at Dexter Park in Queens, New York, the home of the renowned semipro Brooklyn Bushwicks team. After starting pitcher Cecil Cole had allowed four runs in seven innings,

Boyd pitched a scoreless eighth, though he did surrender a base hit and two walks that put him in a tenuous position. The Cubans did not score on Warren Peace in the ninth inning either. They won the game, 4-1.[2]

After Newark clinched the Negro National League's first-half pennant with a doubleheader sweep of the Philadelphia Stars on June 30, Boyd made his lone start, against the New York Black Yankees at Ruppert Stadium on July 2. Larry Doby hit a three-run homer as part of Newark's four-run outburst in the third inning and the Eagles triumphed, 7-1.[3] Although the box score for the game is incomplete, Boyd's season statistics make it clear that he pitched six full innings before being relieved by Len Hooker. Newark's victory was Boyd's sole pitching win as a member of the Eagles.

In spite of Boyd's successful outing, Effa Manley may have decided to reassign him as part of the Eagles' preparations for the NNL's second-half race since manager Biz Mackey had used him so sparingly. She wrote a letter that was postdated July 7 – one day before Boyd was to report to Asheville – to C.L. Moore, the owner and manager of the Negro Southern League's Blues. In a rarity for the Negro leagues, the Blues served as a farm team for the Eagles. Boyd was supposed to present Manley's letter to Moore when he reported to his new team.

Manley's missive made clear the reason for Boyd's reassignment, as she wrote:

> I believe him to be a nice person so far as conduct is concerned, and if he gets his control he will be a good pitcher. I have seen him pitch some good games.

I believe in your league he may not be pressing so hard, and it will give him a chance to loosen up a little.[4]

Boyd's statistics do not seem to indicate that he was performing poorly and Manley appears still to have considered him to be a good prospect, so he might have had a future with the Eagles. However, it is clear that Boyd was not yet prepared to go to Asheville. He may have felt that he had not been given enough of a chance to prove his mettle or that his success in his brief appearances merited keeping him on the Eagles' roster; thus, he took actions to try to invalidate his reassignment to the Asheville club.

Evidence for Boyd's actions is found in another letter that Manley wrote, this time to team attorney Jerome Kessler and also dated July 7, 1946, though the content indicates that it actually was written on July 8. The fact that Boyd was threatening to sue – whether for breach of contract or to have his contract voided – becomes apparent from the second paragraph, in which Manley wrote:

> I am enclosing the letter from the Atty. Also a copy of the letter I had written to Mr Moore of our Ashville N. Carolina farm club. This letter was to have been delivered by Mr. Boyd. Also enclosing the contract. In the contract paragraph 3, and 5, and 5b, seem to me to take care of this situation.[5]

She also informed Kessler that Newark had issued a paycheck to Boyd dated July 7 and that the Asheville club had "agreed to pay him the same salary we were."[6] She expressed her concern that, "(i)n view of what has happened, if Asheville learns about it, I doubt if they will want him. No club wants what is known as a bad actor on the team. They can cause so much trouble."[7] Boyd's actions had obviously changed Manley's earlier opinion of him as "a nice person so far as conduct is concerned."

In reference to the pertinent sections of Boyd's contract that Manley referenced, they are as follows:

3) The player will faithfully serve the Club or any other Club to which, in conformity with the agreements above recited, this contract may be assigned and pledges himself to the American public to conform to high standards of personal conduct, of fair play and good sportsmanship.

5. (a) In case of assignment of this contract to another Club, the Player shall promptly report to the assignee club; accrued salary shall be payable when he so reports; and each successive assignee shall become liable to the Player for his salary during his term of service with such assignee, and the Club shall not be liable therefor. If the player fails to report as above specified, he shall not be entitled to salary after the date he receives notice of assignment.

(b) This contract may be terminated at any time by the Club or by any assignee upon five days' written notice to the Player.[8]

Based upon these clauses in Boyd's contract, it is obvious that he had no legal leg to stand on. However, no further documents exist to confirm whether he finally reported to Asheville or simply quit playing professional baseball; given the lack of any further news accounts or statistics on Boyd, the latter option is more likely.

Little is known of Boyd after the events of July 1946. He eventually married Lillie Bell, the daughter of Henry and Ida Bell of Fairfield County, South Carolina. (Boyd's hometown of Winnsboro is in Fairfield County as well.) It is unknown whether the couple ever had children. James Boyd died of cerebral thrombosis at the youthful age of 47 on October 14, 1965, in a Columbia, South Carolina, Veterans Administration hospital. He is buried in Saint John Baptist Church Cemetery in Winnsboro. His widow, Lillie B. Boyd, died in Winnsboro at the age of 71 on March 3, 2001; she is buried beside James.

ACKNOWLEDGMENT

Gratitude is here expressed to Bob Golon, who made several trips to the Newark Public Library, scanned every document in the Effa Manley Collection, and made them all available to the authors of the present volume. Bob's actions show the spirit of collegiality that is so often present among those who endeavor to research the history of the Negro Leagues.

SOURCES

All player statistics and team records listed in this article were taken from Seamheads.com.

Ancestry.com was consulted for census, military service, and death information.

NOTES

1   Negro National League of Professional Baseball Clubs, Uniform Player's Contract for James Boyd, 1946, Effa Manley Collection, Newark Public Library.

2   "N.Y. Cuban Nine Trounces Eagles in Dexter Game," *Brooklyn Daily Eagle*, June 11, 1946: 14.

3   "Eagles Beat Yanks, 7-1," *Newark Star-Ledger*, July 3, 1946: 15.

4   Effa Manley, Letter to Mr. C.L. Moore, July 7, 1946, Effa Manley Collection, Newark Public Library.

5   Effa Manley, Letter to Atty. Jerome Kessler, July 7, 1946, Effa Manley Collection, Newark Public Library.

6   Ibid.

7   Ibid.

8   Uniform Player's Contract for James Boyd, 1946.

Negro National League of Professional Baseball Clubs

Uniform Player's Contract

Parties   The ......Newark Eagles Baseball Club......

herein called the Club, and ......James Boyd......

of ......Winnsboro S, Carolina Route 8......, herein called the Player.

Recital   The Club is a member of the Negro National League of Professional Baseball Clubs. As such, and jointly with the other members of the League, it is a party to the Negro National League Constitution and to agreements and rules with the Negro American League of Professional Baseball Clubs and its constituent clubs. The purpose of these agreements and rules is to insure to the public wholesome and high-class professional baseball by defining the relations between Club and Player, between club and club, and between league and league.

Agreement   In view of the facts above recited the parties agree as follows:

Employment   1. The Club hereby employs the Player to render skilled service as a baseball player in connection with all games of the Club during the year ......194 6...... including the Club's training season, the Club's exhibition games, the Club's playing season, any all-star games and the Negro World Series, (or any other official series in which the Club may participate and in any receipts of which the player may be entitled to share); and the Player covenants that he will perform with diligence and fidelity and service stated and such duties as may be required of him in such employment.

Salary   2. For the service aforesaid the Club will pay the Player a salary of $ ......225.00...... per month from ......1st...... to ......, as follows:

......in semi-monthly installments after the commencement of the playing season on the ......1st...... and ...... day of each month covered by this contract, unless the Player is "abroad" with the Club for the purpose of playing games, in which event the amount then due shall be paid on the first week-day after the return "home" of the Club, the terms "home" and "abroad" meaning respectively at and away from the city in which the Club has its baseball field.

If the player is in the service of the Club for part of the month only, he shall receive such proportion of the salary above mentioned, as the number of days of his actual employment bears to the number of days in said month.

Loyalty   3. The Player will faithfully serve the Club or any other Club to which, in conformity with the agreements above recited, this contract may be assigned, and pledges himself to the American public to conform to high standards of personal conduct, of fair play and good sportsmanship.

Service   4. (a) The player agrees that, while under contract or reservation, he will not play baseball (except post-season games as hereinafter stated) otherwise than for the Club or a Club assignee hereof; that he will not engage in professional boxing or wrestling; and that, except with the written consent of the Club or its assignee, he will not engage in any game or exhibition of football, basketball, hockey or other athletic sport.

Post-season Games   (b) The Player agrees that, while under contract or reservation, he will not play in any post-season baseball games except in conformity with the Negro Major League Rules, or with or against an ineligible player or team.

Assignment   5. (a) In case of assignment of this contract to another Club, the Player shall promptly report to the assignee club; accrued salary shall be payable when he so reports; and each successive assignee shall become liable to the Player for his salary during his term of service with such assignee, and the Club shall not be liable therefor. If the player fails to report as above specified, he shall not be entitled to salary after the date he receives notice of assignment.

Termination   (b) This contract may be terminated at any time by the Club or by any assignee upon five days' written notice to the Player.

Regulations   6. The Player accepts as part of this contract the Regulations printed on the third page hereof, and also such reasonable modifications of them and such other reasonable regulations as the Club may announce from time to time.

Agreements and Rules

7.   The Negro National League Constitution, and the Negro Major League Agreements and Rules and all amendments thereto hereafter adopted, are hereby made a part of this contract, and the Club and Player agree to accept, abide by and comply with the same and all decisions of the League President or Board of Owners, pursuant thereto.

Renewal

8.   (a) On or before April 1st (or if Sunday, then the succeeding business day) of the year next following the last playing season covered by this contract, by written notice to the Player at his address following his signature hereto (or if none be given, then at his last address of record with the club), the Club or any assignee hereof may renew this contract for the term of that year except that the salary shall be such as the parties may then agree upon, or in default of agreement the Player will accept such salary rate as the Club may fix, or else will not play baseball otherwise than for the Club or for an assignee hereof.

(b) The Club's right of reservation of the Player, and of renewal of this contract as aforesaid, and the promise of the Player not to play otherwise than with the Club or an assignee hereof, have been taken into consideration in determining the salary specified herein and the undertaking by the Club to pay said salary is the consideration for both said reservation, renewal option and promise, and the Player's service.

Disputes

9.   In case of dispute between the Player and the Club or any assignee hereof, the same shall be referred to the League President as an umpire, and his decision shall be accepted by all parties as final; and the Club and the Player agree that any such dispute, or any claim or complaint by either party against the other, shall be presented to the League President within sixty days from the date it arose.

10.   This contract is subject to Federal or State legislation, regulations, executive or other official orders, or other governmental action, now or hereafter in effect, respecting Military, Naval, Air or other governmental service, which may, directly or indirectly, affect the Player, the Club or the League; and subject also to all rules, regulatons, decisions or other action by the Negro National League or the League President, including the right of the League President to suspend the operation of this contract during any National emergency.

Supplemental Agreements

11.   The player expressly covenants and agrees that in the event of his breach of contract the Club shall have the right to apply to any court of competent jurisdiction, domestic or foreign, for an injunction, or for relief, in such manner as shall be deemed necessary.

12.   The Club and Player covenant that this contract fully sets forth all understandings and agreements between them, and agree that no other understandings or agreements, whether heretofore or hereafter made, shall be valid, recognizable, or of any effect whatsoever, unless expressly set forth in a new or supplemental contract executed by the Player and the Club (acting through its duly authorized agent), and complying with all agreements and rules to which this contract is subject.

Signed in duplicate this **25th** day of **May** , A. D. 194 **6**
[SEAL]

Newark Eagles
(Club)

By *Effa Manley*
(President)

James E. Boyd
(Player)

Asheville S C
(Home address of Player)

Witness:

James Boyd signed this standard Negro National League player's contract with the Newark Eagles on May 25, 1946. He was reassigned to the Asheville Blues on July 4, marking the end of his career in the Negro major leagues. *(Courtesy Newark Public Library)*

HARRY BUTTS

BY MARGARET M. GRIPSHOVER

Harry Butts was a left-handed pitcher who played professional baseball from 1946 through 1953. His résumé included stints in the Negro American League, the ManDak League, the Piedmont League, winter-league play in Puerto Rico and Venezuela, and at least two starts in a Newark Eagles uniform in 1946. In the early 1950s he was one of the first African-Americans to be signed by a team in the Piedmont League.

Harry Thomas Butts was born in Whaleyville, Virginia, on February 2, 1922, to Walter Norfleet and Mary (Downing) Butts. Whaleyville is in the southeastern corner of Virginia, in what was once known as Nansemond County, which in 1974 was reorganized as the Independent City of Suffolk. Today, the region in which Suffolk is situated is generally known as Hampton Roads.

Harry Butts's father, who was known by his middle name, Norfleet, was a truck farmer whose land was on the edge of the Great Dismal Swamp. The surname Butts, and his father's middle name Norfleet, were both last names of slave owners in the region, some of whom were among the area's earliest settlers. Norfleet Butts named his son Harry, after his own father. Harry had three brothers and a sister.

While Norfleet operated the truck farm in the 1920s and 1930s, Mary worked in a nearby factory.[1] The Whaleyville area's largest employers were packers of Virginia hams and local peanut processors, including Planters Peanuts, which was founded in Suffolk in 1912.[2] Mary died in 1933, and sometime between then and 1940, the family moved from their farm into the city of Suffolk.[3]

Pitcher Harry Butts, shown here in an Indianapolis Clowns uniform, made two appearances as a Newark Eagle in June 1946 and posted a 1-1 record. *(Courtesy of Jay-Dell Mah/Western Canada Baseball)*

In 1935 Norfleet married Odessa B. Shambley, who was nearly 20 years his junior.

Two of Harry's brothers left Suffolk after 1940 and headed north to Suffolk County on Long Island, New York. It is possible that Harry's brief career with the Newark Eagles was facilitated through visits to the two brothers. It is more likely, however, that the Newark Eagles learned of the left-handed pitching prospect during their frequent exhibition and league games in the Hampton Roads area during the 1930s and 1940s, the earliest visit being a game against Washington's Hilldale Giants in 1938.[4]

Little is known of Harry's life before 1942, when he registered for the World War II draft. Was he the teenager named Harry Butts who was shot in the legs during a late-night fight at a club in Suffolk in 1937?[5] Did he attend Booker T. Washington High School, the first high school for African-Americans in Suffolk? Is it possible that Butts pitched for the Suffolk Giants in the segregated Virginia-Carolina League prior to his service during World War II?[6] With the passage of time and the lack of documentation, the answers to these questions might never be confidently answered. It is unlikely, however, that Butts graduated from Booker T. Washington High School. His Army draft card credits him with only a "grammar school" education.[7]

The 1940s brought tremendous changes to Butts's life. It was a complicated decade replete with triumphs and turbulence. In June 1942, when Harry registered for the draft, he was 20 years old, unemployed, and living with his father in Suffolk.[8] Later that year, he married Carrie Letha Rollins in Suffolk. At the time, both worked at a local packing plant.[9] Four months after their wedding, Butts was a private in the US Army. His enlistment papers list his height as 5-feet-8 and his weight at 148 pounds.[10] Less than nine months later, on September 24, 1943, Butts was honorably discharged with a Certificate of Disability for Discharge, the first formal indication that he suffered from mental illness.[11] Butts was not alone in this regard. In 1942, roughly 40 percent of all early discharges from the Army were CDDs.[12]

It is not known if Butts received any treatment after his diagnosis by the Army, or if he played in any professional baseball games between 1943 and 1945. One thing is certain, however: His life was beginning to change. The first of his nine children, Harry T. Butts Jr., was born in Suffolk in 1946, a few months before Harry made his debut as a left-handed pitcher for the Newark Eagles.

On June 5, 1946, Butts took the mound for the first time for the Eagles, in a game against the Baltimore Elite Giants at Memorial Field in Hagerstown, Maryland.[13] There was another Butts on the field that evening: Tommy "Pee Wee" Butts, the crack shortstop for the Elite Giants, who was unrelated to Harry. It was not a pleasant experience for the rookie southpaw from Suffolk. Harry Butts was roughed up for seven runs in the second inning and the Eagles fell to the Elite Giants 13-2.[14]

A week after his forgettable debut, Butts pitched for the Eagles in an exhibition game against the Lloyd Athletic Club in Chester, Pennsylvania. This time the outcome was more positive. Butts (whose first name was given as Harvey in the Chester newspaper) and the Eagles won, 7-2, with Warren Peace sealing the deal in relief.[15] Butts struck out two and walked two. He scored one of Newark's seven runs, on a double by Clarence "Pint" Isreal.[16]

After the victory over the Lloyd A.C., Butts was never seen in a Newark Eagles uniform again. Why he was cut from the roster is unknown. Possibly he was injured. Perhaps he was a classic example of a "cup of coffee" player – just a temporary hire to fill in a gap in the lineup. Regardless of the cause, Butts did not play another game for Newark.

It was nearly a year before Butts returned to baseball. This time it was for a semipro team, the Norfolk Royals of the Negro Carolina League. On July 15, 1947, Butts took the mound in relief for the Royals in an 8-6 loss to the Durham (North Carolina) Eagles in Durham.[17] Later that season, an account of another Royals game mentioned a pitcher named Walter Butts.[18] This appears to be a reporting error.

Harry Butts returned to pitch for the Royals in 1948. That year the team had a new name, the Norfolk Newport-News Royals, and a new league, the Negro American Association. In July the Royals played Butts's old team the Eagles and Butts was the starting pitcher in the 9-7 victory at High Rock Park in Norfolk.[19] A month later, on August 22, at Mooers Park in Norfolk, Butts was on the losing end of a battle against his former Newark Eagles teammate Warren Peace, who was pitching for the Richmond Giants.[20] Peace and the Giants won, 9-3, over Butts and his Negro American Association All-Stars.[21] That game appears to have been Butts's final start in 1948. The unhappy end to his season was compounded by personal grief: Harry's father, Walter Norfleet Butts Sr., died in Suffolk on October 24, from brain and stomach cancer at the age of 64.

In 1949 Butts pitched for teams in in two distinctly different geographic regions. He started the year by playing for San Juan in the Puerto Rican Winter League.[22] In March he signed with the Indianapolis Clowns of the Negro American League.[23] For Butts, 1949 was also the year in which he reinvented himself as an untested younger man – as a 20-year-old "rookie find" for the Clowns.[24] In truth, he was 27 years old. While it was not uncommon for ballplayers to shave a few years off their ages, not everyone described Butts as a fresh face, and there seemed to be some confusion as to his real age and experience. An article in the *Chicago Defender* called Butts one of the Clowns' "veteran performers."[25] Later in the season, however, the *Defender* ran a photo of Butts and described him as a "prize rookie" and a "youthful southpaw [who] got off to a slow start, which was blamed on a lack of experience, but is hitting winning form. ..."[26]

After the Clowns season ended, Butts traveled with the team for a barnstorming tour in the South. He played in several games in Florida, including one against the Miami Giants in which he was described in the local newspaper as a "prize rookie" and a "stellar sepia" hurler.[27] His last start and win for the Clowns in 1949 was a sparkling five-hitter against the Miami Giants on October 9 at Miami Stadium.[28] Although he had some tough losses for Indianapolis in the summer of 1949, he was good enough to represent the East in the annual East West All-Star Game and was asked to return to the Clowns for the 1950 season.[29]

For Butts the early 1950s were hallmarked by familiar surroundings, new beginnings, and an abrupt end to his professional baseball career. In 1950 he was one of the top hurlers for the Clowns. He struck out 107 batters, second only to a teammate, 19-year-old Cuban native Raul Galata, who led the NAL with 120 strikeouts.[30] Again Butts also was named to the East All-Star squad.[31] As the 1950 season came to a close for the Clowns, it was widely reported that Butts had caught the attention of major-league baseball. In September rumors were swirling that Butts was being scouted by the Boston Braves after a one-hit performance against the Philadelphia Stars.[32] Were the Braves really interested in Butts, or was this just a public-relations stunt orchestrated by Clowns owner Syd Pollock? News of the possible signing of Butts by the Braves was picked up by dozens of newspapers. Such an addition to the Braves roster was not outside the realm of possibility; the team had already signed an African-American player, Sam Jethroe, earlier in the year.[33] Pollock later lamented that Butts "missed out on an opportunity to move up," and claimed that he had been scouted by the Chicago White Sox and Brooklyn Dodgers.[34] After the 1950 NAL season was over, Butts joined the Clowns on a barnstorming tour facing Jackie Robinson's All-Stars. One notable performance for Butts was his 7-6 victory over the All-Stars in Miami.[35] When all was said and done, at the end of 1950 no major-league club had made an offer to Butts.

Butts returned to play for the Clowns in 1951 but left the team in midseason, jumping to the Brandon Greys of the semipro ManDak League.[36] At the time he was one of the NAL's leading pitchers with a 6-1 record.[37] It was reported that Pollock was incensed at Butt's defection, but he was not the only Clowns player to head northward to play in the ManDak League, presumably for a better payday and a higher quality of life.[38] Pollock, however, may have also been a bit disingenuous with his outrage. According to the *Minot* (North Dakota) *Daily News,* three players were furnished to the Minot Mallards by "Syd Pollock of the Indianapolis Clowns, who supplies colored players to Brandon."[39]

Butts was one of dozens of African-American baseball players (many from then-failing Negro League teams) who headed north to the Mandak League, which straddled the US-Canadian border. Even Satchel Paige was lured to the league after he was released by the Cleveland Indians. Paige pitched a handful of games for the Minot Mallards – all that the team's owners claimed they could afford.[40] Butts played for the Brandon (Manitoba) Greys in 1951 and 1952. In 1951 Lloyd "Pepper" Bassett, former star catcher for the Birmingham Black Barons, was his backstop.[41] Butts finished his first season with an impressive 9-0 record, one of only three Mandak League pitchers with perfect seasons through the mid-1950s.[42] When the 1951 League season ended, Butts played one season in the Dominican Summer League, for the Estrellas Orientales.[43] After his hitch in the Caribbean was over, he barnstormed as a member of the Negro League All-Stars, traveling with Jackie Robinson's Major League Negro League All-Stars.[44]

Butts embarked on a new baseball adventure in 1952 when he signed with the Vancouver Capilanos of the Class-A Western International League. He was the fourth African-American to sign with the Capilanos.[45] As he had done when he had joined the Indianapolis Clowns, Butts shaved a few years off his real age. He was advertised as a 23-year-old "rookie" even though he had turned 30 the month before.[46] Vancouver classified Butts as a rookie because it was his first year in Organized Baseball, and touted his 1.94 ERA with the Clowns and recent success pitching in winter leagues.[47] The club claimed that Butts had amassed an impressive 20-4 record while playing for three different teams in 1951.[48] The Capilanos actively promoted Butts as their next star player, describing him as a "left-handed hurler who comes off the mound as though jet propelled."[49] In a preseason article, the *Vancouver Sun* heaped praise on the southpaw.[50] Capilanos manager Robert "Bob" Brown noted Butts's diverse résumé and powerful physique and observed that "all that jumpin' didn't hurt his throwin'" and as a "5-foot-11, 168-pounder, Butts is regarded as major league timber, especially if he ever stops bouncing around like a Mexican jumping bean."[51] The descriptions of Butts's physical characteristics were likely as accurate as his age. It is unlikely that Butts grew three inches taller after he was measured by the Army in 1942, and again in 1943, as being 5-feet-8.[52]

Butts was unable to live up to the Capilanos' hype. His brief association with Vancouver in the spring of 1952 was not a memorable one. During spring training, Butts showed some promise as a starter and reliever but as the regular season unfolded, his wildness on the mound became a more frequent occurrence. It was not uncommon for Butts to hit a batter with a pitch, and at least once, he clocked two.[53] In addition to his control problems, by early May of 1952, Butts seemed to be "running out of gas with each of his starts."[54] Manager Brown's frank assessment: "I am disappointed in Harry

Butts … a young man with all the ability in the world."[55] Brown felt that Butts "doesn't concentrate enough on the club he's with."[56] He added that Butts, "always has aspirations elsewhere, a habit that could cost him a wonderful career."[57] Butts appears to have been unmoved by his manger's criticisms and embraced his vagabond lifestyle. In a letter he wrote to former Capilanos teammate Paul Jones, he said that he "liked the wheat country just fine."[58]

By the third week in May, Butts was released.[59] He headed 1,200 miles east to Brandon, to play for the Greys in the Mandak League. His lack of success in Vancouver was not a fluke. His glory days as a marquee pitcher were in his rear-view mirror and the road ahead was not an easy one to travel. The control problems that plagued Butts in Vancouver continued to haunt him in 1952 season in the Mandak League. In a game against the Carman Cardinals in June, Butts gave up 10 runs in three innings in a relief appearance.[60] Later in the season, he threw a workmanlike six-hitter to give the Greys a 4-3 win over the Cardinals.[61] But his walks were starting to outnumber his strikeouts and he was losing more games than he was winning. Butts's struggles were mirrored by the financial challenges faced by the Mandak League and the Greys. By early summer there were concerns that the Greys would not be able to field a nine-man roster.[62] The club finished the 1952 season $18,000 in the red.[63]

Butts earned the dubious honor of leading the league in losses – nine, against five victories.[64] He pitched 111 innings and gave up 103 hits, walked 73 batters, struck out 96, and tossed seven wild pitches.[65] There are several possible reasons for Butts's decline in 1952. First, as historian Barry Swanton concluded, Butts underperformed in the Mandak in 1952 because opposing hitters were "catching up to him."[66] But two other factors may have also played a role: the stress from being 1,800 miles away from his family in Suffolk, which, by 1952 included four young children, and possibly his struggles with mental illness that had been diagnosed by Army physicians a decade earlier.

After the Mandak season ended in August 1952, Butts returned home to Virginia and pitched a handful of games for the Newport News Royals. On September 14, 1952, at Peninsula War Memorial Stadium. Butts threw a one-hitter against Vic Zodda's All-Stars, winning the game 8-1.[67] Some of the batters he faced were former minor-league players Pres Elkins and Ed Wopinek, the latter of whom spoiled Butts's no-hit bid with a two-out double in the ninth inning.[68] Although the attendance was just 594, Butts's nearly flawless nine innings on the mound were so memorable that the game was included in the year-end list of Newport News sports highlights.[69] Chances are that few of the 594 in attendance came to see Harry Butts. The real star of the game was Willie Mays, who played for the Royals during his Army service at nearby Fort Eustis.[70] It is worth noting that Vic Zodda, who was the catcher

for his All-Stars, was in 1952 the general manager of the all-white Newport News Dodgers minor-league team. In March Zodda predicted that 1952 was the year in which the color line would be broken in the all-white Piedmont League.[71] Zodda said, "I know of one club that is already dickering with two Negro players in an attempt to sign them for this season," and that it will be accomplished because "none of the Piedmont League cities have laws against Negroes playing on white teams."[72] Actually the Piedmont League did not integrate its squads for another year. It was not until 1953 when Butts and a handful of other black players helped make Zodda's prediction come true.

In the spring of 1953, for the first time in its 34-year history, Piedmont League teams started signing African-American players.[73] It should be noted, however, that with the addition of the York White Roses (formerly of the then-defunct Interstate League), a team that already had African-American players on its roster, the Piedmont League was integrated by default.[74] York had at least two African-American players on its roster prior to joining the Piedmont League. Samuel Green was added to York's bullpen in 1951 and William "Bill" Springfield, was assigned by the St. Louis Browns to the White Roses in the spring of 1952.[75] Springfield signed with the White Roses on February 12, 1953, which made him the first African-American to play for a Piedmont League team.[76]

The first Piedmont League team that was member of the league prior to 1953 to "officially drop the color bar" and invite black players to tryouts was the Portsmouth Merrimacs.[77] Harry Butts was one of them and thus helped to make Piedmont League history. His tenure with Portsmouth, however, was brief and unsatisfying. After Butts took spring training with the Merrimacs, he lost his first and only game for Portsmouth, on May 1, 1953, against the Roanoke Red Sox, 3-2.[78] Butts was called out of the bullpen in the bottom of the 10th with the score tied, 2-2.[79] Butts issued two walks in the 10th which helped Roanoke to score the winning run.[80] Less than two weeks later, Butts was gone from the Merrimacs and signed with the league's Richmond Colts (also known as the Mustangs).[81] Butts was not the first black player for Richmond. A month earlier, the Colts had signed their first African-American player, right-handed pitcher Whit Graves, Butts's former Indianapolis Clowns teammate.[82] The two had something else in common: Both were suspended from playing in the Negro American League when they jumped from the Clowns to teams in the Mandak League in 1951.[83]

Butts lost his first start for Richmond, on May 23 against his former Portsmouth Merrimac teammates.[84] In the 6-3 loss before 887 spectators, Butts issued six walks, struck out four, and hit one batter.[85] His first win for the Colts came five days later, when Richmond edged York, 5-4.[86] It was true that the only team with a worse record in the Piedmont League than the "Hapless Colts" was the York Roses, but for Butts, a win was a win.[87]

By July 1953 Butts had developed a reputation in the Piedmont League; his flashes of brilliance were diminished by his chronic control problems. Such was the case in a start on July 14, when he threw a "sparkling four-hit, 3-0 shutout" against the Hagerstown Braves.[88] It was just his second win of the season. One reporter wrote that Butts, a "lefty whose usual characteristic is wildness, settled down tonight," and issued one walk and struck out nine.[89] The *Petersburg Progress-Index* agreed and noted that "Hagerstown fell victim, more or less, to an oddity, a steady, almost walk-less performance by the Richmond wild man, lefty Harry Butts … who usually walks himself right out of the box."[90] Sportswriter Steve Guback of the *Richmond Times-Dispatch* described Butts as a, "slender Negro left-hander," who was a "habitually wild" pitcher, and that it was "rumored before the game that [Butts] might be released if he failed to come through, and apparently he knew it."[91] Hagerstown manager Dutch Dorman was likely neither impressed by Butts nor surprised at his nine's poor performance. In June, he expressed his disappointment in the level of play the Piedmont League by blaming the Korean War draft for the lack of good players, the lure of jobs with better paydays than "B" leagues could offer, and television for lack of fan support.[92] Dorman may have just been venting his frustrations with his team's lack of success and tasting some sour grapes. He and his Hagerstown Braves were the Interstate League champions prior to migrating to the Piedmont League.[93]

The summer of 1953 was a roller-coaster for Butts's career as a pitcher in the Piedmont League. There were more valleys than peaks, and the ride came to screeching halt in September. After a few promising performances early in the season, the expectations dimmed significantly. By August, Butts had lost 11 starts and earned the title of "losingest pitcher" in the Piedmont League.[94] On September 7, 1953, in a losing effort against the Norfolk Tars (the eventual League champions), Butts "couldn't find the plate [and] threw eight bad pitches to walk [two players]."[95] With the loss, 31-year-old Harry Butts's tenure with the Tars ended with a dismal 3-13 won-lost record. It was also his last start as a professional ballplayer. The season finale was a bitter end for Butts and the Richmond Colts. The team finished in last place in the Piedmont League.[96] Not only had Butts played his last game, but the Richmond team itself said farewell to the Piedmont League. In December 1953, owner Eddie Mooers sold the Richmond club to Harry C. Seibold, who changed the team's name to the Richmond Virginians and it became a member of the Triple-A International League.[97]

After his baseball career ended in September 1953, Butts faded into baseball anonymity. It is possible that he could have con-tinued playing for one of the local amateur nines in the Suffolk area, but if he pitched in another game, it was not reported. His days playing for teams from such far-flung locations as San Juan and Vancouver behind him, Butts and his wife, Carrie, focused on raising their nine children in their house in Suffolk. As adults, five of their nine children remained in southeastern Virginia. Four of their seven sons headed northward to New York, eventually settling on Long Island.

Harry Thomas Butts died on April 7, 1977, at the Veterans Administration Hospital in Hampton, Virginia. He was just 52 years old. Before being admitted to the hospital, he was employed at the Virginia Packing Company, a meat packing and processing plant in Suffolk.[98] The cause of his death was cardiac arrest as a result of a collapsed lung (pneumothorax).[99] Two conditions that contributed to his death were "encephalomalacia of the left parietal lobe" and "chronic schizophrenia."[100] Butts was survived by his wife Carrie, all nine of his children, and two siblings.[101] His obituary mentioned that he "played baseball with several leagues."[102] Butts is buried in the George Washington Carver Memorial Cemetery in Suffolk with a bronze veteran's marker to honor his Army service.

Harry Butts overcame many challenges to pursue a career in baseball. He spent eight years as a pitcher in semipro and professional baseball, and played for teams in at least four countries. One of those teams was the Newark Eagles. Butts played in only two games in an Eagles uniform and did not play for Newark in the 1946 Negro World Series. His association with the Eagles was so brief that his full name is rarely mentioned in the team's records. When his name did appear on the sports pages, it was sometimes misspelled as Harvey Butts, as it was in a newspaper account of his second start for Newark.[103] Others referred to him as Hank, Henry, or sometimes as Lefty Butts.[104] Based on the numbers, Butts will likely be remembered more for his peripatetic career, wild southpaw pitches, and inconsistent performances than for his periodic flashes of brilliance. Those memories, however, should not obscure his legacy that has been overlooked by sportswriters and baseball historians. And that is that he was one of the first African-American players to take the field in the Piedmont League in 1953, and helped to integrate what had been an all-white league. That accomplishment, more than any won-lost statistic, is his enduring contribution to baseball.

NOTES

1   US Census Bureau, 1920 Census; US Census Bureau, 1930 Census.

2   Patrick Evans-Hylton, *The Suffolk Peanut Festival* (Charleston, South Carolina: Arcadia, 2004), 38.

3   Commonwealth of Virginia, Certificate of Death, August 31, 1933; US Census Bureau, 1940 Census.

4   "Hilldale Play Two," *Richmond Times Dispatch,* June 29, 1938: 12; "Crack Negro Nines to Play Here Tonight," *Newport News Daily Press,* September 10, 1941: 8.

5   "Negro Youth Shot, Another Arrested," *Norfolk Virginian-Pilot,* September 28, 1937: 15.

6   "Tidewater Giants Defeat Suffolk in Loop Opener," *Newport News Daily Press,* May 6, 1940: 5.

7   US Army World War II Draft Record, January 28, 1943.

8   US Army, Selective Service Enlistment Record, Registrar's Report, June 30, 1942.

9   Commonwealth of Virginia, Certificate of Marriage, September 28, 1942.

10 US Army, Selective Service Enlistment Record, Registrar's Report, June 30, 1942.

11 US Army Selective Service Enlistment Record, Discharge Document, September 24, 1943.

12 Hans Pols and Stephanie Oak, "War and Military Mental Health: US Psychiatric Response in the 20th Century," *American Journal of Public Health,* December 2007: 2132-2142.

13 "Elite Giants Win," *Daily Times* (Salisbury, Maryland), June 6, 1946: 14.

14 Ibid.

15 "Lloyd Falls Prey to Newark Eagles, 7-2," *Delaware County Times* (Chester, Pennsylvania), June 13, 1946: 26.

16 Ibid.

17 "Durham Eagles Win," *Durham* (North Carolina) *Morning Herald,* July 15, 1947: 9.

18 "Johnson Hurls Victory Over Royals by 4 to 3," *Richmond Times Dispatch,* September 5, 1948: 26.

19 "NN Down Jersey City Nine," *Newport News Daily Press,* July 14, 1948: 8.

20 "Giants Divide Pair of Games with All-Stars," *Richmond Times Dispatch,* August 23, 1948: 13.

21 Ibid.

22 Center for Negro League Research, "Negro Leaguers in Puerto Rico," accessed online, cnlbr.org/Portals/0/RL/Negro%20Leaguers%20in%20Puerto%20Rico.pdf.

23 "Clowns Ready for Workouts," *Chicago Defender,* March 5, 1949: 14.

24 "Expect a Crowd at Flaherty Field Tuesday Night," *New Castle* (Pennsylvania) *News,* July 23, 1949: 15.

25 "Clowns Ready for Workouts," *Chicago Defender,* March 5, 1949: 14.

26 "No Buts About It," *Chicago Defender,* July 23, 1949: 16.

27 "For [sic] Top Hurlers Here as Clowns," *Miami* (Florida) *News,* October 3, 1949: 19.

28 "Negro Teams Play Second Game Here," *Miami News,* October 10, 1949: 17.

29 "Chandler to Open East, West Game," *Chicago Tribune,* August 14, 1949: 67.

30 "NAL Revises Plans for College Stars," *Pittsburgh Courier,* March 10, 1951: 8; "Indianapolis Clowns Win Three Exhibition Games," *Atlanta Daily World,* April 7, 1951: 5.

31 Russ J. Cowans, "Fans Storm Chicago for East-West Game," *Chicago Defender,* August 19, 1950: 1.

32 Les Matthews, "Sports Train," *New York Age,* September 30, 1950: 27.

33 Bob Holbrook, "Streakin' Sam Proud of His Speed, Hopes to Be Worthy of Braves Cap," *Boston Globe,* March 1, 1950.

34 "Peeples Sold to Dodger Farm Club," *Pittsburgh Courier,* July 7, 1951: 14.

35 Howard Kleinberg, "Clowns Nose Out All-Stars by 7-6," *Miami News,* November 6, 1950: 18.

36 Peeples Sold to Dodger Farm Club," *Pittsburgh Courier,* July 7, 1951: 14.

37 Ibid.

38 Ibid.

39 "Pitcher to Appear in 3 [sic] Tilts," *Minot* (North Dakota) *Daily News,* May 11, 1950.

40 "Caps' Hitters Take Command," *Regina* (Saskatchewan) *Leader-Post,* May 22, 1950: 18; ("Satch's Back," *Regina Leader-Post,* May 26, 1950: 19.

41 "Leafs Capture Baseball Gravy," *Regina Leader-Post,* July 26, 1951: 20.

42 John Owen, "The Bucket," *Bismarck* (North Dakota) *Tribune,* May 25, 1955: 20.

43 Center for Negro League Baseball Research, "Negro League Players Who Played Baseball in the Dominican Summer League, accessed online, cnlbr.org/Portals/0/RL/Negro%20Leaguers%20in%20the%20Dominican%20Republic.pdf.

44 "Major League All-Stars Play Here Tonight," *Asheville* (North Carolina) *Citizen-Times,* October 22, 1951: 10.

45 "Capilanos Have Four Negro Players," *Nanaimo* (British Columbia) *Daily News,* March 4, 1952: 6.

46 "Meet Harry Butts," *Vancouver* (British Columbia) *Sun,* March 4, 1952: 10.

47 "Capilanos Have Four Negro Players."

48 Keith Matthews, "Vancouver Capilanos Will Be Favored to Take Western International Honors," *Roseburg* (Oregon) *News-Review,* April 16, 1952: 8.

49 Dick Beddoes, "Caps Rooks Look Good, Says Carse," *Vancouver Sun,* April 8, 1952: 10.

50 "Meet Harry Butts," *Vancouver Sun,* March 4, 1952: 10.

51 Ibid.

52 US Army World War II Draft Record, January 28, 1943: 2; US Army Selective Service Enlistment Record, Discharge Document, September 24, 1943: 2.

53 Dick Beddoes, "Lundberg Shatters Ol' No. 13 Hoodoo," *Vancouver Sun,* May 6, 1952: 8.

54 "WIL Baseball – 1952," Blog, accessed online: wilbaseball52.blogspot.com/2007/12/sunday-may-11-1952.html.

55 Don Carlson, "Caps Best Ever," *Vancouver* (British Columbia) *Province,* May 27, 1952: 8.

56   Ibid.

57   Ibid.

58   Al Cottrell, "But Listen!" *Province*, June 28, 1952: 14.

59   Clancy Loranger, "Heat Haunted Snyder," *Province*, May 20, 1952: 8.

60   "Players Swing Fists," *Regina Leader-Post*, June 17, 1952: 22.

61   "Out of the Cellar for One Hour," *Leader-Post*, August 14, 1952: 22.

62   "Lou Tost to Boss Brandon," *Leader-Post*, June 5, 1952: 22.

63   "From the 4 Corners," *Leader-Post*, September 20, 1952: 17.

64   Western Canada Baseball, "1952 Statistics, Mandak League," Accessed online: attheplate.com/wcbl/1952_2.html.

65   Ibid.

66   Barry Swanton, *The Mandak League: Haven for Former Negro League Ballplayers* (Jefferson, North Carolina: McFarland, 2006), 83.

67   Dick Welsh, "Royals Rout 'Stars,' 8-1; Butts Misses No-Hitter," *Newport News Daily Press*, September 15, 1952: 5.

68   Ibid.

69   Day-by-Day Chronology of Busy 1952 Year in Peninsula Sports Circles," *Daily Press*, December 31, 1952: 13.

70   James S. Hirsch, *Willie Mays: The Life, the Legend* (New York: Simon and Schuster, 2010), 157-159.

71   "Piedmonters May Break Color Line," *Richmond Times-Dispatch*, March 24, 1952: 18.

72   Ibid.

73   "Colts are Fourth Piedmont Club to Get Negro Player," *Newport News Daily Press*, April 20, 1953: 5.

74   Ed Young, "Piedmont League Negro Stars Show Up Well," *Petersburg* (Virginia) *Progress-Index*, July 29, 1953: 16-17.

75   "York Roses Acquire Bill Springfield, First Negro Player on Local Roster," *York* (Pennsylvania) *Gazette and Daily*, April 8, 1952: 22.

76   First of Roses on the Line," *Gazette and Daily*, February 13, 1953: 29.

77   "Portsmouth Club Tryout 10 Players," *Atlanta Daily World*, April 8, 1953: 5.

78   "Roanoke Red Sox Nip Macs in Ten Inning Hill Battle, 3-2," *Roanoke* (Virginia) *Daily Press*, May 2, 1953: 9.

79   Ibid.

80   Ibid.

81   "Macs in 5th Straight Win, Bounce Colts," *Daily Press*, May 24, 1953: 25.

82   "Colts Are Fourth Piedmont Club"; Swanton, 207.

83   "Peeples Sold to Dodger Farm Club," *Pittsburgh Courier*, July 7, 1951: 14.

84   "Macs in 5th Straight."

85   Ibid.

86   "Dewey Wilkins Doing Usual Fine Job for Hapless Colts," *Staunton* (Virginia) *News Leader*, May 29, 1953: 6.

87   Ibid.

88   "Colts Slow Up Hagerstown on 4-Hit Job," *Newport News Daily Press*, July 15, 1953: 11.

89   Ibid.

90   Colts Slow Up Hagerstown."

91   Steve Guback, "Left-Hander Claims Nine on Strikes," *Richmond Times Dispatch*, July 15, 1953: 22.

92   Shelley Rolfe, "War, Higher Pay Elsewhere Cited by Dorman for Poor 'B' Baseball," *Richmond Times-Dispatch*, June 4, 1953: 26.

93   "Hagerstown Cops Interstate Loop Playoff Crown," *York* (Pennsylvania) *Gazette and Daily*, September 22, 1952: 18.

94   "Johnson Comeback Helps Norfolk in Bid to Cop Piedmont Pennant," *Staunton* (Virginia) *News Leader*, August 4, 1953: 9.

95   "Dodgers Open Playoffs Tonight in Hagerstown," *Newport News* (Virginia) *Daily Press*, September 8, 1953: 5-6.

96   "Piedmont Playoffs Begin Tonight as Norfolk Tars Capture Pennant," *News Leader*, September 8, 1953: 9.

97   "Offer Possessions to Save Richmond Club," *Ottawa Journal*, January 6, 1954: 22.

98   Commonwealth of Virginia, "Certificate of Death" for Harry Thomas Butts, April 7, 1977.

99   Ibid.

100   Ibid.

101   "Obituaries," *Suffolk* (Virginia) *News-Herald*, April 10, 1977: 2.

102   Ibid.

103   "Lloyd Falls Prey to Newark Eagles, 7-2," *Delaware County Daily Times* (Chester, Pennsylvania), June 13, 1946: 26.

104   Dick Beddoes, "Caps Rooks Look Good, Says Carse," *Vancouver Sun*, April 8, 1952: 10; Keith Matthews, "Vancouver Capilanos Will Be Favored to Take Western International Honors," *Roseburg* (Oregon) *News-Review*, April 16, 1952: 8; "Newark Eagle [sic] Plays Royals Here Tonight," *Newport News Daily Press*, July 21, 1948: 10.

CECIL COLE

BY RICHARD BOGOVICH

Cecil Cole only pitched for the Newark Eagles during the 1946 season. He later spent numerous years as a regional scout for the Pittsburgh Pirates. *(Courtesy of Seamheads.com Negro League Database)*

After his playing days, Cecil Cole watched a lot of baseball games in his hometown of Connellsville, Pennsylvania, with local sportswriter Jim Kriek. "A brief chat with him could make the day brighter," Kriek recalled. "We had a lot of good conversations and laughs, not only about baseball, but everything in general." Kriek was well aware that Cole's pitching career peaked with the Negro National League's Newark Eagles the year before

Jackie Robinson broke baseball's color barrier. Kriek once asked Cole whether he ever pondered the possibility of having become a major leaguer himself if he'd been a few years younger.[1]

The question made Cole smile. "Yeah, on occasion I wonder what I might have done if I had had the chance, but you can't dwell on things like that," he replied. "I had my chance to play professionally with the Eagles and I had a good time doing it."[2]

Cecil Edward Cole was born in Connellsville on September 23, 1919, to Virginia and Andrew Jackson (A.J.) Cole. His brother, Elmer, had been born about a year earlier. The 1920 and 1930 censuses show that the four of them lived with A.J.'s parents, Reuben and Minnie, on Connellsville's west edge among Italian immigrants and their families. Connellsville, which is about 45 miles southeast of Pittsburgh, had a population hovering around 13,500 during the 1920s.[3] Minnie Cole ran a laundry business out of their home. Reuben had lost his right arm in a mining accident around the turn of the century but was a dairyman on the side.[4]

A.J. Cole had made a name for himself by mid-1914 while attending Dunbar Township High School. In March he appeared with four white students in a photo on the front page of nearby Uniontown's *Morning Herald*. They were members of the Fricksonian Society, a competitive speech team.[5] His oration, a tribute to mothers, was so highly regarded that it was reprinted in Connellsville's *Daily Courier* 35 years later.[6] Soon enough, he was mentioned in the context of a committee of Union Baptist Church, and then served a few months in the military in 1918, at the end of World War I.[7]

Between the 1919 and 1921 city directories the family's address changed from 206 North Twelfth Street to 201, where Cecil Cole lived at least until his marriage in 1946.[8] As a result, he had easy access to Connellsville's Twelfth Street Field for baseball games and the like. A game of "mushball" (16-inch softball) at that field in mid-1932, when Cecil was 12, was reported in the *Daily Courier*, and that may have been the first time the Cole brothers were mentioned in any newspaper. Cecil and Elmer's H.D. Club defeated a "junior" team of the Betters Athletic Club, 7-6.[9] The Cole brothers' team may have been attached to a local Home Demonstration Club, an equivalent to the 4-H Clubs that still exist today.[10] In any case, less than a month later the brothers were again on the winning side of a mushball game, except with the U.B. Juniors. That may have been a Union Baptist team. In both instances the newspaper helped drum up additional contests for the Cole brothers. "Teams desiring games with the Juniors are requested to call No. 986 on the telephone and ask for Cecil or Elmer Cole," the latter account concluded.[11]

Based on first initials, it appears that in 1933 Cecil Cole pitched for the Liberty Heights Juniors (caught by a kid from his same block, Mickey Delligatti), while in 1934 both Cecil and Elmer were on the DePaul All Stars. In November of that year a C. Cole and E. Cole were also in the lineup of the Liberty Heights Juniors' football team.[12]

Connellsville High School didn't have a baseball team while Cecil Cole attended, so as an athlete he was known there primarily as a javelin thrower.[13] In May of 1936 he was among the 52 students who represented his school at a county track and field competition.[14] About a year later, in a summary of a dual meet against Georges Township High School, Cole was listed among the top three finishers in the pole vault and high jump as well as the javelin.[15] Three weeks later he repeated that performance against Scottdale.[16] On June 5, 1937, Cole graduated from Connellsville High.[17]

The very next month he burst onto the local baseball scene. In a seven-inning Works Progress Administration-YMCA Junior Baseball League game on July 7, 20 of the 21 outs he recorded on the mound were by strikeout and he yielded only one hit. From the box score it appears that the remaining putout was a baserunner thrown out by Cole's catcher. Cole's Bowmans upset the "highly touted Cubs," 14-2. "He completely baffled the hard hitting Cubs with his curves and blinding speed," wrote the *Daily Courier* after calling Cole the "new pitching sensation in the Junior League" and crediting him with "one of the most dazzling performances of twirling yet seen at Fayette Field." The paper characterized attendance as very high.[18] Less than two weeks later, in another seven-inning game but against a different team, he struck out 17 opponents and gave up only two hits. Then, on August 9, he again dominated the Cubs. In a six-inning nightcap he struck out 14 and again limited them to one hit in a shutout.[19]

In 1938 Cole wore two different baseball caps. During the first half of May he was twice listed by his local newspaper on the roster of the Connellsville Tigers. It was only after a game later in May that the *Courier* mentioned the fact that the Tigers were a "Negro" nine. Cole played shortstop in that game against a Merchants team. In mid-June Cole was the winning pitcher against the Scottdale Grays at that foe's ballpark. He also pitched the Tigers to victory in Normalville during July.[20]

Cole's other team that summer was the American Legion's squad in the WPA-YMCA Junior Baseball League. On June 28 he reminded fans of his success a year earlier by striking out 11 Dunbar batters on his way to a four-hit shutout that the *Courier* called "masterful." He followed that up on July 5 with a one-hit shutout in which he struck out 16.[21]

On July 19 Cole continued to astound, with a 5-0 no-hitter against a team called the Pirates in which he fanned 17. One walk kept him from a perfect game. He began August with a 2-0 two-hitter in which he whiffed 12 foes. In a game on August 24 he suffered an ankle sprain that forced him to leave the mound in the fourth inning of his start the next day, and that signaled the end of his staggering accomplishments for the season.[22]

Oddly, Cole was hardly mentioned by first name during the 1939 season. His time on area diamonds was seemingly limited to the local Church Softball League, hurling for a new team organized by the Payne African Methodist Episcopal Church.[23] Cole was their pitcher in the box score printed by the *Daily Courier* on June 2; most of his teammates' surnames match the rosters of the Connellsville Tigers a year earlier.[24]

Reuben Cole was in poor health throughout the first half of 1939, but he and Minnie celebrated 50 years of marriage in May. He died in July at the age of 77. The family was so overwhelmed by the resulting sympathy, kindness, and floral tributes that it placed a classified ad to express its gratitude. Minnie died in February of 1943, at the age of 67 or 68, days after suffering a stroke.[25]

In 1940 Cecil was working 44 hours a week as a janitor for a retail grocery, according to the federal census. His military draft card that year specified his height as 5-feet-10 and his weight as 161 pounds. He apparently pitched for two teams that summer, as he had two years earlier. "C. Cole" pitched for Payne A.M.E. again,[26] but by the end of June he also debuted with the West Side team of the City Recreation Center-YMCA Schoolboy Baseball League. In his first outing he immediately re-established his credentials as a pitching star by not yielding a hit in a 1-1 tie. He struck out 12 opponents in the seven-inning contest, and their only run resulted from an error.[27]

On August 20 Cole his match against his league's Davidson team, when both pitchers tossed a two-hitter and struck out 19. Cole's team was shut out and Davidson scored three times with the aid of three errors, four walks, and a hit batsman. Nevertheless, Cole impressed enough that season to be one of only two pitchers to hurl for "Team One" in both league all-star games on consecutive days in late August.[28]

In November Cole was named in a *Daily Courier* article about local men who were potentially facing military service, and in February of 1941 the paper identified him among 13 new volunteers. Word of this reached a newspaper in New York, where it was noted that the Newark Eagles had been working to recruit "the promising rookie hurler."[29] According to Cole's Application for World War II Compensation, filed in 1950, he began domestic service on February 24, 1941.

On August 2, 1941, the *Daily Courier* printed a letter that Cole wrote from Fort Huachuca, Arizona, to Fred Snell, assistant county supervisor of the WPA recreation program. Cole was assigned to the 368th Infantry. The newspaper prefaced the letter by noting that for the previous three summers Cole "was the leading pitcher in the Recreation Center-Y.M.C.A. Baseball League which is a city playground loop for boys of high school age. At the time Cole was inducted into the service he was under contract to play for the colored Elks [*sic*] of Newark, N.J." Cole began with an upbeat tone, and then described his duties. "I'm attached to Headquarters Company, and my work consists of map reading and radio coding," Cole wrote. "We go to school for radio coding. I am a radio operator."

After remarking about the beauty of the Arizona landscape, he reported on baseball: "I am now playing on the Regular 368th baseball team and we are undefeated in the six games played," he wrote, and listed the opponents, noting that he limited the Tucson Air Corps team to two hits. "Since I've been on the team here in camp, I have really learned a few things in baseball that will help me," Cole added. "I have developed a little more speed and control and my batting is a great deal improved." In closing, he asked Snell to say hello for him to colleagues Walter Miskinis and Joe Mullen.[30]

In October a profile of the 368th team was published in a few papers around the country, and Cole was one of three pitchers named. The article also noted his contract with the Eagles. The starter at first base was Sergeant Thomas Turner, formerly of the Dayton (Ohio) Monarchs, who played for the Chicago American Giants in 1947.[31] That same month, the *Arizona Republic* reported

on a loss by the 368th team in which "Coles" was one of their two pitchers.[32]

Later in October a *Daily Courier* columnist summarized another letter from Cole to Snell. Enclosed with the letter was a clipping from a Tucson paper that sang Cole's praises. "The club won 20 out of 24 games," wrote John H. Whoric. "Cole pitched 11 and won nine." One of those victories was a one-hitter. "The local lad hopes he'll still be in Arizona around the first of the year when he'd like to attend the Rose Bowl in Pasadena next January 1," Whoric concluded.[33]

A photo of Staff Sgt. Cecil E. Cole holding a rifle was printed in a "souvenir edition" of the *Daily Courier* on July 17, 1942, and one month later the paper confirmed his promotion in a story about him. In November the paper reported that both Cecil and brother Elmer, a corporal stationed at Camp Edwards, Massachusetts, were back in Connellsville on furlough.[34] On February 19, 1944, Cecil Cole was shipped to the Pacific Theater, according to the Application for World War II Compensation.

At some point Cole was assigned to the 318th Engineer Combat Battalion and spent considerable time in the Solomon Islands, New Guinea, and Morotai Island (off the Dutch East Indies).[35] In a letter to Cole, Brigadier General Leonard R. Boyd of the 93rd Infantry Division expressed his appreciation for "outstanding performance of duty as first sergeant," specifically from March 31 to April 2, 1945. "The manner in which you accomplished all assignments of duties was a material aid to the accomplishment of the division's missions," Boyd wrote.[36] On April 4 the decision was made for the 93rd to invade Morotai.[37] World War II in the Pacific ended on September 2, 1945, with Japan's formal surrender, and Cole continued overseas until December 27. The extra service time allowed him to play some additional baseball; during his military service, he reportedly hurled five no-hitters.[38]

Cole's active duty ended on January 9, 1946, and thus began the most momentous year of his life. Three days later the *Daily Courier* announced that both Cecil and Elmer had returned home. The paper noted that each brother had received "decorations for meritorious service."[39]

Cecil Cole soon received a letter, dated January 19, from Newark Eagles co-owner Effa Manley. She informed him that Charles C. Williams, his baseball manager in the Army, had visited her and recommended Cole to her. "I told him you had agreed to play with us just before you entered the army, and I was expecting to hear from you when you were discharged," she wrote. She passed along Williams's address in case Cole wanted to contact him. Cole wrote a reply on January 26, stating, "I was more than glad to hear from you, as anxious as I am to try out for the team." He informed her that he was 26 years old, 5-feet-10½-inches tall, weighed 175 pounds, and threw and batted right-handed. He summarized his baseball experience and concluded by asking if a frequent teammate in Connellsville, James Keith, could also try out. Mrs. Manley replied four days later. In response to Cole's inquiry about pay she wrote, "On the strength of your recommendations I feel safe in saying I will start you at $200 a month." She added that Keith could try out if he paid his own way. "It costs about $25.00 a week for a man in camp," she wrote.[40]

In the meantime, Cecil Cole married another Connellsville High School graduate, Rose Perie Carter, an elevator operator in the Second National Bank Building. On February 20, the day before the ceremony, the *Daily Courier* reported in detail about a shower held in her honor. A few days later the paper also reported details of the wedding itself, and even the *Pittsburgh Courier* devoted four paragraphs to the event. The best man was one of Cole's cousins, Connol Reid.[41]

An article in the *Newark Sunday Call* on March 24 may have contained the earliest print reference connecting Cole to the Eagles that year. The focus of the article was the abundance of military veterans on the team's roster. On April 13 the *Newark News* reported on spring training in Jacksonville, Florida, and named Cole among three rookie pitchers "showing great promise." Alas, the next day the *Call* reported that Cole "was confined to his room with an attack of chickenpox." Nevertheless, the paper asserted that he was "almost certain to win a starting assignment with the Eagles."[42] Other papers praised Cole as well, reporting that he had "fine control, a good fast ball and handle[s] himself like a veteran on the mound. He is also a powerful hitter and can be used in the outfield."[43]

The first regular-season game for Newark was on May 5, but Cole didn't debut until May 30, against the Philadelphia Stars. Accounts in three newspapers differed in some respects, but Biz Mackey apparently broke a 3-3 tie in the bottom of the eighth inning by driving in a runner from third base while pinch-hitting for starting pitcher Rufus Lewis. Cole retired the first two Stars he faced in the ninth and reached a full count against the third. Accounts state that this batter was opposing pitcher Henry McHenry, but one box score indicates that Goose Curry batted for him instead. Whichever man batted, the result was a home run. Cole then allowed additional runs before Max Manning came on in relief to secure the final out. Thus, Cole's debut resulted in a blown save and a loss.[44]

Cole's second game – and first start – came on June 10 against the New York Cubans at Dexter Park in Queens, New York. Cole lasted six innings in a 4-1 loss. "Three of the four runs the Cubans scored came with the aid of errors and bases on balls," said the *Brooklyn Daily Eagle,* "but his lack of control proved to be his downfall." A

wild pitch plated the first run for the Cubans, and the six walks Cole issued hurt as well.[45]

Cole started again on June 15, this time against the Baltimore Elite Giants at Dunn Field in Trenton, New Jersey. Cole and the Eagles won, 7-4. Details are scarce. One newspaper said Leon Ruffin pitched at some point, but Ruffin was a catcher; also, statistics published in the *New York Amsterdam News* on July 7 suggest that Cole pitched most of the game, if not all of it, and was the winning pitcher.[46]

More details about Cole's next game are available. He started against the New York Black Yankees in the second game of a doubleheader at Newark's Ruppert Stadium. The Eagles scored at least twice in four different innings, and the Yankees never had a chance. "Cecil Coles [*sic*] turned in a brilliant two-hit shutout in the nightcap," wrote the *Newark News.* "Alex Newkirk singled in the second inning and Emil [actually Ameal] Brooks touched his offerings for another single in the sixth for the Yanks' only two hits of the game." The final score was 11-0.[47]

Over the next few weeks Cole started and relieved at least twice each, but his next noteworthy outing was on July 28 at Griffith Stadium in Washington, when he started the second game of a doubleheader against the Homestead Grays in front of a crowd of 6,000. He scored the game's first run after tripling to left field and came home on a teammate's single. He pitched six scoreless innings in Newark's 4-3 win, but credit for the victory likely went to either Warren Peace or Max Manning after the Grays tied the score late in the game.[48] This was presumably the only time Cole pitched in that ballpark, and he recalled the site and occasion vividly many years later.

Cole was asked how many homers he surrendered to Josh Gibson. "I can truthfully tell you that Gibson never hit one home run off me," he replied, then paused, chuckled, and added, "and for two very good reasons. We were playing Gibson's team in Griffith Stadium, and I think the only field that had a deeper centerfield was the Polo Grounds in New York City. Anyway, I put a fastball up there, a little on the outside, about belt high, and Josh got hold of it. I thought the ball was going to clear the fence in center, but fortunately there was a lot of room to run and Larry Doby was playing center for us. Doby went back as far as he could, leaped, and gloved the ball. So, thanks to Larry Doby and that deep centerfield, I can always say that Gibson never homered off me."[49]

For the next four weeks Cole was used sparingly, but he made an important relief appearance in Wilmington, Delaware, on August 26 against the New York Cubans. Cole entered the game in the eighth inning with the Cubans in the midst of a four-run rally that tied the score. In Cole's two-thirds of an inning he kept them from taking the lead. Newark soon pushed across two runs, and Cole was the winning pitcher.[50]

Cole's last hurrah for 1946 was apparently on September 6 at Dunn Field in Trenton. This was another game for which details are scant, but Cole received credit for the 11-7 win against the Cubans. Seven of the Cubans' nine hits were for extra bases. Monte Irvin helped counter that with four hits in five times at bat. The attendance was reported as 1,427.[51]

A sportswriter's profile of Cole in 2012 noted that there was inconsistent reporting of his record for 1946. "For example, the *Negro Baseball Encyclopedia* lists Cole with a record of 2-2," wrote George Von Benko in the *Uniontown* (Pennsylvania) *Herald-Standard*. "Baseball-Reference.com lists Cole with a record of 0-3 and a 9.00 ERA. In a Nov. 5, 1946, newspaper story, Cole is credited with a record of 6-2." All told, documentation compiled by SABR researchers exists for at least 13 games pitched by Cole, of which he won four and lost three. "Cole said his record was 4-3," Von Benko noted, and he had "earned three of the victories in starting assignments."[52] As far as is known, Cole did not play in the 1946 Negro World Series, which Newark won. Nevertheless, he was one of seven pitchers on the Manleys' list of players who were to receive commemorative tie clasps bearing their surname and a letter or two designating their position.[53]

On December 15, 1946, Cecil and Rose Perie welcomed their first child, Cynthia.[54] "If you don't have it made in baseball at 26, you'd better find something else to do," Cecil decided at that point. "I was making $350 a month and that wasn't enough to be dragging a new wife and a baby all over the country." Therefore, he quickly set aside further pursuit of a professional baseball career. After a short stint at a local enamel plant, he worked for the Connellsville Housing Authority for 40 years as a maintenance man.[55]

On the side, though, Cole always maintained a passion for baseball. By mid-1947 he was an all-star pitcher in the local Fay West Baseball League, and he continued to pitch for teams in Connellsville until at least 1967.[56] A poignant high point occurred in 1955, when he was named to a local all-star team that played a reconstituted Homestead Grays squad. One of his teammates, who was also named an all-star, was the father of major-league pitcher Bob Galasso.[57]

As his pitching career wound down in the Connellsville area, Cole began a long tenure as a regional scout for the Pittsburgh Pirates. His most notable signing occurred early on. Bruce Dal Canton recalled, "[O]ne of my teammates was a guy named Cecil Cole and he was a bird dog for the Pirates and he kept bugging them to take another look. Finally it was arranged for me to have a private workout at Forbes Field. The result of that workout was a contract."[58] Dal Canton began in the minors in 1966 and de-

buted with the Pirates the next year. He had an 11-year career as a major-league pitcher and spent more than 25 years as a pitching coach. Cole's work for the Pirates also created opportunities to reminisce with 1946 teammates and opponents. For example, on separate occasions in 1971 he was in a position to reconnect with Larry Doby and Monte Irvin for the first time in many years.[59]

The Coles became parents again in mid-1951 with the birth of daughter Marva Jo. Late that decade he was ordained a deacon of the Union Baptist Church. By the early 1960s he and his brother Elmer were members of a singing group called the Amalgam Male Chorus.[60]

By the mid-1960s Cecil Cole had become a popular magician locally, sometimes billed as "The Silent Knight of Magic."[61] This sideline happened to connect with his scouting in a 1979 article about a Pirates good-luck charm. Executive Vice President Harding Peterson was a bit embarrassed to confess that when the Pirates faced trouble, he turned to a rectangular red pen that Cole gave him about five years earlier. "When Cecil gave it to me he told me, 'Anytime things aren't going too good, just pull out this pen and hang onto it,'" Peterson said. "So a couple weeks ago when things weren't going too good (during the Pirates' stretch race with Montreal in the National League East), I got it out of my drawer and I've been using it ever since."[62]

In 1968 the Cole family celebrated Cynthia's graduation from Alderson-Broaddus College in Philippi, West Virginia, and did likewise in 1973 when Marva Jo graduated from Lock Haven State College in Pennsylvania.[63] Elmer Cole died in 1969 and A.J. in 1970. Virginia died in 1975. Cecil Cole had three grandchildren and lived long enough to know three great-grandchildren. Marva Jo died in 1999. Three years later, Cecil died at the age of 82 on June 21, 2002.[64] Jim Kriek had written much about his friend Cecil Cole over the years, and on this occasion he declared that "the world in general, but the world of baseball in particular, is so much the poorer for his passing."[65]

NOTES

1   Jim Kriek, "After Talking with Cole, Day Got Brighter," *Uniontown* (Pennsylvania) *Herald-Standard,* June 25, 2002.

2   Ibid.

3   "Connellsville Will Come Back Stronger Than Ever," *Connellsville* (Pennsylvania) *Daily Courier,* May 10, 1930: 4. The city's population declined by more than 500 residents from 1920 to 1930.

4   One source for Cecil's date of birth is his military draft registration card in 1940. One source for Virginia Cole's maiden name is her Social Security Death Index entry. Information about Reuben Cole is partly from his obituary (in which his first name was misspelled as Reuban): See "The Grim Reaper," *Daily Courier,* July 10, 1939: 6.

5   *Uniontown* (Pennsylvania) *Morning Herald,* March 21, 1914: 1. See also "Dunbar Societies" on page 8 for praise about "Andrew Coles." For earlier instances of his developing and deploying leadership skills, see Lavada Burd, "Connellsville," *Pittsburgh Courier,* March 21, 1911: 2 (where he was presumably the "Andrew Coles" mentioned), and "Connellsville," *Pittsburgh Courier,* January 6, 1912: 2.

6   "Oration of 35 Years Ago Has Mother's Day Message," *Connellsville Daily Courier,* May 7, 1949: 8. The 1940 census confirmed that Andrew did in fact complete four years of high school.

7   "Card of Thanks," *Connellsville Daily Courier,* April 3, 1916: 7. Regarding his military service, Pennsylvania WWI Veterans Service and Compensation Files indicate that Andrew J. Cole of Connellsville was inducted on August 3, 1918, and honorably discharged on December 26, 1918, without overseas service. He was also listed in "Negro Draftees Bound for Camp Get an Ovation," *Connellsville Daily Courier,* August 3, 1918: 1.

8   That was identified as his address a month before his marriage, in "Area Soldiers Get Discharges at Fort Knox," *Connellsville Daily Courier,* January 18, 1946: 5. His parents lived there until their deaths in the 1970s. His mother died after his father, and Virginia's address was mentioned in an announcement of her hospitalization just before her death. See "Mount Pleasant," *Connellsville Daily Courier,* March 10, 1975: 13.

9   "H.D. Club Beats Betters Juniors," *Connellsville Daily Courier,* July 15, 1932: 12.

10   For one overview (available on the internet) of how the Home Demonstration and 4-H programs engaged and served African-Americans in Eastern states at the time, see the Atlanta University thesis of Lillian Camilla Weems, "A Study of the Negro Home Demonstration Program in Georgia, 1923-1955" (1956). *ETD Collection for AUC Robert W. Woodruff Library.* Paper 692.

11   "U.B. Juniors Win Mushball Contest," *Connellsville Daily Courier,* August 8, 1932: 8.

12   "Sipe's Specials Conquer Juniors of Liberty Heights," *Connellsville Daily Courier,* June 20, 1933: 10. "DePauls Conquer Findley Club, 9-1," *Connellsville Daily Courier,* August 16, 1934: 9. "Liberty Heights Juniors Win Ninth Gridiron Contest," *Connellsville Daily Courier,* November 19, 1934: 8.

13   George Von Benko, "Cecil Cole Enjoyed His Time in Baseball," *Uniontown* (Pennsylvania) *Herald-Standard,* August 21, 2012: C3.

14   "Announce Entries and Officials for Track Meet," *Uniontown* (Pennsylvania) *Daily News Standard,* May 8, 1936: 15.

15   "Cokers Win over Georges in Dual Meet," *Connellsville Daily Courier,* April 24, 1937: 5.

16   "Cokers Triumph over Scottdale Hi [sic]," *Connellsville Daily Courier,* May 13, 1937: 12.

17   "Class of 1937, C.H.S.," *Connellsville Daily Courier,* June 5, 1937: 10.

18   "Cole Whiffs 20; Bowmans Upset Cubs," *Connellsville Daily Courier,* July 8, 1937: 9. Cole's catcher was named Marcondi, which was the surname of C. Cole's catcher on the 1934 DePaul All Stars.

19   "Bowmans Top Bears, Occupy First Place," *Connellsville Daily Courier,* July 20, 1937: 7; "Bowmans Win, Lose in Junior Loop," *Connellsville Daily Courier,* August 10, 1937: 8.

20   "Tigers Baseball Team Seeks Games," *Connellsville Daily Courier,* May 5, 1938: 10; "Tigers Baseball Team Will Meet Wednesday," *Connellsville Daily Courier,* May 10, 1938: 10; "Merchants Win Exhibition Game from Tiger Club," *Connellsville Daily Courier,* May 28, 1938: 10; "Tigers Topple Scottdale Grays," *Connellsville Daily Courier,* June 16, 1938: 8. "Tigers Annex Two Victories," *Connellsville Daily Courier,* July 11, 1938: 10.

21   "Legion Moves Ahead, Spills Dunbar Team," *Connellsville Daily Courier,* June 29, 1938: 8; "Cole Allows One Hit, Legion Wins," *Connellsville Daily Courier,* July 7, 1938: 8.

22   "Cecil Cole Has No-Hitter, Legion Ahead," *Connellsville Daily Courier,* July 22, 1938: 13; "Cole Blanks Dunbar Team," *Connellsville Daily Courier,* August 3, 1938: 5; "Dunbar Whips Legion, St. Rita Ties for Lead," *Connellsville Daily Courier,* August 27, 1938: 8.

23   There was no American Legion team in the City WPA-YMCA Schoolboys League standings during 1939 e.g., see Daily Courier, August 12, 1939: 8. The Davidson team had an outfielder named Cole in box scores occasionally but he apparently never pitched. The fact that the Payne team was new to the church league was reported in "Church Softball Loop to Open Season Friday with Exhibition Game," *Connellsville Daily Courier,* May 17, 1939: 7.

24   "Christians Trip Paynes in Softball," *Connellsville Daily Courier,* June 2, 1939: 13. "C. Cole" was also their pitcher in a brief account a few days later, "Christians, Paynes, Methodists Capture Church Loop Games," *Connellsville Daily Courier,* June 6, 1939: 8. Two other examples of Cole pitching: "Payne A.M.E. Defeats Christians in Second Game of Church Series," *Connellsville Daily Courier,* July 14, 1939: 12; "Christians Win First Half Softball Crown; Beat Payne Method-ists," *Connellsville Daily Courier,* August 23, 1939: 10. (The game to decide the first-half championship kept getting delayed, and ultimately was played close to the end of the second half.) In late August "Cecil Cole" was assigned to umpire some league playoff games, as reported in "Brethren Defeat I.C. for Participation in Second Half Play-Off," *Connellsville Daily Courier,* August 24, 1939: 10.

25   "The Grim Reaper," *Connellsville Daily Courier,* July 10, 1939: 6; "Announce-ments," *Connellsville Daily Courier,* July 14, 1939: 14; "The Grim Reaper," *Connellsville Daily Courier,* February 15, 1943: 2. Minnie's obituary stated her date of birth as May 22, 1875, but her findagrave.com entry shows May 22, 1874.

26   As examples, see box scores accompanying these two articles: "May's Softball Club Shuts out Payne A.M.E.," *Connellsville Daily Courier,* May 13, 1940: 7; and "Paynes Topple Merchant Team in Second Game," *Connellsville Daily Courier,* September 27, 1940: 16.

27   "Pitches Hitless Ball Yet Gets Only Deadlock in City Softball Group," *Connellsville Daily Courier,* June 26, 1940: 10.

28   "Gough, Back in Line-Up, Wins Game," *Connellsville Daily Courier,* August 21, 1940: 10. Accounts of the two all-star games were printed on the same day and page: "Team One Victor in First Game" and "Team Two Evens All Star Ball Series," *Connellsville Daily Courier,* August 30, 1940: 14.

29   "50 More Conscriptees Given Questionnaires for Selective Service," *Connellsville Daily Courier*, November 8, 1940: 13; "13 Volunteers Fill Next Draft Quota; Will Report Monday," *Connellsville Daily Courier*, February 18, 1941: 1; Dan Burley, "Confidentially Yours," *New York Amsterdam Star-News*, March 15, 1941: 18.

30   "Map Reading and Radio Coding Work Done by Cecile [sic] Cole, Who Writes He Likes Life in Army," *Connellsville Daily Courier*, August 2, 1941: 10. See also "Fred Snell Member of Advisory Body, Allegheny Fair," *Connellsville Daily Courier*, August 27, 1940: 7.

31   "Army Camp News," *Evansville* (Indiana) *Argus*, October 3, 1941: 2, 7. A shortened version of this article was printed in the *New York Age* on October 11, 1941: 11, under the headline, "Baseball Popular at Ft. Huachuca." For more on Turner and this team, see thomasturnernegroleague.org/fort-huachuca-arizona.php and Brent Kelley, *Voices from the Negro Leagues: Conversations with 52 Baseball Standouts of the Period 1924-1960* (Jefferson, North Carolina: McFarland & Company, 1998), 244-249.

32   "Birds Rout Soldiers, 9-3," *Arizona Republic* (Phoenix), October 6, 1941, section 2, page 2.

33   John H. Whoric, "Sportorials," *Connellsville Daily Courier*, October 23, 1941: 6.

34   "Men of Region Battling for Perpetuation of American Way of Life," *Connellsville Daily Courier*, July 17, 1942: Section 2, page 3. "Cecil Cole Made First Sergeant," *Connellsville Daily Courier*, August 17, 1942: 1; "Brothers Get Furloughs," *Connellsville Daily Courier*, November 4, 1942: 2. On June 26, 1943, the *Courier*'s front page featured an eloquent letter from Elmer, by then a Staff Sergeant with an engineer battalion in North Africa, appealing to a reported "400,000 slackers" to consider volunteering for military service. See "Soldier at Front Asks Miners for 'Break,'" *Connellsville Daily Courier*, June 26, 1943: 1.

35   "Former Local Boy Pitches for Newark," *Connellsville Daily Courier*, June 27, 1946: 9.

36   "Sgt. Cecil E. Cole Wins Warm Praise," *Connellsville Daily Courier*, March 11, 1946: 1.

37   See Stephen D. Lutz, "The 93rd Infantry Division: The Only African-American Division in the Pacific Theater," warfarehistorynetwork.com/daily/wwii/the-93rd-infantry-division-the-only-african-american-division-in-the-pacific-theater/, December 15, 2017.

38   Von Benko: C3; see also note 34 above.

39   "Personal Mention," *Connellsville Daily Courier*, January 12, 1946: 2. Elmer served in Tunisia, in the Rome-Arno campaign of 1944, and in Central Europe.

40   On February 7 Cole typed up a brief reply, and on March 21 Manley sent him a one-page letter confirming details about traveling as a team to their camp from Newark. Thanks to SABR member Bob Golon for providing scans of these letters from the Manley Papers at the Newark Public Library.

41   "Rose Carrie [sic] Carter, Bride-Elect, Honored," *Connellsville Daily Courier*, February 20, 1946: 2; "Miss Rose Perie Carter Weds Cecil E. Cole, Former Sergeant," *Connellsville Daily Courier*, February 25, 1946, 2; "Popular Pair Marries at Bride's Home," *Pittsburgh Courier*, March 9, 1946: 9. Among the out-of-town guests named was Lieutenant Scipio White. See Chris Buckley, "Retired Monessen Mail Carrier, Veteran, Still Loves to Travel the World," *Pittsburgh Tribune-Review*, September 1, 2015 at triblive.com/neighborhoods/yourmonvalley/yourmonvalley-more/9010287-74/monessen-war-army, which sheds light on Cecil Cole's service in the South Pacific.

42   Fred Bailey, "Leon Day, ETO Star, Back to Newark," *Newark* (New Jersey) *Sunday Call*, March 24, 1946: part II, page 2. "Rookie Pitcher Impresses Eagles," *Newark News*, April 13, 1946. "Fast Pitcher with Eagles," *Newark Sunday Call*, April 14, 1946.

43   "2 Rookie Slabmen Bolster Eagles," *Baltimore Afro-American*, April 20, 1946: 30. The same text also appeared in that day's *New York Amsterdam News*.

44   Only a short narrative was provided in "Stars, Eagles Split, 7-4, 6-3," *Philadelphia Inquirer*, May 31, 1946: 31. However, the accompanying box score seems to indicate that Curry batted for McHenry. On June 8 the *New Jersey Afro-American* printed two narratives about the doubleheader, under the headlines "Eagles Break Even with Philly Stars" and "Eagles, Philly Stars Divide Two." The former wasn't accompanied by a box score but provided the most detail about Cole's inning. It named Lewis as the pitcher, but at the end of the preceding paragraph the account noted that Mackey had batted for Lewis. That paper's other account did name Cole, and added the details about Manning, though it omitted Cole from the box score (not particularly surprising given that he didn't bat). Both Cole and Manning were included in the box score that accompanied "Eagles Split," *Newark Star-Ledger*, May 3, 1946: 17.

45   "N.Y. Cuban Nine Trounces Eagles in Dexter Game," *Brooklyn Daily Eagle*, June 11, 1946: 14.

46   "Eagles Win 3 Games, Move Closer to First Half Title," *New Jersey Afro American*, June 22, 1946. See also "N.Y. Cubans Tighten Lead in N.N. League," *Pittsburgh Courier*, June 22, 1946, 35. League statistics published in the *New York Amsterdam News,* July 7, 1946: 10 showed Cole having pitched in four games, totaling 25 innings, and that he had decisions in all four: two wins and two losses. Outings of approximately one, six, nine, and nine innings would total 25.

47   "Eagles Win Two," *Newark News*, June 22, 1946.

48   Ric Roberts, "Grays and Newark Eagles Divide Twin Bill 3-0, 4-3; Fields Blanks Newark," *Pittsburgh Courier*, August 3, 1946: 17. "Grays Split with Eagles," *New Jersey Afro American*, August 3, 1946.

49   Kriek, 2002.

50   "Eagles Nose out Cubans, 8 to 6, *Wilmington* (Delaware) *Morning News*, August 27, 1946: 16.

51   "Eagles Down Cubans," *Trenton* (New Jersey) *Evening Times*, September 8, 1946: 28.

52   Von Benko: C3.

53   Manley Papers at the Newark Public Library. Cole was shown sporting a 1946 Newark Eagles Negro World Series *ring* late in his life. See *New Pittsburgh Courier*, January 10, 1998: 7. Its origin is uncertain. REA catalog description auction preview tells a fascinating story about a unique ring: The 1946 Newark Eagles Negro League World Championship Ring, sportscollectingnews.com/excl1.htm.

54   "Starting Down Baby Lane," *Uniontown Morning Herald,* December 17, 1946: 5.

55   Von Benko: C3.

56   Herman Welsh, "Fay-West Baseball Stars Will Clash Sunday Afternoon at Scottsdale," *Connellsville Daily Courier*, July 18, 1947: 6; Jim Kriek, "Sports Notes," *Connellsville Daily Courier*, August 2, 1967: 6. For a particularly long profile while Cole was still pitching, see Jim Kriek, "Sports Notes," *Connellsville Daily Courier*, August 8, 1964: 6.

57   The game received steady buildup: "Big Ten All-Stars Meet Grays June 26," *Uniontown Morning Herald,* June 15, 1955: 18; "Youth, Speed Characterize Homestead Gray Aggregation," *Uniontown Evening Standard,* June 23, 1955: 10; "Big Ten, County Stars to Face Stellar Visitors in Exhibition," *Connellsville Daily Courier*, June 25, 1955: 4. For the results, see "Big Ten All-Star Club Downs Homestead," *Connellsville Daily Courier,* June 27, 1955: 6. In August Cole's own team was scheduled to face the Grays. See "Homestead Grays Will Field Diamond Stars in Clash with Levin's," *Connellsville Daily Courier*, August 4, 1955: 6 and "Levin's to Host Grays Tomorrow at Trotter," *Connellsville Daily Courier*, August

6, 1955: 4. On August 8 the *Courier* reported that the game was rained out; despite stated intentions, it apparently wasn't rescheduled. This obscure Homestead Grays aggregation was managed by Walt Hughes, who played on at least two teams in the short-lived United States Baseball League and was the brother of an early member of the Pittsburgh Crawfords, Charlie Hughes. "Galasso's father, Bob Galasso Sr., pitched in the Pittsburgh Pirates chain in 1949," according to baseball-reference. com/bullpen/Bob_Galasso.

58   Von Benko: C3. It's possible that Cole played baseball with another future Pirate, Bob Robertson, shortly before that slugger's pro debut. See "Two Fay-West Grads Playing for Pirates," *Connellsville Daily Courier*, September 19, 1970: 7. When Cole's Negro World Series ring – see note 52 above – was auctioned off, the auctioneer's profile of Cole said, "After [a] five-year stint with the Baltimore Orioles as a scout, he enjoyed the same position with the Pittsburgh [Pirates] for 35 years." See robertedwardauctions.com/auction/2010/spring/1723/1946-newark-eagles-negro-league-world-championship-ring/. However, Cole's name wasn't in any of the lists of Baltimore Orioles scouts printed in that team's media guides from 1954 through 1967. See mlb.com/orioles/history/media-guides.

59   Jim Kriek, "Sports Notes," *Connellsville Daily Courier*, November 3, 1971: 6.

60   "Three Births at Hospital," *Connellsville Daily Courier*, June 29, 1951: 1; "Baptists Will Ordain Deacon at Service," *Connellsville Daily Courier*, May 22, 1959:

24; "Musical Program Given at Meeting of Cameron PTA," *Connellsville Daily Courier*, December 6, 1962: 18.

61   For example, see "50 Attend WSCS Dinner and Program," *Connellsville Daily Courier*, March 23, 1965: 5. He was identified as "a member of the International Brotherhood of Magicians." See especially "Black Arts events," *Lock Haven* (Pennsylvania) *Express,* March 9, 1972: 6, above which was a large photo of Cole.

62   Pohla Smith, "Charms Big with Pirates," *Huntingdon* (Pennsylvania) *Daily News,* October 12, 1979: 5.

63   "English Major," *Connellsville Daily Courier*, June 18, 1968: 3; "Accepts Position," *Connellsville Daily Courier*, September 12, 1974: 24.

64   "Death Notices," *Uniontown Evening Standard,* October 16, 1969: 29; "Obituaries," *Connellsville Daily Courier*, August 5,1970: 17; "Funeral Notice," *Daily Courier,* March 24, 1975: 4. Regarding Marva Jo, see billiongraves.com/grave/ MARVA-JO-cole-DEBEARY/3731648. See also "Cole," *Pittsburgh Post-Gazette,* June 22, 2002, D4.

65   Jim Kriek, "After Talking with Cole, Day Got Brighter," *Uniontown Herald-Standard,* June 25, 2002.

JOHNNY "CHEROKEE" DAVIS

BY DAVE WILKIE

Johnny "Cherokee" Davis was a dual threat for the Eagles. He batted over .300 as a starting outfielder and posted a 2-0 record as a pitcher for Newark's 1946 championship squad. *(Noir-Tech Research, Inc.)*

Hall of Famer Monte Irvin, speaking to Negro League historian James Riley, had this to say about his teammate Johnny Davis's talent: "Perhaps too many gifts. Had Davis not divided his time between pitching, catching and playing the outfield, Johnny might have starred in the Majors."[1]

John Howard Davis was probably born on February 6, 1918.[2] In a questionnaire he filled out for the Hall of Fame in 1975, he listed this date and apologized for not knowing his place of birth.[3] Davis grew up an orphan, spending most of his childhood in a Catholic protectory in the Bronx.[4] He would often run away, get caught and be placed with a family, and then run away again. "I'd run away from the homes. I was probably looking for something, but who in the heck knows what I was looking for?" he said. "Maybe I was trying to find my mother. I was seven or eight. Just take off and run. Cops'd find me. OK, back in another home."[5] Davis played stickball and, later, baseball at the protectory. He claimed to be the biggest kid in his division.[6]

At 17, Davis left the protectory and joined the merchant marine. Between 1936 and 1939 he sailed the world, overcoming seasickness, learning Spanish, and experiencing life in way that he would fondly look back on later. "I always wanted to see what's on the other side of the street, different people, different places, different foods. Eighteen years old, and I'd seen half the world already."[7]

After leaving the merchant marine, Davis returned to baseball in Schenectady, New York. His play soon attracted the attention of the Brooklyn Dodgers' Al Campanis. Campanis sent Davis to the Mohawk Giants in the Upper New York State Independent League and also secured him a job at American Locomotive to help make ends meet.[8]

In 1940 Abe and Effa Manley, the husband-and-wife owners of the Negro National League's Newark Eagles, expressed an interest in Davis and attempted to acquire him from the Giants. The Giants' white owner, Henry Bozzi, was willing to sell Davis, but Davis was on parole for a crime committed as a minor and he wasn't allowed to move from the state.[9] Effa Manley campaigned hard, later giving credit to the unnamed "biggest negro politician in New Jersey" in the transfer of Davis's parole to New Jersey.[10] Halfway through the 1941 season, her persistence paid off and Davis became a full-time member of the Newark Eagles.

Davis often referred to himself as part Cherokee Indian and his nicknames reflected a Native-American heritage.[11] His Newark teammates called him Cherokee; in Puerto Rico he was known as Chief; and thanks to the legendary Josh Gibson, the Homestead Grays called him Geronimo. This came about when, after a mammoth home run at Ebbets Field early in his career, Davis jumped onto home plate after rounding third and Gibson shouted, "Geronimo."[12]

The 1942 season saw Davis hitting his stride with a .310 average. Teammate and future Hall of Famer Leon Day said of Davis's hitting style: "He was a good fastball hitter. Don't try to throw the fastball by him. He hit the ball a long way."[13]

Davis had a solid 1943 season, hitting .324 and settling in nicely with the star-studded Newark Eagles. Newark pitcher Max Manning described his teammate this way: "He used to act kind of wildish, he was a really big kid more than anything else. He'd do a lot of kiddish things. He loved to drive the bus. He liked to be alone, but he was a good mixer too."[14]

With some of their best players, including superstar outfielder Monte Irvin, off to war, the 1944 Newark Eagles finished in fifth place, nine games behind the champion Homestead Grays.[15] This didn't stop Davis from having one of his finest seasons. He batted .353 and chipped in on the mound with a 3-3 record. Davis was also honored with the starting center-field spot in the 1944 East-West All-Star Game, in which he rapped out two hits while sandwiched between greats Josh Gibson and Sam Bankhead.[16] Davis, power-hitting Hall of Famer Mule Suttles, and a few other veterans were able to take the field during wartime thanks to 4-F classifications by their draft boards.[17]

The 1945 season brought more success for Davis as he hit .333 and earned another trip to the East-West All-Star Game. He spent the offseason barnstorming for a team called [Biz] Mackey's All-Stars, when they played a five-game series against the [Charlie] Dressen All-Stars, a white major-league team that included Ralph Branca, Virgil Trucks, Eddie Stanky, and Tommy Holmes. Standouts Roy Campanella, Monte Irvin, and Willie Wells also suited up for the Mackey team.[18] Davis went 3-4 in limited action in the series.

Newark Eagles publicist J.L. Kessler wrote of Davis for the 1945 season: "John Davis, No. 31 – OF. Johnny is a fence buster and has been banging them to the far corner, but some of his longest 'wappos' have been long outs. He still sports a .300 batting average, and when they start falling where they ain't, watch out for Davis!"[19]

The 1946 Eagles were the stuff that legends are made of, and the squad became one of the greatest teams in baseball history. They ran away with the Negro National League with a 56-24-2 record[20] for a .700 winning percentage, finally ending the Homestead Grays' nine-year grip on the title. Davis was a member of what was known as the "Big Four" – the power-hitting quartet that also included Monte Irvin, Larry Doby, and Lennie Pearson.[21] The team also featured pitching standouts, Rufus Lewis, Leon Day, and Max Manning. Together the three pitchers combined for an other-worldly 42-8 record.[22]

The 1946 Negro League World Series was a nailbiter between the Eagles and the Buck O'Neil-led Kansas City Monarchs. The series went down to a deciding seventh game in which Davis delivered one of his career-defining moments. In the bottom of the sixth inning, with the score tied, 1-1 after an O'Neil homer in the top of the inning, Davis laced a double to left field that scored Doby and Irvin and put the Eagles up 3-1.[23] Irvin's run turned out to be the game-winner as the Eagles took the game, 3-2, and the championship, four games to three. Davis was 7-for-24 in the series for a .292 average. He said about his legendary team: "The 1946 Eagles would have beat anybody. We wanted to play the Brooklyn Dodgers. Wouldn't play us, would not play us."[24]

Davis managed to squeeze another highlight into an already memorable 1946 when he signed on with the Satchel Paige vs. Bob Feller barnstorming tour. The two star-studded teams played 12 games between September 29 and October 17. Feller's team was made up of such stars as Stan Musial, Mickey Vernon, Charlie Keller, Phil Rizzuto, Spud Chandler, Johnny Sain, Dutch Leonard, and Bob Lemon. The Paige All-Stars fielded a team that included Buck O'Neil, Quincy Trouppe, Hank Thompson, Ed Steele, Howard Easterling, Hilton Smith, and Davis. It was truly a heavyweight bout.[25] The white major leaguers took a very competitive series, nine games to seven. Davis's heroics happened in game nine on October 12.[26]

Davis described that day's game: "In Kansas City in '46 Bob Feller's team was leading us in the ninth inning with two outs and a man on, and I hit Spud Chandler's fastball over the left-field fence. I picked Phil Rizzuto up at shortstop and carried him piggy-back from shortstop to third base, and we both slid in at home plate together."[27] Davis experienced another career highlight during the tour when he stroked two hits off Bob Feller in a game at Yankee Stadium.[28] As if that wasn't enough, Davis rounded out the year playing for league champion Matanzas of the Cuba Federation.[29] He batted a paltry .238 (26-for-109), but chipped in with 12 runs for the winning club.[30]

The 1947 Newark Eagles were not able to recapture the magic of their championship season, possibly due to the uncertainty of superstar players jumping to the now-integrating major leagues. Newark did manage to do well in the first half of the season, but took a nosedive in the second half when Larry Doby was snatched up by the Cleveland Indians, becoming the first black player to play in the American League. Davis had another stellar year smacking 13 home runs, second in the league, and hitting 17 doubles, two behind the leader.[31]

Davis enjoyed a tremendous amount of success in the Latin American winter leagues, where he was more famous as a pitcher than a hitter. For the 1947-48 season, Davis hooked up with the iconic Mayaguez Indians of the Puerto Rican League and immediately felt right at home. "To me, the best thing was just going from city to city. I just wanted to see the next town. I like to go from here and see what's on the other side of the street. That's what intrigued me, going to different places to play baseball. I guess that's why I liked it so much."[32]

Davis went 12-7 with a 3.22 earned-run average and led the league with 100 strikeouts for the 1947-48 Mayaguez team. In what he described as his most outstanding achievement in baseball, Davis pitched a no-hitter on February 8, 1948, beating the Aguadilla Sharks 1-0.[33] Joining sluggers Luke Easter, Wilmer Fields, and Alonzo Perry, Davis also slugged 11 home runs and played an integral part in leading the Indians to their first of many Puerto Rican championships.[34]

The Negro Leagues began to struggle mightily during the 1948 season and records became even more scarce. The integration of the major leagues and the Negro Leagues' uncertain future were no doubt factors. The Homestead Grays finished the year winning the Negro National League title with a record of 44-23-1, but only seven games of statistics have been found for Johnny Davis.[35] With the league barely hanging on, the Eagles were sold and moved to Houston after the season ended. Looking back on her team with a tinge of melancholy, Effa Manley talked about her players: "We had others who would have developed into great stars had they been given the chance. Leon Day, Rufus Lewis, Willie Wells, Johnny Davis, Terris McDuffie, Joe Ruffin, Mule Suttles, Dick Seay. There were a dozen Newark Eagles who would have been major league stars, not just major league material, but stars."[36]

Johnny Davis' powerful batting stroke the resulted in a .319 average for the season and a .292 mark in the Negro World Series. *(John W. Mosley Collection, Temple University)*

Davis headed south for the winter again for the 1948-49 season, returning to the Mayaguez Indians. He drove in over 50 runs in the 80-game season.[37] Star players Artie Wilson, Wilmer Fields, Luke Easter and Alonzo Perry all rapped out over 100 hits for player-manager Wilson and his championship Indians. Davis returned to Mayaguez for the winter of 1949-50 and managed the team for a short stint.[38]

Davis spent his last two seasons in the Negro Leagues playing for the Houston Eagles. In 1949 he led the league with 14 home runs[39] and played in his third and final East-West All-Star Game. Although the season started out well enough – in one May game Davis hit a homer completely out of the park while also pitching a 4-0 shutout – the Houston incarnation of the Eagles performed poorly.[40] By midsummer the local press had turned on the team and was blaming the players, including Davis. A *Houston Informer* reporter wrote, "Johnny Davis's bat has wilted. Of all things Tuesday night, he had the audacity to strike out when he knows his public expects him to knock one over the left field fence every time he comes to bat."[41] Things did not get any better in 1950, when the team was almost entirely ignored by Houston reporters; no statistics are available for the 1950 season.

With baseball opportunities dwindling in the United States during the steep decline of the Negro Leagues, Davis, along with many other former Negro League players, headed north to Canada. In 1951 he starred for the Drummondville Cubs of the Quebec Provincial League. Davis finished the year batting .347 with 31 home runs and 116 RBIs, all second in the league.[42]

Davis joined the Santurce Crabbers for the 1951-52 Puerto Rican Winter League season, playing the outfield and pitching. The following year he would take the field with 17-year-old Roberto Clemente.[43]

The closest Davis ever came to the major leagues was a stint with the Lefty O'Doul-led San Diego Padres of the Pacific Coast League in 1952.[44] Davis had this to say about his experience:

They wanted me to go to the Chicago White Sox to hit behind Eddie Robinson, but I broke a leg. Before I broke my leg I was hitting about .400 and I was only one home run behind Max West for the league lead. When I came back my average dropped, but the way I started the season, I believe that I could have gone up there (to the majors) and kept on doing what I was doing. I regret not going to the majors … just a little. I'd love to go up there in August or September just to see what it was like.[45]

It wasn't all bad news for Davis in 1952. He was married to Adamit Hasselmyer in Puerto Rico on September 9, 1952.[46]

Davis wasn't quite ready to hang up his spikes and signed with the Pepper Martin-led Fort Lauderdale Lions of the Florida International league for the 1953 season.[47] Proving he still had some fight left in him, while wielding his 35½-inch, 33-ounce bat,[48] Davis broke the league home-run record with 35, drove in 136 runs, and batted .331.[49]

Davis closed out his professional baseball career in 1954 with the Montgomery Rebels of the South Atlantic League. He walloped 8 home runs in 40 games and batted .263.[50]

Davis spent his post-baseball days living in Fort Lauderdale, Florida, with his wife and their two daughters, Diana and Camille. He worked as an auctioneer's assistant at the Galt Plaza Gallery. Davis died on November 18, 1982. He was 64. Probably.[51]

A powerful slugger and pitcher, Johnny Davis stood 6-feet-2 and is listed as weighing 215 pounds during his playing career. He batted and threw right-handed.[52] Davis had a remarkable career and a genuine zest for life, and he deserves more recognition for his accomplishments. Davis reflected on his career shortly before his death: "I had a ball. I really had a ball. Baseball has been very good to me."[53]

SOURCES

All statistics, unless otherwise noted, are from seamheads.com or John B. Holway's *The Complete Book of Baseball's Negro Leagues: The Other Half of Baseball History* (Fern Park, Florida: Hastings House Publishers, 2001). In three places where the stats differed, the more recent Seamheads stats are presented.

NOTES

1   Timothy M. Gay, *Satch, Dizzy & Rapid Robert: The Wild Saga of Interracial Baseball Before Jackie Robinson* (New York: Simon & Schuster, 2010), 237.

2   February 16 is also listed as Davis' birthdate by numerous sources.

3   Clifford Kachline, questionnaire of Davis for the National Baseball Hall of Fame, 1975. Seamheads.com lists Davis's birthplace as Ashland, Virginia.

4   John B. Holway, *Black Diamonds: Life in the Negro Leagues from the Men Who Lived It* (New York: Stadium Books, 1991), 158.

5   Ibid.

6   Holway, *Black Diamonds,* 160.

7   Holway, *Black Diamonds,* 160-161.

8   James A. Riley, *The Biographical Encyclopedia of the Negro Leagues* (New York: Carroll & Graf, 1994), 216.

9   James Overmyer, *Effa Manley and the Newark Eagles* (New Jersey: The Scarecrow Press, Inc., 1993), 194.

10   Ibid.

11   Kachline questionnaire.

12   James A. Riley, *Of Monarchs and Black Barons* (Jefferson, North Carolina: McFarland & Company, Inc., 2012), 188.

13   Ibid.

14   Holway, *Black Diamonds*, 157.

15   John B. Holway, *The Complete Book of Baseball's Negro Leagues: The Other Half of Baseball History* (Fern Park, Florida: Hastings House Publishers, 2001), 415.

16   Larry Lester, *Black Baseball's National Showcase: The East-West All-Star Game, 1933-1953* (Lincoln: University of Nebraska Press, 2001), 237.

17   Bob Luke, *The Most Famous Woman in Baseball: Effa Manley and the Negro Leagues* (Dulles, Virginia: Potomac Books, Inc., 2011), 103.

18   William F. McNeil, *Black Baseball Out of Season* (Jefferson, North Carolina: McFarland & Company, Inc., 2007), 105.

19   Robert L. Cvornyek, *Baseball in Newark* (Charleston, South Carolina: Arcadia Publishing, 2003), 96.

20   Seamheads.com

21   Riley, *Of Monarchs and Black Barons*, 189.

22   John Holway, *The Complete Book of Baseball's Negro Leagues*, 437.

23   Overmyer, 207.

24   Holway, *Black Diamonds*, 163.

25   Holway, *The Complete Book of Baseball's Negro Leagues*, 441-443.

26   Holway, *The Complete Book of Baseball's Negro Leagues*, 442-443.

27   Holway, *Black Diamonds*, 165.

28   Riley, *Of Monarchs and Black Barons*, 190.

29   Holway, *The Complete Book of Baseball's Negro Leagues,* 444.

30   Jorge Figueredo, *Cuban Baseball: A Statistical History 1878-1961* (Jefferson, North Carolina: McFarland & Company, Inc., 2003), 284-85.

31   Figueredo, 447-448.

32   Riley, *Of Monarchs and Black Barons*, 190.

33   For Davis's valuation of his game, see Clifford Kachline, questionnaire of Davis for the National Baseball Hall of Fame, 1975. For the game itself, see "Davis Pitches Second Puerto Rico No-Hitter," *The Sporting News*, February 18, 1948: 24,

34   Thomas E. Van Hyning, *Puerto Rico's Winter League* (Jefferson, North Carolina: McFarland & Company, Inc., 1995), 140.

35   Van Hyning, *Puerto Rico's Winter League*, 211.

36   John Holway, *Voices From the Great Black Baseball Leagues* (New York: Da Capo Press, Inc., 1992), 318.

37   Van Hyning, *Puerto Rico's Winter League*, 140.

38   Lou Hernandez, *The Rise of the Latin American Baseball Leagues, 1947-1961* (Jefferson, North Carolina: McFarland & Company, Inc., 2011), 243.

39   Dick Clark & Larry Lester, *The Negro Leagues Book* (Cleveland: SABR, 1994), 276.

40   Rob Fink, *Playing in Shadows: Texas and Negro League Baseball* (Lubbock: Texas Tech University Press, 2010), 115.

41   Ibid.

42   Barry Swanton & Jay Dell Mah, *Black Baseball Players in Canada* (Jefferson, North Carolina: McFarland & Company, Inc., 2009), 56-57.

43   Thomas E. Van Hyning, *The Santurce Crabbers: Sixty Seasons of Puerto Rican Winter League Baseball* (Jefferson, North Carolina: McFarland & Company, Inc., 1999), 223-224.

44   Holway, *Black Diamonds*, 163.

45   Riley, *Of Monarchs and Black Barons*, 191.

46   Kachline questionnaire.

47   Riley, *Of Monarchs and Black Barons*, 191.

48   Dick Meyer, "Time Out for Sports," *Fort Lauderdale Daily News*, June 3, 1953.

49   Riley, *The Biographical Encyclopedia of the Negro Baseball Leagues*, 217.

50   Ibid.

51   Kachline questionnaire.

52   Ibid.

53   Riley, *Of Monarchs and Black Barons*, 191.

LEON DAY

BY THOMAS KERN

"If we had one game to win, we wanted Leon to pitch."
— Monte Irvin

So much of Leon Day's story is caught up in his last years and his long wait for the Hall of Fame call. For Day, who spent a lifetime exceeding at his professional calling, punching his card at every level of baseball but one, the word from the Hall came in what were to be his final days. "I thought this day would never come. I'm feeling pretty good," he said when he received word from the Hall at his hospital bed on March 8, 1995. "I'm so happy, I don't know what to do. I never thought it would come." He was joined that day in the hospital (where he had been admitted for diabetes and heart troubles) by his wife, family, teammates, and friends to share the good news of his induction with him.[1]

There had been times when he said this accolade was not important. He had said as much about the money, too. "When they told me they was gonna pay me to play baseball, I said they must be crazy. I said I'd play for nothing." He valued his career in the Negro Leagues, especially knowing that it gave him the memories and sense of accomplishment it did. "I was glad to play in the Negro Leagues. I wouldn't trade it for anything in the world."[2] However, in a 1992 interview in conjunction with his throwing out the first ball at a September 24, 1992, Baltimore Orioles game, Day acknowledged that "it would mean a lot to me to get into the Hall of Fame, to be grouped with some of the greatest players in history."[3]

Ace pitcher Leon Day threw a no-hitter on May 5 to kick off the Eagles' march to the 1946 Negro League championship. Day was inducted into the National Baseball Hall of Fame in 1995. *(National Baseball Hall of Fame)*

In the end, the call meant everything to him, perhaps giving him the impetus he needed to enter the next world. For Day died on March 14, 1995, at the age of 78, five days after he got word of the ultimate honor. "I think that's what he was waiting for," said his sister Ida May Bolden.[4] And so it was his wife, Geraldine, who tearfully spoke on his behalf at the induction ceremony in Cooperstown that summer, surrounded by the many Hall of Famers on stage Day wanted to have as peers.

With his induction, Leon Day became the 12th Negro League representative in the Hall and the first to be voted in since 1987, when Ray Dandridge was inducted.

Timing is everything or nothing, and Day's overdue induction in 1995 came after an increasingly more demonstrative campaign on his behalf over several years that finally bore fruit. In 1993 Day fell one vote shy in Veterans Committee deliberations, star-crossed by the unfortunate absence due to sickness of Veterans Committee member Roy Campanella (a former Negro leaguer himself and three-time MVP for the Brooklyn Dodgers). In 1995, the votes were there.

***

Leon Day's signature was the matter-of-fact, low-key manner through which he approached his craft. This was evident both in terms of his pitching style and his personality.

Day was often overshadowed by more colorful players. Most notable was Satchel Paige, whom, records show, he defeated in three of four head-to-head pitching contests. Paige's delivery was over the top, both in terms of mechanics and showmanship. In the eyes of some, it was all about self-promotion. In contrast, according to Monte Irvin, "Leon was as good as Satchel Paige, as good as any pitcher who ever lived, but he never made any noise. Leon was never the promoter Satch was."[5] Max Manning, a former Newark Eagles teammate of Day's, said, "If Satchel Paige is like the Negro League icon, Leon Day is the warrior."[6]

When it came to Day's pitching, his famous no-windup delivery was his trademark. It masked an intensity and effectiveness that likely won him around 300 games. "Day could throw as hard as anyone. I didn't see anyone in the major leagues who was better than Leon Day. If you want to compare him with Bob Gibson, Day had just as good stuff. Tremendous curveball and a fastball at least 90-95 miles an hour. You talk about Satchel. … I didn't see anyone better than Day."[7] These were the words of Larry Doby, who played alongside Day on the Newark Eagles and who later broke the American League color barrier by joining the Cleveland Indians in 1947 after Jackie Robinson debuted with the Brooklyn Dodgers in the National League.

The Satchel Paige comparison was common—on all levels. Paige's flamboyance versus Day's quiet, workmanlike approach; Paige's tall stature versus Day's 5-feet-8, 170-pound frame; Paige's self-promotion versus Day's reluctance to draw attention to his exploits. And perhaps most important, the infrequent but remarkable head-to-head competition that had Leon winning three of four games against Satchel.

Day admitted that he did not remember the details of that many of his games, but he did recall the Paige/Day matchups. "I faced him about four times. I beat him three. They were all low-scoring games. … [In one game] we were playin' and the score was 0-0. My team wouldn't get me a run, so I came into the ninth inning, got lucky, and hit a home run to win it 1-0."[8]

According to Negro league historian Todd Bolton, "He was never a self promoter. If he were, he might have been elected [to the Hall of Fame] years ago. But he was a humble man and let his record speak for itself."[9] In Leon's own words, "I could hold my own."[10]

Buck O'Neil's "scouting report" on Day, filled out on a Kansas City Royals scouting form years later described his pitching as follows, "Front line starter, short arm type, everything quick, strike out pitcher, very durable, worked with three days rest, played 2B or LF between starts, top athlete, very desirable."[11] O'Neil's reference to short-arming merits a little more elaboration.

Gene Benson, an infielder with the Philadelphia Stars and a friend of Day's, described Leon's pitching method of throwing the ball from his ear, as he did when he was an infielder when playing as a youth in Baltimore's Mount Winans neighborhood. This short-arming, as it was called, went something like this, according to Benson: "He threw that ball more or less from his hip. He didn't rear back and come right over his shoulder. He came right from his thigh, but he would whistle the ball and make it move. He could bring it!"[12] Day admitted the motion was not natural. "I think I pitched that way from the way I threw the ball from second base. I think that's where that came from."[13] Said Day, "When I threw overhand, it would hurt my shoulder…but from here [his ear], I'd feel nothing. I threw my fast ball straight up. I couldn't throw overhand, so I jerked it at them. It fooled a lot of hitters." [14]

After a dozen years of professional ball, with only sporadic play during his time in the armed forces, the delivery might have expedited his arm troubles in 1946.

Leon, like many Negro League pitchers, played on his "offdays." Second base, left field, center field—Leon provided good, consistent fielding and a decent bat to go along with his pitching every third day. Monte Irvin said, "He's played center field as good as or better than or starting center fielder did. The center fielder at that time was me."[15]

***

Born in Alexandria, Virginia, on October 30, 1916, Leon Day was of an age to take part in some stellar years of the Negro Leagues, from 1934 to 1946. Yet, as fate would have it, the color line was broken too late and he was too old to be seriously considered for the majors. His only chance might have come just as he returned from his military service. As the story goes, Jackie Robinson asked Day to join him in the Dodgers organization with the Montreal Royals in the spring of 1946. Day demurred, having already signed with the Newark Eagles so that he could return to his old ballclub, which had been very good to him over the years. Who knows what might have happened for Day had he joined Robinson in Montreal?

Looking further back in Leon's life, to his earliest years, it was his family's move from Alexandria to Baltimore when he was 6 months old that would pair him forever with what would become one of his two hometowns—Baltimore (with Newark as the other). His father, Ellis Day, got a job at the Westport glass factory so that he and his wife, Hattie, could make enough to help raise their six children. They lived in nearby Mount Winans, then a poverty-stricken, all-black community in Southwest Baltimore in a house with no electricity or running water. For Leon, baseball became an early fixture. He would do anything to see the Baltimore Black Sox play at Maryland Baseball Park in Westport (another Baltimore neighborhood). "I had to go over the fence, under the fence. … I got in there some kind of way," he said.[16]

By the time Day was 12 he was playing with the Mount Winans Athletic Club. He was good at ball and in the tenth grade, much to the disappointment of his mother, he left Frederick Douglass High School because it had no baseball team. This was 1934, when Day was 17. He began playing with a semipro team, the Silver Moons, and soon his second base and pitching skills caught the attention of Rap Dixon, the manager of the Baltimore Black Sox. Dixon signed Day to play the rest of the 1934 season with the Black Sox, who were now playing in nearby Chester. For Day the significance of this move was the mentoring he received from Lamon Yokeley, a pitcher for the Black Sox. According to Yokeley, "I'd tell him what to do, hate not to do. He was my boy."[17] One can only imagine the tutoring that an impressionable teenager received about the Negro Leagues and pitching.

The instability of the Black Sox franchise led Dixon, Yokeley, and Day to jump to the Brooklyn Eagles in 1935. Ben Taylor, the Eagles manager, liked Day's pitching and used him almost exclusively as a starter. The luxury of being able to refine his delivery and pitch consistently must have helped Leon; he pitched a one-hitter that year, compiled a 9-2 record, and pitched in his first of seven Negro League All Star games. Max Manning, his teammate of five seasons, recognized early that Day's fastball-curve- changeup assortment was lethal. Manning said, "I still think that the players, if you said to the team at any given time, who would you like to pitch, they would all choose Leon. When he was right, I don't think there was anybody his equal."[18]

Doubtless Manning appreciated this as it propelled the Eagles into the upper echelon of the Negro Leagues for quite a few years.

The Eagles moved to Newark in 1936 and there they stayed – and Day with them for much of the next decade, save for arm troubles in 1938, brief stays with Philadelphia and Homestead, his brief foray in search of a higher salary to Vargas, Venezuela, and then Vera Cruz, Mexico, in 1940 (where he helped both teams win their league championships), and then military service. As for 1938, Leon told the story this way: "Well, I was in Cuba in the winter of 1937. I was playing in Cuba, and I'm in the shower and I slipped and caught myself with my right arm. I felt something pull right then. Then, in '38, when I came back, my arm was messed up."[19]

***

Negro League seasons were short, at 40 to 60-plus games, only about a third or more the length of a 154-game major-league schedule. That did not mean there was no other baseball to be had for Leon and his peers. The rest of the time was filled with barnstorming exhibitions, sometimes against a mix of major-league talent, and invariably winter-league ball. For Leon, Puerto Rico and Cuba were his offseason havens. The records that exist show that he played for Almendares (1937-38) and Santiago (1947-48), winning two-thirds of his games. Statistics are spotty for these campaigns, but Day's Puerto Rican sojourn is the stuff of celebrity. He played winter ball for six years in Puerto Rico, most notably with the Aguadilla Sharks. Records show that he went 34-26 for the team, struck out 19 in one game in 1939-40 (a Puerto Rican baseball record), batted over .300 each year, and struck out a league record 168 in 1941-42. In 1993 the Puerto Rico Baseball Hall of Fame stole a march on Cooperstown and inducted Leon in recognition for his exploits.

Day's decade of Negro League excellence had several signature moments. Best of all, according to Day himself, was 1937, which he considered his best all-around season. A 13-0 record and 3.02 ERA went along with his .320 average and eight home runs. The Eagles and their all-star (million-dollar) infield of Ray Dandridge, Willie Wells, Dick Seay, and Mule Suttles came in second to the Homestead Grays, led by Josh Gibson and Buck Leonard.

On July 31, 1942, Day set a Negro League record by striking out 18 Baltimore Elite Giants in a one-hitter. The only hit was a bloop single by Pee Wee Butts to short left field.

Also in 1942, after Game Three in one of the quirkier Negro World Series stories, Cum Posey, owner of the Homestead Grays, signed four players (three Newark Eagles and one Philadelphia Star) to fill out a depleted roster. The primary signing was Leon Day, who pitched Game Four (the Grays were down three games to none at the time) against Satchel Paige. Day pitched a complete-game five-hitter and won, 4-1. The game was subsequently protested by Kansas City and overturned by league officials because of Homestead's use of ringers. Game Four was replayed and won, along with the Series, by the Monarchs.

The *Pittsburgh Courier*, one of the most respected African American papers covering the Negro Leagues, ranked Leon Day ahead of Paige as best pitcher in 1942 and 1943. In 1942 the article naming its All American Team for the Negro Leagues said, "Leon Day is the best pitcher in Negro baseball … despite the fact he is used daily either as a pitcher, outfielder, or infielder."[20] And again in 1943 the *Courier* named him the "outstanding moundsman in Negro baseball [over Satchel Paige]."[21]

Much is made, and for good reason, of Ted Williams, Bob Feller, and others who sacrificed the prime of their baseball careers for their country. Leon Day belonged to this fraternity, too. He was drafted into the Army on September 1, 1943, and served America during the Normandy invasion and its aftermath. Leon served with a segregated amphibious unit (the 818th Amphibious Battalion), and helped land supplies at Utah Beach on June 12, six days after D-Day. "I was scared as hell. I'll never forget Jun 12th. I lost a lot of good friends."[22]

Day served until February 1946 and while under military orders, wore a second uniform as a pitcher for the integrated Overseas Invasion Service Expedition (OISE) All Star Baseball team, an aggregation run by Philadelphia Phillies pitcher Sam Nahem that competed against teams from other units. He and his team were good enough to play in and win the European Theater of Operations World Series against the 71st Infantry Division team featuring a number of major leaguers led by Ewell Blackwell. Day was 1-1 against the 71st in OISE's 3-2 series victory. Records show that crowds in excess of 50,000 watched each of the games, held at Nuremberg Stadium in Germany. If barnstorming wasn't proof that Negro League players could hold their own against white players, Day's performance in Game Two of the Series, a 2-1 four-hit, ten-strikeout victory, should offer strong evidence.

Day returned to the US in 1946 in time to rejoin his Newark Eagles teammates for the season. His first game back was the stuff of legends—a May 5 Opening Day no-hitter against the Philadelphia Stars. However, Leon said that owing to the combination of a decade of pitching and two years missed because of military service, he was past his prime as a pitcher. He knew his arm didn't feel right. "It wasn't the same no more."[23] And, in fact, he hurt his arm more in that May 5 game on a fielding play, but nonetheless finished the no-hitter to the acclaim of the hometown crowd. Remarkably, despite Day's arm troubles, he compiled a 13-4 record, led the league in wins, strikeouts, innings pitched,

and complete games that year (all of this and a batting average of .469), and led Newark to the Negro National League pennant.

Despite his dead arm, Day pitched in Game One of the 1946 World Series for Newark, the Negro National League winner, against Kansas City (the Negro American League champion), but came out of the game after the seventh inning with the game tied at 1-1. The game took place in front of what might have been a major-league audition before many baseball scouts who also were seeing the likes of Satchel Paige, Larry Doby, Monte Irvin, Hank Thompson, and Willard Brown, all of whom eventually played in the majors. Day pitched in another game, but was ineffective and did not play again in the Series. Newark won the World Series in seven games, with the last matchup noteworthy due to Satchel Paige's unknown whereabouts.

The season of 1946 was not the end for Leon Day. He would go on to play in Mexico and Cuba in 1947 and 1948, drawn by the financial remuneration he could obtain. He played for the Mexico City Red Devils both seasons with an 18-20 combined record and an ERA around 4.00. "I made more money in Mexico than I did here in the States," he said. "I played about four months a year and made about $5,000."[24] Although Negro League officials banned players for five years for going to Mexico, the ban was lifted after one year and Day returned to the US to play in what would be his last year for a Negro League team. In 1949 he returned to Baltimore to help lead the Baltimore Elite Giants to the Negro American League Eastern Division pennant and then playoff victory over the Chicago American Giants by four games to none. The following year, his journey took him to the semipro ManDak League in Canada, where he played for the Winnipeg Buffaloes.

Perhaps the most compelling legacy that Day left in the annals of Negro League history was his record seven appearances in the East West All-Star Game: 1935, 1937, 1939 (two games), 1942, 1943, and 1946. In addition to appearing in more games than anyone else, he held the record of 14 total strikeouts. This acknowledgement by the Negro League hierarchy that the All-Star Game was better off with Day in it spoke volumes.

Day's next-to-last career move in 1951 placed him for the first time in Organized Baseball, albeit the minors. He and a number of other Negro Leaguers, some young and others past their prime, are credited with the hard work of integrating the minors, just as Jackie Robinson, Larry Doby, and their peers did so on the major-league stage.

To be involved in any part of Organized Baseball at all remained important to him and when the chance to play in the minors arose, Leon signed with Toronto of the Triple-A International League in 1951, pitching in 14 games with a 1-1 record and an ERA of 1.58. He played two more years in the minors (Scranton, Double-A

Eastern) in 1952 and Edmonton (Class-A Western International) in 1953. This must have been an immeasurably harder task for Day and his black brethren, for they had to ply their trade at times in deeply segregated towns without the gratification of major-league status or a decent paycheck. "We didn't worry about that," he said of playing in segregated ballparks. "See, we loved to play baseball. As long as we played, we didn't care where we played."[25]

When asked if he was upset that he did not make it to the majors, Leon said that he and other Negro Leaguers who played minor-league ball "never talked about it. We figured we were in the major leagues [by playing in the minors]. We were as high as we could go."[26]

Day's career ended back in the semipro ManDak League, where he played for Winnipeg in 1954 and Brandon in 1955.

In the years after his retirement from baseball, Day lived first in Newark, where he worked as a bartender, and then returned to Baltimore, the town to which his family moved when he was a child. He continued to work, mainly as a security guard, and retired in 1979. A widower, he remarried and upon his death on March 14, 1995 in Baltimore was survived by his wife and sister.

NOTES

1   Brad Snyder, "'You made it, man': Day named to Hall of Fame," *Baltimore Sun*, March 8, 1995: 1A.

2   Tom Keyser, "It's Day's turn to throw again," *Baltimore Sun*, September 24, 1992: 6D.

3   "Baltimore's Day had Hall of Fame numbers," *Daily Mail*, September 25, 1992.

4   Brad Snyder, "Day dies a week after greatest honor," *Baltimore Sun*, March 14, 1995: 1A.

5   "Leon Day, Selected Last Week for Hall of Fame, is Dead at 78," *New York Times*, March 15, 1992.

6   Brad Snyder, "Day dies a week after greatest honor."

7   Rick Hines, "Leon Day: the man Cooperstown forgot," *Sports Collector's Digest*, March 13, 1992: 70.

8   Ibid., 71.

9   Brad Snyder, "Day dies a week after greatest honor."

10   Tom Keyser.

11   The Baseball Hall of Fame holds copies of a number of Buck O'Neil's scouting reports on Negro League ballplayers, completed on forms routinely used by the Kansas City Royals for whom O'Neil served as a scout from 1988 to 1998. The report noted that Day's overall makeup was a 4 or excellent.

12   Tim Wendel, "In His Day, Leon Day was the Best," National Pastime Museum, March 5, 2013. https://www.thenationalpastimemuseum.com/article/his-day-leon-day-was-best

13   Rick Hines, 71.

14   John Holway, *Blackball Stars* (Westport, Connecticut: Meckler Publishers, 1988), 345.

15   Brad Snyder, "Negro League Star Leon Day Waits for Fame,' *Baltimore Sun*, March 5, 1995.

16   James A. Riley, *Dandy, Day, and the Devil* (Cocoa, Florida: TK Publishers, 1987), 78.

17   John Holway, 347.

18   Brad Snyder, "'You made it, man': Day named to Hall of Fame," *Baltimore Sun*, March 8, 1995: 1A.

19   Rick Hines, 70.

20   Cum Posey, "Kansas City, Homestead Grays Stars Dominate 'Dream Team'," *Pittsburgh Courier*, November 7, 1942" 17.

21   "To Make Plans for 1943 at Meeting," *Pittsburgh Courier*, January 23, 1943, 16.

22   John Steadman, "Integration couldn't keep up with Day's best fastball, either," *Baltimore Sun*, February 3, 1992.

23   James A. Riley, 75.

24   John B. Holway, "Day Crossed a Road Less Traveled to Cooperstown," *Washington Post*, March 19, 1995.

25   Tom Keyser.

26   Ibid.

LARRY DOBY

BY JOHN MCMURRAY

Larry Doby is best remembered for becoming the first black player in the American League and the second in modern history in major-league baseball. When Doby made his major-league debut for the Cleveland Indians on July 5, 1947, he broke the league's color barrier less than three months after Jackie Robinson first played for the Brooklyn Dodgers.[1] In the face of racial prejudice, Doby remained a superior hitter and outfielder during his 13-season career, with selection to seven American League All-Star teams. "I had to take it," Doby said, "but I fought back by hitting the ball as far as I could. That was my answer."[2]

Lawrence Eugene Doby was born on December 13, 1923, in Camden, South Carolina. Larry's father, David, met his future wife, Etta, while playing baseball on the street in front of her home.[3] Biographer Joseph Thomas Moore wrote that the Dobys were "one of the most prosperous black families in Camden."[4]

David Doby was a stable hand, grooming the horses of many wealthy New Jersey families. The marriage, however, was strained because of David's frequent travel and Etta's strong attachment to her own mother, leaving young Larry often in the care of his grandmother, Augusta Moore. She recounted how Doby said that Augusta "made me go to church with her all the time. I liked what I heard in the Twenty-Third Psalm and the Ten Commandments. Somehow I got the feeling that the church helped black people to be themselves. I liked that feeling."[5]

When Larry was eight years old, his father died in a tragic accident.[6] David had gone fishing on a day off, and he drowned after falling from a boat while fishing on Lake Mohansic, in upstate

Larry Doby and the 1946 Newark Eagles won the Negro League championship. In 1947 he integrated the American League as a Cleveland Indians player; the next season he won the World Series with Cleveland. *(Noir-Tech Research, Inc.)*

New York.[7] His death began a tumultuous time for Larry, during which he moved frequently and was cared for by his aunt and uncle.[8] Four years after his father's death, Larry and his mother left South Carolina and moved to Paterson, New Jersey.[9]

It wasn't easy for Doby in Paterson. "I was lonely living alone," he said. "But I just kept trying to be me."[10] In Paterson, Doby began following in the footsteps of his father, who had been a semipro ballplayer. He developed his skills playing sandlot baseball close to home, at the Newman Playground and on Twelfth Avenue. Doby lettered in baseball at Paterson Eastside High School, where he was one of about 25 black students in the school. He won letters in three other sports, a total of 11 in all. Initially, Doby had thoughts of finishing high school and then becoming a physical education teacher or perhaps a coach.[11]

Doby was more introspective than demonstrative, and his personality could confuse his teammates. As recounted by biographer Moore, high-school teammate Al Kachuadurian never felt he could slap Doby on the back, and thought Doby kept his teammates at a distance.[12] "I remember distinctly that if things didn't go just right, he'd sulk. Deep down, he's a warm-hearted guy. But you didn't know if he was sulking at you personally, or whether he was sulking inwardly at himself."[13] Doby, however, later countered that he wasn't sulking at all but had gotten accustomed to being alone based upon the circumstances in his life.[14] In some sense, Doby's self-reliance may have been mistaken for aloofness.

Even before graduating from high school, Doby began playing second base under the assumed name of Larry Walker in the Negro Leagues for the Newark Eagles.[15] He was an immediate star, and team owners offered him $300 to play between high school and college.[16] Although statistics from his first season are inexact, Doby believed he had batted around .400 during that summer.[17]

Doby enrolled at Long Island University. Part of his motivation was to play for renowned basketball coach Clair Bee. Another reason was to be able to visit Helyn Curvy, whom Doby had begun dating at Eastside High School when he was a sophomore.[18] Curvy's father had died, however, and responsibilities for taking care of her siblings prevented Curvy from attending any of Doby's high-school baseball games.[19] "But when I had a game," Doby recalled, "I'd take her brother George to the game with me, then I'd bring him back to her house."[20]

At the time, Doby had concern about being drafted into the military during World War II.[21] He made the difficult decision to transfer from Long Island University to Virginia Union College, where he would play basketball for coach Henry Hucles.[22] Doby believed he could transfer into an ROTC program there.[23] Yet he was drafted into the Navy at the conclusion of the basketball season. The mandated racial segregation of the military at the time left a deep impression on him.[24] He was assigned to Camp Robert Smalls, the black division of the Great Lakes Naval Training Station, outside Chicago.[25]

Due in large part to his outstanding physical condition, Doby was able to become a physical education instructor there.[26] He kept his baseball and basketball skills sharp by playing in the afternoons. Doby got to know future NFL Hall of Famer Marion Motley

while on his tour of duty.[27] Later, while stationed in the Pacific, Doby began what became a lifelong friendship with Washington Senators star Mickey Vernon.[28] Vernon wrote to Senators owner Clark Griffith, touting Doby's playing abilities. After their military service was done, "[Vernon] sent me a gift of some bats when I started the 1946 season with the [Newark] Eagles," Doby recalled.[29] "It was a gift I'll never forget."[30]

In 1945, general manager Branch Rickey of the Brooklyn Dodgers signed Jackie Robinson to a contract to play baseball in Montreal. The move made Doby reconsider his options, as playing baseball in the major leagues now seemed a possibility. "My main thing was to become a teacher and coach," Doby said. "But when I heard about Jackie, I decided to concentrate on baseball. I forgot about going back to college."[31]

Doby was honorably discharged from the military in January 1946. After playing two months of winter ball with the San Juan Senators for $500 a month at the invitation of Monte Irvin, a prewar teammate on the Newark Eagles, Doby subsequently rejoined the Eagles. Being close to home also allowed him to date Helyn again. "She told me if we didn't get married that year, 1946, to forget it," Doby said.[32] "We got married on August 10, 1946, in Paterson."[33] The night of their wedding, the couple drove to Trenton, where Doby was scheduled to play.[34] The game was rained out.[35] A few days later, Doby played in a Negro Leagues All-Star game against a team including Josh Gibson.

The Eagles went on to win the Negro Leagues World Series in 1946. Doby batted .272 with one home run in that series against the Kansas City Monarchs of the Negro American League. He tagged a runner out at second base for the second out of the ninth inning of the seventh game, and he caught a popup for the final out of the series. "To play the Monarchs in the World Series!" Doby later exclaimed. "They had Satchel Paige and all those guys. That was a great team. To beat those guys, you were in the upper echelon of baseball."[36]

With Doby's notoriety high after the 1946 championship season, Bill Veeck, the owner of the Cleveland Indians, took notice. Veeck, who had long been eager to racially integrate the American League, hatched a plan for Doby to join Cleveland right after the 1947 All-Star break. Doby had played the first half of the season with the Eagles, and he had hit a home run in his final Newark at-bat. The Cleveland team quietly purchased Doby's contract and brought him to Cleveland. A scoop by local writer Bob Whiting forced the team to move up Doby's first game from July 10, which was the original intention, to July 5.[37]

Teammates, however, did not immediately welcome Doby, averting their eyes and not speaking to him as he made his entry to the clubhouse at Comiskey Park to meet with player-manager

Lou Boudreau.[38] "Shrug it off," Boudreau reportedly said.[39] Still, Doby in 2002 recalled, "I knew it was segregated times, but I had never seen anything like that in athletics. I was embarrassed. It was tough." As Bill White later noted, Doby had to go to the Chicago clubhouse to get a first baseman's glove since none of his Cleveland teammates offered him one.[40]

Pinch-hitting for Bryan Stephens against Earl Harrist of the White Sox, Doby struck out in his first major-league at-bat. On July 6, in the second game of that day's doubleheader, Doby made his only start of the season at first base. He got his first major-league hit, a single off Orval Grove in the third inning that also gave him his first RBI.[41] During that difficult first season, Doby batted only .156 in 29 games with two RBIs. "It was 11 weeks between the time Jackie Robinson and I came into the majors. I can't see how things were any different for me than they were for him," Doby said.[42]

He had to wait until the start of the 1948 season to win a starting job in Cleveland's outfield. During his first full season, Doby hit 14 home runs and had 66 RBIs. That fall, Doby became the first black player to hit a home run in the World Series when he connected off the Boston Braves' Johnny Sain in Game Four. His blast helped lead Cleveland to a 2-1 win and a lead of three games to one in the Series. A photo taken after the game showing Doby embracing Cleveland pitcher Steve Gromek has become one of the most famous in baseball history, symbolizing an erosion of racial divisions and Doby's acceptance as a member of his new team.

The 1948 season was the first of 10 consecutive years in which Doby hit at least 14 home runs and drove in at least 50 runs. He was selected to the All-Star team in every year between 1949 and 1955 and finished in the top 10 in the American League MVP voting in 1950 and 1954. Doby's finest statistical season was 1952, when he led the American League in slugging percentage (.541), home runs (32), and runs scored (104). He hit for the cycle that year against Boston on June 4 at Fenway Park. The last time an American Leaguer accomplished that feat until Mickey Mantle did it in 1957.[43]

In 1954, Doby was Cleveland's most dominant offensive player, leading the American League in home runs (32) and runs batted in (126). He also played a stellar center field, committing only two errors in 153 games while finishing second in the league in putouts. Doby's regular season success that year, like that of many of his teammates, did not extend into the World Series, as he was able to manage only two singles in the four games against the New York Giants. Still, for his regular-season efforts, Doby finished second in the 1954 American League Most Valuable Player award voting to Yogi Berra.

After the 1955 season, during which Doby battled a wrist injury, he was traded to the Chicago White Sox for Jim Busby and

Newark Eagles teammates Monte Irvin and Larry Doby (at right) went on to Hall of Fame major-league careers with the New York Giants and Cleveland Indians respectively. *(Noir-Tech Research, Inc.)*

Chico Carrasquel. At the time, Chicago manager Marty Marion said that Doby's arrival was "the end of the search for a No. 4 hitter."[44] Marion later said, "This guy used to murder us when we played Cleveland. Last year, I definitely felt that, when we could get him out, we could handle the Indians. But we couldn't – and the record shows that they had a season break on us, 12-10."[45]

Doby immediately delivered with Chicago, hitting 24 home runs and knocking in 102 runs. During a nine-game winning streak in June 1956, Doby hit five home runs, leading White Sox owner Charles Comiskey to remark, "Larry Doby, he's our guy. You know, when we dealt for Doby, we weren't worried about Larry. We knew he'd come through."[46]

Doby was involved in one of the bigger melees of the 1957 season. In a game on June 12, Art Ditmar of the Yankees threw a pitch inside, causing Doby to fall to his knees. Both benches emptied, and Doby knocked Ditmar down with a punch to his jaw. Doby also got into an on-field fight with Billy Martin after the umpires had restored order. Doby, teammate Walt Dropo, and the Yankees' Enos Slaughter and Martin were all thrown out of the game. The Yankees, feeling that penalties against their players by the league were unjustified, paid all fines of their players assessed after the incident.[47]

After his power numbers faded a bit during the 1957 season, Doby was traded to Baltimore that December with Jack Harshman, Russ Heman, and Jim Marshall in return for Tito Francona, Ray Moore, and Billy Goodman. Manager Al Lopez explained the deal, saying, "We wouldn't start another season with Doby because the fans are down on him."[48] A contemporary article noted that the fans often booed Doby at Comiskey Park, leading to resentment on Doby's part.[49] Doby never played with the Orioles, being traded again before the season began on April 1. This time he went back to the Cleveland Indians along with Don Ferrarese for Dick Williams, Gene Woodling, and Bud Daley.

By then, however, injuries had taken their toll, and Doby was a part-time player. In 1958, he hit 13 home runs and batted in 45 runs in only 89 games. Just before the 1959 season, Doby was traded to the Detroit Tigers for Tito Francona. Finally, on May 13, 1959, he was purchased from Detroit by the Chicago White Sox for $30,000.

Chicago was Doby's last major-league stop as a player. By then 35 years old, he played in only 21 games, batting .241 with no home runs and only nine runs batted in. His final game in the major leagues was on July 26. Sent down to the White Sox' San Diego farm team in the Pacific Coast League, Doby fractured an ankle sliding into third base on a triple on August 23.[50] Doby finished his major-league career with a .283 batting average, 243 doubles, 253 home runs, and 970 RBIs.

In 1960, Doby signed with the Toronto Maple Leafs of the International League, but because of the lingering effects of his ankle injury, he was released in May without getting into a game. In 1962 he played for the Nagoya Dragons in Japan. He went on to coach with Montreal, Cleveland, and the White Sox.[51] He also owned a lounge and a liquor store in Newark, and he worked in the Essex County prosecutor's office in New Jersey for three years.[52]

During that time, Doby wrote letters to major-league teams seeking the opportunity to be a major-league manager.[53] In 1971, when he was a batting coach for the Montreal Expos, Doby spoke of the possibility of managing in the major leagues in an interview: "The Expos know what I want to do," he said. "But they want me to work my way up. …They want me to wait. I don't mind waiting because right now I'm learning. But I can't wait for the rest of my life."[54] Doby remarked that he enjoyed working with kids in part because he had good training – he had five children of his own.

Doby received the chance to manage in 1978, becoming the second black manager in major-league history when he took over the White Sox. He succeeded Bob Lemon, who was fired, but took over the Yankees and led them to the pennant. Doby's time managing was filled with frustration, however, as he had a record of only 37-50 during the portion of the one season in which he managed during his career. Doby cited injuries for the team's failures, saying, "When you have to use people you hope can play, rather than those you know can play, you are in a bad situation."[55]

He also maintained strong feelings about why he had to wait until the age of 53 to receive the Chicago managerial job: "Why did it take this long? You tell me. I don't mean to sound prejudiced, but you can look at the system and see that, until I was named

(to replace Lemon on June 30), there was no black manager in the major leagues."[56]

After the 1978 season, Doby was fired as the team's manager. "I can't truly say what kind of manager I was or could've been because I didn't have enough time," he said.[57] "I thought I could have been successful. I thought I had those intangibles."[58]

After his managerial career was over, Doby remained active with major-league baseball. He was an administrator for the Former Players Licensing Branch of Major League Baseball, helping to license people or companies that wanted to use players or their trademarks for card shows or speaking engagements.[59] In 1995, Doby was named special assistant to American League president Gene Budig, who said at the time, "Few have done more for Major League Baseball than Larry Doby, and we are excited about having him associated with us."[60] Doby later was also named to the Baseball World board.[61]

In 1997, the Indians retired Doby's number 14 on the 50th anniversary of his major-league debut.[62] He became the fifth Cleveland player to be so honored, joining Bob Feller, Earl Averill, Mel Harder, and Lou Boudreau.[63] A banner was displayed in left field on July 5, 1997, at Jacobs Field, showing Doby and Jackie Robinson, saying "50 years: 1947-1997."[64] At the ceremony, Hank Aaron said to Doby, "I want to thank you for all that you went through, because if it had not been for you, I wouldn't have been able to have the career that I had."[65] In 1998, Doby was elected to the Baseball Hall of Fame by the Veterans Committee.[66]

Doby's health plagued him in retirement. He battled a cancerous tumor in 1997 and had to have a kidney removed.[67] Helyn, his wife of 55 years, died in 2001 after a six-month battle with cancer.[68] Larry Doby died of cancer in Montclair, New Jersey, on June 18, 2003. More than 300 mourners attended his funeral at Trinity Presbyterian Church.[69] He is buried in Montclair. He was honored posthumously by appearing on a U.S. postage stamp released in July 2012.[70]

NOTES

1   Kevin Kernan, "Larry is the stuff of legends: Struggles of Doby a lesson for any time," *New York Post*, July 28, 2002.

2   Kerman.

3   Joseph Thomas Moore, *Pride Against Prejudice: The Biography of Larry Doby* (Westport: Praeger Publishers, 1988), 7.

4   Moore, 6.

5   Moore, 9.

6   Doby, Lawrence Eugene "Larry," in David L. Porter, ed. *Biographical Dictionary of American Sports* (Westport, Connecticut: Greenwood Press, 2000).

7   Ibid.

8   Ibid.

9   Ibid.

10   Moore, 12.

11   Moore, 12-17.

12   Moore, 16.

13   Ibid.

14   Ibid.

15   Moore, 19-20.

16   Moore, 20.

17   Ibid.

18   Moore, 23.

19   Dave Anderson, "A Pioneer's Hall of Fame Wife," *New York Times*, July 26, 2001.

20   Anderson.

21   Moore, 24.

22   Ibid.

23   Ibid.

24   Moore, 24-25.

25   Moore, 25.

26   Ibid.

27   Ibid.

28   Ibid.

29   Ibid.

30   Ibid.

31   Moore, 29.

32   Anderson.

33   Ibid.

34   Ibid.

35   Ibid.

36   Dave Hutchinson, "Doby relives past, the good and the bad: Indians retire his number today." No publication given. Clipping from Doby's file at the Hall of Fame Library.

37   Moore, 41-45.

38   Moore, 47.

39   Ibid.

40   Jerome Holtzman, "Doby's Rightful Recognition," *Chicago Tribune*, March 4, 1998, available at https://chicago.tribune.com/sports/whitesox/article0,1051,ART-4566,00.html.

41   Sam Goldaper and Jack Cavanaugh, "Sports World Specials; Honors for Doby," *New York Times.* July 6, 1987.

42   Dave Hutchinson, "Doby relives past, the good and the bad: Indians retire his number today." No publication given. Clipping from Doby's file at the Hall of Fame Library.

43   Daniel, "Mick Thought Homer Cleared Stadium," July 24, 1957. No publication given. Clipping from Doby's Hall of Fame file.

44   United Press, "Carrasquel, Busby Acquisitions 'Round 1' for Trading Tribe." Clipping from Doby's Hall of Fame file.

45   "Doby Now Tonic to Old Foe: Ex-Indian Esteemed by Chicago Pilot," May 5, 1956. No author or publication given. Clipping from Doby's Hall of Fame file.

46   Doby connects: Jersey Vet 'Finds Range' for Chisox," June 23, 1956." Clipping from Doby's Hall of Fame file.

47   "Police Grab Martin After Fighting Doby: Drysdale and Logan Swap Punches in Brooklyn Free-for-All," June 13, 1957. Clipping from Doby's Hall of Fame file.

48   "Chisox Fans Sour on Doby; Forced Deal with Baltimore," December 11, 1957. Clipping from Doby's Hall of Fame file.

49   Ibid.

50   "Doby to Enter Johns Hopkins, Career in Danger, August 25, 1959." Clipping from Doby's Hall of Fame file.

51   Porter, *Biographical Dictionary of American Sports.*

52   Bob Decker, "Doby's next goal—manage in majors." *Newark Star-Ledger*, January 24, 1971.

53   Ibid.

54   Ibid.

55   Hutchinson, "Doby relives past, the good and the bad: Indians retire his number today."

56   Tom Melody, "Doby's dream now a nightmare," *Akron Beacon Journal*, August 21, 1978.

57   Hutchinson, "Doby relives past, the good and the bad: Indians retire his number today."

58   Ibid.

59   Ibid.

60   American League Press Release, "Doby Named Special Assistant to the American League President," April 17, 1995.

61   "Doby among 3 named to Baseball World board," *Cooperstown Crier*, July 8, 1999. No author or page number given. Clipping from Doby's Hall of Fame file.

62   Kevin Kernan, "Larry is the stuff of legends: Struggles of Doby a lesson for any time," *New York Post*, July 28, 2002, 97.

63   Ibid.

64   Associated Press, "Finally a hankering to honor Doby: Aaron says thanks to barrier-breaker on 50th anniversary of his AL debut," *Newark Star Ledger*, July 6, 1997, Section 5, 8.

65   Ibid.

66   Jerome Holtzman, "Doby's Rightful Recognition," *Chicago Tribune*, March 4, 1998, available at https://chicago.tribune.com/sports/whitesox/article0,1051,ART-4566,00.html.

67   Holtzman.

68   Anderson.

69   Steve Politi, "Doby recalled as a Hall of Famer in Life," *Newark Star Ledger*, June 24, 2003: 53.

70   Baseball Hall of Fame press release, "Postal Service to Unveil New Stamps Depicting Hall of Fame Legends on Friday in Cooperstown," July 16, 2012. Clipping from Doby's Hall of Fame file.

CHARLES ENGLAND

BY MARGARET M. GRIPSHOVER

Charlie England's baseball story is intertwined with the vagaries of growing up as an African-American in North Carolina in the Jim Crow era and beyond. His brief tenure with the Newark Eagles was bookended by longer careers as a college and semipro baseball player and later as a college coach, mentor, and much-lauded community leader who broke the color barrier to achieve success on and off the field.

Charles Macon England was born on September 21, 1921, in Newton, the county seat of Catawba County in the uplands of west-central North Carolina. His parents were Guy Leroy and Katie (Duncan) England. His grandparents were born into slavery not long before the end of the Civil War. England's family has deep roots in Catawba County. Charlie had two brothers and two sisters who survived to adulthood. His older brother, Horace, enlisted in the US Army during World War II. He re-enlisted to serve in the Korean War, was captured by the enemy in North Korea, and died as a prisoner of war. His remains were never found. Charles's younger brother, Warren, also served in the Army during World War II. After he was discharged from the Army, he returned to Newton. Charles's two sisters were Marion England Burgin and Betty Jean England Gibbs. His parents and all of his siblings except Horace are buried in Catawba County.

Life for the England family in Newton during the Jim Crow era was full of challenges, setbacks, tragedies, and accomplishments. Guy England worked a variety of jobs. He was the janitor for the Catawba County Courthouse and a fireman at a textile mill, where he had the backbreaking job of stoking the mill's boilers.

Charles England was 0-2 in his brief tenure with Newark in 1946. His greatest impact came as a high school science and physical education teacher and football coach. (Courtesy of W.A. Pattillo High School, Tarboro, North Carolina)

Katie also did tedious labor – she was a laundress in the days before modern washing machines. Their hard work paid off and by 1930, they owned their home in Newton and made sure their children attended school.

During the 1930s the England household began to unravel. In 1933, when Charles was 12 years old, his mother died at age 39 from pneumonia, a complication of influenza. A year later his father was remarried to Vanda Hewitt Frye, also recently widowed. Less than a year later, Vanda's son, Richard Frye Jr., was killed in a truck accident that also took the lives of nine other African-Americans who were on their way to a picnic. In the midst of family turmoil and grief, Charles England went to live with his maternal grandparents, Warren and Alice Duncan. Warren was a house painter and Alice Duncan toiled as a washerwoman.[1] Charles was living with his grandparents when he graduated from Central High School in Newton.[2]

The first mention of a baseball game in the *Newton Enterprise* came on July 14, 1883, when the Newton Nine lost the first game of the season to the Statesville Nine.[3] As early as the 1870s, "colored nines" competed in organized leagues at the local, regional, and state levels. Some cities, like Asheville, had more than one team. The success of black baseball teams in the decade after the Civil War prompted the *Tarboro Enquirer Southerner* to complain, "Is it not time that the whites retire from the game?"[4]

Coverage of colored baseball teams continued sporadically in Catawba County newspapers through the early 1900s. One such nine, the Newton Colored Base Ball [sic] Team, traveled throughout western and central North Carolina to play local and college teams, often playing their home contests on the now-defunct Catawba College diamond.[5] By the 1930s, numerous colored nines were playing in local and regional leagues.

Local newspapers' attention to sporting events at Charles's Central High School were virtually absent. The school offered little in the way of extracurricular activities. In the late 1930s, when Charles attended the segregated school, it was described as having "broken windows, bare light bulbs suspended from the ceiling, and only one pot-bellied stove."[6] Athletic facilities were nearly nonexistent save an outdoor patch of dirt that passed for a basketball court – there was no gym.[7] Any opportunities for Charles to play competitive baseball came from elsewhere. While records are scarce and evidence slim, it is likely that England had his first baseball experiences in the 1930s with one of the colored nines in Catawba County before he graduated from Central High School to head off to college.

England enrolled at the historically black Shaw University in Raleigh, North Carolina, for the 1940-1941 academic year. He was a star pitcher for the Bears and played on the basketball team. Shaw engaged in intercollegiate baseball skirmishes as early as 1898 against their crosstown rival, St. Augustine's School (now St. Augustine's University). Shaw began fielding an intercollegiate-conference baseball team in the 1910s. All of their games were against black colleges and most were in North Carolina.

England was a student at Shaw University in 1942 when he registered for the World War II draft. At the time he was unmarried, and he named his grandmother Alice as the "person who will always know your address."[8] Besides attending the university, he took welding classes at a vocational-technical school in Rocky Mount. When he enlisted in the US Army at Fort Bragg on January 19, 1945, England had two years of college and a skillset that included welding and "flame cutting." He was described as being 5 feet-7½ inches tall, and weighing 150 pounds. But it was not his welding skills that got him through his military service – it was his firepower on the mound.

England completed all of his Army service in the United States. Fourteen months after he joined the Army, he was a sergeant in the Quartermaster Corps. At Camp Lee, Virginia, he was a pitcher for the Travelers, the Camp Lee baseball team.

The Travelers played military and civilian teams throughout the mid-Atlantic region. (Its home field was Nowak Field, named in honor of Sgt. Henry "Hank" Nowak, a St. Louis Cardinals minor-league pitcher who was killed in action in Belgium on January 1, 1945, during the Battle of the Bulge.)

Major-league players who played for the Travelers included Jim Greengrass, Granny Hamner, Johnny Lindell, and Porter Vaughan, as well as two future Hall of Famers, Luke Appling, who was a player-manager for the Travelers in 1944; and Red Ruffing, who pitched at least one game for Camp Lee in the spring of 1945.

During World War II, US military bases organized traveling baseball and football teams that played against military and civilian squads. Four years before Jackie Robinson broke major-league baseball's color barrier, the Army was already fielding mixed-race teams. The relatively progressive attitudes of the military stood in stark contrast to the segregated teams on college campuses and civilian life. But the Army saw integrated sports teams as a means to foster unity and patriotism, and promote some semblance of racial harmony in its forces.[9] Camp Lee, named for the Confederacy's Robert E. Lee and situated in the heart of Jim Crow country, was among the Army installations that allowed white and black players on the same teams. (The baseball team, the Travelers, was nicknamed for Lee's favorite horse.) Cpl. Ernest R. Rather in the *Chicago Defender* observed, "On the buses, though segregation is the rule in Virginia, it is not observed in practice within the Camp Lee limits"[10]

According to a 1967 newspaper article, Charles England was the first African-American to play on the Travelers baseball team.[11] That assertion is likely incorrect. Before England arrived at Camp Lee in 1946, other black ballplayers had integrated the squad. As early as 1943, George Crowe played first base on what had previously been an all-white nine. After World War II Crowe played for the New York Black Giants (1947-1949) and played nine major-league seasons (1952-1953; 1955-1961) for the Boston and Milwaukee Braves, Cincinnati Reds, and St. Louis Cardinals. Crowe also played professionally for several basketball teams including the

Harlem Globetrotters and the Los Angeles Red Devils in the National Basketball League, where one of his teammates was Jackie Robinson. In 1944, two years before Charlie England reported to Camp Lee, former Negro League player William McKinley "Sug" Cornelius was pitching for the Travelers. Sug's résumé included stints on the mound for the Nashville Elite Giants, Memphis Red Sox, Birmingham Black Barons, Chicago American Giants, and Cincinnati Buckeyes. So clearly England was not the first African-American to play for the Travelers. But that historical correction does not diminish his baseball accomplishments or his contributions to racial equality and the civil-rights movement.

The first mound appearances by Sgt. Charles M. England for the Camp Lee Travelers took place in the spring of 1946. In his first outing, on April 10, he pitched two innings in relief in a losing effort against the Wilkes-Barre (Pennsylvania) Barons of the Class-A Eastern League, a farm team of the Cleveland Indians.[12] The winning pitcher for the Barons was Joe Tipton, who after the war played seven seasons for American League teams between 1948 and 1954. The losing pitcher for the Travelers was Bob Chakales, who also spent seven seasons in the majors, pitching for several American League teams. About two weeks later, Charlie England pitched in relief against the Binghamton (New York) Triplets of the Eastern League, a New York Yankees farm team. This time, England and the Travelers came out on top, 4-3, before a crowd of 5,000 at Camp Lee.[13] England gave up 11 hits but yielded just two runs to notch the win.

The last mound appearance by England in a Travelers uniform came on June 29, 1946. He pitched a three-hitter against Quantico as the Travelers defeated the Marines, 8-1. Less than three weeks later, England was honorably discharged. He spent his Army service – one year, eight months, and two days – as an "athletic instructor." Clearly, some of his instructing took place on the pitcher's mound. His service awards included the American Theater Ribbon, the Good Conduct Medal, the Meritorious Unit Award, and the World War II Victory Ribbon. His final mustering-out pay was $265.92, including compensation for his travel costs to return home to Newton.[14]

Less than a month after his discharge, England was in Newark making his debut on the mound for the Eagles. His first start, at Ruppert Stadium on August 15, 1946, was not a memorable game for England or the Eagles. The game was scheduled on the same day as the Negro League All-Star Classic at Griffith Stadium in Washington, three days before the East-West Game was to take place at Comiskey Park in Chicago. Eagles stars Larry Doby, Monte Irvin, Leon Day, and Lennie Pearson were absent from the lineup; they were slated to play in the Washington and Chicago games. England and the Eagles lost to the Memphis Red Sox, 11-4. An account of the game in the *Atlanta Daily World* noted

that in the fourth inning the Red Sox "launched their bunting attack and combined six hits, along with three Eagles errors to score eight runs and clinch the contest."[15] The *Chicago Defender* also noted that the "sensational bunting attack" by Memphis was what won the game.[16]

On August 19, the day after the Comiskey Park game, England made his second start for Newark. The outcome again was not in his favor: a loss to the Baltimore Elite Giants, 7-1, in the first game of a doubleheader. England gave up 12 hits and his teammates committed five errors. He walked five and made a wild pitch before a crowd of 3,000 at Bloomingdale Oval Park in Baltimore. (Today this field is known as Leon Day Park, named in honor of the former Negro League standout and England's teammate and leading pitcher for the 1946 Eagles.)

On September 1 the Eagles were in first place in the second half of the season with a record of 14-3. Two of the three losses were charged to England. By then England was no longer with the team. In all likelihood he had been hired by the Eagles to help replace the missing players. After Doby and the others returned from their all-star appearances, England was released. He headed back to Raleigh and re-enrolled in Shaw University. Although it appears that his Negro League career ended with those two Newark losses, some newspaper articles decades later said that England also pitched for the Philadelphia Stars. Even the Baseball in Wartime website links him to the Stars.[17] While these assertions are not beyond the realm of possibility, no box scores and/or game summaries exist to support them.

After his stint in the military and his brief career with the Eagles, England resumed his life as a student-athlete on the Shaw Bears' 1947 and 1948 championship football and baseball teams. He was the team captain and place kicker for the Bears when they won the Central Intercollegiate Athletic Association football championship by defeating South Carolina A&T in the title game in Washington, DC.[18] In 1948 England was the team captain and most valuable player for the Shaw team that captured the CIAA baseball crown. He also played basketball at Shaw and was an active member of the Omega Psi Phi fraternity. But one has to wonder how England was eligible to play collegiate baseball after his stint, albeit brief, with the Eagles. This is especially puzzling given this entry in the 1948 Shaw University yearbook: "We find Charles Macon England playing hand to hand with Jackie [Robinson] on the world's greatest baseball team."[19] The yearbook's writers were likely referring to Jackie Robinson's All-Stars, who barnstormed across the country in 1947, the roster including England's former Eagles teammate, Larry Doby.

England graduated from Shaw University in 1949 with a bachelor's degree. He was recognized for his academic and athletic accomplishments with a biographical entry in *Who's Who in American Colleges and Universities.* England's nickname at Shaw was "Life," and he "willed" his ability to "keep cool" while pitching to an underclassman. But England was not done with baseball. After graduation, he left Raleigh and picked up a pitching gig with the North Carolina Twins, a semipro team based in Winston-Salem and playing in the Carolina Baseball Association. He had played in the same league in 1940 when he appeared on the roster for the Raleigh Grays. On July 10, 1949, he took the mound for the Twins in a game against the Asheville Black Tourists. He was billed as the "well known former pitcher for Shaw University and later the Philadelphia Eagles [sic]."[20]

In the fall of 1949 England was hired to teach science and physical education and coach football at W.A. Pattillo High School in Tarboro, North Carolina. He was on the faculty at Pattillo through 1958 and continued to play baseball during his summer breaks. On April 16, 1950, described as a "former Shaw star who now plays with the Chicago American Giants," he was scheduled to pitch three innings for the Raleigh Grays in a charity game against the Central Prison Giants.[21] That same month, England was among "six collegians" who joined the Giants in their spring-training camp in Columbus, Mississippi.[22] His tenure with the team was brief and likely ended shortly after the team broke camp in Mississippi because his name was not mentioned again that season as part of the Giants' regular lineup.

The 1950s brought many changes to England's personal and professional life. As a newly minted college graduate, he embarked on what would be a long career as an educator and high-school sports coach. In 1951 he pitched for two semipro baseball teams in North Carolina. In May he took the mound for the semipro Rocky Mount All-Stars. By June he was pitching for the Asheville Blues, formerly of the Negro Southern League. England was touted as an all-star twirler for the Blues and "one of the top hurlers in Negro baseball."[23] Given that Rocky Mount and Asheville are more than 300 miles apart, it is unlikely that he played in too many games.

England's most remarkable year in baseball was 1952, when he coached his Pattillo High School baseball team to the North Carolina state championship.[24] He also garnered headlines for integrating the Rocky Mount Leafs of the Class-D Coastal Plain League. He was signed to a contract with the Leafs by owner Charles Franklin "Frank" Walker, an outfielder for five seasons between 1917 and 1925 for the Detroit Tigers, Philadelphia Athletics, and New York Giants. Walker's motivation for integrating the Leafs was more of an effort to boost attendance than a brave challenge to racism and Jim Crow, as evidenced when he announced that England would not travel with the team, and would pitch only at home in Rocky Mount.[25]

Walker's decision to use England to integrate the Rocky Mount Leafs was not a random choice. England was well-known in the community for his play in the Negro Leagues and semipro circuits, his meritorious military service, his college baseball triumphs at Shaw University, and his roles at a teacher and coach at Pattillo High School. Howard Criswell Jr., a white sports columnist for the *Rocky Mount Telegram,* wrote that Walker was "not averse" to signing an African-American player, but that "finding one who would be able to take the proper attitude in playing and have the ability" was the challenge.[26] According to Criswell, Walker "was not the first one to look at England. … [T]he St. Louis Browns showed a great deal of interest in [England] and had him at a tryout camp they held in Asheville."[27] Criswell said that England turned down a chance to play for the Browns because it would have "interfered with [his] coaching at (Pattillo)," and that after his debut game, England was emotional, understood the historic importance of the moment, saw his chance with the Leafs as a "great honor," and did his best to "live up to the code of the club and the league. …"[28]

England made two starts for Rocky Mount. Things did not go well. In both outings, he was knocked out in the fourth inning. For his debut, on June 18, 1952, England stood on the mound before nearly 3,100 boisterous fans, nearly one-third of whom were African-Americans.[29] He struck out the first Kinston Eagles batter and retired the second on a routine fly ball. But the third Kinston batter, Herb Grissom, blasted a home run and then the flood gates were wide open. By the time England got the hook in the fourth inning, the Eagles had scored 16 runs, not all of them earned. England was understandably nervous and his teammates didn't do much to help. The Leafs fielders made three errors in the first four innings. There were also a variety of distractions including a pregame beauty contest, multiple arguments between players, managers, and umpires, and a "negro boy" described as an "illegal person," who broke the rules by warming up a Kinston player on the field."[30]

For England's second start, on June 24 in Rocky Mount, against the Tarboro Tars, the crowd was noticeably smaller – about 2,000. England had a better outing, giving up six hits in four innings but the Leafs lost, 3-2. And despite his marked improvement over his first outing, two days later he was released. Walker declared that "England didn't have enough on the ball to pitch in the Coastal Plain League."[31] England brushed off being cut from the team by saying that he was treated fairly, was appreciative for the opportunity, and in short order was planning to leave Rocky Mount for New York University, where he was working on a master's degree in physical education.[32] R.D. Armstrong, in his "News About Negroes" column in the *Rocky Mount Telegram,* wrote, "England's short stay here was a credit to himself, his race, and to organized baseball and his anxiety to get in school for the remaining summer months is indicative of his determination to go forward.[33] (Within days Walker signed another African-American pitcher, Lafayette Stallings, a native of Nash County, North Carolina. Like England, Stallings did not win a single start with the Leafs and was likewise released.

Charles England was the first African-American to play for the Rocky Mount Leafs but was not the first to be signed by a Coastal Plain League team. That credit went to Charlie T. Roach, a 29-year-old graduate of Winston-Salem Teachers College (today Winston-Salem State University), who made his debut as the first black player for the New Bern Bears on June 10, 1952, eight days before England's debut,[34] and was gone after playing in one game. England and Roach had much in common. Both were grandsons of slaves and lifelong residents of North Carolina. Each served in the Army during World War II, earned bachelor's degrees at historically black colleges, attended graduate schools, and had successful careers as educators.

England's and Roach's fleeting tenures in the Coastal Plain League received similar coverage by the white press. The *Rocky Mount Telegram's* Criswell wrote that England "didn't get rattled" by the large crowd at his debut game and that "Everyone in the stands were behind him."[35] Criswell added that England was not permitted to share the locker room with his white teammates and that there were "only a few minor boos." The columnist's sanitized perception of England's debut did not go unchallenged. Criswell neglected to mention that some Leafs players refused to take the field with an African-American. A "letter to the editor" by a white writer defended England's poor showing by noting, "(T)he Rocky Mount team presented a makeshift lineup with a pitcher playing left field and a third baseman – who last year fielded like a sieve and batted less than .200 – filling in at shortstop."[36] The letter writer summed up his disgust with the uncritical press coverage of England's performance by adding that he heard "one Negro fan [comment] quite bitterly that Bob Feller couldn't have won with such a team behind him."[37] White sportswriters made similar assumptions regarding Charlie Roach's one-and-done appearance. Local newspapers reported that Roach, in his performance for New Bern, "fitted into the club without friction." Reality was quite different.[38] Roach endured racial slurs and boos from the majority white crowd and was sold three days later to the Danville Leafs of the Class-B Carolina League.[39] England and Roach made headlines in the summer of 1952 for breaking the color barrier for their respective teams. Their performances generated a momentary spike in gate receipts and public interest, but in the end, they were used for little more than a failed publicity stunt and then were summarily dismissed. The average attendance at Leafs games in 1952 had slumped to just 600 and Frank Walker predicted that

the Coastal Plain League would fold and fail to field any teams in 1953.[40] And he was right.

After his brief career in the Coastal Plain League, England returned to his teaching and coaching duties at Pattillo High School in Tarboro.[41] But he did not quit baseball. Through the 1950s he sporadically pitched games in local leagues. One of his last appearances on the diamond was in 1957, when he managed the Rocky Mount native and Hall of Famer Buck Leonard and an aggregation called the Eastern North Carolina All Stars in an exhibition game in Tarboro against the Kansas City Monarchs. He left Pattillo for teaching and coaching assignments at Dunbar High School in Lexington, North Carolina, until the school closed in 1967. England coached Dunbar's baseball and football teams to numerous titles and in 1960 was named Coach of the Year in Davidson County, North Carolina.[42] In 1968 England was hired to teach and coach at the integrated Lexington Senior High School, where he enjoyed similar success as an assistant football coach and head baseball coach.

The 1960s also marked a major change in England's personal life. On April 15, 1960, he married Julia May Chisholm in Mecklenburg, North Carolina. She had graduated summa cum laude with a bachelor's degree in elementary education from Johnson C. Smith University in her hometown of Charlotte, North Carolina. Like her husband, she went to New York City for her graduate education and earned a master's degree at the Teachers College of Columbia University. She was a teacher for 32 years when she retired in 1985. Charles and Julia raised three children in Lexington. They had something else in common – their commitment to the civil rights movement. Both were members of the NAACP and activists for racial equality and social justice in their community. In the early 1990s, Charles England tried unsuccessfully to convince the Davidson County Commission to recognize MLK Day as an official holiday for county employees. After England's death in 1999, members of a committee created by England continued the fight for recognition. One committee member said of England that he "taught me how to walk with dignity" and that he saw England as a "replica" of Dr. Martin Luther King.[43] Another three years elapsed before Davidson County acknowledged MLK Day in 2002 as a legitimate holiday, one of the last of North Carolina's 100 counties to do so.

After England retired from teaching and coaching in the 1980s, he received numerous awards and accolades for his athletic achievements and dedication to education and serving the community. In 1982 he was inducted into the Shaw University Hall of Fame. In 1988 he received the A. Odell Leonard Humanitarian Award from the Lexington Civitan Club. Even after his death in 1999, England continued to be honored. Less than a month after he died, the Dunbar Intermediate School, where he began his teaching career, was renamed the Charles England Intermediate School.[44] In 2000 he was inducted into the North Carolina High School Athletic Association Hall of Fame.[45] When a new Charles England Intermediate School was built in Lexington in 2008, his son, Charles Macon England Jr., recalled one of his father's favorite sayings: "A man never stood so tall as when he stooped to help a child."[46] In 2016 the nonprofit Charles and Julia England Foundation was created to provide grants for teachers who are engaged in "creative learning opportunities for students" in the Lexington city schools.[47] The theme for the Charles England school and foundation is based on another frequent exhortation by Coach England – "Be somebody."

Charles M. England died on January 23, 1999, in Salisbury, North Carolina. He was 77 years old. He was survived by his wife, Julia, and their three children. Only one of his siblings survived him, his sister Marion Evelyn England Burgin, who lived her entire life in Catawba County. Julia Chisholm England died in 2015. Charlies and Julia are buried in Forest Hill Memorial Park in Lexington.

Charles Macon England lived a dignified and meritorious life in difficult times. In spite of the barriers placed before him in the Jim Crow South, he graduated from college, excelled in his academic and athletic pursuits, and helped break down racial barriers in US Army baseball teams and the Coastal Plain League. England had a dismal two-start career with the Newark Eagles in 1946 but was not daunted by the defeats. He moved forward in his life and made quantifiable differences in the lives of hundreds of students and student-athletes who benefited from his tutelage and tried their best to "be somebody." England was a sterling role model in the classroom and on the baseball diamond. It is quite possible that he is one of the most lauded former Negro League players in history who was not a superstar on the mound but was a stellar member of society as a whole. Charles England did not make a major mark in the Negro League record books, but his name, his wide-ranging contributions, and his reputation are still very much present.

NOTES

1   US Census Bureau, 1940 Census.

2   Ibid.

3   "Base Ball," *Newton* (North Carolina) *Enterprise*, July 14, 1883: 3.

4   "Base Ball," *Enquirer Southerner* (Tarboro, North Carolina), October 2, 1874: 4.

5   "Locals," *Newton Enterprise*, June 5, 1903: 3; "Locals," *Newton Enterprise*, April 15, 1909: 3; "Locals," *Newton Enterprise*, April 11, 1912: 2; "Locals," *Newton Enterprise*, March 27, 1913: 3.

6   Betty J. Jamerson, *School Segregation in Western North Carolina: A History, 1860s-1970s* (Jefferson, North Carolina: McFarland, 2011), 213.

7   Jamerson, 215.

8   World War II Draft Registration Card, 1942, for Charles Macon England, Order No. 10170.

9   Wanda E. Wakefield, *Playing to Win: Sports and the American Military, 1898-1945* (Albany, New York: State University Press of New York, 1997), 128.

10   Ernest R. Rather, "Camp Lee Training Band," *Chicago Defender*, September 15, 1945: 11.

11   "Lexington Dunbar Coach Speaks at Final Carver Sports Banquet," *Daily Independent* (Kannapolis, North Carolina), April 30, 1967: 11-A.

12   "Wilkes-Barre Nine Trips Camp Lee," *Washington Post*, April 11, 1946: 13.

13   "Rally by Camp Lee Defeats Binghamton Nine by 4-3 Count," *Richmond* (Virginia) *Times Dispatch*, April 25, 1946: 18.

14   US Army, *Enlisted Record and Report of Separation Honorable Discharge*, for Charles Macon England, July 17, 1946.

15   "Memphis Red Sox Top Newark Eagles, 11-4," *Atlanta Daily World*, August 15, 1945: 5.

16   "Memphis Trims Eagles," *Chicago Defender*, August 17, 1945: 11.

17   baseballinwartime.com/negro.htm.

18   *1948 Shaw Bear Yearbook* (Shaw University), 54. The CIAA is a collegiate athletic conference of mostly historically black colleges.

19   *1948 Shaw Bear Yearbook*, 33.

20   "Asheville Black Tourists Face N.C. Twins Today," *Asheville* (North Carolina) *Citizen-Times*, July 10, 1949: 36.

21   "Raleigh Grays Play Prison Squad Today," *Raleigh News and Observer*, April 15, 1950: 19.

22   "Gate Attractions Sought on College Campuses," *Atlanta Daily World*, April 18, 1950: 3.

23   "Firefighters Play Blues," *Jersey Journal* (Jersey City, New Jersey), June 22, 1951: 17.

24   R.D. Armstrong, "News About Negroes," *Rocky Mount* (North Carolina) *Telegram*, June 22, 1952: 5.

25   "Leafs Lose but Turkey Protests Game in Ninth," *Rocky Mount Telegram*, June 19, 1952: 14.

26   Howard Criswell Jr., "Sports Talk: The First One," *Rocky Mount Telegram*, June 17, 1952: 10.

27   Ibid.

28   Ibid.

29   "Full House," *Rocky Mount Telegram*, June 19, 1952: 15.

30   Ibid.

31   "England Released," *Rocky Mount Telegram*, June 27, 1952: 10.

32   R.D. Armstrong, "News About Negroes: Two Big Events," *Rocky Mount Telegram*, June 22, 1952: 5.

33   Ibid.

34   "Negro Makes Debut in Coastal Plains," *Asheville Citizen-Times*, June 10, 1952: 14.

35   Howard Criswell Jr., "Sports Talk: Big Night," *Rocky Mount Telegram*, June 20, 1952: 10.

36   W.G. Williams, "Charlie England," *Raleigh News and Observer*, July 10, 1952: 10.

37   Ibid.

38   "Negro Makes Debut in Coastal Plains."

39   Bill Hand, "New Bern Hosted the First Black Player in an All White League," *New Bern* (North Carolina) *Sun Journal,* November 4, 2012. newbernsj.com/article/20121104/Opinion/311049940.

40   "Closed Out," *Rocky Mount Telegram*, September 2, 1952.

41   "Monarchs Will Play All-Stars at Tarboro, *Raleigh News and Observer,* July 3, 1957: 12.

42   "Charlie England Coach of the Year," *Chicago Defender*, January 23, 1960: 24.

43   "In Memory of Coach Charles England," *Lexington* (North Carolina) *Dispatch,* January 27, 1999. the-dispatch.com/news/19990127/in-memory-of-coach-charles-england.

44   Deneesha Edwards, "New Charles England Intermediate School Opens," *Lexington Dispatch*, August 21, 2008. the-dispatch.com/news/20080821/new-charles-england-intermediate-school-opens.

45   "Charlie England, *Lexington Dispatch*, September 6, 2002. the-dispatch.com/news/20020906/born-thomasville-may-22-1946.

46   "New Charles England Intermediate School Opens."

47   besomebodyfund.com.

William "Benny" Felder

BY BRYAN STEVERSON AND FREDERICK C. BUSH

Shortstop Benny Felder was a member of the 1946 Eagles for two months. In 1954, he batted .302 and helped lead the minor-league Pampa Oilers to the West Texas-New Mexico League crown. *(From the Collection of Bill Nowlin)*

Newark Eagles shortstop Benny Felder was born on December 9, 1926, in Tampa, Florida.[1] Little is known of his family. In an interview with Brent Kelley, Felder said, "My family was brick masons."[2] Benjamin Franklin Felder was the ninth of 10 children born to Porter Henry Felder (1882-1944) and Minnie Lee (Fluker) Felder (1886-1979). The couple had seven sons and three daughters, and they seemed to favor naming the sons after public figures – among Benny's brothers were Frederic Douglas Felder and Booker T. Felder.[3]

Porter Felder worked as a roofing tie contractor in Argyle, Georgia, at the time of the 1920 Census, but by 1930 was listed as a brick mason in Tampa, as was his eldest son, Mitchel. Minnie worked as a servant for a private family. Porter Felder's father, Dow Felder, had been a farm laborer. Porter was an Alabaman and Minnie a Georgian by birth.

Growing up in Tampa during the late 1930s, Felder played baseball, which was a popular sport among his African-American friends. He played for the Pepsi-Cola Giants, an independent Negro team. Felder recalled, "I really just got out on the field when I was around 13, 14 years old. I played with Pepsi-Cola about three or four years."[4] Higher-level Negro League teams trained in Florida and – just as was the case with his friends and fellow Giants John and Walter "Dirk" Gibbons, Raydell Lefty Bo Maddix, and Clifford "Quack" Brown – Felder's skills were soon recognized. All five of these men made it to the top levels of the Negro Leagues.

On Easter Sunday and Monday, April 21 and 22, 1946, Felder's Giants played exhibition games against the Negro National League's

Newark Eagles in Port Tampa. The Eagles had finished third in the six-team NNL the previous year with a squad led by backstop and future Hall of Famer Raleigh "Biz" Mackey. Future Brooklyn Dodgers ace Don Newcombe had been their top pitcher in 1945, having posted an 8-2 record.[5]

Felder related that he had two good games in the series against Eagles pitching stars Leon Day and Rufus Lewis, both of whom were returning from military service. Felder fielded well in the games and recorded multiple hits each day. Abe Manley, owner of the Eagles, took notice of his performance. After a dinner at the Felder home in Tampa, Manley persuaded a skeptical mother to let her son join the club. Felder explained, "You know how it is. You want to get away to see how things are. Abe told her to let me give a try 'cause I wanted to try it anyway, so she agreed."[6] Thus, the 19-year-old Felder – who batted and threw right-handed and was listed as 5-feet-9 and 170 pounds – entered the Negro Leagues in 1946 as an infielder with the Newark Eagles.

One of Felder's biggest thrills in baseball involved an Eagles teammate, future Hall of Famer Leon Day.[7] On Opening Day in 1946, after returning from a 2½-year stint in the Army, Day hurled a no-hitter against the Philadelphia Stars at Ruppert Stadium in Newark. Day faced 29 batters, with no baserunner reaching second base. One batter was walked and two reached first base as a result of Felder's errors. One error was erased by an Eagles double play. "Felder was just a young kid. He could field pretty good but he wasn't that sure and he might overrun anything," Day recalled.[8] One of the recorded errors may have been questionable. After fielding the ball cleanly, Felder took three or four bunny hops before making the toss to first. In so doing, he made a bad throw. The runner may have been out. The scorer also could have classified it a hit. It was officially recorded as an error, thereby saving Day's notable no-hitter. The miscues could not erase Felder's thrill in playing behind the great right-hander on this special day.

Though Felder began the season with the Eagles, he was released in early June to make way for Oscar Givens.[9] Felder was back with Newark at the beginning of the 1947 season but then was traded to a team in North Carolina. According to Felder, "I went down there to spring training, but I didn't stay. I didn't like it." He returned to Tampa, where he again played for the Pepsi-Cola team."[10]

In 1948, thanks to his friend and former Pepsi-Cola Giants teammate Walter "Dirk" Gibbons, Felder joined the Indianapolis Clowns. The Clowns had become a barnstorming team, and Felder recalled how exhausting his stint with that franchise was, especially in regard to finding time to eat in order to maintain any stamina. He related:

> We was getting $2.50 a day for meals. I learned how to eat pork and beans and sardines. A lot of times, like when we were playing with the Clowns, the Clowns played *every* day,

sometimes two and three games a day, and you didn't get a chance to stop to eat. You got to run in a grocery store and get a loaf of bread and lunch meat or stuff like that to eat.[11]

In spite of such conditions, Felder enjoyed himself, saying, "I didn't make no money, but I got a lot of experience."[12]

After spending the 1948 season with the Clowns, Felder was out of baseball in 1949. The following season he entered white baseball with the Fort Lauderdale Braves (who moved the franchise and became the Key West Conchs of the Class-B Florida International League). He became one of the first blacks to play in the league.[13] In 1951, he performed at both shortstop and third base for the Philadelphia Stars, and then he returned to Key West in 1952. Felder moved to a different minor league as a member of the Pampa Oilers of the Class-C West Texas-New Mexico League for the 1953 and 1954 seasons; he also spent part of 1954 with the Artesia Numexers of the Class-C Longhorn League.

On June 4, 1953, Felder was playing second base for Pampa and was beaned in the second inning by Lubbock pitcher Benny Day and fell unconscious to the ground. The next day's *Lubbock Morning Avalanche* provided a detailed account of the frightening incident:

> Felder, after regaining consciousness, walked off the field, supported by Oiler teammates, and walked from the dugout to the stretcher.

> At the hospital, x-rays showed that he had no fracture and at midnight, he had no headache. He probably will be released today, but probably won't see action for a few days. The ball hit him high on the crown at the back of his head as he ducked away from an inside pitch, turning his back to the mound.[14]

Felder returned to the lineup for a game in Plainview three days later.[15] He also had a 3-for-4 game against Albuquerque on June 9. Two days later, however, he suffered a broken finger in a pregame workout. A few weeks after returning to action, he was hit in the head by a pregame grounder on August 4 and was removed from that day's lineup.[16]

Pampa's August 19 game was a noteworthy event, but not because of the game itself. The *Pampa Daily News* explained what the big occasion was:

> The first Negro wedding in West Texas-New Mexico League history will take place tonight at Oiler Park where Oiler second baseman, Ben Felder, will wed Miss Irene Boyd in a homeplate ceremony.

> The wedding will precede clash between the Oilers and the Amarillo Gold Sox. Time of the wedding has been set for 8 p.m.

The bride-to-be is member of the Carver High School faculty. ... Sad Sam Williams, who will pitch tonight's game for the Oilers, will serve as best man.[17]

The paper also reported that local merchants were showering gifts upon the couple and that the Oilers' owner, Doug Mills, was giving them 10 percent of that night's gate receipts as a wedding gift. In a baseball questionnaire that Felder filled out in June or July of 1953, prior to his marriage to Irene Boyd, he listed his status as "divorced" and stated that his son from his first marriage, Michael, was 2 years old.[18] It is unknown how long Felder's marriage to Boyd lasted or how it ended – since his obituary listed a woman named Miriam as his companion – and it is also unknown whether Felder's other children all came from their union.

The state of Texas and his marriage both appear to have agreed with Felder in 1953 as he batted a career high .312 with 26 doubles and stole 13 bases.[19] Pampa finished in fifth place with a 77-65 record. In spite of the fact that he had been having his best season, by this point Felder appeared to realize that he was unlikely to achieve his goal of making it to the majors. In fact, this is probably the reason why he had shaved five years off his age on his questionnaire, listing his birthday as December 9, 1931. At his actual age of 26, he was not truly prospect material anymore, but if he could convince people that he was only 21, then he might still be given a longer chance to try to develop major-league skills.

Sure enough, notwithstanding the great season he had for Pampa in 1953, the Oilers traded Felder to the Artesia Numexers for infielder Joe Calderon.[20] As it turned out, it was reported in March that Felder would be returned to the Oilers because Calderon, who had received a promotion on his "hi-way job in San Antonio," had decided to quit baseball.[21]

Although James Riley claims that Felder spent the latter part of the 1954 season with Artesia, game articles and box scores in the *Carlsbad Current-Argus* show that Felder spent the early part of the season with the Numexers.[22] Since it was already certain in March that Felder would be returned to Pampa, it is unknown why he spent any time with Artesia, but he did. Felder played in 23 games for the Numexers, batting .295 with 2 homers and 18 RBIs.[23] The Carlsbad newspaper referred to him as Billy Felder, another name by which Benny was known. Brent Kelley explained the confusion, writing, "As a small boy, his playmates called him Billy, and it sort of stuck. As he grew, people came to believe his name must be William. As a result, he was called Billy by some and Benny by others, but for the record, his name is Benjamin."[24]

Felder returned to the Pampa Oilers squad and picked up where he had left off the previous season. He is credited with batting .302 with 21 doubles, 6 homers, and 69 RBIs as the Oilers finished with an 81-54 record. Pampa's season ended as a rousing success

on September 23, and Felder was in the Oilers' lineup for the final time that evening. The *Pampa Daily News* enthused:

> It was all over but the shouting for the Pampa Oilers today after the locals eked out a 3-2 decision over the Clovis Pioneers last night at Oiler Park to nail down the West Texas-New Mexico Shaughnessy Playoff title.
>
> The playoff title gave the Oilers a complete sweep of the WT-NM crowns for the year as the Pampans also won the straightaway flag.[25]

Longtime Negro League pitcher Jonas Gaines, who had preceded Felder at two of his stops – the Newark Eagles in 1937 and the Philadelphia Stars in 1950 – was the winning pitcher for Pampa in the playoff-clinching game.

Felder began the 1955 season under contract for the Eugene (Oregon) Emeralds.[26] His time in the Pacific Northwest was short-lived, however, as the *Eugene Guard* reported on May 3 that "(t)he Emeralds were forced to release Ben Felder, a fine third baseman, because of an overload of vets."[27] Felder then finished his playing career with the Tampa Rockets of the Florida State Negro League, playing for the team from 1955 through 1957.[28]

After baseball, Felder returned to the family occupation as a brick mason. He subsequently purchased a service station in Tampa called Billy Felder's Fina Station.[29] Felder did not talk about his baseball experiences much unless prompted. In fact, a 1997 feature article noted, "The young guys who run an auto detail business next to Felder's shop say they had known him for years before they found out about his professional baseball career."[30] In his later years, Felder was more forthcoming about his experiences as he attempted to educate younger generations about what he and other black players experienced in the Negro Leagues and in the early days of Organized Baseball's integration. Felder remarked, "There's a lot of kids who don't know anything about it. ... We caught a lot of hell in our days. We couldn't stay where the white ballplayers stayed. We had to eat in the back of restaurants. The kids can't believe it when we tell them."[31]

Eventually, bad legs led Felder to have vascular surgery; rather than amputating his right leg, surgeons removed a vein from his left leg and placed in his right leg.[32] Later it was reported that he experienced health and financial problems. After suffering a heart attack, Felder struggled with hospital bills and prescription costs. He reportedly lived in a house owned by his brother. At the time he was taking as many as eight prescriptions, including those for his heart, an ulcer, and blood pressure. Eye drops were need for his blurred vision and insulin for diabetes.[33]

In 2007 Felder was among a number of former Eagles honored at Newark Bears and Eagles Stadium in a tribute organized by the

Newark Historical Society. He joined Monte Irvin, James "Red" Moore, and Willie "Curly" Williams in throwing out the first pitch.

Felder died on October 2, 2009, at home in Tampa. Following a funeral at Beulah Baptist Institutional Church, he was buried at Rest Haven Memorial Park Cemetery. He was survived by his longtime companion Miriam, and seven children – Barbara, Shirley, W. Michael, Andre, Billy, Alicia, and Reggie, as well as three siblings, Lela, Booker, and Bobby.[34]

NOTES

1   In his interview with Benny Felder in *The Negro Leagues Revisited, Conversations with 66 More Baseball Heroes*, Brent Kelley has Felder's birth date as December 9, 1926, in Tampa, Florida. The Negro Leagues Baseball Museum and historian Wayne Stivers also list the same birth date, year, and place. Historians Dick Clark and Larry Lester as well as James Riley give Felder's birth year as 1925 but with no date. Kelley also notes that many Negro League publications have listed him as William or Billy Felder.

2   Brent Kelley, *The Negro Leagues Revisited, Conversations with 66 More Baseball Heroes* (Jefferson, North Carolina: McFarland & Company, Inc., Publishers, 2000), 207.

3   Spellings are as per United States Census data.

4   Kelley, 205.

5   John Holway, *The Complete Book of Baseball's Negro Leagues: The Other Half of Baseball History* (Fern Park, Florida: Hastings House Publishers, 2001), 424.

6   Kelley, 205.

7   When asked in 2002 who were the best players he saw during his years in the Negro Leagues, Felder responded:

1st Base:	Buck Leonard
2nd Base:	Larry Doby
Shortstop:	Willie Wells
3rd Base:	Ray Dandridge
Catcher:	Roy Campanella
Outfielders:	Willard Brown, Johnny Davis, Monte Irvin, and Bob Thurman
Left-handed Pitcher:	Pat Scantlebury, Jonas Gaines, and Vibert Clarke
Right-handed Pitcher:	Satchel Paige and Leon Day

8   James A. Riley, *Dandy, Day, and the Devil* (Cocoa, Florida: TK Publishers, 1987), 68-69.

9   "Player Shift," *Newark Star-Ledger*, June 6, 1946: 18.

10   Kelley, 206.

11   Kelley, 207.

12   Ibid.

13   Kelley, 206.

14   Joe Kelly, "Hubs Slam Pampa, 12-10, as Fernandez Homers Twice," *Lubbock Morning Avalanche*, June 5, 1953: 10.

15   Felder told Brent Kelley that his first game back after the injury came in a return visit to Lubbock. With the bases loaded, he said, Pampa manager Ted Pawalek approached him and asked if he could swing the bat. Recently reunited with his team and elated to be back, he replied, "Yeah, let me try." He stepped to the plate. "And the Lord helped me. I hit a grand slam home run that night and that was one of the best feelings I had in baseball." Kelley, 206. We were unable to find any support for this story in any of the Texas newspapers that covered the league. His first game was said to be against Plainview, not Lubbock. Felder also told Kelley that he hit about 12 or 13 home runs a year, but his stats show him with five in 1953 and eight in 1954, so perhaps there was some embellishment involved.

16   "Hubbers Edge Pampa, 12-10," *Lubbock Evening Journal*, June 5, 1953: 12; Buck Francis, "Press Box Views," *Pampa Daily News*, June 12, 1953: 12.

17   "Wedding at Oiler Park on Tap Tonite," *Pampa Daily News*, August 19, 1953: 6.

18   "U.S. Baseball Questionnaires, 1945-2005 for Benjamin Felder," ancestry.com, accessed January 10, 2019.

19   "Artesia Trades for Ben Felder," *El Paso Times*, February 28, 1954: 45.

20   Ibid.

21   Buck Francis, "Press Box Views: Harvester Sprint Relayers Undefeated; Ben Felder to Be Returned to Oilers," *Pampa Daily News*, March 28, 1954: 7.

22   "Six Homers Help Artesians Beat Broncs 22-8 in Opener," *Carlsbad Current-Argus*, April 21, 1954: 7; "Artesia Belts Wichita Falls by 14-4 Count, *Carlsbad Current-Argus*, April 25, 1954: 11.

23   Kelley, 208.

24   Kelley, 205.

25   Buck Francis, "Oilers Bring WT-NM Flag Back to Pampa," *Pampa Daily News*, September 24, 1954: 7.

26   "Emeralds to Launch Spring Training," *Eugene Guard*, April 3, 1955: 28.

27   Dick Strite, "Highclimber," *Eugene Guard*, May 3, 1955: 14.

28   Wayne Stivers email to W.B. Steverson, February 7, 2018.

29   Taylor Ward, "Leagues of Their Own," *Tampa Bay Times*, February 7, 1997: 1T.

30   Ward: 8T.

31   Ibid.

32   Kelley, 207.

33   Dan Steinberg and Dave Sheinin, "Empty-Handed," *Washington Post*, August 23, 2003.

34   Obituary, *Tampa Tribune*, October 8, 2009: 15.

OSCAR GIVENS

BY SKIP NIPPER

Backup shortstop Oscar Givens excelled in his limited playing time in 1946 as he batted .327 in 17 games. Givens gained greater notoriety on the gridiron at Morgan State University and with semipro football teams. *(Courtesy Seamheads. com Negro League Database)*

The Newark Eagles' May 5, 1946, season-opening game against the Philadelphia Stars, a 2-0 no-hit victory for Eagles pitcher Leon Day, soon spelled opportunity for a multi-talented college player named Oscar Givens. Shortstop Benny Felder made two errors in the game,[1] and when the two teams moved from Ruppert Stadium to Delaware's Wilmington Park the next day, the 19-year-old Felder made two more errors in the Eagles' 14-6 win over the Stars.

Seeking Felder's replacement, team owner Abe Manley and manager Biz Mackey turned their eyes to Givens, an outstanding athlete at Morgan State Teachers College in Baltimore.[2] Aware of his maturity and athleticism, they had viewed him as a prospect for Newark prior to World War II, but that conflict had delayed his being signed to a contract. This time, Givens joined the Eagles as soon as his spring semester ended.[3]

The 6-foot-2, 190-pound all-around player was 23 years old and became the heir-apparent to Felder. His athletic ability was his calling card, but in his first professional game with Newark, on June 9, at Wilmington Park against Homestead, he was hitless in three plate appearances though he did not make an error.

During the season Givens appeared in only 17 games at shortstop and moved to third base in one of them. He collected 17 hits in 52 at-bats, including a double and home run, and had five RBIs, but his potential was overshadowed by his lack of production. The July 3 *Brooklyn Eagle* listed Givens as shortstop for that night's game between Newark and the Brooklyn Bushwicks,[4] but the published box score showed Calvin Irvin at that position.[5] On July 5 Mackey gave Felder another chance at shortstop.[6]

It appears Mackey had given up completely on Givens by then, and was unsure about who his starting shortstop would be. Felder was named to the position on July 17 for two games the next day against the Cleveland Buckeyes in Rochester,[7] but he was replaced by Monte Irvin, who was brought in from the outfield to finish the season at shortstop.[8] Givens returned to Morgan State for the fall semester and resumed playing football, the sport that would give him his most fame.

Oscar Cornellnes (possibly Cornelius) Givens was born on July 5, 1922, and grew up in Linden, New Jersey,[9] 11 miles from Newark. His mother, Florida, a homemaker, and father, Jasper, an oil refinery worker, were born in Georgia. His siblings were Rosears (Rosie), the eldest, who was born in 1910, Nathaniel (Noonie), born in 1912, Freddie (1913), sister Mattie (1915), and Jackson (1919). When Oscar was 17 and in his third year of high school, there were 11 other family members living in the Givens home. Oscar followed in the footsteps of his older brothers at Linden High School, where every brother had played nearly every sport; he played multiple sports and starred in basketball and football.

Oscar, like his brothers, was destined to develop into a notable Linden High graduate. The school boasts a list that includes Tiffany Andrade, Miss New Jersey 2008; John Charles, a former cornerback and safety who played eight seasons in the National Football League; Eddie Kasko, an infielder, manager, scout, and front-office executive in major-league baseball; Vincent Obsitnik, an American diplomat of Slovak descent; Jon Rua, an actor, singer, and choreographer who appeared in the Broadway hit *Hamilton*; Troy Stradford, who played for six seasons in the NFL; Craig Taylor, a running back for three seasons for the Cincinnati Bengals; and Muhammad Wilkerson, a defensive end for the New York Jets.[10]

Linden's football coach, Ted Cooper, noting that he may have been the first coach in the state to coach six brothers, said, "They were all great men."[11]

Nine-year-old Oscar represented his hometown in a marbles tournament in Elizabeth, New Jersey, and went to the semifinals, where he was defeated and was awarded the bronze medal.[12]

Oscar began to excel at sports in junior high school, even as a reserve. When the Linden High junior varsity met the Plainfield reserves on October 8, 1934, it was Givens who led the way. With the score tied 0-0, he tossed two touchdown passes in a 13-0 triumph.[13] In the fall of his sophomore year, he was a steady fullback.[14]

As a junior on his high-school basketball team, he was known for his ball-handling skills and teams were aware of his being a team leader. A sportswriter noted, "He is an extremely clever ball handler. He is remembered rather for his method of commanding the team and setting up plays than for his individual scoring prowess."[15] Linden's basketball team finished 21-1 and captured the Union County championship.[16]

When the baseball season began, Givens held down third base and was a good hitter. Against North Plainfield High School on May 1, he had a single, double, and triple in his team's 8-3 win.[17] He added a single and another triple against Carteret on May 22,[18] and hit another triple on May 30.[19]

A bruising fullback on the Linden football team his senior year, Givens was called "the spearhead of the Terriers attack and bulwark of the defense in every game."[20] He was named Honorable Mention on the Writers All-State Football Team.[21]

Once Linden's basketball season began, his reputation on the court picked up where it had left off the previous year, but with an added dimension: scoring. With nine points against North Plainfield in a blowout, others took notice: "Givens, although not the high scorer, was the big gun of the visitors, making plays, setting up his teammates and then for a change scoring himself almost at will."[22] After a successful run during the regular season, Linden lost in the semifinals of the Group III state tournament to Bound Brook High School, 42-22. Both Givens and teammate Butch Woytowicz had 280, combining for 500 points during the year.[23] Both made Honorable Mention on the Writers All-State Basketball Team.[24]

At Morgan State, Givens immediately established himself on the football team. In a 22-0 win over Virginia Union on October 12, 1940, he ran for a touchdown,[25] and on November 9 he paced the team to its sixth straight victory in a win over North Carolina A&T, 34-0. He scored two touchdowns and kicked three extra points in the game.[26]

Named an All-American in football in 1941, Givens was almost as good on the court as he was on the football field. Elected captain of the basketball team, he was instrumental in getting his team to the top of the Colored Intercollegiate Athletic Association standings. But on March 2, 1942, before the season ended, Givens and six basketball teammates were called up to military service.[27]

In the fall of 1946 Givens returned to Morgan State and resumed his position on the football team as a passing fullback and punter. Memorably, he led the squad to a 13-12 win over West Virginia State in Baltimore, a team that included Linwood Greene, a 1945 All-American selection, who was tossed from the game for fighting.[28]

In the third game of the season, in Baltimore, Morgan State thumped Grambling 35-0. The Bears' second touchdown was scored when Givens "whipped a perfect strike to Joe Black in the end zone."[29] Black, the future major-league pitcher, was on a football scholarship (there was no baseball program at Morgan State), and played the same position as Givens. When Black realized he would never beat out Givens for the position, he became an end.[30]

On Thanksgiving Day in Petersburg, Virginia, Morgan State won the CIAA championship by a 6-0 score when Givens "dug his cleats into the soft turf and then rammed his way through left guard from the one-foot line and over for the most precious touchdown Morgan has scored all season."[31]

In 1947 the Los Angeles Dons of the All-America Football Conference signed Givens, who had been named to the Negro All-American team in 1941 and 1942.[32] When the Dons opened camp, there were 40 players, including eight blacks. Givens was one of them, listed at 6-feet-2 and 200 pounds.

In *Gridiron Gauntlet: The Story of the Men Who Integrated Pro Football in Their Own Words,* Andy Piascik quotes John Brown, one of the first black players to play pro football, on Givens' abilities:

> We had another black guy in camp, a quarterback from New Jersey, Oscar Givens, and he could throw with both arms. He went to Morgan State, and I played basketball against him in college. DeGroot wanted to keep him but somebody higher up made some decisions and they got rid of him. DeGroot was a fair-minded person. … [T]hey sent Givens to Hawaii to play and he played over there for a year, but he never came back to the pros. Oscar Givens was one hell of a football player.[33]

Givens could win neither the starting quarterback position nor the backup slot. When a team in Honolulu, the Hawaiian Warriors of the Pacific Coast Professional Football League, let it be known they were searching for backfield help, the Dons loaned Givens and Charles Price to the Warriors. Los Angeles wanted them to return to the Dons for the 1948 season.[34]

Givens impressed F.J. Brickner, general manager of the Warriors, in his first two workouts. "Givens has been particularly impressive in passing and he looks like a good bet to replace Joe Kaulukukui at the quarterback spot," said Brickner.[35]

The unusual schedule against the San Francisco Clippers, Sacramento Nuggets, Salt Lake Seagulls, and Los Angeles Bulldogs allowed the Warriors to play all 10 of their games at home. Givens led his team to a 14-12 opening day win against the Clippers. When the team played Sacramento on October 30, Givens was not dressed.[36] It was later revealed that he had a leg injury but that he would be in the lineup against Sacramento on November 7.[37] The injury was more serious than first determined, as he did not return to action until November 14 against Salt Lake City, when he played as a backup.[38]

The team had a 7-2 record for the season. (Its final game of the season was canceled.) Givens' finished with 38 rushing yards, and 549 passing yards on 36-for-59 passing.[39]

The season may have been successful for the Warriors, but there had been trouble looming. On December 13, 15 members of the team were fined in district court for betting on football games, though Givens was not one of them.[40] On the 15th league Commissioner Rufus Klawans announced that four of the Hawaiian Warriors were suspended from professional football for life: halfbacks Melvin Abreau and Ray Scussel, guard Floyd M. Rhea, and center Jack Keenan.[41] The two backs were the league's leading ground gainers.

In February 1948 Effa Manley signed Givens to a second tryout with Newark. The *Pittsburgh Courier,* reporting the signing, said Givens had "showed considerable promise as a shortstop on the [1946] championship team. In fact, the Eagles started their pennant spirit as soon as Givens was placed into the lineup at shortstop in June of that year."[42]

While noting that Givens would be heading south with the team to begin spring training, Manley also announced that he would marry Hazel J. Hill of Baltimore on February 20.

When the team bus pulled out of Newark on March 29, heading to Jacksonville for a month, Givens was on it.[43] However, during the team's Florida games, 22-year-old Willie "Curly" Williams appeared to be upstaging Givens. Wrote the *Pittsburgh Courier,* "Manager [William] Bell has especially been impressed with the playing of Curley [sic] Williams at shortstop. This rookie has been covering ground like a veteran and also packs a terrific punch at the plate."[44]

At some point the entire Newark team was evaluated by New York Yankees scouts. The assessment probably took place during spring training, as both Williams and Givens are mentioned in their report. Neither was seen as of major-league caliber, with Williams noted as "only fair ability" and Givens as "can't hit, fair fielder."[45]

When the 1948 season began on May 2 in Baltimore against the Elite Giants, Givens was nowhere to be found. In fact, he is given credit for appearing in one game during the entire season, and on August 29, 1949, he signed with the Wilmington (Delaware) Clippers of the American Football League.[46] According to the *Wilmington News Journal,* he was the team's first black player.

The newspaper said of Givens, "He lives in Baltimore, working there for the Bethlehem Steel Corporation. He is married and his wife is a school teacher in the Maryland metropolis."[47]

After a delay waiting for the steel plant in Baltimore to transfer him to daytime work so he could play football,[48] he joined the Clippers and was on the practice field as the team prepared to visit the Erie Vets. Although he was "unfamiliar with some of the plays, Givens looked right at home in the key signal-calling slot and put on an impressive exhibition of ball-handling and passing control during dummy scrimmage," the *Morning News* reported.[49]

At that point, the trail ends on Givens' career, although he was inducted into the Morgan State Athletics Hall of Fame in 1974. The university's website contains a glowing description of what type of athlete he had been:

Oscar "Gip" Givens, a quiet deadly efficient quarterback, became Morgan's foremost triple-threat player. A master at T-formation, excelled as a left-handed passer and right-footed kicker. In addition to his many prowess's [sic] on the football field, the deceased "Gip" Givens also played basketball with great skill and poise during his career at Morgan.[50]

Givens died on October 25, 1967, and was buried in Rosedale and Rosehill Cemetery in Linden.

ACKNOWLEDGMENT

The author wishes to thank Mike Cooney and Nick Diunte for providing reference materials.

SOURCES

In addition to the sources cited in the Notes, the author also consulted Ancestry.com, Baseball-Reference.com, Profootballarchives.com, Seamheads.com, and one book:

Ross, Charles K. *Outside the Lines: African Americans and the Integration of the National Football League* (New York: NYU Press, 2009.)

NOTES

1   "Day Beats Stars in No-Hitter, 2-0," *Philadelphia Inquirer*, May 6, 1946: 22.

2   "Brief History of Morgan State University," Morgan State website, morgan.edu/about/history.html, retrieved October 29, 2018.

3   James Overmyer, *Effa Manley and the Newark Eagles* (Lanham, Maryland: Scarecrow Press, 1993): 200.

4   "Bushwicks Tackle Newark Eagles at Dexter Tonight," *Brooklyn Daily Eagle*, July 3, 1946: 14.

5   "Madison Faces Bushwicks Under Lights Tonight," *Brooklyn Daily Eagle*, July 5, 1946: 12.

6   "Lloyd Nips Newark Eagles in Seventh, 6-5," *Delaware County Daily Times* (Chester, Pennsylvania), July 6, 1946: 10.

7   "Newark Pilot Picks Infield, Outfield Trio," *Rochester* (New York) *Democrat and Chronicle*, July 17, 1946: 20.

8   Ibid.

9   His middle name is rendered as Cornelius in "Dons Sign Negro Star Quarterback," *Honolulu Advertiser*, April 24, 1947: 16.

10   "Famous Alumni Linden High School," PeopleMaven Website, peoplemaven.com/l/X5wOn9/Famous-Alumni-Linden-High-School-(Linden%2C-NJ), retrieved October 28, 2018.

11   Lauren Pancurak Yeats, *The Making of America Series: Linden, New Jersey* (Charleston, South Carolina: Arcadia, 2002).

12   "Marble Play Tourney Will Decide Champs," *Plainfield* (New Jersey) *Courier-News*, April 17, 1931: 36; "Hillside Boy Wins County Marbles Title," *Courier-News*, April 21, 1931: 20.

13   "NPS Junior Varsity Drops One to Linden," *Bridgewater* (New Jersey) *Courier-News*, October 9, 1935: 17.

14   "30-Second Deadlock!," *Asbury Park* (New Jersey) *Press*, September 26, 1937: 13.

15   "Card Cagers Meet Linden Five Tomorrow," *Bridgewater Courier-News*, January 19, 1939: 12.

16   "Linden Five Tops Plainfield, 30-20," *Bridgewater Courier-News*, March 2, 1939: 17.

17   "Bernardsville, Linden Supply Opposition for Borough Squads," *Bridgewater Courier-News*, May 2, 1939: 14.

18   "Carteret Trips Linden, 5 to 3," *Central New Jersey Home News* (New Brunswick, New Jersey), May 23, 1939: 12.

19   "Canucks Drop 2 of 3 Matches – Bears Nose Out Red Caps," *Bridgewater Courier-News*, May 31, 1939: 14.

20   "Prisco Worried as Rain Keeps Squad Indoors," *Central New Jersey Home News*, November 1, 1939: 12.

21   "Writer's All-State Team," *Asbury Park Press*, December 12, 1939: 12.

22   "Givens, Mulhall Lead Goodwin Quintet in 43-22 Victory," *Bridgewater Courier-News*, January 4, 1940: 16.

23   "Bound Brook Gains Tourney Final, Owls Lose," *Central New Jersey Home News*, March 15, 1940: 26.

24   "Champion Fives Fail to Place Man on Writers' All-State Selections," *Bridgewater Courier-News*, March 21, 1940: 20.

25   "Morgan Gridders Run Wild in Two Periods To Defeat Va. Union," *Baltimore Sun*, October 13, 1940: 27.

26   "Morgan State Romps Over N.C. Gridmen, 34-0 for Sixth Triumph," *Baltimore Sun*, November 19, 1940: 28.

27   Martha Joe Black and Chuck Shoffner, *Joe Black: More Than a Dodger* (Chicago: Chicago Review Press, 2015), 69.

28   Ric Roberts, "Morgan Shades W.V. in 13-12 Thriller," *Pittsburgh Courier*, October 19, 1946: 13.

29   "Younger Stars in Morgan Victory," *Pittsburgh Courier*, October 26, 1946: 12.

30   Black and Shoffner.

31   Wendell Smith, "Morgan Beats Va. State, Unruly Crowd to Win CIAA Crown," *Pittsburgh Courier*, December 7, 1946: 16.

32   "L.A. Dons Sign Oscar Givens, Ex-Morgan Star," *Pittsburgh Courier*, April 26, 1947: 15.

33   Andy Piascik, *Gridiron Gauntlet: The Story of the Men Who Integrated Pro Football in Their Own Words* (Lanham, Maryland: Taylor Trade Publications, 2009), 23.

34   "Gridders Will Arrive This Week," *Honolulu Advertiser*, August 24, 1947: 17.

35   "Ex-Don Quarterback Impressive in Drills," *Honolulu Advertiser*, September 5, 1947: 15.

36   Wildred Rhinelander, "Rhiney's Roundup," *Honolulu Star-Bulletin*, November 1, 1947: 3.

37   "Molesworth Expects Battle From Sacramento on Friday, *Honolulu Star-Bulletin*, November 5, 1947: 24.

38   "Warriors Find Stubborn Foe in Salt Lake City Gridders," *Honolulu Star-Bulletin*, November 15, 1947: 22.

39   "Statistics of Warriors Released," *Honolulu Star-Bulletin*, December 7, 1947: 26.

40   "15 Grid Players Fined for Pro Game Gambling," *Honolulu Star-Bulletin*, December 14, 1947: 1.

41   "3 'Outsiders' Charged With Betting on Football Here," *Honolulu Advertiser*, December 16, 1947: 4.

42   "Givens Signed for Trial at Short," *Pittsburgh Courier*, February 21, 1948: 16.

43   "Newark Eagles Winging Way to Sunny Jacksonville Camp," *Pittsburgh Courier*, April 3, 1948: 15.

44   "Manning Signs, but Newark's Pitcher Lewis Still a Holdout," *Pittsburgh Courier*, April 17, 1948: 14.

45   National Baseball Hall of Fame, Manuscript Archives Collection, Integration correspondence and clippings, collection.baseballhall.org/PASTIME/new-york-yankees-memorandum-and-scouting-reports-circa-1948-0#page/1/mode/1up, retrieved November 1, 2018.

46   This was not the American Football League that eventually merged with the National Football League to form the current NFL. It was a post-World War II resurrection of the American Association, a minor professional league that was based in New York City.

47   "Clippers Sign Negro Star Who Played for L.A. Dons," *Wilmington* (Delaware) *Morning News,* August 30, 1949: 22.

48   "Clippers' Squad Cut to 35 for Game With Hawaiians," *Wilmington* (Delaware) *News Journal,* August 31, 1949: 22.

49   "Quarterback Givens Excels as Clippers Prep for Erie," *Wilmington Morning News,* September 6, 1949: 14.

50   Morgan State Athletics Hall of Fame, morganstatebears.com/hof.aspx?hof=34, retrieved November 1, 2018. Givens' nickname may have changed over the years. Earlier, he was known as Gibby.

VERNON HARRISON

BY MARGARET M. GRIPSHOVER

The story of Vernon Randolph Harrison and the 1946 Newark Eagles is a case of "did he or didn't he?" Did Lefty Harrison pitch for Newark during the 1946 season, or was the Harrison whose name appeared in at least one box score Vernon Harrison or someone else? Negro League baseball research on teams and individuals is fraught with two major problems – the lack of records of persons and/or events makes it difficult to find reliable information, or errors in the records of persons and/or events may lead to questionable conclusions. In the case of Vernon Harrison, he did indeed play for the Newark Eagles. He signed a contract with the team in 1939.[1] That can be verified through newspaper accounts and baseball statistics. The question is, was the Harrison who was credited with playing in at least one game with the Newark Eagles in 1946 really Vernon R. Harrison, another player named Harrison, or not a Harrison at all? This is one of many baseball mysteries that may never be solved, but Vernon Harrison's story before and after his baseball career is worth telling, and, with any luck, the answer to the real identity of the Harrison who played for the Newark Eagles in 1946 may eventually be resolved.

Vernon Randolph Harrison was born on July 13, 1919, in Norfolk, Virginia. His parents, Henry J. Harrison Sr. and Anna (Milteer) Harrison, were both born in Nansemond County, Virginia (today the independent city of Suffolk), situated in the Hampton Roads region of southeastern Virginia. Vernon had seven siblings, one of whom died as an infant from measles. Six of the seven were born in Virginia and spent their early childhoods in Portsmouth, where their father, Henry J. Harrison Sr., was a carpenter and contractor. In the early 1920s, Henry's business was successful enough that

Pitcher Vernon Harrison (at left) enrolled in Jersey City's Lincoln High School in 1937 and became the only African American player on the school's varsity baseball team. He made his Newark Eagles debut in 1939. *(Courtesy of Lincoln High School, Jersey City, New Jersey)*

it warranted paying to have his name appear in boldface as an advertisement in the Portsmouth City Directory.[2]

In 1923 Henry and Anna moved their family to Pleasantville, New Jersey, a town about eight miles west of Atlantic City. That same year, Vernon's youngest sibling, Emmett H. Harrison, was born in Pleasantville. Coincidentally, one of the Harrisons' neighbors in Pleasantville was Maxwell C. "Max" Manning, who played for the Newark Eagles. Vernon and his family lived just one block away from the Mannings, on McKinley Street. Manning, who signed with Newark in 1939, was with the team in 1946 and pitched two games in the Negro League World Series.[3]

The lives of Vernon Harrison and his family were shattered on September 10, 1933, when Vernon's father was killed in an automobile accident that also seriously injured Vernon's two youngest brothers, Henry and Emmett Harrison.[4] Harrison's car collided head-on with another vehicle, then "bounded into a ditch and overturned" near the town of Port Republic, about 10 miles north of Pleasantville.[5] Henry Sr., 45 years old, died shortly after being taken to the Atlantic City Hospital. Henry Jr. and Emmett suffered lacerations and head injuries.[6]

Shortly before the accident the family had moved to Atlantic City, where Vernon started his high-school education. Four years later, in 1937, Vernon's mother moved the family to Jersey City and Vernon began attending Lincoln High School, where he was the only African-American on the varsity baseball team.[7] His coach, J. Warren "Warnie" Young, told a reporter that he was "especially enthusiastic over the fine pegging turned in by Vernon Harrison, a colored southpaw … [who] has a fine fastball and in addition to his hurling ability is also a dangerous man with the willow."[8] Young's assessment was prescient. Harrison was named to the first team Hudson County all-star high-school team at the end of his first year at Lincoln High, an honor he repeated the following year in both baseball and basketball,[9] when he was described as "the slickest and most brilliant passer to appear in our midst in some time [and] is a star baseball pitcher with a trick knee."[10] Harrison chose baseball over basketball and football for his senior year, however, perhaps to protect himself (and his knee) for what he foresaw as a possible professional career.

While attending Lincoln High, Harrison also pitched for various local nines including Selmod Athletic Club of the Fifth Ward Twilight League, and the Jersey City Colored Athletics.[11] He took the mound in the summer of 1937 as a member of the Loew's Jersey theater team for a charity event at the Polo Grounds against a team representing Metro-Goldwyn-Mayer.[12]

Quitting the basketball team to concentrate on baseball paid off when Harrison was signed by the Newark Eagles shortly after graduating from Lincoln in 1939.[13] He was described as "one of the best looking prospects to enter the [Negro National League] in a number of years."[14] (A week earlier, Max Manning, Vernon's former neighbor in in Pleasantville, had been added to the Eagles' roster.[15]

Harrison made his Eagles debut on July 4, 1939, in a 7-0 loss to the New York Black Yankees at Dexter Park in Queens, New York.[16] He pitched two innings in relief after the Black Yankees knocked out Newark's starter, Jim Brown, and his reliever, Big Train Cozart.[17] Harrison gave up three runs but struck out two Black Yankees. The

outcome did not bode well for his future with Newark. Harrison's next start came the following day, but not for the Eagles. He was back in his old uniform for the Jersey City Frank Association of the semipro Twilight League, and pitched a no-hitter, against the McDermott Association, missing a perfect game by one walk.[18] Harrison was with the Franks the rest of the summer. He did not pitch for the Eagles for the rest of the 1939 season.

In the spring of 1940, Harrison was working as a baggage porter at the Central Railroad of New Jersey terminal, not far from the home he shared with his mother, sister, and two brothers in Jersey City.[19] His pitching was limited to a handful of appearances on the mound for the semipro Jersey City Negro Athletics. By August, cracks in Harrison's game were beginning to show. In a 7-1 loss to the West Haverstraw Dunnigans, Harrison's pitching was so unsteady that it earned him the headline "Jersey Pitcher's Wildness Ruins Game He Tried Hard to Win."[20] In October Harrison married Althea Van Croft in Jersey City. Their expected betrothal must have been the talk of the town. Earlier that year, a cheeky gossip column in the New York Age speculated about their impending engagement by popping a question of its own: "Say, do you know when Lefty Harrison and Althea Van Croft will say I do?"[21]

In 1941 the couple became parents with the birth of son Vernon J. Harrison. Also, he joined the Brooklyn Royal Giants, a team that had seen better days. It had been 10 years since the Royal Giants were a member of the Negro Leagues Eastern division.[22] In the intervening years, they had devolved into a semipro organization without a league and played against increasingly less prestigious opponents. In 1941 Harrison spent much of the season in the bullpen along with a teammate, Marlon "Sugar" Cain. Brooklyn played mostly local nines, regional semipro clubs, and the barnstorming House of David. At least once Harrison went on the road with the Royal Giants for a June 27 game against the Lloyd Athletic Club of Chester, Pennsylvania.[23] He was the starting pitcher and was removed after giving up four runs in the first three innings.[24] (His replacement, Sugar Cain, pitched six shutout innings; the Royal Giants fell, 4-2.[25]) After the foray to Chester, Harrison's name did not appear in Brooklyn's game results for the rest of the season.

Harrison resurfaced in August 1942, starting a game for his old team, the Jersey City Colored Athletics.[26] The game, a World War II fundraiser for the USO, pitted the Athletics, against Local 16, a group of shipyard workers.[27] Harrison started out strong but flagged by the fifth inning when he gave up five earned runs as the Colored Athletics lost, 12-5.[28]

Sometime later Harrison served in the US Navy, sailing mainly on patrol vessels along the Pacific Coast, searching for enemy submarines."[29] After his discharge in August 1945, he returned to Jersey City. He remained active in veterans affairs, and in 1946 he helped establish the United Negro Veterans of World War II, serving as the organization's first treasurer.[30] In 1946, he also went back to playing baseball.

Harrison joined the newly constituted Jersey City Minor Leaguers in the spring of 1946, and stayed with the team through 1947. The Minor Leaguers were mostly World War II veterans, some of whom, like Harrison, had played in organized ball.[31] Harrison was the only African-American on the team.[32] He started a game against the Puerto Rican Stars in May and was described in the *Jersey Journal* as a "Negro southpaw who hurled for Lincoln High School and served in the armed forces during World War II."[33] It was not unusual for sportswriters to mention his high-school pitching accomplishments, even though he had graduated from Lincoln High School nearly a decade earlier. There was no mention, however, of Harrison's stint with the Newark Eagles in 1939, or of any contract offers in the offing for him for the 1946 season.

Did Vernon Harrison pitch for the Newark Eagles in 1946? An account of an Eagles game played on July 28, 1946, suggested that he did.[34] The *Pittsburgh Courier* reported that "Harrison" (no first name given) played in the first game of a doubleheader against the Homestead Grays in Washington. But this particular Harrison turned out not to be Vernon Harrison: He played third base and batted second in the lineup. Vernon Harrison was a left-handed pitcher with no history of being used as a position player, even going back to his high-school days. Why would the league-leading Eagles call upon Vernon Harrison to play third base when he had not appeared in an Eagles uniform since 1939? In a game being played in Washington, 225 miles from Jersey City. The answer is that they wouldn't have. If Newark's starting third baseman, Andrew "Pat" Patterson wasn't available, Clarence "Pint" Isreal could have stepped in to take his place. In fact, Isreal was in the dugout that night and came in as a pinch-runner in the first game and then played third base in place of "Harrison" in the nightcap. So it is highly improbable that the Harrison who played third base for Newark was Vernon Harrison. In all likelihood, there was an error in the reporting of the game and Harrison was actually Newark's regular third baseman, Pat Patterson; the misidentification was simply a typo in the box score, something that was not at all unusual in that time.

The closest that Vernon Harrison came to having an actual association with the Newark Eagles in 1946 was when he pitched for the Jersey City Minor Leaguers against the Newark Buffaloes. The Buffaloes' manager was Mule Suttles, Harrison's former teammate from the 1939 Eagles. The two teams faced each other multiple times during the summer of 1946. Harrison was mostly relegated to the role of a reliever, although he did enjoy occasional success as a starter.[35]

Harrison resumed his pitching duties for the Jersey City Colored Athletics in the spring of 1947. Newspaper coverage of semipro baseball leagues was in 1947 spotty at best and the results of just a handful of Colored Athletics games were reported in which Harrison played, none with box scores. The 1947 season became Harrison's baseball swan song. He had some memorable highlights to savor such as a one-hitter he tossed against the East Orange Red Sox, but after the 1947 Colored Athletics' season was over, Vernon Harrison's name vanished from the sports pages.[36] Although it is not out of the question that Harrison continued to play on some local or amateur teams, for all intents and purposes, he pitched his last professional game in 1947. After leaving baseball, Harrison pursued careers as a firefighter and police officer in Jersey City.[37] By the time he started training as a fireman, his family had expanded to four with the birth of a daughter, Christine.

When Vernon Randolph Harrison died in Jersey City on March 18, 1978, at the age of 58, he was survived by his wife, Althea, his two children, three grandchildren, and three of his seven siblings.[38] He is buried in the Bay View Cemetery in Jersey City. Although he was not a member of the Newark Eagles during their memorable 1946 season, he made his own contributions to baseball history, as well as serving his country, fellow veterans, and his community.

NOTES

1 "Rookie Looks Good," *Pittsburgh Courier,* July 8, 1938: 17.

2 *Norfolk and Portsmouth City Directory* (Norfolk, Virginia: Hill Directory Company, 1922), 1197.

3 "Newark, Black Yanks Go on Barnstorming Trip," *New Amsterdam News,* July 1, 1939: 19.

4 "The Dead," *Courier-News* (Bridgewater, New Jersey), September 11, 1933: 10.

5 "2 Die, Scores Hurt in South Jersey Weekend Crashes, *Camden* (New Jersey) *Courier-Post,* September 11, 1933: 10.

6 "The Dead."

7 *The Quill, Lincoln High School Yearbook,* 1937), 89.

8 "Scholastic News," *Jersey Journal* (Jersey City, New Jersey), April 2, 1937: 16.

9 "Three All-County Players of 1936 Retain Berths," *Jersey Journal,* June 17, 1937: 12; James H. Haygood Jr., "All-Star Basketball Team chosen by Staff Writer of the New York Age for 3rd Time," *New York Age, April 9, 1938: 11.*

10 Haygood.

11 "Monmouths Clash with Selmod A.C.," *Jersey Journal,* July 10, 1938: 11; "Cakeaters to Play Sunday," *Jersey Journal,* June 23, 1937: 17.

12 "Loew Nine Plays in Polo Grounds," *Jersey Journal,* September 17, 1937: 15.

13 "Newark, Black Yanks."

14 "Rookie Looks Good," *Pittsburgh Courier,* July 8, 1938: 17.

15 "Newark, Black Yanks."

16   "Black Yankees, Eagles Divide," *Brooklyn Daily Eagle,* July 5, 1939: 17.

17   Ibid.

18   "Harrison Hurls Near Perfect Game in Tioga Twilight Loop," *Jersey Journal,* July 6, 1939: 15.

19   US Census Bureau, 1940 Census.

20   "Jersey Pitcher's Wildness Ruins Game He Tried Hard to Win," *Rockland County (New York) Times,* August 24, 1940: 7.

21   Andy Goldman and Harold Baker, "Soil Tiller," *New York Age,* March 16, 1940: 11.

22   John Holway, *The Complete Book of Baseball's Negro Leagues: The Other Half of the History* (Fern Park, Florida: Hastings House Publishers, 2001), 276-279.

23   "Lloyd Scores Impressive Win Over Brooklyn," *Delaware County Times* (Chester, Pennsylvania), June 28, 1941: 14.

24   Ibid.

25   Ibid.

26   "Local 16 Conquer Athletics," *Jersey Journal,* August 17, 1946: 11.

27   Ibid.

28   Ibid.

29   US Navy, USS PC-800, Muster Roll of Crews, April 1, 1946.

30   "Jersey Negro Vets Form Local Group," *New Amsterdam News,* March 9, 1946: 5.

31   "Minor Leaguers Make Debut Against Puerto Rican Stars," *Jersey Journal,* May 4, 1946: 7.

32   "Mule Suttles' New'k Buffaloes Coming Here Sunday Afternoon," *Jersey Journal,* June 6, 1946: 17.

33   "Minor Leaguers, Puerto Rican Stars in Twin Bill Tomorrow," *Jersey Journal,* May 19, 1946: 9.

34   Ric Roberts, "Fields Blanks Newark," *Pittsburgh Courier,* August 3, 1946: 17.

35   "Minors Face Nutley Team in Twin Bill," *Jersey Journal,* June 29, 1946: 7; "Local Club Takes Pair of Clashes," *Jersey Journal,* June 10, 1946: 11; "JC Minor Leaguers in Twin Bill," *Jersey Journal,* July 3, 1946: 14; "Minor Leaguers Defeated," Jersey Journal, August 13, 1946: 11.

36   "Harrison's Hurling Is Big Feature," *Jersey Journal,* April 28, 1947: 11.

37   "Funds Tight, City May Name Only 25 Cops, Less Firemen," *Jersey Journal.* February 11, 1954: 6.; "Death Notices," *Jersey Journal,* March 20, 1978: 3.

38   "Death Notices."

BOB HARVEY

BY JEB STEWART

Outfielder Bob Harvey garnered six hits against the Monarchs in the 1946 World Series. In 1945, he had led the Eagles with a .389 batting average. *(Noir-Tech Research, Inc.)*

Bob Harvey was a menacing hitter, who reliably anchored right field for the Newark, Houston, and New Orleans Eagles from 1943 to 1951. Harvey was a large man, who stood 6-feet tall and weighed 220 pounds but was a capable fielder and possessed a deadly throwing arm.[1] He threw right-handed but was a left-handed hitter, and consistently batted over .300 during his professional career.

Robert Alexander Harvey was born on May 28, 1918, in Saint Michael's, Maryland, a town of less than 1,500 residents along the Miles River on Maryland's Eastern Shore. There is some uncertainty about his lineage. A 1930 Census record from St. Michael's says his mother may have been a widow named Dacurcy Harvey and that he had three siblings, George, Lillian, and Lafayette.[2] However, his death record from Archives.com suggests that his parents may have actually been John Hall and Lillian Harvey.

Harvey attended the Julius Rosenwald School[3] in St. Michael's, where he quickly developed beyond his peers as an athlete.[4] As a teenager, he joined the St. Michael's Red Sox, a local men's baseball team, and was one of the club's best players.[5] After graduating from high school, Harvey enrolled at a teacher's college across Chesapeake Bay, the Maryland Normal and Industrial School at Bowie, in 1936;[6] he attended the school until 1938, when he left because of finances.[7]

At Bowie, Harvey played on the baseball, football, and basketball teams. Photographs show him wearing catching gear for the Bulls baseball team.[8] He also starred in basketball; in the winter of 1937, Harvey scored 18 points as Bowie defeated Storer, 41-6.[9]

But it was in football that Harvey's skills shone the greatest. On Thanksgiving Day 1936, in a game against rival Princess Anne, Harvey intercepted a pass on defense early in the game. On offense, he was a bruising running back. On one running play, "[l]ike a powerful machine Harvey went across for first touchdown of the game"; then he "smashed the line like a steam roller and went over for the second touchdown."[10] In the second half, Harvey caught a long reception and carried the ball to the goal line to set up the final score as the Bulls won 18-0, but failed to convert a single extra point.[11] Harvey's duties expanded the next year as he also became the Bulls' place-kicker and performed well.[12] In 1939, the school named Harvey to its Hall of Fame for football.[13]

After leaving college, Harvey moved back to the Eastern Shore and took up residence in Cambridge, Maryland, less than 30 miles from his hometown of St. Michael's.[14] He "took a job in the shipping department of Phillips Packing Co., a canned goods processor," and played catcher for the company's baseball team.[15] By 1943, Harvey's performance on the diamond attracted the attention of Webster McDonald, a manager and part-time scout for Abe and Effa Manley, the owners of the Newark Eagles.[16]

After receiving McDonald's report, the Eagles invited Harvey to audition. He slammed two home runs in the 1943 tryout and the Manleys eagerly signed the 25-year-old slugger to a contract for $135 a month.[17] The team was already deep at catcher, so Harvey moved to right field.[18] He joined a talented squad, which included five future Hall of Famers including second basemen Larry Doby, center fielder Monte Irvin, catcher Biz Mackey, and player-manager Mule Suttles. The club played its home games at Ruppert Stadium when the Newark Bears of the International League were on the road. For Harvey, Ruppert's right-field fence, which was just 305 feet down the line, must have been an enticing sight, although he could hit to all fields.[19]

The Negro leagues presented a chance for young black men to make a living playing baseball, although Harvey recalled life on the road was often hard:

> The traveling was really rough, says Harvey, who recalls having to board the team bus immediately after games and travel all night – often hundreds of miles –to get to the next game on time. All our traveling was done by bus.[20]

> Sometimes we played tripleheaders, where we'd play a pair (of games) at Yankee Stadium, keep our uniforms on and then drive to Trenton (New Jersey) for a night game.[21]

The Eagles finished fourth in the NNL in 1943 behind the eventual Negro League World Series champions, the Homestead Grays.

Bob Harvey (wearing catcher's gear) roamed the outfield for the Eagles, but he had been a backstop at Maryland Teacher's College at Bowie. The institution was also known as Bowie Normal School (BNS). *(Photograph courtesy of the University Archives and Special Collections Department, Thurgood Marshall Library, Bowie State University, Bowie, Maryland 29715)*

Harvey batted .323 with one homer and 10 RBIs in 17 games,[22] as sportswriters were already recognizing him as a key run producer.[23] In 1944, while Doby and Irvin served in the military, Newark added another future Hall of Famer, Ray Dandridge, but fell further in the standings to fifth place. Harvey again performed well, hitting .307 with 25 RBIs and a team-leading five home runs.[24]

After Suttles' departure, future Hall of Famer Willie Wells became player-manager for 1945, although his tenure did not last long. After a dispute with owner Abe Manley over his use of pitcher Terris McDuffie, Wells resigned; Manley later traded him to the New York Black Yankees.[25] Biz Mackey replaced Wells and was player-manager until the end of 1947. Under Mackey, Newark improved to finish third in the NNL, despite Doby's absence. The 1945 campaign also proved to be memorable for Harvey. He married Catherine "Kay" Lewis, who would be his wife for 47 years until he died in 1992; the couple had a daughter named Cynthia.[26] Now 27, Harvey had arguably his finest performance as a Negro Leaguer in 1945. According to the Howe News Bureau's official statistics for the NNL, he led the Eagles with a .389 average, which was his career high, and finished behind only Josh Gibson (.393) among everyday players in the league.[27] He struck 3 home runs and 12 doubles, and drove in 29 runs.[28]

In late September, New York's Polo Grounds hosted a doubleheader showcasing four Negro League clubs closing out their schedules. In the first game, the Eagles played the Baltimore Elite Giants and won, 5-2, behind the strong pitching of teenage phenom Don Newcombe.[29] The Birmingham Black Barons faced the New York Cubans in the second game. The game was unremarkable, except for the name Harvey in the box score as the center fielder for the Black Barons.[30] "Bill Harvey [had already] pitched for the Elite Giants" and it appears the Eagles loaned Bob Harvey – who occasionally played center field[31] – to Birmingham, as the Black Barons did not have another player on the roster with that surname.[32] Harvey went 0-for-3 and recorded one putout in the loss.[33]

Later that fall, Harvey played for the Negro National League All-Stars with Mackey, Irvin, Newcombe, Roy Campanella, and Sam Bankhead, among others, in a five-game exhibition series against an all-white National League all-star team managed by Chuck Dressen.[34] The results were expected to be presented to the New York State Committee Against Discrimination as part of a coming debate about whether to compel the major leagues to integrate.[35] Dressen's All-Stars opened with a sweep of a twin bill in tight contests at Brooklyn's Ebbets Field, 5-4 and 2-1.[36] After scoring a 10-0 victory in Ruppert Stadium behind the pitching of Ralph Branca, who matched his major-league teammates' run production with 10 strikeouts, the series returned to Flatbush for a doubleheader. The major leaguers won the fourth game, 4-1, as Virgil Trucks cruised.[37] In the final game, Johnny Wright – pitching under the alias Leroy Leafwich (because he was still in the Navy) – held the major leaguers scoreless for those five innings, but the game ended in a scoreless tie.[38] Despite losing the series, Bob Harvey believed Negro League players could compete with their white counterparts, maintaining, "I don't think they were any better than us."[39]

At the start of 1946, the Eagles had high hopes as Doby returned, and Mackey believed they were ready to compete for a pennant.[40] On Opening Day, Leon Day threw a no-hitter against the Philadelphia Stars.[41] Newark streaked to wins in its next two games, and a double by Harvey punctuated an 8-2 win against the New York Black Yankees.[42] The defending NNL champions, the Homestead Grays, were next; the Grays featured stars Josh Gibson, Buck Leonard, and Cool Papa Bell.[43] After falling behind 3-0, Mackey's men battled back to tie the score, thanks in part to a sacrifice bunt by the versatile Harvey, before the umpire declared the game a tie at dusk.[44]

Despite the fast start, the Eagles lost four games in a row and sank to fourth place by the end of May.[45] Monte Irvin and Bob Harvey suffered hitting slumps and were blamed for the sudden downturn.[46] Mackey was reportedly frustrated with Harvey's performance:

> Another player who has also been in a slump is Bob Harvey, who was the second-best hitter in the league last year. Bob has been woefully weak at the plate and may be benched in an effort to get more batting punch in the lineup and give Harvey a chance to regain his batting eye, Bob is also overweight and may be forced to undergo a serious siege of reducing by Manager Mackey.[47]

However, the slide ended as quickly as it began; by June 9 the Eagles nested into first place.[48] They played well and claimed the first-half

league title by the end of June after sweeping a doubleheader from Philadelphia; Harvey's three-run triple against the Stars proved to be the championship-clinching hit.[49]

In the second half, the Eagles avoided any inconsistency, flew to a 17-4 start, which included a 14-game winning streak, and easily won the league championship again.[50] Newark finished with a combined record of 56-24-3.[51] For his part, Harvey saw his batting average plummet to .284.[52]

Harvey played an immediate role in deciding the Negro League World Series against the formidable Kansas City Monarchs, champions of the Negro American League. He is remembered more for his glove and baserunning than his bat in the series, however. At the Polo Grounds, in Game One of the Series, Satchel Paige relieved Hilton Smith for the Monarchs and shut down the Eagles' bats for four innings, as Kansas City won 2-1. Kansas City had taken an early 1-0 lead after Harvey allowed a ball to roll between his legs to the right-field wall in the first inning.[53] After Harvey led off the fifth inning with a single, Leon Ruffin grounded out. Harvey slid hard into second and "blocked [shortstop Jim] Hamilton on the double play throw and the contact with the heavy Newark outfielder broke Hamilton's leg in two places."[54]

The Series was a back-and-forth affair that went a full seven games with the Eagles claiming their first and only Negro League World Series championship after a 3-2 victory at Ruppert Stadium in the finale. Based on the box scores, which are available for five of the contests, Harvey collected six hits in the Series, but was not mentioned in the summaries after Game One. Harvey fondly remembered the 1946 championship as "one of the best times of my life."[55]

The following summer one of Harvey's most memorable moments occurred in a doubleheader in Yankee Stadium against the Black Yankees, although his own memory of the game was probably fuzzy:

> A freak play in the first game put the officials at a test for a rare ruling that drew a "protested game" beef from the Yankee manager, Marvin Barker. Dick Seay, Yank third sacker, walked to lead off the fourth inning. Bud Barbee poled a long fly over the right field barrier. Bob Harvey galloped over fast, snared the ball and crashed waist high into the stands. Seay tagged up and went all the way home.
>
> Dusty Rhodes, plate umpire, ruled the hitter out and the runner safe, but Barker maintained Harvey took the ball out of the playing field and Barbee was entitled to a home run.[56]

Harvey did not attempt a throw home on the play after being knocked unconscious when he smashed into the stands, but he held onto the ball, and Newark won the game, 9-8.[57] By July 4 Harvey had shaken off any aftereffects from the play as he and

Doby homered in a win over the Philadelphia Stars in Doby's final NNL game before he joined the Cleveland Indians.[58]

With the loss of Doby's offensive production, the Eagles' championship reign quietly ended.[59] They finished 1947 with a respectable record of 50-38-1, including the best record in the first half, but in the second half the Birds fell behind their rivals, the New York Cubans, who were declared the NNL champions without a playoff series.[60] There was bad blood with the Cubans as the players brawled in early May during a 10-2 Newark win.[61] Harvey rebounded, batting .335 (seventh among qualifiers) with 17 doubles and 3 home runs.[62] He spent the winter playing baseball in Puerto Rico for a monthly salary of $1,500, which was his highest ever.[63]

Change was in the air in 1948. It would be the last season the Eagles played in Newark, the end of the NNL, and the final Negro League World Series, although it is unlikely anyone realized what was happening as the campaign got underway. The transition began in the winter, as the Manleys released Mackey, who they believed lacked discipline, and installed William Bell as the manager.[64] The move did not help their fortunes, however, as the Eagles tumbled to a disappointing third-place finish.[65]

Despite the decline in the standings, columnist Dan Burley noted "dependable Bob Harvey, who while rather portly, can still wallop the ball and manage to get under flies."[66] Now 30, Harvey led the Eagles with a .363 batting average, fourth among the league's hitters;[67] and for the first time in his career, he was chosen for the East-West All-Star Game.[68] In the game, played at Comiskey Park in Chicago, Harvey had one plate appearance for the East, but failed to reach safely, as the West won, 3-0.[69]

The Eagles played their final game at Ruppert Stadium on September 8, 1948, and their last league games as the Newark franchise four days later in Yankee Stadium.[70] The Manleys lost their interest in continuing and sold the club to "Dr. W.H. Young, a Memphis dentist, and Hugh Cherry of Blytheville, Arkansas, for a reported $15,000. That was a fraction of the $100,000 often reported as the sum Abe had invested in the team."[71] By late fall, the NNL dissolved as a result of declining attendance; the Eagles joined the Negro American League and relocated to Houston, Texas.[72] During the winter, the new owners sold Monte Irvin to the New York Giants.[73]

Harvey brought his steady bat to Houston as he hit .299 in 1949.[74] Goose Curry invited him to be an instructor for Curry's Delta Negro Baseball School the following February.[75] In two seasons in Houston, the Eagles, who played their home games at Buffalo Stadium, suffered back-to-back fourth-place finishes.[76] The 1949 squad finished just under .500. The next year was a disaster as Houston crashed to 23-41-1.[77] Harvey performed well, hitting a team-leading .367 in 1950, sixth in the NAL batting race.[78] He

was an All-Star again, this time as a member of the West squad.[79] Harvey batted twice in the contest, drawing a walk and scoring a run on an error "when Ben Littles of Philadelphia lost [a] lazy fly ball in the sun."[80] Later in the game, Harvey returned the favor as he also lost a ball in the sun, which led to a run for the East. The West won, 5-3.[81] Harvey barnstormed against a group of black major leaguers in the offseason.

The 1951 season was Harvey's last in the Negro leagues. Before the season, the Eagles moved to New Orleans.[82] The change of venue did not improve the results, however, as they started 9-17.[83] The 33-year-old Harvey hit at a furious pace, however, and posted a .474 batting average into June.[84] He abruptly left the club to join the Elmwood Giants in the semipro Manitoba-Dakota Baseball League.[85] Harvey led the Man-Dak League with nine home runs and batted .306 with 43 RBIs.[86]

Back in New Orleans, the Eagles were in last place of the NAL's Western Division with a 13-22 record on July 4,[87] and management soon began to cut its losses. Jehosie Heard and Curley Williams were sold to the St. Louis Browns in late August.[88] In January the end finally came as the Eagles withdrew entirely from the league.[89] Owners Martin and Young offered to sell the contracts of the remaining players to other NAL franchises and announced Harvey's availability.[90]

In February 1952, the Birmingham Black Barons purchased Harvey's contract.[91] Throughout the early spring, the *Birmingham World* published reports of the Black Barons' expectation of Harvey reporting for spring training.[92] However, his name never appeared in a box score or game story for the Black Barons in 1952. In Canada the newspapers also anticipated Harvey's return to the Man-Dak League for the Winnipeg Giants.[93] However, it appears he never actually reported. Barry Swanton and Jay Dell-Mah concluded that "(h)e retired after the '51 campaign"[94] and Harvey told Ross Forman, "I played in Canada for a year."[95]

Based on the incomplete statistics available from the Howe News Bureau, Harvey had a lifetime batting average of .338 during his career in the Negro Leagues. Seamheads.com assesses him as having an OPS+ of 119, although the calculation is based solely on his performance in the NNL.[96] Although he did not face Harvey often, pitcher Bill Greason remembered him as a dangerous left-handed slugger.[97]

After his baseball career, Harvey and his wife, Kay, settled in Montclair, New Jersey, where the couple liked to entertain in their home.[98] He spent 32 years working in the shipping department for Hoffmann-LaRoche, a pharmaceutical company, before retiring in 1983.[99] Despite his retirement, he worked part-time as a crossing guard at an elementary school.[100] Late in his life, Harvey's baseball accomplishments were remembered by the public as he regularly appeared at autograph signings, reunions, and Negro League appreciation days at major-league ballparks, including Memorial Stadium, Veterans Stadium, and Shea Stadium.[101] On one occasion, Harvey remarked, "Society must have had a guilt trip because it's taken close to 40 years for them to recognize the former players of the Negro League."[102] However, he denied any bitterness over not playing Organized Baseball, adding, "Baseball gave me the opportunity to see the world and I wouldn't have traded it for anything."[103]

Harvey died from a blood disorder on June 27, 1992, at the age of 74.[104] He is buried at the Rosedale Cemetery in Montclair, New Jersey.

ACKNOWLEDGEMENTS

Like a pitcher with a collection of all-star defenders behind him, the author is grateful for all the help he received on this project. Everett "Ev" Cope of Bozeman, Montana, provided a copy of Ross Forman's *Sports Collectors Digest* article on Bob Harvey. Thomas Zocco and Larry Lester provided Jonathan Welsh's excellent 1991 feature on Harvey from the *Montclair Times*. John Zinn even offered to drive to the Montclair Public Library to search for the same article. Paul Brennan, a staff member of the library, provided the author with a copy of Harvey's obituary. Gary Ashwill of Seamheads. com helped explain Harvey's 1945 appearance for the Birmingham Black Barons. Jay-Dell Mah and Rick Bush provided research on Harvey's time in Canada. Charles Ruberson, a volunteer in the Maryland Room of the Talbot County Library, provided useful information about Harvey's education in St. Michael's. Finally, Katherine Hayes and Arlene Creek of Bowie State University provided invaluable help with Harvey's college years, including photographs, which have not been seen for decades.

NOTES

1   "Two Big League Negro Baseball Teams Here Soon," *Daily Standard* (Sikeston, Missouri), June 25, 1951.

2   Maryland. Talbot County. 1920 U.S. Census.

3   Julius Rosenwald Schools were established by Rosenwald, an early owner of Sears Roebuck & Co., to serve African-American children in the South.

4   James A. Riley, *The Biographical Encyclopedia of the Negro Baseball Leagues* (New York: Carroll & Graf Publishers, 1994), 368.

5   Dr. Carole Marks, *Lift Every Voice: Echoes from the Black Community* (Wyes Mill, Maryland: Chesapeake College Press, 1999, Kindle Edition), 84-85.

6   In 1938 the school changed its name to the Maryland Teachers College at Bowie and later became Bowie State University. "The Eye Salutes President James," *The College Eye*, Vol. 6, No. 1, September-October, 1938: 1 accessed at bowiestate.edu/academics-research/library/departments/archives-and-special-collectio/the-college-eye-1935-1967/.

7   Katherine A. Hayes, archivist, Department of Archives & Special Collections, Thurgood Marshall Library, Bowie State University, email correspondence with author, October 10, 2018; Jonathan D. Welsh, "Bob Harvey Recalls: Race Line Clouded His Season in Sun," *Montclair* (New Jersey) *Times*, May 23, 1991: A1. There is some speculation that Harvey may have attended Bowie in 1939, but in a preview of the coming basketball season *The College Eye* reported the loss of Harvey. Thelma Hawkins, "Outlook for Basketball," *The College Eye*, Vol. 6, No. 2, November-December, 1938: 12. Additionally, Harvey's name was absent on the roster of the baseball team in 1939. Robert "Pope" Mack, "Sports Review," *The College Eye*, Vol. 6, No. 4, June 1938: 10.

8   Today Bowie State's athletic teams are nicknamed the Bulldogs, but the contemporaneous student newspaper during Bob Harvey's playing days – *The Normal Eye*, later renamed *The College Eye* – referred to all athletic teams as the Bulls.

9   "Storer Topples to Bowie," *The Normal Eye*, Vol. 4, No. 4, March 1937: 7.

10   Francis Nool, "Bulls Top Princess Anne," *The Normal Eye*, Vol. 4, No. 3, December 1936: 4, 6.

11   Ibid.

12   Charles Frisby, "Cheyney Traps Bowie Bulls 48-0," *The Normal Eye*, Vol. 5, No. 2, December 1937: 8.

13   Arlene Creeke, associate athletic director for internal affairs/senior woman administrator, email correspondence with author, November 1, 2018; Ross Forman, "Bob Harvey Recalls Negro League Days," *Sports Collectors Digest*, June 21, 1991: 108; Riley. Harvey is not listed as a member of the Bowie State Athletic Hall of Fame on the school's website. Nevertheless, the university has a plaque identifying him as a member of the Hall of Fame for football in 1939.

14   Welsh.

15   Ibid; James Overmyer, *Queen of the Negro Leagues: Effa Manley and the Newark Eagles* (Lanham, Maryland: Scarecrow Press, Inc., 1998), 195.

16   Overmyer, 195.

17   Riley, 368; Welsh; Forman, 108.

18   Overmyer, 195.

19   Alfred M. Martin, *The Negro Leagues in New Jersey* (Jefferson, North Carolina: McFarland, 2008), 63.

20   Welsh.

21   Forman, 108.

22   seamheads.com/NegroLgs/player.php?playerID=harve01bob.

23   "Eagles and Philly Clash in Twin Bill," *Pittsburgh Courier*, August 14, 1943: 18.

24   Official Negro National League Statistics for 1944, compiled by Howe News Bureau (Chicago). Seamheads.com reckons Harvey's batting average as an incredible .426 over 27 games for the 1944 season, but Howe's statistics included 41 games played.

25   Oyermyer, 81-82; Bob Luke, *The Most Famous Woman in Baseball: Effa Manley and the Negro Leagues* (Washington: Potomac Books, 2011), 110.

26   "Obituaries," Robert A. Harvey, *Montclair Times*, July 2, 1992 B4.

27   Ibid.; Official Negro National League Statistics for 1945, compiled by Howe News Bureau.

28   Official Negro National League Statistics for 1945, compiled by Howe News Bureau.

29   "Eagles Defeat Elites, Cubans Upset Barons," *New York Amsterdam Times*, October 6, 1945: 22.

30   Ibid; Gary Ashwill, Seamheads.com, email correspondence with author, October 16, 2018.

31   Martin, 63; "Eagles Top Giants In Doubleheader," *Norfolk* (Virginia) *Journal and Guide*, August 9, 1947: 20 ("The second double by Bob Harvey, Eagles' centerfielder, drove in the winning run in a seven-run rally").

32   Ashwill email.

33   "Eagles Defeat Elites."

34   Dan Burley, "Big Leaguers Play Negroes," *New York Amsterdam Times*, October 6, 1945: 1, 3.

35   Ibid.

36   "Dressens Cop Two From Negro Stars," *The Sporting News*, October 11, 1945: 13.

37   "Dressenmen Annex Four in Rover Over Negro Stars," *The Sporting News*, October 18, 1945: 17, 18.

38   Dressenmen: 17.

39   "Former Players Visit Black Baseball Exhibit," *Courier-News* (Bridgewater, New Jersey), September 28, 1984: A-12.

40   "Eagles Satisfy," *Newark News*, April 9, 1946.

41   "Fireworks at Eagles Game," *Newark News*, May 6, 1946.

42   "Test Ahead for Eagles," *Newark News*, May 13, 1946.

43   "Eagles Hold Top in 3-3 Tie Game," *Newark News*, May 13, 1946.

44   Ibid.

45   "Negro National League Standings (as of May 26)," *New Jersey Afro-American*, June 1, 1946.

46   "Biz Mackey Irked Over Slump; Cracks Whip Over Newark Eagles," *Philadelphia Tribune*, June 1, 1946: 11.

47   Ibid.

48   "Eagles Move to the Top," *Newark News*, June 10, 1946.

49   "Eagles Clinch Midway Title," *Newark News*, July 1, 1946.

50   Diamond Dust (Standings)," *New Jersey Afro-American*, September 7, 1946; "Eagles Streak Reaches 14," *Newark News*, September 3, 1946.

51   seamheads.com/NegroLgs/team.php?yearID=1946&teamID=NE.

52   Official Negro National League Statistics for 1946, compiled by Howe News Bureau (Chicago).

53   Sam Lacy, "19,423 Fans See Paige in Brilliant Performance," *New Jersey Afro-American*, September 21, 1946.

54   Lem Graves Jr., "Paige Leads K.C. to Series Victory 2-1," *Norfolk Journal and Guide*, September 21, 1946: A1.

55   Forman, 108.

56   "Yanks and Eagles Split Doubleheader, 9-8, 5-6," *Norfolk Journal and Guide*, July 4, 1947: 5.

57   Haskell Cole, "Doby Stars for Newark," *Pittsburgh Courier*, July 5, 1947: 15.

58   "Doby Hits Homer in Final Game with Newark Eagles" *Atlanta Daily World*, July 9, 1947: 5.

59   Overmyer, 239.

60   Luke, 139; seamheads.com/NegroLgs/year.php?yearID=1947&lgID=NN2.

61   "Johnson Fines Cuban-Newark Brawlers," *New York Amsterdam News*, May 3, 1947: 13; "Photo Standalone 40," *Chicago Defender*, May 10, 1947.

62   Official Negro National League Statistics for 1947, compiled by Howe News Bureau (Chicago).

63   Forman, 108.

64   Luke, 141.

65   seamheads.com/NegroLgs/year.php?yearID=1948&lgID=NN2.

66   Dan Burley, "Confidentially Yours," *New York Amsterdam News*, May 29, 1948: 20.

67   Official Negro National League Statistics for 1948, compiled by Howe News Bureau (Chicago).

68   "Newark Eagles Play Chicago Giants Sunday, *New York Amsterdam News*, August 7, 1948.

69   Larry Lester, *Black Baseball's National Showcase, The East-West All-Star Game*, 1933-1953 (Lincoln: University of Nebraska Press, 2001), 313.

70   "Eagles, Cubans Play Last Doubleheader in Stadium," *New York Amsterdam News*, September 11, 1948: 15.

71   Luke, 145.

72   A.S. "Doc" Young, "Negro Leagues Reorganize in 10-Club Group," *The Sporting News*, December 8, 1948: 31.

73   "Giants Mum on Reports They Signed Monte Irvin," *The Sporting News*, January 26, 1949: 6; "Giants Get Three Negroes for Trials at Jersey City," *The Sporting News*, February 9, 1949: 7.

74   Official Negro American League Statistics for 1949, compiled by Howe News Bureau (Chicago).

75   "Baseball School to Open Feb. 27: Goose Curry Heads Set-Up in Greenville," *Pittsburgh Courier*, February 11, 1950: 22.

76   cnlbr.org/Portals/0/Standings/Negro%20American%20League%20(1937-1962)%20 2018-04.pdf.

77   Ibid.

78   Official Negro American League Statistics for 1950, compiled by Howe News Bureau (Chicago).

79   "West All-Star Team Roster Completed," *Norfolk Journal and Guide*, August 12, 1950: D20.

80   Lester, 347.

81   Lester, 348-49.

82   Russ J. Cowans, "Clowns Start with a Rush to Lead NAL," *The Sporting News*, May 16, 1951: 16.

83   Russ J. Cowans, "Monarch Lefty Setting Record Strikeout Pace," *The Sporting News*, June 13, 1951: 10.

84   Ibid.

85   "Turk Sends 'Em, Haas Grabs 'Em," *Winnipeg Free Press*, June 8, 1951.

86   Barry Swanton and Jay-Dell Mah, *Black Baseball Players in Canada: A Biographical Dictionary, 1881-1960* (Jefferson, North Carolina: McFarland, 2006), 80-81.

87   Russ J. Cowans, "K.C. Monarchs and Clowns Win First-Half Titles," *The Sporting News*, July 4, 1951: 33.

88   Emmett Maum, "Brownies Obtain Four Performers in Negro Leagues," *The Sporting News*, September 5, 1951: 22.

89   Russ J. Cowans, "Negro League Cut From Eight Clubs; Will Go With Six," *The Sporting News*, January 9, 1952: 19; Russ J. Cowans, "Negro League Claims Players of New Orleans," *The Sporting News*, January 23, 1952: 17.

90   Cowans, "Negro League Claims Players."

91   "Birmingham Black Barons Have Tradition of Great Performers" *Atlanta Daily World*, February 20, 1952: 5.

92   "New Players Expected to Join B'ham Black Barons" *Birmingham World*, April 1, 1952: 3; "Birmingham Black Barons Kickoff Training Drills," *Birmingham World*, April 8, 1952: 5; "Black Barons to Meet Chi American Giants Sunday," *Birmingham World*, April 11, 1952: 6.

93   "Winnipeg Giants Release Names of Probable Lineup," *Brandon* (Manitoba) *Daily Sun*, April 22, 1952; "Minot Thumps Giants," *Winnipeg Free Press*, May 27, 1952; attheplate.com/wcbl/negro_3.html.

94   Swanton and Mah, 81.

95   Forman, 108.

96   seamheads.com/NegroLgs/player.php?playerID=harve01bob.

97   Interview with author at the Southern Negro Baseball Conference, October 4, 2018.

98   "Mrs. Kay Harvey Entertains in Montclair Home," *New York Amsterdam News*, February 7, 1959: 12.

99   Forman, 108; Welsh, A-10; Martin, 63; Riley, 368.

100   Forman, 108.

101   "Former Players Visit Black Baseball Exhibit," *Courier-News*, September 28, 1984: 12; Carl Babati, "The Other Game," *Courier-News*, August 16, 1988: 19; Peter Genovese, "Black Players Were a Hit When the Big Leagues Were Foul," *Central New Jersey Home News* (New Brunswick), February 5, 1989: 15; "Former Negro Major League Baseball Stars Feted by the Baltimore Orioles," *Atlanta Daily World*, June 12, 1990: 5; "Upper Deck Heroes to Honor Negro Leaguers," *Atlanta Daily World*, August 4, 1991: 8; Howie Evans, "Mets Honor Stars from Negro Leagues," *New York Amsterdam News*, May 30, 1992: 48; Kenneth Meeks, "Ex-Negro League Baseball Players Sign Autographs," *New York Amsterdam News*, June 6, 1992: 51.

102   Meeks.

103   Forman, 108.

104   "Obituaries," Robert A. Harvey, *Montclair Times*, July 2, 1992 B4; Martin, 63.

FRED HOBGOOD

BY RICHARD BOGOVICH

The assertive teenager's pro baseball career began with a simple letter, jointly submitted with a friend and mailed from his hometown of Kinston, North Carolina. "We would like to seek a job or a tryout with your ballclub. We are now at the age of nineteen years old, we have had two years of experience with a semi-pro club which were the state champions," they wrote. "Frederick Hobgood, pitcher, has record of 19 victories and 2 defeats, has excellent control, bats and throws on left side," they continued, and for good measure they added that "neither has habits of smoking or drinking." Hobgood composed that letter with teammate James Waters in early 1941 and sent it to the Newark Eagles.[1]

Frederick Douglass Hobgood was born on October 1, 1921, to Cuder and Zylphia (Bryant) Hobgood, about two years after his brother, John Bryant Hobgood.[2] Fred was a lifelong resident of Kinston, which a 2018 ESPN article called "the NBA capital of the world," asserting that "this town of some 21,000 residents is most surely, per capita, the greatest producer of NBA players in America."[3] As a result, it is reportedly called "Basketball Heaven" by many locals, but back when Hobgood joined the Newark club, Kinston was advertising itself as the "world's foremost tobacco center."[4]

According to the county marriage register, Cuder and Zylphia were wed on April 24, 1918.[5] Two days later Cuder began military service, during the final year of World War I. His military service card dated November 22, 1919, indicated that he did not serve

Pitcher Fred Hobgood, an Eagle from 1941 to 1944, apparently rejoined Newark for one game against the Baltimore Elite Giants on June 3, 1946, in Norfolk, Virginia. *(Noir-Tech Research, Inc.)*

overseas. He was honorably discharged on February 3, 1919, 12 weeks after the end of the war.[6]

Minimal information about Fred Hobgood's youth is available, but the 1920 census reports that shortly before Fred's birth, Cuder worked at a tobacco factory. Cuder was listed in the city's 1920 directory. In the 1930 census the family's entry consisted of Zylphia Hobgood and her two sons, both of whom attended school. Zylphia, a servant in a private home, was identified as a widow, which was also the case in the 1940 census. However, Cuder had apparently remarried: In the 1940 census he and a different wife were living in Washington, D.C., with children Eugene, Loretta, and Cuder Jr. (The latter was born around 1925.) Kinston's 1923 city directory had an entry for "Delphia" Hobgood, a laundress, who had presumably become a single mother by then.

The 1940 census entry for Zylphia and her two sons indicates that John had completed high school and Frederick had completed two years.

At the time of the 1930 census they would have been attending Tower Hill Elementary School. The only public high school for African-Americans in Kinston was Adkin High School, which opened in 1928. Twelfth grade wasn't added to Adkin until 1942, after both Hobgood brothers attended.

The semipro team to which Hobgood alluded in the 1941 letter to the Newark Eagles was the Kinston Greys (sometimes called the Grays). They were founded in 1939, and initially their home games were played at Adkin High Park.[7] On June 3, 1939, the *Pittsburgh Courier* did the Greys a big favor by publishing an announcement that they were "anxious to book games with teams traveling in this section. To date this strong nine has won eight out of twelve games." Anyone interested in challenging the Greys was to contact a Miss Margaret Bryant (Zylphia's maiden name), whose address was across the street from the team's organizer, Oscar Cannon.[8]

One game that first season was a 6-5 loss to the Durham Black Sox on August 8. The game was covered by the *Carolina Times*, Durham's African-American newspaper, though without a box score. The Greys used two pitchers, but neither was Hobgood.[9] However, Lefty Hobgood was the winning pitcher for the Greys at home in a game early the next season. They hosted the Charlotte Hornets toward the end of April on a day that the *Carolina Times* described as cold and damp, "better suited for football than baseball."[10] The Greys led the entire game and had a comfortable cushion late "but received a terrific scare in the ninth inning when the visitors scored four times on four hits and a trio of errors after one man was out and the game ended with the tying run on base."[11] The *Times* added that Hobgood had been "master of the game until the fatal ninth when he weakened but he managed to pull through before too much damage was done."[12]

After the Kinston nine's first two years, Hobgood jumped to the professional ranks at the age of 19 with the Eagles, though his addition to the roster flew under the proverbial radar before Opening Day. For example, he wasn't among the six pitchers named in a *New York Age* report in mid-April of 1941 from Newark's spring-training camp in Daytona Beach, Florida. Similarly, he was not one of the five pitchers named in the *Newark Sunday Call*'s preview of the May 11 opener, against the Cuban Stars at home.[13] When the *New York Age* summarized the outcome of that contest, a 10-7 Eagles loss before a crowd of 12,500, it noted that Leon Day was the starting pitcher and Maxwell Manning relieved him in the eighth inning, then added that other pitchers on Newark's staff included Jimmie Hill, James Brown, Len Hooker "and several rookies."[14]

Due to the spotty coverage of Negro National League games in newspapers, it is difficult to state with confidence when Fred Hobgood made his regular-season debut, but it was no later than May 18. On that Sunday, Newark hosted the Philadelphia Stars for a doubleheader. Jimmie Hill apparently pitched a complete game in the first contest, won by the Eagles, 5-2. According to the *New York Age*'s account, Manning was Newark's starting pitcher in the "abbreviated" second game but "was relieved in the seventh by Rookie Fred Hopgood [sic]." (Hobgood's surname was often misspelled that way during his pro career.) His team trailed 4-2 heading into the bottom of the seventh inning but Francis Matthews led off with a walk and Clarence Isreal homered into the left-field bleachers to tie the game. Monte Irvin then walked but the next two Eagles were retired. That brought up Day, who played center field in both contests. His triple in the first game was a crucial blow, and this time he tripled again to plate Irvin with the winning run.[15]

The next day Hobgood was the starting pitcher in a game against the Stars at Elks Park in Chester, Pennsylvania. Hobgood was one of six Eagles who scored in the second inning, which knocked opposing pitcher Henry McHenry out of the game, but the Stars replied with six runs in the second and third innings to tie it. Ultimately the Eagles won, 12-7. According to the box score, Hobgood scored two runs and had a single in five times at bat. Manning relieved him late in the game but Hobgood was the winning pitcher.[16]

Hobgood had another noteworthy outing about a month later against Philadelphia. In the second game of a doubleheader, the *Pittsburgh Courier* said, he "took top honors" in a 6-3 win, though he didn't pitch a complete game. Another month or so later, in the second game of a doubleheader against the Baltimore Elite Giants toward the end of July, he struck out six opponents and limited them to one run on his way to a five-hitter.[17] Outside of NNL competition, Hobgood's peak performance presumably came on September 5 against the Springfield Greys of New York when he hurled a three-hit shutout. "The Eagles southpaw had the Spring-field club completely baffled as he spun a masterful pitching job to triumph 4-0," wrote a Long Island newspaper.[18]

A rookie pitcher will commonly have his fair share of rough or rocky outings, and all told, Hobgood's statistics for 1941 were decidedly average. One source shows his record as 5-4 with a 5.08 ERA in 15 games, nine of which he started and two of which he completed. Another source shows his record as 5-5 and his total starts as 10, but it credits him with only one complete game.[19]

In February 1942, not many weeks after the United States entered World War II, Hobgood filled out a draft registration card. His height was listed as 5-feet-11½ and his weight as 160 pounds. He listed his employer as Abe Manley, the co-owner of the Eagles, so Hobgood may already have had reason to believe he'd continue with the team in 1942. An obvious factor was the loss of players to military service, but the Mexican League was also aggressively recruiting African-American players. "The squad that Abe Manley had so painstakingly assembled by the late 1930s came apart rapidly after 1941," concluded Effa Manley biographer James Overmyer.[20] As the Eagles prepared for spring training, the *New York Age* declared that Newark's staff for 1942 would "consist of Hill, Day, Hooker, Brown, Hopgood [*sic*] and Manning."[21] Sure enough, he earned a starting assignment early in the regular season. At Philadelphia on May 17 he pitched a complete game against the Stars but was on the losing end of a 4-1 score when the Eagles managed only four hits.[22]

During the first game of a doubleheader at Washington's Griffith Stadium on June 28, the 20-year-old Hobgood demonstrated his durability. Jimmie Hill started for the Eagles against the Homestead Grays but was taken out in the third inning, down 3-1. "Frederick Hobgood, another lefthander, took over and held the Grays to two runs and nine hits for the remaining 12 innings, blanking them over the final five innings and stranding 17 men," reported the *Baltimore Afro-American*. The Eagles almost won it in the ninth inning. They trailed 4-3 but rallied for two runs. But Hobgood walked the leadoff batter in the bottom of the inning, "and East-erling's smash to First Baseman Pearson put both runners on when nobody covered first. Benjamin fanned but Ches Williams tied it up, 5 to 5, by singling to right and scoring Whatley." In the 14th inning, doubles by Willie Wells and Leon Day off starter Ray Brown produced the winning run. Though Hobgood walked eight and was 0-for-5 at bat, he earned the victory.[23]

Another high point for Hobgood in 1942 came on August 23 in the second game of a doubleheader against the New York Blank Yankees. The final score was 8-6 and the *New York Age* noted that Hobgood "won his first home game of the season with four-hit pitching."[24] Overall, though, his statistics were again so-so, with

a record of 4-4 in 11 games, eight of which he started. He did, however, increase his complete games from two to four and lowered his ERA somewhat, to 4.57.

A notable preseason start for Hobgood in 1943 was in an exhibition doubleheader on April 25, Easter Sunday, before 11,000 spectators in Washington. After singling in two runs as a pinch-hitter in the first game, he pitched a complete-game loss to the Homestead Grays in the second game. The Grays tormented him more in another doubleheader there on July 4. "The Eagles went into the last inning with a 5 to 4 margin to protect and Hobgood, pitching carefully, retired both Bell and Benjamin," the *Pittsburgh Courier* detailed. "He walked Leonard, however, and Josh Gibson, next up, leaned on one of his serves for a 430-foot line drive homer to win the game, 6 to 5."[25]

On August 1, Hobgood apparently pitched for a different team, the Philadelphia Stars. A pitcher named "Hopgood" took over in the second inning of a game at Dexter Park, Queens, against the semipro Bushwicks of New York.[26] Regardless, on August 7 and 8 Hobgood played for the Eagles against the Homestead Grays, and later in the month he was the second of three Newark pitchers in a game against the Stars.[27]

The 1943 season ended up being a financial success for the Eagles. "Solid profitability may still have been elusive in 1942, for Effa later told how a brisk attendance on the road had been needed to counter low home," wrote James Overmyer.[28] "But 1943 was reported to have been 'the year the Eagles hit the black.'"[29] On the other hand, that season was unsuccessful for Hobgood; his record was just 1-4 in six games. Five were starts and he completed three of them, but his ERA ballooned to 9.20.[30]

During NNL meetings in March of 1944, Newark negotiated a three-team trade with the Black Yankees and the Stars that resulted in Hobgood and outfielder Ed Stone ending up with Philadelphia.[31] Hobgood's statistics for 1944 consist of just one appearance for the Stars, lasting 1⅔ innings, plus a complete-game win back with Newark.[32] He pitched less than an inning for the Stars against the Bushwicks in mid-June, but about a month later a newspaper in New Jersey reported that he was with "the Morristown Memorials, a colored club that are tied with the Knights of Columbus of that place for first position in the G.M.C.B. [Greater Morristown Community Baseball] League." Early in a game against the Madison Colonels of New Jersey, Memorials Manager Buddie Ransome called upon reliever "Jim Hopgood, who recently left the Newark Eagles."[33] Hobgood also played semipro ball in New Jersey from June to October of 1945, as an outfielder and first baseman for the Orange Triangles.[34]

On May 13, 1945, a player named "Hopgood" played first base for the Hilldale A.C. club of Branch Rickey's United States League in a doubleheader against another team in that short-lived circuit, Oscar Charleston's Brooklyn Brown Dodgers. Because coverage of that league was so minimal, there may be no way to confirm that this player was indeed Fred Hobgood.[35]

On June 3, 1946, the Newark Eagles traveled to Norfolk, Virginia, for a game against the Baltimore Elite Giants. Despite chilly weather, 1,500 people watched Newark deploy 16 players in the close contest, which wasn't decided until late. Lem Graves Jr. described the turning point for Norfolk's African-American newspaper:

> Ahead 2 to 1 in the eighth inning, Byrd got off to a bad start by issuing a pass to Hobgood, Newark pinch batter, after getting the Newark lead-off man down 2 strikes to no balls. Hobgood was way behind when he decided to wait Byrd out. When Hobgood drew the freebie, Wilkes laid a bunt down the third base line. Russell, Baltimore third baseman, was up on the green for the play at first with plenty of time. However, he threw the ball away, making Wilkes safe at first on an error and allowing Hopgood [sic] to score. Then Pat Patterson hit a triple to right field scoring Wilkes.

Newark scored one more run in the inning, and the final score was 4-2 in what Graves said twice was an official game.[36] If that was indeed Fred Hobgood rejoining his old team, it was quite possibly the final game of his pro career.

The Kinston Greys continued for about two decades, although whether Hobgood ever rejoined them is unknown. Five members of the team tried out with the St. Louis Browns at a camp in Kinston in August of 1948, but Hobgood wasn't among them.[37]

By 1951 both of Fred Hobgood's parents had died. His father, who is buried in Arlington National Cemetery, died in 1943. Zylphia died in December of 1950. The next month Fred Hobgood married Cecil (often spelled Cecile) Loftin, and a daughter, Frieda, was born in 1956, followed by daughter Melba in 1963.[38]

From 1953 to the end of the decade, city directories listed Hobgood's job as a driver and later a salesman for the Carey-Perry Oil company, also known as the A.J. Carey Oil Company. Starting in the 1960 directory, he owned his own Hobgood's Oil Service and in at least one of those directories he took out an ad specifying mobile fuel oil and printed meter service, for which his business would "assure accuracy."

Hobgood wouldn't enjoy having his own business for very long. He died on September 23, 1965. The cause specified on his death certificate was coronary occlusion, a common cause of heart attacks. He was a week shy of his 44th birthday.

NOTES

1   James Overmyer, *Effa Manley and the Newark Eagles* (Lanham, Maryland: Scarecrow Press, Inc., 1993), 84.

2   This spelling of his middle name is from his draft registration card dated February 16, 1942, though it is sometimes rendered as "Douglas" instead. Both of his parents' first names were spelled differently in various sources, his father's as "Cruder" and his mother's as either "Zilphia" or "Zelphia." One source for John Bryant Hobgood's date of birth, November 11, 1919, is the North Carolina Birth Index, 1800-2000, available online via Ancestry.com.

3   "Since the 1972-73 NBA season, 1 out of every 52.7 players to suit up for Kinston High School's varsity squad has reached the league, meaning the odds to do so in Kinston are, since the early 1970s, about 63 times [better] than the national average. Baxter Holmes, "America's Basketball Heaven," February 20, 2018. espn.com/espn/feature/story/_/id/22467698/how-kinston-north-carolina-became-greatest-producer-nba-talent-america.

4   Ibid.

5   Kinston is the seat of Lenoir County, and its register identified the couple's parents as John and Letitia Hobgood and John and Fannie Bryant. One witness was Ethel Loftin, whose surname is the same as that of Frederick's future wife.

6   See also his individual entry at blacksoldiersmattered.com/soldier?id=WW-I-Card_World-War-I-Service-Card-3-a_01165.tif. His service was confirmed in a list – as "C. Hobgood (colored)" – in "Kinstonians in Arms," *Kinston Daily Free Press*, September 3, 1918: 4.

7   "Played Ball! The Greys Showed Baseball Was Colorblind," *Kinston Free Press*, February 18, 2006: C1.

8   "Kingston [sic] Greys Booking," *Pittsburgh Courier*, June 3, 1939: 16. The city's name was spelled correctly within the short article.

9   "Black Sox Take 2," *Carolina Times* (Durham, North Carolina), August 12, 1939: 8. The starting pitcher for the Greys was named Green and at some point he was relieved by an underhand pitcher named Williams. The hitting star for the Greys was named Price, who tripled. A column on the same page by Wm. A. Tuck, "The Sports Bazaar," noted that at third base for the Greys was Dynamite Brewington, a former North Carolina College fullback. Based on "N.C. College Athletes Honored With Letters at Reception and Smoker," *Carolina Times*, June 11, 1938: 3, Brewington's first name was John, and he also lettered in basketball.

10   "Turn Back Charlotte Hornets," *Carolina Times*, April 27, 1940: 2. Hobgood's catcher was named Mills. On April 28 the Greys were scheduled to play the Greensboro Blue Sox.

11   Ibid.

12   Ibid.

13   "Newark Eagles Have New Pitching Star in James Brown,' *New York Age*, April 19, 1941: 11. In addition to Brown, the article said, other pitchers in or expected at the camp included Leon Day, Maxwell Manning, Haywood Cozart, Len Hooker, and Jimmie Hill. "Negro Loop Opens Here Next Sunday," *Newark Sunday Call*, May 4, 1941: Part 2, page 3. "On the pitching staff Manager Mackey will have Jimmy Hill and Leon Day battling for the No. 1 berth, in addition to James Brown, Len Hooker and Max Manning."

14   "12,500 Fans Atttend [sic] Opening at Ruppert Stadium in Newark," *New York Age*, May 17, 1941: 11.

15   "Newark Eagles Take Two from Star[sic]; Go Into First Place," *New York Age*, May 24, 1941: 11. May 24, 1941, was a Saturday, and this newspaper was reporting on the previous Sunday, which was May 18.

16   "Newark Eagles Rout Phila. Stars," *Chester* (Pennsylvania) *Times*, May 20, 1941: 15.

17   "Eagles in Stride; Top Philly Stars," *Pittsburgh Courier*, June 21, 1941: 16. "Baltimore Giants, Newark Divide," *Philadelphia Inquirer*, July 27, 1941: 4.

18   "Greys Blanked with Three Hits," *Nassau Daily Review-Star* (Long Island, New York), September 6, 1941: 11.

19   See seamheads.com/NegroLgs/player.php?playerID=hobgo01fre (which, as of this writing, is the source that provides an ERA for him and shows his record as 5-4) and baseball-reference.com/register/player.fcgi?id=hobgoo000fre.

20   Overmyer, 191.

21   "Newark Eagles to Train in Florida," *New York Age*, February 28, 1942: 11.

22   "Eagles, Stars Divide Bill," *Baltimore Afro-American*, May 23, 1942: 22.

23   "Eagles Nip Grays in 14th Inning," *Baltimore Afro-American*, June 30, 1942: 22.

24   "Eagles Beat Black Yankees Twice at Ruppert Stadium," *New York Age*, August 29, 1942: 10.

25   "Grays Win Twin Bill from Newark in D.C.," *Pittsburgh Courier*, July 10, 1943: 19.

26   Bill Bloome, "Bushwicks Top Philly Stars in Two Games," *Long Island Daily Press*, August 2, 1943: 11. "Hopgood" was mentioned three times in the article. This surname also appeared in the box score beneath "Dexters Dim Philly Stars in Two Games," *Brooklyn Eagle*, August 2, 1943: 10.

27   Al Dunmore, "Jud Wilson Paces Grays in Two Wins," *Pittsburgh Courier*, August 14, 1943: 19. "Hopgood [*sic*] was replaced in the fifth for Newark by the elongated Elam after giving up eight runs to the Grays." Dunmore said the game was played on a Saturday, presumably referring to August 7. An article by Ric Roberts on the same page, "Grays and Eagles Split 2 Games," was about a Sunday game, undoubtedly on August 8, in which "Hopgood" was a pinch-hitter. See also "Phila. Stars Beat Newark, 12-11," *Philadelphia Inquirer*, August 20, 1943: 25.

28   Overmyer, 177.

29   Ibid.

30   seamheads.com/NegroLgs/player.php?playerID=hobgo01fre.

31   "National League Set for Season," *Pittsburgh Courier*, March 11, 1944: 12. See also "Judge Paige Plans Parade to Games," *Brooklyn Eagle*, May 14, 1944: 18.

32   seamheads.com/NegroLgs/player.php?playerID=hobgo01fre.

33   "Bell's Single in 9th Gives Dexters 2 Wins," *Brooklyn Eagle*, June 19, 1944: 12. "Local Team Continues Their Winning Streak," *Madison* (New Jersey) *Eagle*, July 20, 1944: 10.

34   For example, see "Brookdale Weak with Stick in Two Loop Losses," *Independent Press* (Bloomfield, New Jersey), June 29, 1945: 22. Hobgood played outfield while Joe Black pitched for the Orange Triangles.

35   "Twin Bill Swept by Dodgers Here," *Harrisburg* (Pennsylvania) *Evening News*, May 14, 1945: 16. Information compiled by baseball historians about the United States League can vary considerably. For example, contrast the teams listed at baseball-reference.com/register/league.cgi?code=USBL&class=Neg with those named at cnlbr.org/MuseumGallery/Programs/tabid/83/mid/402/ProjectId/62/wildRC/1/Default.aspx.

36   Lem Graves Jr., "Newark Tops Baltimore 4-2 As Doby Hits Ball Out of Park, *New Journal and Guide* (Norfolk, Virginia), June 8, 1946. Thanks to SABR member Drew Noe for tracking down this article. Though Graves said Newark used 16 players, only 15 were listed in the box score. Though Hobgood's first name was never identified, Norfolk is only 150 miles from Kinston. Also, in the 1940 census, every male named Hopgood or Hobgood in Virginia was white, and there was nobody by either surname in Norfolk's city directories for 1946 or 1947.

37   See David E. Dalimonte, "Kinston Has a Rich Tradition in Baseball," at milb.com/. "St. Louis Browns Try Five Players," *Baltimore Afro-American*, August 21, 1948: Section 2, page 13. "Five colored players were among 50 young baseball hopefuls working out last week here at the St. Louis Browns' tryout camp at Grainger Park. The five players, members of the Kinston Greys, a semi-pro team, were infielders William Randolph, Hubert Collins and Robert L. Smith, catcher Sam Coefield and pitcher Arthur Collins. Their ages range from 18 to 23. Scouts George Stis and George Staten said the colored players were smooth ball handlers, but did not say whether they would get contracts."

38   Most of this information is from North Carolina death, birth, and marital records, but regarding Cuder Hobgood, see ancexplorer.army.mil/publicwmv/#/arlington-national/search/. John Hobgood, who outlived brother Fred by a few decades, served in the US Army for 23 years, and in 1964 "received a commendation from the American ambassador to Ethiopia for his outstanding volunteer work with Ethiopian youth," according to his obituary. See legacy.com/obituaries/dispatch/obituary.aspx?n=-john-bryant-hobgood&pid=15160199.

LENIEL HOOKER

BY TIM TASSLER AND FREDERICK C. BUSH

L eniel Charlie Hooker was a right-handed pitcher from 1940 to 1948 with the Newark Eagles of the Negro National League. A 6-footer who weighed about 169 pounds, Hooker had a decent fastball and also threw a knuckleball. He was also considered a fair hitter and an excellent fielder.

Hooker was born on June 28 in Sanford, North Carolina, but the year is as foggy as some of the statistics from this time in history. Hooker put 1916 on his draft card, but his death certificate shows 1919, his Social Security Death Index shows 1921, and the 1930 Census lists Hooker – with his first name spelled as "Lyniel" – as being 15 years old, which would make his birth year 1915 or even 1914, depending upon exactly when the census was taken. Hooker was one of nine sons and three daughters of James and Sallie Hooker. The family lived on a farm just outside Sanford. James ran the farm, with all the children working to make ends meet. Sallie kept everyone fed and clothed. Little is known about Hooker's early life.

Sanford, in North Carolina's Piedmont country about 40 miles southwest of Raleigh, was the birthplace of three major-league baseball players. Bill Harrington pitched three years with the Philadelphia A's, and Albie Hood played one season at second base with the Boston Braves. Dick Such pitched one season with the Washington Senators and spent 25 years in the big leagues as a pitching coach.

Len Hooker was the fourth starter on the 1946 Eagles' pitching staff. He posted a 1-1 record in the World Series, winning Game Six with a stellar eight-inning relief effort. *(Noir-Tech Research, Inc.)*

The first newspaper account in which Hooker is found noted him playing baseball for Captain Cole's Giants in North Carolina's prison league in 1936. He pitched a 12-inning complete game, giving up six hits and beating the Print Shop Devils, 3-2, for the Giants' sixth consecutive victory.[1] Hooker's team represented Central Prison, a state prison in Raleigh. Why Hooker was serving time is unknown. By 1939 Hooker was out of prison, living in a rented room in Raleigh, and working as a dishwasher at the Sir Walter Hotel.

Hooker's pitching gained notice and in 1940 he was signed by the Eagles. Right around the beginning of the season – on April 27, 1940 – Hooker's father died in Sanford at the age of 75.[2] Hooker started 11 games for the Eagles; he pitched two complete games and finished the year with a 3-5 record.[3] The Eagles battled for the pennant that year, but ended up in third place in the Negro National League finishing with a 26-21-1 record.

Before the 1941 season began, Hooker staged a holdout. In his biography of Eagles co-owner Effa Manley, Bob Luke relates that Hooker returned his contract unsigned, noting, "terms not acceptable." In turn, Manley fired off a missive stating that she was "quite surprised." She felt that there had been outside influence on him in returning the contract, adding, "I cannot believe it was your idea. I cannot even understand you permitting it to be done." According to Luke, "Effa told Hooker that anyone familiar with his record last year would certainly feel 'you had been treated more than fairly. I expect you to sign the enclosed contract, return it, and be ready to meet the bus in Raleigh about mid-night April 3.'"[4] Hooker was waiting suitcase in hand, and rejoined the Eagles' rotation, which included Jimmy Hill and Max Manning. He pitched in 13 games, starting seven of them, and finished the season with a record of 4-2 and a 3.64 ERA as Newark once again finished third in the NNL with a 27-23-1 ledger.

Hooker's 1942 season was one of his best in terms of his won-lost record. He pitched in 17 NNL games, starting 10 of them, and finished 6-1 with a 4.42 ERA. The team finished in third place again. After the season Hooker returned to Raleigh and on December 30 he married Bettie E. Jones, who was listed as being three years his senior, which indicated a birth year of 1919 for Hooker; in truth, Bettie actually may have been a year or two younger than her husband.

The war years continued to be lean ones for the Eagles. In 1943 the squad finished in fourth place with a 26-32 record. Notably, Hooker and Jimmy Hill delivered a one-two knockout punch in a doubleheader against the New York Black Yankees at Ruppert Stadium in Newark on June 10. In the opener, Hooker hurled a seven-hit, 4-0 shutout in which he "rose to great heights in the 8th inning when he struck out three straight batters with the

bases loaded to prevent a score."[5] Hill was even better; he "turned in a brilliant no hit no run game in the seven-inning nightcap."[6] Hooker led the Eagles in pitching victories, posting a 6-4 record with a 3.79 ERA in league play. He also made a two-inning start for the North All-Stars that season.

Things did not improve much for the Eagles in 1944 as they dropped to fifth place with a 27-35 record in NNL play (32-35 overall). Hooker again led all Newark pitchers in wins with only five, and he finished with a losing mark of 5-6 to go with his 4.41 ERA.

In 1945 Newark improved slightly to a 25-24 record and a third-place finish in the NNL, but Hooker fell to 2-5 in spite of a vastly improved 2.62 ERA. He started the season in a more exotic locale than Newark: on May 26, the *Wilmington (Delaware) Morning News* reported that "[Ray] Danbridge [sic] and Len Hooker have succumbed to the 'south of the border' offers."[7] Hooker's stay with the Veracruz team in Mexico was brief, and he did not pitch effectively there, going 2-5 with 16 strikeouts and a 6.54 ERA in 52⅓ innings pitched in 12 games.[8] By July, Hooker was back with Newark as is evidenced by an article that said, "Newark will count on Len Hooker" in a game against the Black Yankees at Victory Field in Indianapolis.[9]

After the 1945 season Hooker joined Biz Mackey's Negro All-Stars as they played a five-game series against Brooklyn Dodgers coach Chuck Dressen's All-Stars. Hooker started two games and was the losing pitcher in both, although he pitched adequately. In 13 innings he allowed 11 hits and six runs (two of them unearned) for a 2.77 ERA.[10] Mackey's All-Stars ended up with a 0-4-1 record, and Hooker's performance was not enough for the Brooklyn Dodgers to become interested in him. (The Dodgers' Branch Rickey eventually did sign three of Mackey's All-Stars, Johnny Wright, Don Newcombe, and Roy Campanella.)

In January 1946 Hooker joined Joe Lillard, a football star, as he led an all-Negro baseball team on a Pacific tour as part of the USO Camp Shows. Players from the Black Yankees, New York Cubans, and some Puerto Rican players also took part. Over three months they played 30 games against service teams in the Central and Southwest Pacific.[11]

Hooker returned from the USO tour in time to join the Eagles for the 1946 season. The Eagles also welcomed back numerous players who had been away during World War II, including Leon Day, Larry Doby, Monte Irvin, Oscar Givens, Clarence "Pint" Isreal, Charles Parks, and Leon Ruffin. The infusion of talent led the Eagles to soar to their greatest heights as they finished 50-20-2 for the season and won both the first- and second-half NNL pennants. Day, Manning, and Rufus Lewis were all aces that year, and Hooker was relegated to a lesser role than he had played for the team during the war years. Hooker posted a 4-4 mark with a 3.62 ERA in league play; he finished at 5-5 with a 3.86 ERA against all competition that season.

Though his role had diminished somewhat, Hooker was far from an afterthought and he ended up seeing action against the Kansas City Monarchs in the 1946 Negro League World Series. He started Game Three against the Monarchs' Jim LaMarque at Kansas City's Blues Stadium on September 23. He had a rough time, surrendering six runs in four innings before reliever Cotton Williams entered the game in the fifth. Hooker was tagged with the loss as the Eagles suffered a humiliating 15-5 defeat. Hooker found redemption in Game Six, on September 27 at Newark's Ruppert Stadium. After the Monarchs knocked Leon Day's pitches around the park for five runs in the first inning, Hooker took over in the top of the second inning and went the rest of the way, earning the win as the Eagles evened the Series with a 9-7 triumph.[12] Hooker received fielding help from Day, who had moved from the mound to center field. Monte Irvin recalled that "Buck O'Neil hit a deep line drive to right center field and Leon made a great over-the-shoulder catch to save the game."[13]

After the World Series, Hooker pitched for the Havana Reds during the 1946-47 Cuban League winter season. He was 0-1 in three games, and the Reds lost a one-game playoff to Matanzas for the league championship.[14]

The 1947 season found Hooker back in Newark. On May 30 the Eagles took part in a Negro League showcase doubleheader that also featured the Homestead Grays. Branch Rickey was to attend both games as he had an interest in watching both Monte Irvin and Larry Doby play.[15] Hooker was not used in either game of the doubleheader, and missed out on another opportunity to try to impress the Dodgers' general manager. Newark (50-38-1) finished in second place behind the New York Cubans. Hooker's performance dropped off dramatically. In 14 games – 10 starts – he managed only a 2-6 record and he had a 4.18 ERA.

Hooker finished 1948 with a 6-5 record and a 3.06 ERA. The Eagles, having lost many of their future Hall of Famers, fell to third place in the NNL with a final ledger of 29-28-1 in league play (33-31-3 overall). Hooker pitched in 14 NNL games, starting 11 in what ended up being his final season with the Eagles.

In February 1949 Hooker returned to Havana to play ball. This time, rather than playing in the Cuban winter league, he was a member of Panama's Spur Cola team in the Caribbean Series. He pitched in only two games (9⅓ innings, 0-0) as Panama placed third in the series.[16] Returning to the United States, Hooker barnstormed with the Brooklyn Cuban Giants before he made his way to Organized Baseball, pitching for the Farnham Pirates and then the Drummondville Cubs of the Class-C Quebec Provincial League; no statistics are available from this season.[17]

In the spring of 1950 Hooker joined the semipro St. Joseph (Michigan) Auscos for a brief barnstorming stint.[18] Then he returned to Drummondville for the 1950 and 1951 seasons. During his first full year with the Cubs he posted a record of 11-6 with a 2.53 ERA. He followed that up in 1951 with a 10-9 mark and a 3.79 ERA, after which his professional baseball career came to an end.[19]

By 1965 Hooker owned a tavern in Newark, New Jersey, that he named Hooker's Elbow Room. His application for a liquor license listed himself as the president of the corporation and his wife, Bettie, as secretary-treasurer.[20] Hooker apparently made a good living from the tavern. By August 10, 1976, when the officers of the United Licensees Beverage Association of Newark were installed at an association dinner, Hooker was listed as one of the organization's trustees.[21]

Hooker died in Newark on December 18, 1977. He was survived by his wife; two sisters, Anna Glover and Nordelle Hooker; and a brother, Melvin Hooker. Leniel and Bettie had no children. The funeral service was held at the New Hope Baptist Church in Newark and burial was at the Glendale Cemetery in Bloomfield, New Jersey.[22]

SOURCES

In addition to the sources cited in the Notes, the author consulted the following:

Ancestry.com.

Baseball-Reference.com.

Riley, James A. *The Biographical Encyclopedia of the Negro Baseball Leagues* (New York: Carroll & Graf Publishers, Inc., 1994).

Seamheads.com was used for Negro League statistics and team records. (It should be noted that statistical variances can be found in different sources, which is quite common for most Negro League players).

NOTES

1. "Prison Teams Battle in Overtime Contest," *Raleigh News & Observer,* August 20, 1936: 9.

2. *Raleigh News & Observer*, October 14, 1940: 13.

3. Baseball-Reference.com has Hooker's statistics at 3-4 starting 10 games with two complete games.

4. Bob Luke, *The Most Famous Woman in Baseball: Effa Manley and the Negro Leagues* (Dulles, Virginia: Potomac Books, 2011), 70.

5. "Newark Pitchers Blank New York Black Yanks Twice in Twin Bill," *Pittsburgh Courier*, June 12, 1943: 19.

6. Ibid.

7. "Newark Eagles Boast Fine Squad of Baseball Stars," *Wilmington* (Delaware) *Morning News*, May 26, 1945: 12.

8. Pedro Treto Cisneros, *The Mexican League: Comprehensive Player Statistics, 1937-2001* (Jefferson, North Carolina: McFarland & Company, Inc., 2002), 473.

9. "Negro National League Clubs Will Vie Tonight," *Indianapolis Star*, July 26, 1945: 12.

10. "1945 Negro All Stars," seamheads.com/NegroLgs/team.php?yearID=1945&teamID=NST&LGOrd=2&tab=pit, accessed February 2, 2019.

11. "Negro Baseball Stars to Make Pacific Tour," *Baltimore Sun*, January 26, 1946: 11.

12. The brief summaries of the World Series presented here were culled from Richard Puerzer's comprehensive account of the series that appears in the present volume and from Kyle McNary, *Black Baseball: A History of African-Americans & the National Game* (New York: Sterling Publishing Company, Inc., 2003), 120-24.

13. Monte Irvin with James A. Riley, *Nice Guys Finish First: The Autobiography of Monte Irvin* (New York: Carroll & Graf, 1996), 106.

14. Jorge Figueredo, *Cuban Baseball: A Statistical History, 1878-1961* (Jefferson, North Carolina: McFarland & Company, Inc., 2003), 283-85.

15. *Brooklyn Daily Eagle*, May 29, 1947: 16.

16. Figueredo, 313-14, 317.

17. Barry Swanton and Jay-Dell Mah, *Black Baseball Players in Canada: A Biographical Dictionary, 1881-1960* (Jefferson, North Carolina: McFarland & Company, Inc., 2009), 85.

18. *St. Joseph* (Michigan) *Herald Palladium,* May 20, 1950: 7.

19. Swanton and Mah, 85.

20. "Announcements: Notice of Application," *Newark Star Ledger*, July 23, 1965: 34.

21. 'Officers Named by Tavern Owners," *Newark Star Ledger*, August 10, 1976: 28.

22. *Newark Star Ledger*, December 20, 1977: 72.

CALVIN IRVIN

BY BRYAN STEVERSON

Calvin Coolidge Irvin was born on November 28, 1924, in Haleburg, Alabama, to Cupid Alexander (C.A.) and Mary Eliza Henderson Irvin, the youngest of 13 children.[1] Haleburg is a small town in the southeastern part of the state, near the Georgia state line. Like many in the area, C.A. was a sharecropper. After being cheated and mistreated by the local landowner, the family relocated to New Jersey, initially to Bloomington and then to Orange. It was in Haleburg, however, that family interest in sports had its beginnings. Working only a half-day on Saturdays, Cal's father gathered with other men and older boys to play baseball in the afternoon. It was in this setting that the family's love of sports, and baseball specifically, was nurtured. Cal's older brother, Monte, became a multi-sport high-school athlete and later starred in both the Negro Leagues and the major leagues. Monte, who was elected to the National Baseball Hall of Fame in 1973, served as a role model for his younger brother Cal in academics, athletics, and behavior.[2]

Calvin Irvin was the graduation speaker in 1942 for his senior class at Orange High in Orange, New Jersey. During his high school years, Cal had won the highest award for excellence in scholarship and athletics.

Although basketball proved to be his highlight sport, Cal Irvin played baseball in the Negro Leagues, alongside Monte, for the 1946 Negro National League and World Series champion Newark Eagles. In correspondence in 2001, Cal noted that he had played shortstop for Newark for only three-quarters of that season.[3]

Cal Irvin, Monte's younger brother, had a cup of coffee with the 1946 Eagles. After baseball, he taught and coached basketball at North Carolina A&T University; eventually he became the school's athletic director. *(Courtesy of Kathryn Irvin)*

Negro League historian Wayne Stivers has located box scores for two games in 1946, one against the Kansas City Monarchs and another against the Cleveland Buckeyes, in which Cal played shortstop for the Eagles.[4] While he played for Newark's 1946 championship team, he was teamed with four future members of the Baseball Hall of Fame: catcher and manager Biz Mackey, pitcher and outfielder Leon Day, second baseman Larry Doby, and Monte Irvin, who played shortstop as well as the outfield.[5]

Playing the same position as his brother and being a double-play partner with Doby proved to be exciting. When asked in 2001[6] who were the best players he saw in the Negro Leagues, Cal answered with an all-star lineup:

1st Base: Buck Leonard, Homestead Grays

2nd Base: Larry Doby, Newark Eagles

Shortstop: Willie Wells, Newark Eagles

3rd Base: Ray Dandridge, Newark Eagles

Catcher: Josh Gibson, Homestead Grays

Outfield: Monte Irvin, Newark Eagles
(only one named)

Left-handed Pitcher: Jimmy Hill, Newark Eagles

Right-handed Pitcher: Satchel Paige,
Kansas City Monarchs

Each of these players, except Jimmy Hill, is in the Hall of Fame. Interestingly, Cal placed his brother in the outfield and not at his primary position with Newark, which was shortstop. The fact that a number of Eagles were listed was not unexpected since they were the 1946 champions.

In 1947, Irvin played for the Raleigh Grays of the Negro Southern League. He turned down a contract with the major-league New York Giants, refusing the Giants' wish to assign him to Phoenix in the Class-C Arizona-Texas League.[7]

Cal would have an influence on another future Negro Leaguer and major leaguer, Joe Black. At Morgan State University in Baltimore, Irvin was a halfback and Black was a receiver on the 1942 CIAA (Colored Intercollegiate Athletic Association) championship football team. The two also played together on the Bears' basketball team, for which Irvin was a starting forward and Black a reserve.

Morgan State had no baseball team, but Irvin and Black obtained summer jobs that year working on the campus grounds. It was Irvin who suggested the two teammates attend a NNL game between the Newark Eagles and the homestanding Baltimore Elite Giants at nearby Bugle Field. Hearing bragging about how good each (i.e., Black and Irvin) was compared with what was evident on the field, Vernon Green, Baltimore's secretary and business manager, approached the two and offered them a tryout. Calvin Irvin declined the opportunity, not wanting to risk losing his amateur status.[8]

Joe Black, who was 19 years old, accepted the Elite Giants' offer and went on to become a three-time Negro League All-Star pitcher

(1947, '48, and '50) for Baltimore. He entered the major leagues with the Brooklyn Dodgers in 1952 and posted a 15-4 record with 15 saves for the pennant-winning Dodgers. He was named the National League's Rookie of the Year. Pitching in Game One of the 1952 World Series at Ebbets Field in Brooklyn, Black became the first African-American pitcher to win a World Series game when he hurled nine innings in a 4-2 Dodgers victory over the New York Yankees.[9]

Returning to Morgan State, Irvin continued his education. He had been a three-sport high-school star athlete and valedictorian of his Orange, New Jersey, high-school class. In college he earned All-CIAA honors in basketball and football. After a leg injury ended his playing days, Irvin left Morgan State in 1945, and finished his education at the University of Illinois, where he received a bachelor's degree.[10]

From Illinois, Irvin's educational pursuits led him to Columbia University in New York and in 1948 he received a master's degree in physical education. He then returned to Orange and obtained a job as a recreation supervisor for East Orange's Department of Recreation.[11] A friend of Irvin's, who lived across the street from him, was on the board of Johnson C. Smith College in Charlotte, North Carolina, and he advised Irvin of an opening at the college. Irvin soon accepted a position as a teacher, basketball coach, and assistant football coach at the college. After three years, he moved to Atkins High School in Winston-Salem to teach and coach basketball. He later went to North Carolina A&T in Greensboro, where he taught and coached until his retirement.[12]

Irvin coached the North Carolina A&T basketball team to the 1959 NCAA College Division Final Four as the first historically black university to earn a bid to the NCAA tournament. As head coach for 18 of his 35 years at A&T, he never had a losing season, and his teams won 308 basketball games in the 18 years, including CIAA titles in 1959, 1962, 1964, and 1967.[13] Irvin also became North Carolina A&T's athletic director, and he was chair of the Health, Physical Education, and Recreation Department for seven years. The college's basketball court was named for him.[14]

After retirement from A&T, Irvin worked as a scout for the National Basketball Association's Charlotte Hornets and later as a scout evaluating college football game officials to identify potential candidates to officiate in the National Football League.

Calvin Irvin was inducted into the Newark Athletic Hall of Fame in 1995, five years after his brother Monte and one year after the Newark Eagles had received the team award.[15] The recognition was based on his accomplishments at Orange High School and with the 1946 Newark Eagles.

In addition to the Newark HOF, Irvin has been inducted into the sports halls of fame at Morgan State University; Johnson C. Smith University; North Carolina A&T; CIAA; Mid Eastern Athletic Association; National Association of College Athletic Directors; Guilford County, North Carolina; New Jersey; and North Carolina.[16]

On November 25, 2017, another Eagle flew home. Calvin Irvin died at the Morningview Assisted Living facility in Greensboro after a 16-year battle with Alzheimer's disease.[17] He was survived by his wife of 59 years, Kathryn W. Irvin.

NOTES

1   Monte Irvin with James A. Riley, *Nice Guys Finish First, The Autobiography of Monte Irvin* (New York: Carroll & Graf Publishers, 1996), 11.

2   Ibid.

3   Written correspondence to the author from Calvin Irvin, postmarked July 27, 2001.

4   Email from Wayne Stivers to the author, January 16, 2018.
     Box scores found: Calvin Coolidge Irvin; Shortstop, Newark Eagles, Age 21, Height: 5'10", Weight: 175, Bats: R, Throws: R

Date	Opponent	AB	R	H	HR	RBI	BB	SAC	E
7/16/46	Kansas City Monarchs	2	1	0	0	0	1	0	1
7/18/46	Cleveland Buckeyes	1	0	1	0	0	0	0	1

5   Dick Clark and Larry Lester, editors, *The Negro Leagues Book* (Cleveland: Society for American Baseball Research, 1994).

6   Written correspondence to the author from Calvin Irvin, postmarked July 27, 2001.

7   Stivers. Monte Irvin entered Organized Baseball with the Jersey City Giants in 1949.

8   Martha Jo Black and Chuck Schoffner, *Joe Black, More Than a Dodger* (Chicago: Academy Chicago Publishers, 2015), 93.

9   baseball-reference.com/teams/BRO/1952.shtml.

10   Irvin with Riley, 24; and Calvin Irvin obituary, *Greensboro* (North Carolina) *News & Record,* November 30, 2017. Calvin Irvin left Morgan State College (which became a university in 1975) after injuring his knee in football. The football coach wanted him to play anyway and said he would take his scholarship away if he didn't play. At that point, Cal left and worked his way through the University of Illinois.

11   Ibid.

12   Kathryn Irvin, phone interview with the author, January 17, 2018.

13   Irvin obituary, *Greensboro News & Record.*

14   Larry Lester, editor, *The Courier,* a publication of SABR's Negro Leagues Committee, December 2017.

15   Newark Athletic Hall of Fame website, at newarkathletichalloffame.org/wp-content/uploads/2016/03/NAHF-Souvenir-Journal-2015.pdf. Accessed January 18, 2018.

16   Irvin obituary, *Greensboro News & Record.*

17   Ibid.

MONTE IRVIN

BY DR. LAWRENCE HOGAN

A young Monte Irvin strikes a pose in his Newark Eagles uniform. He later played eight seasons in the major leagues and was inducted into the Hall of Fame in 1973. *(John W. Mosley Collection, Temple University)*

Of all those who proudly wore the uniform of the Newark Eagles of the Negro National League, Monte Irvin, at 95, and James "Red" Moore were the last of the Eagles still alive in 2014. Of the two, Irvin went on to a Hall of Fame career as a pioneering African American player in the major leagues.

Montford Merrill Irvin was born in Haleburg, Alabama, on February 25, 1919. He was the eighth of 13 children of Cupid Alexander Irvin and Mary Eliza Henderson Irvin. His father, like so many blacks in the American South of the early 20th century, earned a living, if it could be rightly called that, as a sharecropper. Sharecroppers were caught up in an exploitative system of tenant farming where you worked land that you did not own, and had the sale of the crop you raised controlled by the landowner. In such a system there was little opportunity to secure your own land. Besides the economic push that was central to the decision of so many blacks in what historians refer to as the great migration to leave the South for the hope of better times in the North, Irvin described in his autobiography an incident in which the threat of violence that was a constant for blacks in the South of his youth figured into his family's move to the North.

The Irvin family came north to New Jersey primarily for the better opportunities present there for their children. His mother and father must have been surprised when one of those opportunities turned out to be a baseball career that began in high school, advanced to the Negro Leagues, and led to his being one of the group of black pioneers we credit with the integration of our national pastime. As Monte told his baseball story, it actually began when as a youngster on the way to purchase a saxophone at a local music store, he saw a baseball glove in a sporting goods store window that proved too tempting to resist. And so he ended up playing center field with the Eagles of Newark rather than first sax with all-time favorite Jimmie Lunceford band.

That first baseball glove led to a high-school career that would be the envy of any athlete.

Arguably, Irvin was the finest all-around athlete ever to graduate from a New Jersey high school, earning 16 varsity letters in four sports at East Orange High while setting a state record for the javelin throw. His athletic prowess made no difference on senior prom night when he and his date, and a friend and his date, were refused service at a late-night eatery in their hometown because of the color of their skin. The year was 1937.

While Irvin took great pride in his track and field and football accomplishments, he recollected a childhood filled with dreams of playing baseball.

> I just wanted to be a real good ball player. I didn't know if I'd ever play professionally. I didn't know if I'd ever play in the major leagues. I certainly wanted to play in the Negro Leagues. You see at that time we aspired to play in the Negro Leagues. That was as high as our aspirations could go. I would say, now one of these days I would like to play for the Homestead Grays; I would like to play for the Newark Eagles; I would like to play for the Pittsburgh Crawfords, or the Lincoln Giants. If you were a baseball player you did aspire to play for those clubs. We never knew that later on we would get a chance to play in the majors. But those were our inspirations at that time.[1]

After a tryout at Hinchliffe Stadium in Paterson, where he was playing while still in high school with that city's semipro Smart Set team, Irvin joined the Newark Eagles of the Negro National League. He played under the assumed name of Jimmy Nelson to preserve his amateur status, allowing him to continue to play high-school and college ball. He is most remembered from his major-league days as a fine outfielder. But in the Negro Leagues his athleticism translated into a versatility that saw him as a sure-handed infielder with a strong throwing arm from third base and shortstop, with quality time in center field as well. During the Eagles' championship season of 1946, they could boast of a second-base/shortstop combination who would turn out to be Hall of Famers, with Irvin at short combining with teammate Larry Doby at second for strength up the middle.

From 1937 through 1940, Irvin established himself as one of the best in the Negro Leagues. After a strong 1941 season in which he compiled a batting average of .401 in league play, he was refused what he thought was a reasonable salary increase for 1942 from Eagles co-owner Effa Manley. With a salary offer from Mexican baseball magnate Jorge Pasquel well in excess of anything the Eagles were willing to offer, it was an easy decision for Irvin to succumb to the lure of Mexican baseball.

His record with the Vera Cruz Blues was all the more outstanding considering that his move from Newark caused him to miss almost a third of the Mexican season. It included a league-leading 20 home runs and a league-leading .397 batting average.

One of those 20 homers was especially interesting. In a game in Mexico City when it was Monte's time to bat, the Blues owner, Pasquel, called him over to his box seat and in effect ordered him to hit a home run. Monte demurred, saying the best he could do was to keep the rally going. Pasquel insisted that it be a home run. When Roy Campanella, catcher for the Monterrey team, learned from Monte what was going on, he said, "No way." After taking a strike, and fouling off the second pitch, Monte, guessing fastball, caught one on the fat of the bat for a game-winning shot over the center-field fence. Campanella was beside himself until Monte came over and said that Pasquel had given him $500 and told him to split it with Campy. "My man, my man," said Campy in reply.[2]

Irvin referred to his year in Mexico City (1942) as the best year of his life. "For the first time in my life I felt really free. You could go anywhere, go to any theater, do anything, eat in any restaurant, just like anybody else, and it was wonderful. The Negro League owners and players took a poll that year asking which player would be the perfect representative to play in the major leagues. They said I was the one to do it, the perfect representative. I was easy to get along with, and I had some talent."[3]

Irvin's plan to be back in Mexico for the 1943 season was thwarted by the wrong answer from the Newark draft board when he asked for permission to join Vera Cruz for spring training. He expected that a knee injury would have him fail the required physical examination. Besides, he was married with a child. Neither his "football knee" nor his wife, Dee (Dorinda Otey), and daughter, Pamela, worked to secure a deferment for him in this instance.

Monte Irvin was the 1946 Newark Eagles' RBI leader. As a member of the New York Giants in 1951, he led the entire National League with 121 RBIs. *(Noir-Tech Research, Inc.)*

Irvin was in the Army and away from baseball for three years during World War II. His outfit was the all-African American 1313th General Services Engineers, which served in England and France, where, with no chance to play baseball, he told historian Jim Riley "he built bridges and roads, and did guard duty."[4] Irvin went in as a private and was honorably discharged as a private, having been demoted on his last day from buck sergeant for being an hour late in returning to base.[5]

Irvin recounted his war experience at some length to Peter Golenbock: "When I went into the war I was treated very shabbily. I was with a black unit of engineers in England, France and Belgium. More than anything else we weren't treated well in the army. They wouldn't let us do this. We couldn't do that. The guys said, 'If they weren't going to give us a chance to perform, to reach our potential, why did they induct us into the army?'"

"All our commanding officers were white. In England we had a southerner who had no business being a company commander. He made some remarks about no fraternization with whites. We couldn't do this, couldn't that. After he spoke, we had a company chaplain who got up and said, 'Men, you are members of the United States Armed Forces. You can do anything anybody else can do. I assure this company commander will be gone in two weeks.' And he was. He was replaced by a lieutenant, a black company commander. This was 1944 in England in a little town called Red Roof in southern England."

"We felt like we were thrown away. We built a few roads, and when the German prisoners started to come in, we guarded the prisoners. We thought it would have been better if they hadn't inducted us, and just let us work in a defense plant. We were just in the way.

"I got home on September 1, 1945. In October, I started playing right field for the Newark Eagles. I had been a .400 hitter before the war. I became a .300 hitter after the war. I had lost three prime years. I hadn't played at all. The war had changed me mentally and physically."[6]

The Eagles team Irvin returned to in 1946 was poised to have a great season with a pitching staff led by fellow returning Army veterans Leon Day and Max Manning. The high hopes of team owners Abe and Effa Manley to win the Negro National League pennant were boosted by an opening game no-hitter pitched by Day. Irvin played a major role in the team's entry into postseason play with a league-leading .404 batting average. A tight seven-game Negro League world series saw him lead the Eagles to victory with three home runs while hitting .462 against the Monarchs of Kansas City whose pitching staff featured future Hall of Famers Hilton Smith and Satchel Paige.

The Eagles' reign as Negro League champions was the high point for Monte's black baseball career. That same 1946 season marked the debut in white baseball of Jackie Robinson in the uniform of the Brooklyn Dodgers' top farm club, the Montreal Royals. What followed was a painfully slow process of integration that bled the Negro Leagues of its top players, with fans following their stars into major-league stadiums.

While Robinson was first, if Branch Rickey's decision had been based purely on baseball ability, Irvin should have been his choice. Who could be better than "faster than lightning" James "Cool Papa" Bell to tell us who in the eyes of Negro Leaguers should have been first? "Most of the black ballplayers thought Monte Irvin should have been the first black in the major leagues. Monte was our best young ballplayer at the time. He could hit that long ball, he had a great arm, he could field, he could run. Yes, he could do everything."[7] This was a judgment shared by most Negro League owners.

If integration had been just a bit slower in coming, and if he hadn't been so fine a player, all the baseball talent that was Monte Irvin would likely never have been showcased in the big leagues.

When he came up to the majors in 1949, Irvin commented that "this should have happened to me 10 years ago. I'm not even half the ballplayer I was then."[8] His friend Roy Campanella agreed: "Monte was the best all-round player I have ever seen. As great as he was in 1951, he was twice that good 10 years earlier in the Negro Leagues."[9]

Irvin told Golenbock, "On July 8, 1949, Hank Thompson and I reported to the New York Giants. Leo Durocher came over and introduced himself. And when everyone got dressed, he had a five-minute meeting. He said, 'I think these two fellows can help us make some money and win the pennant and the World Series. I am going to say one thing. I don't care what color you are. If you can play baseball you can play on this club. That's all I am going to say about color.' This was two years after Jackie. They had gotten used to seeing an Afro-American on the field. It wasn't a picnic. We heard the names. But we didn't have it as rough as he did."[10]

It is his 1951 season with the New York Giants that defines Irvin's greatness as a baseball player. He was coming off his first full year in the majors, in which he had established himself as a solid, promising cog in the Giants' lineup. At 32 years of age, segregation had cost him his prime. With his .312 batting average, 24 home runs, and 121 runs batted in, he came close to winning the MVP award, finishing third to Roy Campanella and Stan Musial. He scored 94 runs, hit 11 triples, and drew 89 walks while only striking out 44 times, and he went 12-for-14 in steals. In the field, he more than matched his prowess at the plate with his .996 percentage, a product of only one error all season. He was fifth in batting average, fourth in on-base percentage, seventh in slugging, tied for 10th in runs scored, seventh in hits, ninth in total bases, third in triples, tied for 10th in homers, and his league-leading 121 RBIs were 12 better than his nearest competitors. It was an across-the-board outstanding season for what was essentially a rookie campaign for this veteran Negro Leaguer. Irvin finished seventh in walks, tied for eighth in steals, fourth in runs created, fifth in times on base, and tied for third in times hit by a pitch. His outstanding regular-season play more than carried over into the World Series, in which he hit .458, tying a record with his 11 hits. In Game One of the Series, he gave his Giants fans the thrill of a steal of home in the first inning against Yankees ace pitcher Allie Reynolds.

A broken ankle suffered sliding into third base during spring training 1952 limited Irvin's playing time to 46 games. His absence from the lineup could well have made the difference in a close race with the Dodgers, whose 96-57 gave them the National League pennant over Irvin's Giants' 92-62.

The next season, 1953, was a comeback year for Monte Irvin, but decidedly the opposite for his Giants. His .329 batting average with 97 runs batted in could not offset the loss of Willie Mays to Army service, and a pitching staff that had declined considerably from the glory year of 1951. The Giants finished in fifth place, a distant 35 games behind the 105-49 Dodgers.

There was great anticipation in Giants circles as the 1954 season opened with Willie Mays back in the lineup having completed his Army service. That anticipation was more then met when the Giants finished in first place five games better than the Dodgers, and in the World Series bested the heavily favored Cleveland Indians, who were coming off a record-setting 111-win season.

The toll that time takes on a player's performance is clearly apparent when one compares Irvin's 1951 World Series play with his .458 batting average and record-tying 11 hits with his .222 (2-for-9) in the Giants' startling four-game sweep of the heavily favored Indians.

One more season with the Giants in 1955, when he saw action in only 51 games and finished with a .253 batting average, found him in the offseason selected by the Chicago Cubs in the Rule 5 draft. He ended his eight-year major-league career giving the Cubs a more than respectable 111 games played with a .271 batting average.

After retiring as a player, Monte Irvin worked in public relations with Rheingold Brewery, as an assistant to the commissioner of baseball, and as an outstanding public educator as regards the history of the black leagues in which he starred.

He had two daughters, Patricia Denise Gordon and Pamela Irvin Fields.

With the deaths of his teammates Max Manning and Larry Doby, Irvin became the last of the Eagles who soared to the heights of baseball greatness on the 1946 world champion Newark club that bested the Kansas City Monarchs in one of the best of Negro League fall classics. He has been inducted into the baseball halls of fame of Mexico, Cuba, Puerto Rico, and the United States.

Monte Irvin died in Houston on January 11, 2016.

SOURCES

In addition to the sources cited in the Notes, the author also consulted:

Riley, James, *Biographical Encyclopedia of the Negro Leagues* (New York: Carroll & Graf, 1994).

NOTES

1   Interview for *Before You Can Say Jackie Robinson* documentary, copyright 2006, Union County College, Cranford, New Jersey.

2   Monte Irvin with Jim Riley, *Nice Guys Finish First: The Autobiography of Monte Irvin* (New York: Carroll and Graf, 1996).

3   Peter Golenbock, *In the Country of Brooklyn* (New York: William Morrow, 2008), 148.

4   *Nice Guys Finish First*, 101.

5   Interview with the author on June 30, 2014.

6   Golenbock, 148.

7   Jack Lang, *Long Island Press*, February 14, 1974.

8   Monte Irvin quote cited in Hogan, *The Forgotten History of African American Baseball* (Santa Barbara: ABC-Clip Praeger, 2014), 202.

9   Ibid.

10   Golenbock, 150.

CLARENCE "PINT" ISREAL

BY BILL HICKMAN

His name was Clarence Charles Isreal. That's Isreal, not Israel. His name should not be conflated with the country of the Middle East. Most of the newspapers of his time did not grasp that distinction. Consequently, often the misspelling has carried over into subsequent baseball records.

In his six-year professional baseball career, Clarence Isreal spent more than four playing under three managers who now reside in the Baseball Hall of Fame and were well known for their ability to tutor young ballplayers. It was perhaps due to the influence of these men – Ben Taylor, Biz Mackey, and Willie Wells – that Isreal's lasting fame in life was as a mentor to young men in his community. His two other managers, Dick Lundy and Vic Harris, weren't run-of-the-mill names, either. Lundy was among the 39 finalists in the 2006 selection process of Negro Leaguers for the Hall of Fame. Harris was one of the most successful managers in Negro League history, with his Homestead Grays finishing first seven times under his guidance. Isreal had plenty of fine examples from whom he could have learned.

The earliest years of Clarence Isreal were spent in rural Georgia. He was born in Marietta, Georgia, on February 15, 1918. His parents, Frank and Violet Isreal, lived on a farm in a place called Big Shanty in an area of Cobb County near Kennesaw. Frank was a sharecropper and railroad worker whose life spanned from 1886 to 1977, and Violet lived from 1891 to 1985; they were wed in 1911.

Georgia was not a lasting part of Clarence's life. In 1923 Frank and Violet packed up their household and moved to Rockville, Maryland, near Washington, where they hoped their lives would improve. According to the 1920 Census, there were three children

in the family at that point – Louise, age 7; Willie May, 6; and Clarence, 2. By the time of the 1930 Census, the family had expanded dramatically. Clarence was now one of nine children, and there was a grandchild in the house as well.[1]

Infielder Clarence "Pint" Isreal hit two doubles and scored four runs in Newark's 17-5 NNL pennant-clinching triumph against the New York Cubans on September 4, 1946. *(Courtesy of Bill Hickman)*

To feed all these children, Frank and Violet had to work hard, and they took a number of jobs over the years. According to the book *Rockville: Portrait of a City*, Frank initially worked as a caretaker and handyman at Chestnut Lodge in Rockville. Violet was a housekeeper at Rose Hill Farm in Rockville.[2] They also raised some farm animals on their property and grew their own vegetables. Later, Frank was a laborer in a coalyard. He had also been head custodian at Lincoln High School.

Clarence grew up in the Lincoln Park neighborhood of Rockville during a period of segregation. He attended segregated schools, including Rockville Colored Elementary School, and graduated from Rockville Colored High School in 1935. Unfortunately, to families of color the city seemed in many ways like a place in the Deep South until well into the midcentury.

Life also was difficult for Clarence in that he had a falling out with his father. The second oldest son, Clarence felt that he was being given too great a share of the responsibility for the household chores. He rebelled and was punished by his father. As a result, he left home for a period and had to fend for himself. He and his father did not reconcile until Clarence was well into adulthood.[3]

After high school, he played sandlot baseball locally for a few years. A historical marker in Rockville indicated that the first semipro team he signed with was the Washington Royals. In 2018 the year on the marker was being revised, but the team seems to be correct. The Washington Royals traveled up the East Coast to cities like Rochester, New York, and Trenton, New Jersey, to take on all sorts of local arrays, such as YMCA teams. Clarence's nephew, Jackie Smith, said he believed that Clarence joined the Royals in 1938. Then he started to play at a higher level of semipro ball with the Washington Royal Giants in 1939. The Royal Giants played in Griffith Stadium, the home of the American League's Washington Senators. The Royal Giants were in the Negro International League, and they were making their debut under that name in 1939. In 1938 the team had been known as the Washington Black Senators. Teammates of Isreal's on the Royal Giants squad included Rockville pals Mike Snowden and Russell Awkard, Mike's nephew. Also on the team was catcher Thomas "Babe" Snowden, a first cousin of Mike who came from Sandy Spring, Maryland. Since Mike was a pitcher, there were times when the line score showed a battery of Snowden and Snowden.[4]

Isreal was a fine ballplayer. His Royal Giants manager, Ben Taylor, who had been a premier player in the Negro Leagues and who would be inducted into the Baseball Hall of Fame in 2006, described him as "another Dandridge." The reference was to Ray Dandridge, who had a Hall of Fame career as a third baseman and who was generally considered, along with Judy Johnson, one of the two best third sackers in the Negro Leagues. Later on, Clarence Isreal and Ray Dandridge became teammates on the Newark Eagles, and Clarence was the one who held down the third-base spot. That's how good he was. After his death, the *Montgomery Journal* reported that scouts had said of Isreal: "You just can't get anything past him at third."[5]

Clarence was generally known by his nickname, Pint, which came from his diminutive size. According to the website of the Cobb County (Georgia) Hall of Fame, of which Isreal is a member, he was 5-feet-5; Seamheads.com confirms that height. Originally, the nickname was Half Pint, but it was shortened as people verbalized it and used it with more frequency.

In 1940 Isreal made his debut in the Negro Leagues with the Newark Eagles and was positioned at second base as half of the keystone combination with future major leaguer Buzz Clarkson. He took over from 12-year veteran second baseman Dick Seay, as the 1940 Eagles manager Dick Lundy announced on July 29 that Isreal had been doing such terrific work as an understudy that he deserved the top job.[6] According to James Riley's *The Biographical Encyclopedia of The Negro Baseball Leagues*, although never a spectacular hitter, Seay had been the best defensive second baseman in the Negro Leagues during the decade of the 1930s, so Isreal had beaten out somewhat of a legend.[7]

Pint had a highly successful rookie season, batting .294 with 32 hits in 32 games, with an on-base percentage of .347. He hit 4 homers, scored 28 runs, and drove in 22 runs. In the annual benefit game against the House of David team, Pint won the contest by hitting a single with the bases loaded to seal the victory for the Eagles, 7-6. The Salisbury newspaper described him as the "home run king on the team," although that seems to be an exaggeration since by the end of the season three other Eagles had slammed more homers.[8]

Isreal began 1941 by continuing at the second sack, but a couple of changes were in store for him that year. First, he shifted to third base to make room for Leon Day, mostly known as a pitcher in his Hall of Fame career, but who was versatile on the field and with his bat. That move occurred in September as it was announced that "Clarence Israel [*sic*], the smooth-fielding infielder, has shifted over to third."[9] Second, his draft board started taking significant interest in him. In August, Isreal was rejected by the draft board on the basis of flat feet and bowlegs, but that was not the end of his concern about military obligations.

The newspapers and the public had a great deal of praise for Pint's playing ability in 1941. The *Washington Evening Star* said he was "regarded as the sparkplug of the infield" on the Newark team.[10] The *Jersey Journal* of June 18 stated that "the Eagles built their attack around Francis Matthews, Clarence Israel [*sic*], and Monte Irvin." When it came time for the public to select the teams for the East vs. West All-Star Game, Pint came close to securing the second-base slot on the East Team. Ironically, he lost out to an aging Dick Seay, who had moved on to the New York Black Yankees after having surrendered his second-base position with the Eagles to Pint. The top three vote-getting second basemen in the final results were Dick Seay, 182,063 (made the East all-star team); Billy Horne, 179,621 (made the West all-star team); and Clarence Isreal, 179,210.[11]

In total for the 1941 season, Isreal hit .268 with 42 hits in 44 games, with an on-base percentage of .341. He hit two homers, scored 31 runs, and drove in 17 runs while hitting second in the batting order for most of the season.

After the season, Pint was back in Rockville and was representing his community in a baseball game in mid-September. Along with fellow Newark Eagles player Russell Awkard, Isreal was on the Montgomery County All-Stars, an Afro-American team that played the white All-Stars from Howard County at John C. Howard's Green Bridge Inn in Maryland. The Montgomery County All-Stars were managed by Robert Lee "Mike" Snowden, from a Rockville family. Mike was the man who had first influenced Pint to start playing baseball seriously, according to Pint's son Robert.[12] Mike became the high-school baseball coach around 1936 after Pint had graduated. When the high-school season ended, Mike Snowden would organize the teenage boys, along with some older youths and adults, and play them against adult teams, giving them the competitive training they needed to advance their skills. According to Pint's nephew, Jackie Smith, Mike's team was called the Rockville AC's.[13] Mike also managed a semipro team from Baltimore, so he was well equipped to train the young men in advanced concepts of the game. Mike had assumed the leadership position in the Snowden Funeral Home in 1936 when his father, George, the founder, retired. As of 2019 the Snowden Funeral Home remained a prominent fixture in Rockville.

In 1942 Pint returned to the Eagles and continued to receive praise for his play. In late June the *Washington Evening Star* declared that "Newark is reported to have one of the finest infields in Negro baseball, with (Willie) Wells at short, 'Pint' Israel [sic] at third, Ray Dandridge at second, and Lenny Pearson at first."[14] Isreal's batting average declined, but he was solid. He hit .208 with 30 hits and 19 walks in 42 games, scored 24 runs, and drove in 15 from the leadoff spot in the lineup. During the summer he learned that he had lost his draft exemption and on August 18 he reported for induction into the US Army.

Isreal was initially assigned to the 54th Aviation Squadron at Mather Field in California, and was reported to be on the Baseball Stars team from that Army Air Force Base near Sacramento.[15] After that assignment, he was the player-manager of an Army team in Texas. Subsequently, he was reassigned to the Aleutian Islands in Alaska. In 1945 it was reported that he led his team to the Aleutian championships as he hit .450 and was the most feared hitter in the championship series. His Aleutian team topped an Alaskan mainland team in the "Midnight Sun" World Series.[16] He was discharged from the Army as a sergeant on November 25, 1945.

Although Pint had shed his military uniform, he decided to take another job connected to national defense. Pint's personnel record indicates that he worked for the Navy Department from January 4 through March 28, 1946, when he returned to the Eagles.

Perhaps Isreal's most notable games in 1946 were his first and last. At the opening game of the season, which was played in Newark on May 7, Leon Day tossed a no-hitter. The game was a pitchers' duel and scoreless until the sixth inning, when Pint tripled to right-center and subsequently scored as the Eagles beat the Philadelphia Stars and Barney Brown, 2-0. Brown gave up only six hits, and Pint had two of them.

On May 30 Pint was part of a fifth-inning rally in the second game of a doubleheader with the Philadelphia Stars at Ruppert Stadium in Newark. He hit a single and scored a run, contributing to a 6-3 Eagles victory. He was the only Eagles player with two hits in the contest.

Pint was at the center of a controversial game which was the second of a twin bill on Sunday, July 21, 1946. The Eagles were playing the Cleveland Buckeyes in the home park of the latter team. The remainder of the game description comes from Effa Manley, the co-owner of the Eagles:

> The score was tied 1-1 in an extra inning game. (Leniel) Hooker came to bat and got a hit. Mackey (Biz Mackey, the Newark manager) sent Isreal to run for him. The next man to come to bat was pitched one ball by the Cleveland pitcher and Isreal was called out, due to the fact that Isreal did not tell the umpire that he was running for Hooker. Now, there is no question that the umpire should have been told that Isreal was running for Hooker, and the Eagles were at fault for not doing it; but the penalty in the rule book for such an offense is a fine for the captain or the manager of the team at fault. Under no condition is the runner to be called out by the umpire for this offense. I do not like the team to squabble on the field, but I am sure that no one would expect a manager to take a decision like that without arguing.[17]

Mackey had done more than argue. He had pulled the Newark team off the field, causing the Eagles to forfeit the game, 9-0. Effa Manley had stood behind his decision.

Overall, Pint's 1946 regular-season statistics for the Eagles were a .191 batting average with 17 hits and 6 walks in 31 games. He scored 11 runs and drove in 6. Although still mostly a third baseman, he also played part-time in the outfield. At some point during the season, he moved over to the Homestead Grays for one game as the website Seamheads.com credits him with a batting average of .250, chalking up one hit and one RBI for the Grays in 1946. The most likely scenario is that he was loaned to Homestead for one game.

The most important game of the 1946 season for Pint and the Eagles took place on September 4. That was the day on which the Eagles clinched the championship of the National League and assured that they would be playing in the Negro League World Series. The Eagles defeated the Cuban Stars, 17-5. Pint had two hits, both doubles, according to the newspaper write-up, and scored four runs. The account in the *Indianapolis Recorder* cited Larry Doby as the leading Eagles contributor with five hits in the game, but Pint was the second offensive player mentioned.[18]

Pint did not play a more crucial part in the Eagles' 1946 season because in early June they obtained Pat Patterson from the Philadelphia Stars to replace him as the starting third baseman. After that, Pint played utility roles, including some games in the outfield.

In the Negro League World Series of 1946, the Eagles faced the Kansas City Monarchs. In Game One, Pint was the starting third baseman for the Eagles. He had one unsuccessful at-bat before he was injured chasing a pop foul off the bat of Herb Souell into the field boxes along the third-base line; he ended up dislocating his knee. He did not make another appearance until Game Five, which was played in Chicago's Comiskey Park. In that game he was once again the starting third sacker, and he hit a single in three official at-bats. That was the only contest of the World Series in which Pint played for the entire game.

Going into Game Six, the Eagles were down three games to two and were desperate for a win. One more loss and the Monarchs would be the champions. Pint started the game at third base, walked in the first inning, and moved around the bases to score the Eagles' first run. The Monarchs had taken a 5-0 lead in the top of the first, but by the time the inning was over, the lead was narrowed to 5-4. The Eagles ended up winning, 9-7. The two-run edge was slim, so every run was important, and Pint had made a significant contribution in the World Series. The victory enabled the Eagles to advance to Game Seven, which they won, although Isreal did not play. He had been removed from the lineup early in Game Six with one official at-bat and no hits, and had been replaced by Pat Patterson; it is quite possible that his knee injury had started bothering him again after he ran the bases.

James A. Riley asserts that Pint played in three games during the 1946 World Series and he got a pinch hit off Satchel Paige in one of them.[19] This claim is only partially correct. According to the box scores for all seven games, Pint played in three games but never faced Satchel Paige in any of them. He got his sole hit off Hilton Smith.

Pint must have made quite an impression during his lone game for Homestead in 1946 as he played exclusively for Grays in 1947. He hit .206 in 131 at-bats, according to Seamheads.com. Only five players on the team had more plate appearances, so he was playing regularly. He would later call it "one of the greatest teams I've ever seen in my life and that's including black or white."[20] It is assumed that he was referring to the 1946 version of the Homestead Grays, since two of their biggest stars, Josh Gibson and Cool Papa Bell, had departed by 1947.

There were also times during Pint's Negro Leagues career when he joined barnstorming teams of Negro League stars. When he was interviewed for an article in the *National Institutes of Health Record* of July 21, 1978, he recalled, "We used to barnstorm against white

"Pint" Isreal is memorialized by this plaque at the park that bears his name in Rockville, Maryland. *(Courtesy of Bill Hickman)*

teams in various games and most of the time we'd beat 'em." Pint also asserted, "We felt we were as good as the white players, if not better – and this was our chance to prove it."[21]

At a gathering at Glassboro (New Jersey) State College as part of Black History Month in February 1986, Isreal remembered a game against a white all-star team in which the blacks could not hit the ball past the infield, while the whites were clobbering the ball. Pint said: "I couldn't believe they were that much better than us. It turned out that when we were up, their pitchers were throwing balls that they had put in the refrigerator."[22]

In the book *Shades of Glory*, Lawrence Hogan picked up what really motivated Pint to strive to play well in baseball. He quoted Pint as saying: "I guess the only reason I wanted to play was because I wanted to be good like the rest of the ballplayers. It's something that gets in your craw. It sticks with you."[23]

It was clear that Isreal enjoyed the experience of playing in the Negro Leagues, but what brought it to an end was Jackie Robinson's breaking into the major leagues. According to Pint's son Bobby, his father could read that step as the "handwriting on the wall" for the future of Negro Leagues baseball.

Pint's brother Elbert, also known as Al, had a five-year career in the minor leagues in the Philadelphia-Kansas City A's system as Organized Baseball began to integrate. He, too, was an infielder. Elbert hit .301 in 622 games from 1952 through 1957 with a break in 1955 when he did not play. In 1952 he led the Class-B Interstate League in hitting with a .328 batting average. In his book *Brushing Back Jim Crow*, Bruce Adelson details the struggles of Afro-American minor leaguers in the 1950s as they grappled with lingering discrimination in the South, despite Jackie Robinson's already having broken through barriers at the major-league level; the entire discussion about the South Atlantic League in one chapter of the book is devoted to Hank Aaron and Al Isreal.[24] Al played in the Negro Leagues for the Philadelphia Stars in 1950 and, along with his brother Pint, on the Homestead Grays in 1947. Al was born in 1927 and died in 1997.

Pint's wife, Florence, was originally from Leavenworth, Kansas. They were married during World War II while Pint was in the Army. In addition to raising their children, Florence toiled as a domestic worker in houses located in places like Bethesda and Silver Spring. Florence died in January of 1975.

Pint and Florence raised three sons, Michael; Robert (aka Bobby), and Clarence Jr. (aka Butch). Michael died in 1997, Bobby in 2007, and Butch in 2014.[25]

Pint and Florence also had a daughter, Karen, who did not survive through childhood because she suffered from leukemia. In 1958 Satchel Paige staged a benefit game at McCurdy Field in Frederick, Maryland, to raise money to assist in the care of Karen. Pint and his nephew, Jackie Smith, both played in that game.[26]

Isreal had a fulfilling life after his time in the Negro Leagues. He continued to play baseball with a segregated team in Rockville, the Rockville Legionnaires, sponsored by the American Legion. In 1949 the *Frederick News* reported Pint as playing for that team in a game against the Frederick Legion contingent.[27] At one point the Rockville team had Russell Awkard as player-manager plus Pint, Elbert, and Dewey Isreal as players.

Isreal's first experience with the civilian part of the federal government was holding an offseason job as a laborer with the Public Health Service from November 1946 to May 1947. In those days, PHS was in the Federal Security Agency, which was the forerunner of the Department of Health, Education, and Welfare.

From 1948 to 1973 he worked for the National Institutes of Health. He began as an animal caretaker, but for most of his career at NIH he was a lab technician.

Pint offered his baseball prowess to the athletes at the NIH Club. He became player-manager of their baseball team. In 1951 he helped them tally 45 wins and take home the honor of being the best among the Washington area's 233 teams. His NIH group was the first integrated baseball team in Montgomery County.[28] He also continued to apply his baseball skills as a coach in semipro baseball and an umpire for baseball and softball games.

Beyond the ongoing investment of his time in baseball activities, Pint wanted to do even more things for others. In 1968 he and schoolteacher Russell Gordon co-founded the Black Angels Boys Club in Rockville, an organization that served throughout Montgomery County.[29] He collected donations from his colleagues there to support the work of the Boys Club. Pint was active in the Big Brothers program to help young boys who needed guidance. He volunteered with FISH (For Immediate Sympathetic Help), an organization that provides food, transportation, and other services to the needy and elderly. He gave volunteer hours to two day-care centers in Rockville and with the Head Start Program in Lincoln Park, and was active in his church. At the Jerusalem United Methodist Church, he sang in the choir and, showing his ever-present love for children, taught Sunday School.[30]

Pint's longtime friend Michael Johnson shed some additional light on his attributes. Johnson recalled:

> When I was young, Pint got me started in basketball officiating. Pint observed that in the local area, there were no Afro-Americans in officiating roles. He went to the Rockville officials to plead for change, and things changed. If you met him, you would love him. He saw things in people that they didn't see in themselves. Every kid who played baseball knew his philosophy was 'If you had two strikes on you, you had to swing on the third pitch if it was anywhere near the plate.' In other words, never miss an opportunity. Pint would also say: 'Religion is first, family second, everything else next.' If Pint knew you, he was at the game (to be there in support of you). He knew more about you than your parents. It didn't matter what sport you played, football, basketball, or baseball, if you were a friend of Pint, he would be at the game to cheer you on.[31]

Billy Gordon, a basketball star at Rockville's Richard Montgomery High School and the University of Maryland-Eastern Shore, was drafted by the Seattle Supersonics, but a knee injury ended his NBA career before it started. After basketball, he became an administrator in the Montgomery County public school system. He is also the father of former major leaguer Keith Gordon. He said, "Pint was one of my mentors and my heroes."[32]

Most Americans of a certain age have heard numerous conspiracy theories concerning the assassination of President John F. Kennedy. One of those theories involves Pint Isreal as a witness to Kennedy's autopsy. Healthy skepticism should be employed as the origin of this theory is revealed. Returned to Washington, Kennedy's body was taken to the Bethesda Naval Hospital, directly across the street from the NIH campus where Isreal was known to have worked. There is a file with Clarence Isreal's name on it in the collection of the National Archives pertaining to Kennedy's assassination.

The claim comes from the book *Murder From Within: Lyndon Johnson's Plot Against President Kennedy*, by Fred T. Newcomb and Perry Adams. The book was written in 1974 and only about

100 copies were distributed then as a self-printed manuscript. The version relevant to Isreal was the first full publication of the book in 2011. By that time Fred Newcomb was 82 years old and ailing, and Perry Adams was deceased. The passages pertinent to Pint are contained in the foreword by Fred Newcomb's son, Tyler Newcomb. Around 2004, he learned via a document posted online by the National Archives that Clarence Isreal had told NIH biologist Janie Taylor that his brother (unnamed and deceased) had been on duty as an orderly in the autopsy room in the Bethesda Naval Hospital on November 22, 1963, when Kennedy's body was present. Newcomb assumed that the relevant brother was Elbert (Al). Supposedly, there was one point in the process at which many people were forced out of the room, and one doctor manipulated the bullet wounds in some way. Elbert allegedly witnessed this as it happened. Later in the foreword, Tyler Newcomb wrote that a man named Jim Lavin had spoken with Mrs. Elbert Isreal, who verified that her late husband had been on duty in the hospital's morgue on the night of November 22. According to this account, Mrs. Isreal added that Clarence Isreal had also been on duty there that evening.[33] However, neither Jackie Smith nor Michael Johnson had ever heard mention of Pint having had a job at the Bethesda Naval Hospital.

Elbert Isreal, like Pint, was employed by NIH, but no evidence has been found to show that Elbert was employed by the Bethesda Naval Hospital. On the other hand, Dewey Isreal, Pint's older brother, was known to be a Bethesda Naval Center employee in 1963. An issue of the *Naval Medical Center News* of 1963 places Dewey on the Center's intramural softball team in July of that year, but he was a cook, not an orderly.[34] It must be remembered that Pint was reporting on a deceased brother who supposedly was in the autopsy room. It is not known when Pint spoke to Janie Taylor about this story, but Pint died in 1987. Janie Taylor reported the story to the representative of the Kennedy Assassination Records Review Board in 1995.[35] Elbert Isreal was alive until 1996 and Dewey Isreal lived until 1999. The facts just don't line up.

The Clarence Isreal file at the National Archives contains 16 documents, all of which are perfunctory personnel records. They range from job applications to assignment transfers to reports of minor injuries to statements of minor organizational changes. One document contains a signed oath of allegiance by Isreal to the US Constitution, along with an affidavit that he did not advocate the use of force to overthrow the government; that document was dated October 13, 1947. The materials suggest that the staff of the Kennedy Assassination Records Review Board did their assigned duty in trying to accumulate information about Pint that might link him in some way to the Bethesda Naval Hospital or the assassination, but nothing in the file succeeds in doing that.

Pint Isreal died of a heart attack on April 12, 1987, at Shady Grove Hospital in Rockville. He is buried in Gate of Heaven Cemetery in Silver Spring, Maryland, along with his wife, Florence.

In February 1988, the city of Rockville named a park after Pint. A plaque marking the dedication of the Clarence "Pint" Isreal Park hangs on the outside of the Lincoln Park Community Center, next to the entrance to the parking lot for the park. Fittingly, the park contains a baseball field, along with other amenities, such as a picnic area and playground equipment for the younger children.

> James Coyle, a Rockville councilman in 1988 and later the mayor, was present for the dedication of the Isreal Park. Reflecting on the ceremony, Coyle said, "It was an honor to take part in the dedication of the park in the name of this man who was such a positive influence in the Lincoln Park community."[36]

To close the story of Pint Isreal, it is perhaps fitting to use his own words. When asked if he had any advice for future generations, his reply was, "Love God, have faith, and love thy neighbor as thyself."[37]

ACKNOWLEDGEMENTS

Gary Ashwill, moderator of Seamheads.com.

Sheila Bashiri, preservation planner, City of Rockville.

James Coyle, former mayor and councilman, City of Rockville.

Irene Curry, daughter of Mike Snowden and cousin of Russell Awkard.

Bob Golon, member, Society for American Baseball Research.

Billy Gordon, Montgomery County public school system.

Burt Hall, former director, Rockville Department of Recreation and Parks.

Khali Isreal, grandson of Pint Isreal.

Michael Johnson, friend of Pint Isreal.

Mark Kibiloski, Rockville Department of Recreation and Parks.

Peerless Rockville staff.

Jackie Smith, nephew of Pint Isreal (son of Pint's sister Beatrice).

George Snowden, nephew of Irene Curry.

Richard Cuicchi, member, Society for American Baseball Research.

Wayne Stivers, member, Society for American Baseball Research.

Sween Library (Rockville) staff.

SOURCES

In addition to the sources cited in the Notes, the author consulted baseball-reference.com; the Negro Leagues database at seamheads.com; "Negro Leaguers Who served With the Armed Forces in WW II," at cnlbr.org; various newspapers; and the following:

Luke, Bob. *The Most Famous Woman in Baseball: Effa Manley and the Negro Leagues* (Dulles, Virginia: Potomac Books, 2011).

Abstract of interview of Eileen McGuckian with Violet Isreal and Willie Mae Isreal Carey on September 27, 1983, in files of Peerless Rockville, the historical society of Rockville.

Undated tribute document to Clarence Isreal in files of Peerless Rockville.

File with Title "Medical Isreal, Clarence" in Box 3 of Miscellaneous Files of JFK Assassination Records at National Archives, College Park, Maryland; stack location 650L1/67/19/6.

NOTES

1   The children were: Louise, age 17 (F); Willie May, 16 (F); Dewey, 13 (M); Clarence, 12 (M); Goldie, 9 (F); Frank (Mack), 7 (M); Beatrice, 5 (F); Elbert, 2 (M); Violet, infant (F); and Barbara Shelton, 1 (F), Frank Isreal's granddaughter. Frank and Violet became the parents of three additional children following the 1930 census, as Eileen McGuckian in her book *Rockville: Portrait of a City*, reported that there were 12 children in the Isreal family. That number was confirmed by Clarence's son, Robert, in a 2004 interview, in which he stated that there were six boys and six girls. The two additional brothers were Freddie and James. The additional sister was Irene. Also see oral history interview by Shelby Spillers, preservation planner, City of Rockville, with Bobby Isreal, son of Pint, on March 17, 2004 – located in files of Peerless Rockville, the city's historical society.

2   Eileen McGuckian, *Rockville: Portrait of a City* (Franklin, Tennessee: Hillsboro Press, 2001), 102.

3   Author's telephone interview with Michael Johnson in April 2018.

4   *Washington Evening Star,* May 26, 1939; *Hagerstown* (Maryland) *Daily Mail,* May 31, 1939.

5   *Montgomery Journal* (Chevy Chase, Maryland), April 20, 1987.

6   *Jersey Journal* (Jersey City), July 29, 1940.

7   James A. Riley, *The Biographical Encyclopedia of the Negro Baseball Leagues* (New York: Carroll & Graf, 1994), 706.

8   *Salisbury* (Maryland) *Times*, August 21, 1940.

9   *Jersey Journal*, September 9, 1941.

10   *Washington Evening Star,* May 28, 1941.

11   Larry Lester, *Black Baseball's National Showcase: The East-West All-Star Game 1933-1953* (Lincoln: University of Nebraska Press, 2001), 171.

12   Spillers interview with Bobby Isreal.

13   Author's telephone interview with Jackie Smith of Fort Washington, Maryland, in May 2018. Jackie Smith is a nephew of Pint Isreal.

14   *Washington Evening Star*, June 28, 1942.

15   *Sacramento Bee*, March 27, 1943.

16   *Baltimore Afro-American,* August 18, 1946.

17   *Pittsburgh Courier*, August 10, 1946.

18   *Indianapolis Recorder,* September 14, 1946.

19   James A. Riley, 409.

20   *Rockville Gazette,* April 22, 1987.

21   *NIH Record,* July 21, 1978.

22   *Asbury Park* (New Jersey) *Press,* February 28, 1986.

23   Lawrence Hogan, *Shades of Glory: The Negro Leagues and the Story of Afro-American Baseball* (Des Moines, Iowa: National Geographic Books, 2007), 3.

24   Bruce Adelson, *Brushing Back Jim Crow: The Integration of Minor League Baseball in the American South* (Charlottesville: University of Virginia Press, 1999), 83-97.

25   Butch and his wife, Denise, had three children: Nayo Isreal, Omari Isreal, and Kimberly Nash. Bobby and his wife, Pamela, also had three children: Khali Isreal, Hasani Isreal, and Marjani Isreal. Michael's marriage ended in divorce, and they did not have children.

26   Author's telephone interview with Jackie Smith of Fort Washington, Maryland, May 2018.

27   *Frederick* (Maryland) *News*, June 16, 1949.

28   *NIH Record,* July 21, 1970.

29   *Montgomery Journal,* April 20, 1987; *Rockville Gazette,* April 22, 1987.

30   Author's telephone interview with Michael Johnson, April 2018.

31   Ibid.

32   Voice message response left by Billy Johnson on author's telephone, May 2018.

33   Fred T. Newcomb and Perry Adams, *Murder From Within: Lyndon Johnson's Plot Against President Kennedy* (Bloomington, Indiana: AuthorHouse, 2011), xv.

34   *National Naval Medical Center News*, Volume 19, 1963.

35   Newcomb and Adams.

36   Author's telephone interview with James Coyle, January 2018.

37   Document with title "The United Black Cultural Center Presents 'Let's Reminisce with Montgomery County's Black Baseball Players' Dedicated to Clarence 'Pint' Isreal 6/26/1987," located in the Clarence Isreal folder at Peerless Rockville.

Rufus Lewis

BY MIKE MATTSEY

Rufus Lewis was overshadowed by fellow staff members Leon Day and Max Manning in the regular season, but he posted a 2-0 record in the World Series and won the deciding Game Seven. *(Noir-Tech Research, Inc.)*

There is nothing more exhilarating or more intoxicating in baseball than the seventh game of a best-of-seven championship series. It is an unforgiving arena where history is written of both the heroes who carry the day and their vanquished opponents. Winning pitchers in a game seven instantly become legends not only to their own team's fanbases, but to the sport's broader history as well. Johnny Podres pitched in four World

Series in his 15-year career, but it was his 2-0 shutout of the New York Yankees in Game Seven of the 1955 World Series that cemented his fame in Brooklyn long after Ebbets Field came down. Jack Morris was the ace of the Tigers in the 1980s and led them to a World Series crown in 1984, but it was his 1-0, 10-inning triumph in 1991's Game Seven for the Minnesota Twins that was perhaps the tipping point that led to his 2018 enshrinement in the Baseball Hall of Fame.

While Podres and Morris are rightly remembered as Game Seven heroes, the name Rufus Lewis has largely been lost to history. His game seven résumé equals that of Podres and Morris, but due to baseball's former adherence to the practice of segregation, his exploits have been largely lost to history. But his career demands more. Lewis not only pitched the Newark Eagles to the Negro World Series crown in 1946, he won championships with teams around the world while competing with and against some of the greatest players in the history of the game. He served his country with distinction during World War II, during the prime years of his career, and was named to all-star teams that played in the nation's largest stadiums. His career typifies those of so many other pre-integration African-Americans who starred on Negro League diamonds but were forbidden to compete on the game's greatest stage due to the color of their skin.

Rufus Lewis was born on December 13, 1919, in the tiny town of Johnstons Station, Mississippi, a railroad stop between Jackson, Mississippi, and New Orleans an hour west of Hattiesburg.[1] He was the first of four children born to Robert and Mary Beatrice

(Williams) Lewis. The family migrated north to the more urban setting of Jackson in the 1920s. Census records from 1940 list Lewis as a sophomore at Jackson State University. As with most young American men in the 1940s, Lewis's life was changed by the United States' entry into World War II. He registered for the draft in early 1942.[2] He began his tour of duty as an enlisted man in the Army in 1943, serving through 1945 before being discharged. His military obligation completed, Lewis turned his attention back to baseball. His baseball life featured peaks and valleys, as do most players' careers, but the extremes Lewis experienced on both sides of the spectrum during his playing days tell the story of a man who saw it all on the diamond.

Lewis's big break came after the war when he was scooped up by Effa Manley's Newark Eagles, perennial bridesmaids in the Negro National League, for the 1946 campaign. The star-studded roster featured Larry Doby and Monte Irvin patrolling the infield for Newark while Lewis joined Leon Day and Max Manning to anchor the Eagles' pitching staff. Lewis was discovered in the spring of 1946 by Eagles skipper Biz Mackey. Mackey saw potential greatness in the young hurler stating that not only did Lewis possess a great breaking ball, he also had a fastball that was, "[as] speedy as the unpredictable Satchell in his prime."[3] Mackey, a catcher, took Lewis "under his personal supervision" as Lewis prepared to make his NNL debut.[4]

Lewis took the mound for Newark on May 18 against the Homestead Grays. He struggled through a three-run first inning, but he settled down to record seven strikeouts over four innings in a game that was eventually rained out.[5] On May 22, Lewis earned his first victory for the Eagles against the Philadelphia Stars as he handed them a 5-2 loss.[6] Lewis opened June pitching "brilliant ball" in a 4-2 victory over the Elite Giants.[7] As the Eagles battled down the stretch, Lewis continued to shine. On August 25, Lewis ran his record to 8-1 with a 12-5 win over the Homestead Grays in Newark and chipped in with a double of his own.[8] So dominant were the triumvirate of Day, Manning, and Lewis that, in the words of Baltimore pitcher Frank Duncan, "I think [they] went two or three months and a relief pitcher didn't get off the bench."[9] During the regular season, Lewis went 9-3 with 64 strikeouts. The Eagles defeated the Cuban Stars in early September at Ruppert Stadium in Newark to capture the NNL pennant and earned a berth in the Negro World Series against the legendary Kansas City Monarchs. It was this series that saw Lewis reach the pinnacle of his playing days as he stared down Satchel Paige and the Monarchs and refused to blink.

Lewis featured three times in the 1946 Series, the first appearance in relief of Leon Day in a 2-1 Game One loss. Though Lewis pitched well, scattering four hits and one run in four innings of work, Paige came on in relief to outduel him and also sparked the game-winning rally with an infield hit to open the seventh.[10] Getting tagged with the loss in the Series opener might have crushed the spirit of a lesser pitcher, but Lewis was made of sterner stuff. The right-hander was given a tall assignment for his next Series outing, a Game Four start with the Monarchs seeking to take a commanding three-games-to-one lead in their home stamping grounds of Kansas City. With the spotlight on him, Lewis delivered a gem. He gave up a second-inning run to the Monarchs, but shackled them the rest of the way as the Eagles knocked Ted Alexander out of the box early en route to an 8-1 Series-tying triumph.[11] Lewis's performance evened the series at two games apiece. His next game would turn into the biggest one of his career.

Though the Monarchs and Eagles had split Games Five and Six to force a deciding seventh game, Eagles pitchers Max Manning and Leon Day had struggled. Manning had dropped a 5-1 decision to Kansas City in Game Five and though they won Game Six, Day was shelled early for five runs. Neither man was in form heading into the final tilt, so Eagles boss Biz Mackey went with the hot hand. Lewis got the nod for Game Seven. Mackey and the Eagles would not regret the decision.

The Eagles drew first blood in the bottom of the first inning when Pat Patterson reached on an error and scored an unearned run. Lewis, who scattered eight hits throughout the game, held the lead until the sixth inning. In the top half of the frame, Lewis made a mistake to Buck O'Neil, who crushed a game-tying home run into the left-field stands. Newark immediately struck back in the bottom half when Johnny Davis clouted a two-run double to stake the Eagles to a 3-1 lead. Kansas City answered in the seventh on an RBI single by Herb Souell that cut the lead in half, but Lewis escaped the inning with no further damage. A scoreless eighth inning left Newark clinging to a one-run lead, and Mackey sent Lewis out to pitch the ninth and capture the crown.[12]

Lewis rode his luck to open the ninth. Monarchs catcher Earl Taborn laced a single to right-center to lead off the inning, but he was gunned down at second base by center fielder Jimmy Wilkes. This play loomed large as the inning progressed and Kansas City put runners on second and third with two out and Herb Souell again in a position to drive in a run. This time, Lewis got the upper hand. Souell lofted a lazy popup to Lennie Pearson for the final out of the game, and Newark erupted with joy. Eagles owner Effa Manley, watching from the stands with her "head down, eyes closed, arms crossed, and unable to watch," slumped in her seat with relief as those around her offered congratulations on the team's first World Series crown.[13] Manley owed her "hour of triumph" to Lewis.[14] Over two pressure-packed games, Lewis scattered 12 hits and three runs over 18 innings of work. Overnight, Rufus Lewis was a hero to the Newark faithful.

Lewis's Series performance earned him a berth on the barnstorming circuit in the 1946-47 offseason. Satchel Paige, Lewis's World Series foe, signed the young star to feature with his all-star team in games throughout the country.[15] Paige, ever a showman with an eye on the box office, no doubt was glad to have the red-hot Lewis on his roster. Lewis pitched for the Eagles in 1947 and 1948 and in both seasons did well enough to be tabbed the starting pitcher for the East in the East-West Game. Though he took the loss in both all-star stints, his presence in the starting lineup serves to show how respected Lewis was among Negro League moundsmen during his heyday. Lewis spent both winters in the Cuban League with the Habana Leones, for whom he "had a great campaign on the mound" during their 1947 championship season.[16] By 1950, Lewis was plying his trade south of the border in the Mexican League. It was there that he was involved in an on-field incident that nearly cost him his life.

During a regular-season game in 1950, Lewis was pitching for Mexico City against Jalisco. The batter he was facing was no slouch. Adolfo Cabrera of Jalisco was the loop's leading hitter the year before with a .379 average in 1949.[17] He was also a man with a temper. The day before, Cabrera got into an altercation with the Mexico City shortstop and had to be separated from his opponent.[18] Against Lewis, the situation became far more deadly. Lewis hit Cabrera with a pitch, a curveball that didn't break. Cabrera started toward first base, bat in hand, and then sprinted toward Lewis and hit him with the bat, knocking Lewis senseless to the ground. Cabrera raised the bat overhead to strike Lewis, a blow that would have likely killed the pitcher, according to those present.[19]

Lewis's life was saved by the quick reactions of teammate Wild Bill Wright. Wright sprinted from the dugout, his own bat in hand, and used it to split open Cabrera's scalp to end the fracas. Wright's heroics kept Cabrera out of serious legal trouble. Had he landed the second blow, Cabrera "(would have) been put in jail for life," according to league President Jorge Pasquel.[20] For his part, Lewis denied throwing at Cabrera deliberately.[21] The facts seem to support Lewis's position. No pitcher wishing ill intent toward a hitter would use a curveball to do the job. Further, there was some disagreement by players whether Cabrera had been struck by the pitch at all. Wright stated that while Cabrera may have been brushed by the pitch, the ball carried all the way to the backstop as if it had done the batter no physical harm.[22] In any case, the incident was firmly etched in the memories of everyone present.

The affair with Cabrera was without doubt the low point of Lewis's on-field career. He caught on in 1952 with the Chihuahua Dorados of the Class-C Arizona-Texas League, but it was too late in the game for Lewis. His 8-15 record that season belied the brilliance he had shown with Newark, and his time in Organized Baseball came to a close. As with all former Negro League players, one is left to wonder if he could have pitched in the major leagues while in his prime. He was actively scouted by major-league teams during the 1946 World Series, but was never signed.[23] As historian Rob Ruck argues, baseball's informal quota system was working against Lewis. Younger, all-star-caliber players like Larry Doby and Monte Irvin were snatched up quickly by big-league clubs while older journeyman players such as Lewis were left behind to toil overseas or in the low minors.[24] Lewis retired from the game to the Detroit suburbs, where he lived until his passing in Southfield on December 17, 1999, shortly after his 80th birthday.

The career of Rufus Lewis is one that deserves greater recognition. His exploits in the 1946 Negro World Series led the Newark Eagles to their only championship season. He squared off against some of baseball's most legendary players and came out on top. His clutch pitching skills were recognized by Satchel Paige when he asked Lewis to pitch alongside him on his barnstorming tour against all-star aggregations, and he was named to the East-West Game on two occasions, both as a starter. Jim Crow's legacy has left Lewis's career largely forgotten by modern baseball fans as is the case with countless other Negro League stars. Even when his name is spoken, the Mexico City attack is the most enduring story attached to his name. However, when recalled by those watched and played with him in Newark, Havana, and all points in between, Rufus Lewis is remembered best as a guy who pitched on the greatest stages available to him and excelled.

SOURCES

In addition to the sources cited in the Notes, the author consulted Baseball-Reference.com and the US Federal Census via Ancestry.com.

NOTES

1   World War II Draft Registration Card fold3.com/image/607831679 (accessed December 1, 2018).

2   Ibid.

3   "Fast Pitcher With Eagles," *Sunday Call* (Newark, New Jersey), April 14, 1946.

4   Ibid.

5   "Eagles-Grays Tilt Halted in Sixth Knotted at 3-All," *Sunday Call*, May 18, 1946.

6   "Eagles, Philly Split 2 Games; 7-1, 5-2" *Newark Journal and Guide*, May 25, 1946.

7   "Eagles Are Victors Twice In Road Tilts," *Newark News*, June 6, 1946.

8   "Eagles Continue Race to NNL Flag With 2 Victories," *New Jersey Afro American*, August 31, 1946.

9   Brent Kelley, *Voices from the Negro Leagues: Conversations with 52 Baseball Standouts* (Jefferson, North Carolina: McFarland Publishing, 1998), 170.

10   "Eagles Bow," *Newark News*, September 18, 1946.

11   "Series Is Tied as Eagles Win," *Newark News*, September 25, 1946.

12   "Eagles Hit in Clutches," *Newark News*, September 30, 1946.

13   Bob Luke, *The Most Famous Woman in Baseball: Effa Manley and the Negro Leagues* (Washington: Potomac Books, 2011), 1.

14   Ibid.

15   Rufus Lewis, nlbpa.com/the-athletes/lewis-rufus (accessed December 7, 2018).

16   Roberto Gonzalez Echevarria, *The Pride of Havana: A History of Cuban Baseball* (New York: Oxford University Press, 2001), 54.

17   James A. Riley, *Of Monarchs and Black Barons: Essays on Baseball's Negro Leagues* (Jefferson, North Carolina: McFarland Publishing, 2012), 229.

18   Kelley, 30.

19   Ibid.

20   Ibid.

21   Riley, 229.

22   Kelley, 30.

23   "Majors to Scout Eagles' Series," *Sunday Call*, September 15, 1946.

24   Rob Ruck, *Raceball: How the Major Leagues Colonized the Black and Latin Game* (Boston: Beacon Press, 2001), 108.

BIZ MACKEY

BY CHRIS RAINEY

In the summer of 1946, *Pittsburgh Courier* columnist Wendell Smith gave Newark Eagles manager Biz Mackey all the credit for molding "together the best all-around pitching staff in Negro baseball."[1] Assembling talent is one thing, using it wisely and coping with obstacles that arise is a totally different talent. Mackey's ace, Leon Day, opened the season with a no-hitter and led the team in wins. But he struggled with a sore arm and was of little use in the World Series. Mackey used his staff effectively, especially young Rufus Lewis, to capture a championship. His shortstop, Monte Irvin, simply said of Mackey, "As a player, as a manager, and as a personality, he was in a class by himself."[2]

Capturing the Negro League banner in 1946 was the final jewel of Mackey's brilliant career. Generally regarded as the finest defensive catcher in Negro League history, he was no slouch at the plate. The switch-hitter batted .411 in 1922 and .406 in 1930. He captured two World Series crowns in the Negro Leagues, one as a player and one as manager. He also won a championship in his only season in Cuba. In 2006 his life and talent were recognized with his selection to the National Baseball Hall of Fame in Cooperstown.

The journey to the top of his baseball world was not an easy one for Mackey. He was born the son of Texas sharecroppers. The absence of a birth certificate has led to speculation about his birthplace. In the past 30 years various researchers and writers have placed Mackey's birth in Eagle Pass, Texas, as well as Seguin, Kingsbury, Luling, and Eagle Lake, all in Texas.[3] Most current sources (Seamheads.com is a notable exception) accept the Eagle Pass location.

Raleigh "Biz" Mackey was inducted into the Hall of Fame as a catcher. He also distinguished himself as a manager and led the 1946 Newark Eagles to the Negro World Series championship. *(National Baseball Hall of Fame)*

Mackey listed his birthplace as Caldwell County (near Luling) on his World War I and World War II draft registrations.[4]

We do know that James Raleigh Mackey was one of six children born to John Dee (known as Dee to family and friends) and Beulah (Wright) Mackey, joining the family on July 27, 1897. His parents had wed in 1886 in Caldwell County and farmed there. In the 1900 census, Beulah listed herself as married but Dee was not living under the same roof. She was remarried in 1903 to Montgomery

Meriwether, a farmer in a neighboring county. The 1910 census lists them in Guadalupe County between Seguin and Kingsbury. This blended family included Meriwether's three daughters along with Beulah's five surviving offspring.

The town of Luling, Texas, claims Mackey as its native son. He was wed there on October 20, 1917, to Ora Lee Dorn.[5] It is uncertain if Mackey and Ora ever had children. Mackey did have a daughter named Narcissus. She was born in 1914 and later married George H. Odoms. They took up residence in Caldwell County and raised at least three children. Her oldest son, Riley Mackey Odoms, had a long and successful football career with the Denver Broncos.[6]

Biz and Ora Lee moved to Dallas, where he played baseball and worked as a laborer in 1918. They separated in 1919 and divorced a few years later. Ora Lee remarried in 1924. She and her husband, Will Elam, lived in California. Late in his life, Mackey reconnected with Ora Lee and she is listed on his death certificate as "Informant" and appears to have handled his funeral arrangements.[7]

Mackey received his schooling in nearby Prairie Lea, Texas, through the 10th grade. It was common in rural America for students to take an exam when their schooling ended. They would earn the equivalent of today's high-school diploma with a good performance on the "Common Exam." Mackey met the requirements when he completed the test.

The 1910 census noted that Mackey worked as a farm laborer when not in school. A few years later he took a job as a clerk in a railroad warehouse. At age 16 he reportedly joined his brothers Earnest and Ray playing on the Luling Oilers, the local semipro team. Mackey caught and pitched. Most sources claim he joined the San Antonio Black Aces in 1918. It is more likely that he played for the Dallas Black Giants that season.

Before Mackey earned his nickname, he was known to fans and writers as Riley, Rollie, or Raleigh. He appears in box scores sometimes as Mackey and sometimes by his first name.[8] Based upon that information, it is likely that the Dallas catcher/pitcher in 1918 shown as Riley was in fact Mackey.[9] He opened the 1919 season with the Giants but soon joined the Waco Black Navigators. His time with them was short-lived; he joined five other Waco players in jumping to the San Antonio Black Aces in early June.[10]

The addition of six starters to the Black Aces made them into a juggernaut. League standings showed them with a 45-10 record at the end of the Texas Colored League campaign in 1919. The Waco squad, which had started the season as the strongest team, disbanded shortly after the player defections. Dallas finished with a 51-17 mark and took on San Antonio in a postseason five-game championship.

After tight matches decided by a single run, the series came down to the nightcap of a doubleheader. The Aces sent Walter "Steel Arm" Davis to the mound, but he was pounded for three runs in the first. Mackey took the hill and allowed two more runs the rest of the way. In typical Hollywood fashion, Davis (who moved to center field) came to the plate in the eighth with two men on and lashed a double to give San Antonio a 7-5 victory and the title.

In December the leader of the Black Aces, L.W. Moore, announced his hopes of creating a Colorado-Texas-Oklahoma League. He also announced the signing of two catchers "who will fill the vacancy" created when Riley Mackey became a pitcher exclusively.[11] The new league did not materialize, and the Black Aces remained in the Texas Colored League. Mackey took the hill as planned but when one of the catchers left the team, Mackey was returned to occasional catching duties. He highlighted his return with a 5-for-5 performance against the Black Giants on June 11.

A month later Mackey was enticed to leave Texas. On July 13 he and Aces teammate Henry Blackman (mistakenly called Blackburn in the box score) debuted for the Negro National League Indianapolis ABC's against the Cuban Stars. Mackey smacked a double in four trips in the 5-2 victory.[12] Behind the plate he "worked in first-class style." When the Cubans' shortstop Herman Rios tried to steal second, "Mackey got the ball there so far ahead of him" that the second baseman walked up the line to tag Rios.[13] Many authors have said Mackey's contract was sold to the ABC's, but an article in the *San Antonio Evening News* mentioned that Aces leadership was contemplating a lawsuit because the players had jumped their contracts.[14]

The ABC's finished in fourth place. Mackey's work at bat and behind the plate earned him a contract for 1921. He wintered in Texas and played ball there before returning to Indiana for spring training in early April. Indianapolis opened the season with two wins over the Cuban Stars, but quickly fell off the pace after that. Mackey was even forced to take the mound and took three losses during the campaign. At the plate he hit .304, tied for the team lead in triples, and punched three home runs.

The ABC's stayed together after the season and did some barnstorming. Mackey played third base late in the year and during the fall. Russell Powell handled the catching during the regular season. In the fall, Mack Eggleston was recruited to catch. The team also welcomed back Oscar Charleston, who had spent the season with St. Louis.

Charleston remained with the ABC's in 1922 and the team finished second, tied with the Monarchs but trailing the Chicago American Giants. Charleston batted .395 and slammed 14 doubles, 9 triples, and 11 home runs. Not to be outdone, Mackey also mashed 14 doubles and hit a robust .411 while playing some shortstop and outfield along with catching.

In 1923 Ed Bolden, owner of the Hilldale Daisies (also called Giants and Darbys), led the formation of the Eastern Colored League (ECOL). A talent war ensued between the ECOL and the NNL that resulted in Mackey being signed by Hilldale. There he joined future Hall of Famers Judy Johnson, Pop Lloyd, and Louis Santop. Mackey was now 25 years old and had reached his full stature of 6 feet tall and probably 210 pounds.

The ECOL season opener was staged before 17,000 fans in Hilldale's new park. Mackey caught and batted fifth in the lineup behind Lloyd. The game was called because of rain in the sixth with Hilldale up 4-2 over the Bacharach Giants.[15] Mackey split the catching duties that season with Santop and spelled the 39-year-old Lloyd at shortstop. He is credited with leading the team in batting and RBIs. Hilldale posted a league-leading 32-17 record.

The nickname "Biz" first started to appear in 1923. Both the *Philadelphia Inquirer* and *Pittsburgh Courier* were using it by the end of the season. Mackey was a friendly, loquacious fellow with a competitive streak. He was known for giving the batter an earful when at the plate, hoping to break their concentration and focus. This "giving them the business" earned him the nickname of "Biz." It should be noted that he was not the first "Biz" Mackey to make the sports pages. A featherweight boxer who twice had world-championship matches against Abe Attell – yes, that Attell of Black Sox infamy – had appeared in headlines for two decades as the catcher grew up.

Hilldale was the dominant ECOL team again in 1924, posting a 47-22 mark. Mackey led the team in batting and handled the pitching staff of Nip Winters, Red Ryan, and Phil Cockrell expertly. The two black leagues staged a world series after the regular season and the Kansas City Monarchs captured five of the nine games.

After the season Mackey went to Cuba to play for Almendares. He joined Lloyd, Charleston, Wilbur "Bullet" Rogan, and Adolfo Luque on a team that proved to be a juggernaut. The season was ended early because of Almendares' dominance. Mackey batted .309 with a team-leading 11 doubles.[16]

Because the regular season closed early, a postseason series was staged between an all-Cuban team and the "All Yankees" team made up of Negro League players. The All Yankees posted a 5-2-1 record. Mackey faced Cuban pitchers Jose Mendez and Martin Dihigo in the series and reportedly batted .333. Interestingly, Baseball Commissioner Kenesaw Landis attended one of the games.[17]

Unlike many of his contemporaries who played winter ball in the Caribbean and Mexico, this was Mackey's sole trip to the islands. He chose to spend his winters playing in the California Winter League, which featured a mix of black and white teams. Mackey played 18 seasons on the West Coast and eventually made his permanent home in California. He is credited with a .366 batting average and 28 home runs in those seasons.[18]

The Hilldale squad ran away with the title again in 1925, posting a 52-15 record. The players did prove to be human during a week in June when they dropped three to the Harrisburg Giants and then lost a doubleheader to the Baltimore Black Sox. Mackey, who batted cleanup, produced only four hits in the games.[19] Hilldale was knocked out of first place by the losses but regained the lead in mid-July and never looked back.

Hilldale earned a rematch with the Monarchs in an October series. Mackey struggled early in the series. He was 2-for-17 in the first four games and even dropped a ball in a home-plate collision. Baseball takes a team effort and his teammates picked him up as Hilldale captured three of the first four matches. In the final games, in Philadelphia, Mackey's bat came alive and he had three hits, including a home run and double. Hilldale took five of six to capture the crown.[20]

Hilldale returned their core in 1926, and even added John Beckwith but its record dropped to 34-24 and the team finished in third place. In the offseason Mackey joined a barnstorming squad called the Philadelphia Royal Giants. They went to California and played in the winter league, posting a 26-11-1 record to win the crown. The team split up and some players returned to their teams for the regular season.

Mackey, along with Rap Dixon, Andy Cooper, and others, traveled to Japan and played a 48-game tour, the first tour by a black entourage. The Americans entertained the locals with their brand of baseball, which included a pregame "shadow ball" routine. Years of experience in barnstorming had taught Mackey and his teammates the importance of keeping the local fans interested and entertained. Winning 20-0 would dampen enthusiasm and lessen the gate. It was to their advantage to keep the games close. In doing this they "played to the Japanese sense of honor and dignity."[21]

Mackey established himself as a fan favorite. He launched a massive home run at the new Meiji Shrine Stadium in Tokyo. He fascinated and amazed the crowds with his ability to throw from the crouch. He was quick with a smile and genuine sincerity toward opponents and fans alike. After hitting him with a pitch, a Japanese hurler bowed to apologize, as is the style in the country. Mackey returned the gesture and bowed in return.[22]

Biz returned to Japan for a second tour five years later. On this tour he did some pitching and led the American contingent with a .388 batting average.[23] The Japanese Baseball League would begin in 1936. Japanese baseball historian Kazuo Sayama credits the Royal Giants and Mackey with hastening the adoption of the game in his country. Babe Ruth's visit in 1934 certainly created a countrywide sensation, but without the groundwork laid by the Negro Leaguers the game would not have reached its level of influence and popularity.

The lengthy tour in 1927 caused Mackey and his mates to miss the first half of the ECOL season. Hilldale was experiencing a poor first half. Joe Lewis handled the catching, but three players were suspended indefinitely in early June because of their indifferent play. Mackey was threatened with a five-year suspension after his return to the United States in early July. The suspension proved to be a hollow threat and he was in the lineup on July 28 for a 5-3 win over the Bacharach Giants.[24]

The Daisies finished third in the second half after being in fifth at the close of the first half. Mackey batted .284. He was recruited by Cum Posey in the fall and traveled with the Homestead Grays on their extensive barnstorming trip.

Hilldale added Oscar Charleston to the roster but dropped out of the league in March 1928. Playing an independent schedule against all comers, the team covered the East with appearances. Mackey found himself playing shortstop on numerous occasions. In late September he and second baseman Frank Warfield were added to the roster of the Baltimore Black Sox.

Hilldale moved into the American Negro League in 1929 and Mackey returned to the team. He stayed with it through 1931 after they went independent. In 1932 he declined a contract and stayed in California until promoter Lonnie Goodwin left for the Orient with his tour. The team played nine games in Honolulu, then crossed the Pacific to play in Japan. They also had 10 games scheduled in China and 30 in the Philippines.

From 1933 to 1935 Mackey played with the Philadelphia Stars. He was selected by fan vote as the starting catcher in the inaugural East-West All-Star Game, played before 19,000 fans in Comiskey Park in Chicago. He split time with Josh Gibson at catcher in the 11-7 loss by his East team. In 1936 he was traded to the Columbus Elite Giants, but that franchise moved to Washington. Mackey had his first taste as manager when he filled in for Candy Jim Taylor. He also earned a starting spot in the All-Star Game.

The consensus among fans and scholars of the Negro Leagues was that Gibson was the better hitter, but Mackey was by far his defensive superior. Author James Riley said it best: "Considered the master of defense, (Mackey) possessed all the tools necessary behind the plate. … An expert handler of pitchers, he studied people. … [H]e was a master at … framing and funneling pitches. Pitchers recognized his generalship and liked to pitch" to Mackey. His surprising agility for a big man enabled him to play the infield.[25]

Although 48-year old Biz Mackey relegated himself to pinch-hitting duty in 1946, he finished his 23-year Negro League career after the 1947 season with a lifetime .328 batting average. (*John W. Mosley Collection, Temple University*)

In 1937 Mackey took over as Washington manager when Taylor moved on. Mackey was selected by the fans as the manager for the East-West All-Star Game. His East squad emerged with a 7-2 victory. He was tipped off about the talent of a teenager named Roy Campanella. Washington signed Campanella for $60 a month and Mackey began the task of turning him into a professional catcher. When Mackey left the Elite Giants, Campanella was ready to step into his shoes. Campanella recalled, "Biz Mackey was the master of defense of all catchers." Campanella always was quick to give Mackey credit for his development.[26]

Mackey was sold to the Newark Eagles in 1939. He took over as manager from Dick Lundy partway through the 1940 season. Despite a growing waistline and aching knees, Mackey continued to be an asset on the field. In 1942 he had a falling-out with the owners, Abe and Effa Manley, over salary and was replaced by Willie Wells.

Mackey returned to his California home. He supported the war effort by working at North American Aviation in Los Angeles and played baseball with the San Francisco Sea Lions. When the Manleys had a dispute with Wells, Mackey returned to Newark in 1945. He continued to play occasionally, mostly at first base.

The Eagles captured the first-half championship in 1946 with a record of 25-9. They weathered some hard times in the second half, including the demise of the team bus which forced players to drive their own cars to games at one point.

Mackey was renowned for his levelheadedness and emotional control on the field throughout his managerial career. He uncharacteristically lost his cool in a game against the Cleveland Buckeyes in late July of 1946 and pulled the Eagles from the field in protest. The black press took him to task for being unsportsmanlike. Effa Manley came to his defense with a letter to the *Pittsburgh Courier* and the issue blew over.

The Eagles took the second half with a 22-7 mark and met the Kansas City Monarchs in the World Series. Led by Monte Irvin's bat and the pitching of Rufus Lewis, Newark captured the pennant, a triumph that earned each player a diamond ring.

Mackey managed the Eagles again in 1947. The Eagles sold Larry Doby to the Cleveland Indians that year. Mackey recommended moving the youngster from second base to the outfield, which the Indians did. Mackey was named manager of the East squad for the All-Star Game. The game was played on his 50th birthday and Mackey rewarded himself by pinch-hitting in the eighth inning. He had seen very little action that season, and his waistline had grown to where writer Wendell Smith called him paunchy. His girth did not affect his batting eye; he walked. He immediately replaced himself with Vic Harris.

Mackey retired to California, where he continued to play with the Sea Lions and other teams. Fate has an odd way of impacting our lives. When Mackey made his first trip to Japan, he was intrigued to find a large contingent of Afro-Asians living in Tokyo. He met a young woman of mixed ancestry named Lucille and they became friendly. On later trips to Japan he made it a point to contact her. The pair understandably lost contact during the war.

According to Mackey's great-nephew Ray, Lucille and her family came to the United States in the late 1940s or early 1950s. She and Mackey were reunited in San Francisco. They spent the rest of their lives together. Mackey's reputation in baseball was that of a jovial, trash-talker but in his private life he was very reserved. He bordered on reclusive and did very little to publicize his baseball life.

That changed, for one day at least, on the evening of May 7, 1959. A reported 93,000 fans attended an exhibition game in the Los Angeles Coliseum between the Dodgers and the Yankees. The occasion was to pay tribute to Roy Campanella, the longtime Dodgers catcher, who had been paralyzed in a traffic accident the previous year. In the crowd were Mackey and his nephew Ray. In his thank-you speech to the throng, Campy called for Mackey to join him on the field and made sure that everyone there realized how important Biz had been in his development.[27]

After the Campanella tribute, Mackey lived quietly in Los Angeles and worked as a forklift driver for the Stauffer Chemical Company. In those days before the publication of *Only the Ball Was White*,[28] it was commonplace for a former Negro League player to live in anonymity. Lucille, called "Aunt Lucy" by the family, died a few months before Biz. The family wondered if the loss of the love of his life hastened Mackey's demise. Biz died on September 22, 1965, in Los Angeles. He was buried in that city's Evergreen Cemetery. His death received no coverage in *The Sporting News* nor did it appear in the *Necrology of the 1966 Sporting News Official Baseball Guide*. In the 1970s and beyond, Mackey's name would make

newspapers as a Negro League player who deserved Hall of Fame consideration. His time to enter Cooperstown finally came in 2006.

SOURCES

Statistics come from Baseball-Reference.com unless otherwise noted. Standings of teams come from *The Negro League Book* published by SABR in 1994. A big thank-you to Ray Mackey III for his tremendous wealth of information about Biz and the Mackey family. I would also like to extend my gratitude to renowned Negro League historian Larry Lester for his support and guidance in this research. Finally, a tip of the hat to the Allen County Library in Fort Wayne, Indiana, where a researcher named Cristella searched the *Los Angeles Sentinel* for Mackey info.

NOTES

1   Wendell Smith, "The Sports Beat," *Pittsburgh Courier*, July 13, 1946: 16.

2   templepress.wordpress.com/2018/01/24/biz-mackey-a-giant-behind-the-plate/.

3   John Holway listed the birthplace as Seguin in his 1988 book *Blackball Stars*; other sources found in Mackey's Hall of Fame file suggest Kingsbury, which is east of Seguin and Luling; in a correspondence from 2000 there was mention of Eagle Lake.

4   ancestry.com/interactive/6482/005152930_01688?pid=16453080&backurl=https://search. Last accessed February 26, 2019. search.ancestry.com/cgi-bin/sse.dll?db=YMDraftCardsWWII&indiv=try&h=17975243. Last accessed March 11, 2019.

5   search.ancestry.com/cgi-bin/sse.dll?dbid=60183&h=66427&indiv=try&o_vc=Record:OtherRecord&rhSource=8842.

6   Brad Gray, "Biz's Big Day," *Austin American-Statesman*, July 31, 2006: 20.

7   Gary Krause, email exchange from February 2000 found in Mackey's Hall of Fame file. Krause was researching Mackey's personal information and corresponding with a Hall of Fame library researcher, Eric Enders.

8   An example would be the box scores in the *Dallas Express* from August 23, 1919: 11, in which he was listed as Riley in the first game and Releigh (sic) in game two.

9   "Dallas Black Giants Win," *Dallas Morning News*, August 12, 1918: 7. He was also residing in Dallas in August when he signed up for the draft. See Note 4.

10   Gary Ashwill, "Steel Arm Davis," Agate Type, November 3, 2014. agatetype.typepad.com/agate_type/2014/11/steel-arm-davis.html. Last accessed February 26, 2019.

11   *San Antonio Evening News*, December 13, 1919: 10.

12   "New Players Show Class," *Indianapolis Star*, July 14, 1920: 10.

13   Ibid.

14   "Suit May be Filed for Taking Players from Black Aces," *San Antonio Evening News*, August 2, 1920: 7.

15   "Hilldale Opens New Park with Victory," *Philadelphia Inquirer*, April 29, 1923: 20.

16   Jorge S. Figueredo, *Cuban Baseball: A Statistical History, 1878-1961* (Jefferson, North Carolina: McFarland, 2003), 157-59.

17   Figueredo, 162.

18   Geri Strecker, "Winter Baseball in California: Separate Opportunities, Equal Talent," *The National Pastime (SABR, 2011)*, accessed on February 28, 2019 at sabr.org/ research/winter-baseball-california-separate-opportunities-equal-talent.

19   "Harrisburg Sweeps Three-Game Series with Hilldale; Leads Eastern League," *Pittsburgh Courier, June 27, 1925: 12.*

20   Game coverage from the *Pittsburgh Courier* of October 10 and 17.

21   Gary Joseph Cieradkowski, "Biz Mackey: International Man of Clout," Infinite Card Set blog October 2013. Last accessed on February 28, 2019 at infinitecardset. blogspot.com/2013/10/160-biz-mackey-international-man-of.html.

22   Kazuo Sayama and Bill Staples Jr., *Gentle Black Giants: A History of Negro Leaguers in Japan* (Fresno, California: NBRP Press, 2019), 121.

23   William F. McNeil, *Black Baseball Out of Season: Pay for Play Outside the Negro Leagues* (Jefferson, North Carolina: McFarland, 2012), 108.

24   "Mackey's 'Five-Years Suspension' Over, Aids Hilldale in Win Over Seasiders," *Pittsburgh Courier, July 30, 1927: 16.*

25   James A. Riley, *The Biographical Encyclopedia of the Negro Baseball Leagues* (New York: Carroll & Graf Publishers, 1994), 502-03.

26   Gray, "Biz's Big Day."

27   Telephone interviews with Ray Mackey III, March 6 and 11, 2019.

28   Robert Peterson, *Only the Ball Was White (New York: Oxford University Press,* 1992).

Biz Mackey and Japan

By Bill Staples Jr.

Throughout his career. Biz Mackey served as an international baseball goodwill ambassador by competing in Cuba, and crossing the Pacific to play exhibition games in Hawaii, Japan, Korea, China, and the Philippines.

According to Japanese baseball historian Kazuo Sayama, Mackey's tours to Japan as a member of the Philadelphia Royal Giants in 1927 and 1932-33 played an important role in the development of professional baseball in Japan in 1936.[1] To better appreciate Sayama's position, it's important to understand the factors at play during the game's early evolution in Japan.

Baseball was introduced to Japan in the 1870s and by the 1920s it rivaled sumo wrestling as the nation's favorite sport.[2] However, despite their passion for the game, at that time the skill level of Japanese ballplayers did not equal that of the Americans.

Prior to the Royal Giants' initial tour, major leaguers made four visits to Japan – in 1908, 1911, 1920, and 1922. The first three tours were positive and helped establish a stronger baseball bond between the United States and Japan. But all of that goodwill was damaged in 1922 when Herb Hunter's All-Stars disrespected their hosts by intentionally losing a game. "We welcomed the American team because we thought they were gentlemanly and sportsman-like," one Japanese participant told the *Tokio Asahi*, "but they disappointed our hopes and left an unpleasant impression upon us."[3] Major leaguers did not return to Japan for another nine years.

Among the teams filling this major-league void in Japan were the Philadelphia Royal Giants in 1927. Mackey and notable teammates

Andy Cooper, Rap Dixon, and Frank Duncan first won the hearts of Japanese fans and the respect of opposing players by displaying impressive talent and true sportsmanship.

Mackey in particular left a lasting impression. He hit the first home run ever recorded at Meiji Shrine Stadium, and he even made headlines after getting hit by a pitch. The opposing pitcher bowed to Mackey to apologize for hitting him, and in a display of mutual respect, Mackey bowed back.4

Led by team captain Mackey, the Royal Giants returned to Japan in late 1932. Some Japanese players who competed against the Royal Giants told Sayama in *Gentle Black Giants* that the Negro Leaguers' return visit couldn't have come at a better time.

White major leaguers players resumed tours of Japan in 1931, billing themselves as the Herb Hunter & Fred Lieb All-Stars. They won all 23 of their games, many of which were blowouts and/or shutouts. Opposing Japanese players observed that the Americans approached these games with arrogance, and an attitude that said, "We are experts, let us teach you how to play."[5]

Among the All-Stars was Lou Gehrig, who was on year six of a 14-year run toward his consecutive-games-played streak of 2,130. During the 1931 tour, Gehrig was involved in an incident that was a mirror opposite of Mackey's graceful bow. A Japanese pitcher accidentally hit Gehrig on the wrist with an inside pitch. With his streak top of mind, Gehrig removed himself from the game and, to avoid further injury, refused to play for the remainder of the tour.[6]

Unlike the major leaguers of 1931, the Royal Giants approached the games and their opponents with an attitude of "we are friends, let's play ball together." In doing so, Mackey and his teammates created a comfortable, safe, and fun environment for the Japanese players to improve their skills while playing against high-caliber competition. It was for this approach that Mackey and his teammates earned the term of endearment "gentle, black giants."[7]

"We (Japan) yearned for better skill in the game. But if we had seen only the major leaguers, we might have been discouraged and disillusioned by our poor showing," wrote Sayama. "What saved us was the tours of the Philadelphia Royal Giants, whose visits gave Japanese players confidence and hope."[8]

The Royal Giants made a final visit to Japan in late 1933 – this time without Mackey, who most likely remained in the States due to a commitment to his new team the Philadelphia Stars, or declined because of a nagging arm injury, or both.[9] For the players who did make the trip, rainy weather prevented them from competing on the field in Japan. Instead, the team dined and enjoyed time with their Japanese hosts before moving on to the Philippines.[10]

Major leaguers returned to Japan in November 1934. Babe Ruth impressed observers with his powerful home runs, but as in the previous tours the All-Americans disrespected the Japanese players on the diamond. Former player Yasuo Shimazu shared his memories:

> In a game held in the rain at Kokura in 1934, Babe Ruth took to the field as a first baseman with a Japanese umbrella over his head, and Lou Gehrig, who was playing as a left fielder, had rubber rain shoes on. In another game, when Lefty Grove was pitching, left fielder Al Simmons laid himself on the field to show he had nothing to do but lie down and watch what Lefty was doing. They may have been intended their actions to be a show, but many Japanese fans weren't altogether happy.[11]

Two years after Ruth's visit, the first professional Japanese baseball league was founded. According to Sayama, professional baseball was able to materialize in Japan because the Japanese players had what he called "a good shock absorber." Some countries rejected baseball because the visiting professionals left fledgling players disillusioned with the game through defeat. "We were lucky enough to have the chance to neutralize the shock. The Royal Giants' visits were the shock absorber."[12]

In his 1987 article, "Their Throws Were Like Arrows: How a Black Team Spurred Pro Ball in Japan," Sayama concluded:

> Baseball has in it many elements that appeal to the Japanese mind, and it may safely be said that professional baseball would have been born in the course of time. Without the visits of the gentlemanly and accessible Royal Giants,

however, I don't think it would have seen the light of day as early as 1936.[13]

The positive influence of Biz Mackey and the Royal Giants did not end in 1936. Future Japanese Baseball Hall of Famer Shinji Hamazaki competed against the Royal Giants as a member of the Mita Club, the Keio University alumni team, and his interactions with Negro League players left a positive impression on him.[14] Years later he was named manager of the Hankyu Braves, and when foreign players were permitted to play in Japan in the early 1950s, Hamazaki recruited four black players from America: John Britton, third baseman; Jimmie Newberry, pitcher; Larry Raines, shortstop; and Jonas Gaines, pitcher.[15]

In 1962 two of Mackey's former players with the Newark Eagles, Larry Doby and Don Newcombe, followed their manager's footsteps and journeyed across the Pacific to play the final season of their careers in Japan.[16]

Biz Mackey (second from right) and the barnstorming Philadelphia Royal Giants during their 1927 tour of Japan, where he became a fan favorite both for his play and for his respectful attitude toward Japanese opponents. *(Noir-Tech Research, Inc.)*

NOTES

1   Kazuo Sayama, "Their Throws Were Like Arrows–How a Black Team Spurred Pro Ball in Japan," *Baseball Research Journal* 16 (1987): 85–88.

2   newspapers.com/clip/27693002/baseball_national_sport_of_japan_1928/ or N.K. Roscoe, "The Development of Sport in Japan," Japan Society of London, Transactions and Proceedings 30 (1932–33).

3   "Big Leaguers Boot One in Japan, Herbert Hunter Takes Major League All-Stars to Japan," *Fresno Bee*, December 14, 1922: 9. 43.

4   Sayama, " 'Their Throws Were Like Arrows.'"

5   Kazuo Sayama and Bill Staples Jr., *Gentle Black Giants: A History of Negro Leaguers in Japan* (NBRP Press, 2019).

6   Ibid.

7   Ibid.

8   Sayama, " 'Their Throws Were Like Arrows.'"

9   Bob Luke, "Biz Mackey: Catcher, Manager, Mentor Extraordinaire," *Black Ball: A Negro Leagues Journal*, Vol. 1, No. 2, (Fall 2008).

10   Sayama and Staples.

11   Sayama, " 'Their Throws Were Like Arrows.'"

12   Ibid.

13   Ibid.

14   To learn more about Shinji Hamazaki and other members of the Japanese Baseball Hall of Fame, visit: http://english.baseball-museum.or.jp.

15   "The Secret History Of Black Baseball Players In Japan," npr.org/sections/codeswitch/2015/07/14/412880758/the-secret-history-of-black-baseball-players-in-japan.

16   Associated Press, "Doby to Play Jap Baseball," *Baltimore Sun*, June 24, 1962: 104. newspapers.com/clip/27693321/doby_newcombe_in_japan_1962/.

MAXWELL MANNING

BY FREDERICK C. BUSH

Pitcher Max Manning's glasses resulted in two nicknames. In the Negro Leagues, he had the sobriquet "Dr. Cyclops," but in Cuba his scholarly look made him known as "Profesor." *(Courtesy of Jay-Dell Mah/Western Canada Baseball)*

Max Manning was a man of many nicknames. Newark Eagles teammate Jimmy Hill gave him the moniker Dr. Cyclops, by which he became best-known in baseball circles. Hill had just seen the 1940 movie with that title, but he could not recall seeing any other player who wore glasses – especially thick spectacles like Manning's – so the name seemed fitting to him.[1] Eagles co-owner Abe Manley, Manning's longtime employer, developed such a good rapport with him that he called him Milio

– a contraction of the name Maximilian (though that was not Manning's full first name) – so he also became known by that sobriquet.[2] In Cuba, where Manning played four seasons, he was called Profesor,[3] in reference to the scholarly appearance that his glasses bestowed upon him; this particular nickname became most apropos as Manning went on to a lengthy career as a teacher once his tenure as a star pitcher in the Negro and Latin American baseball leagues ended.

Maxwell Cornelius Manning was born on November 18, 1918, in Rome, Georgia. He was the second son born to Robert W. and Helen (Burrell) Manning. The family eventually grew to include not only Max and his older brother Robert Jr., but also younger siblings Helen, Marilyn, John, Loretta, and Richard.

Manning was named after his grandfather, Cornelius Maxwell Manning, who had a distinguished past. Rev. C. Maxwell Manning, as he later became known, was born in 1845 and, at the age of 18 joined the 35th Regiment of the US Colored Infantry in North Carolina during the Civil War. Over the course of his three-year enlistment, he fought in a number of skirmishes in Florida.[4] After his wartime hitch ended, Manning became a minister in the African Methodist Episcopal Church. In 1896 President Grover Cleveland named him secretary of the US Legation in Liberia, a country that had been founded as a settlement in 1822 with the express purpose of resettling freed slaves from North America; he was recalled from that position by President William McKinley in 1898.[5] Rev. Manning's second son, Robert, was born in 1889 and studied to become a teacher. Robert's son, Maxwell – a.k.a. Profesor – eventually followed in his father's footsteps.

Manning had no memories of Rome, Georgia, as his family moved to Mississippi not long after his birth when his father took the job of head schoolmaster at the Vicksburg Industrial School.[6] The 1920 Census shows that the Manning family lived in a rural area of Hinds County, Mississippi, which is next to Warren County, where Vicksburg is located. The Jim Crow South was a harsh environment for African-Americans, and Hinds County had the highest rate of lynching of black people in Mississippi between 1877 and 1950.[7] Although Manning was too young to know how great a role the extreme prejudice his family encountered in the South may have played in his father's decisions, the family soon moved to Philadelphia, and shortly thereafter settled in Pleasantville, New Jersey.

By the time Manning attended Pleasantville High School, his talents were such that he became the only black player on the school's baseball team. Ty Helfrich, a second baseman for the Federal League's Brooklyn Tip-Tops in 1915, was the team's coach. Helfrich "saw potential in Max and helped him to develop into an excellent high school pitcher."[8] Manning credited Helfrich with helping him to develop his fastball. He also said that Helfrich was the person who first told him he believed Manning could make a good living as a pitcher in the Negro Leagues. According to Manning, Helfrich "went on to tell me about them, how he had played against the House of David and all those different clubs. He said that they do pretty good and not only that, they have a chance to go to other countries and play."[9] Helfrich turned out to be equal parts encourager and prophet.

While he was still in high school, Manning also played for the semipro Johnson's All-Stars, a team coached by the legendary John Henry "Pop" Lloyd, in Atlantic City. Lloyd is still considered by many to have been the top shortstop ever to play in the Negro Leagues, and he was inducted into the Hall of Fame in 1977. Manning said of Lloyd, "Pop taught me many things about baseball, how to play and conduct myself off the field."[10] Besides playing for Johnson's All-Stars, Manning also played for the Camden Giants, a team that he said "had old timers who had played in black leagues."[11]

Manning developed his pitching skills so well – and filled out an intimidating 6-foot-4 frame – that he was offered a contract by Detroit Tigers scout Max Bishop upon his graduation in 1937. Bishop – who ironically was known as "Camera Eye" for his ability to locate pitches as a batter – had never actually seen Manning, so he did not know that his prized pitching prospect was black. Manning laughed as he recalled in an interview:

> My father brought me up against the wall and said, "Look. Let me tell you something. You've got to face real life here.

You've got about as much chance of playing for the Detroit Tigers as a snowball in hell. ... You've seen pictures of ballplayers and you don't see any there your color, do you?"[12]

Once Bishop found out about Manning's race, he immediately rescinded his offer. As the elder Manning had observed, the major leagues were not yet ready for black players.

In the fall of 1937 Manning enrolled at Lincoln University in nearby Oxford, Pennsylvania. He played on the school's baseball and basketball teams, and it was there that he met his lifelong friend, future Newark Eagles teammate, and eventual Hall of Famer Monte Irvin. Manning finished one year at Lincoln before both he and Irvin were approached by Abe Manley, who wanted them to play for the Newark Eagles of the Negro National League. Although both players signed with the Eagles late in the 1938 season, Manning does not appear to have played for the team until 1939. He apparently was sent to play for the Ponce team in the Puerto Rican winter league to get some seasoning, but no statistics are available for Manning's time there.[13]

The next year Manning was ready to start his pro career in earnest, and he recalled his first start for Newark in 1939 as the most memorable game of his career. After training in Miami, the Eagles barnstormed their way north to their New Jersey home. In Winston-Salem, North Carolina, they played a game against the defending NNL champion Homestead Grays. Manning said of his starting assignment, "You know they're going to give me a baptism

Although Leon Day was the better known ace of the 1946 Eagles' pitching staff, Max Manning posted the best pitching record in the Negro National League that season. (*Noir-Tech Research, Inc.*)

of fire here, but the thing about it is that I struck out the first five guys and that included anybody that was up there – Josh and Buck and everybody."[14] Josh Gibson and Buck Leonard are now in the Hall of Fame and the Homestead Grays won nine NNL pennants in 11 seasons from 1938 through 1948, so Manning knew after this start that he could compete with the best players in the league.

Manager Dick Lundy piloted a Newark team that included five future Hall of Famers: Mule Suttles, Willie Wells, Raleigh "Biz" Mackey, Leon Day, and Irvin. In spite of all their talent, the Eagles finished in second place, two games behind the Grays, with a league record of 32-21-1; their overall record was 37-21-1. Later in life, Manning said, "I don't know why we didn't do better than we did. ... in '39 we had a hell of a good team," and he asserted that this team was even better than the Eagles' 1946 squad that won both the NNL pennant and Negro League World Series.[15] As for Manning, statistics show that he received limited playing time during his first full season and finished with a 1-4 record, 22 strikeouts, and a 5.80 ERA in 35⅔ innings pitched over seven games.

Although the Eagles fared worse as a team in 1940, Manning made progress toward becoming a star. He was the team's co-leader in wins, along with Jimmy Hill, and finished 9-4 with a team-leading 66 strikeouts and a 4.38 ERA in 98⅔ innings. Newark finished with a 26-21-1 record in the NNL, only good enough for third place. Mackey replaced Lundy toward the end of the season and led the team to a 5-2 record during his brief tenure as manager. Several sources show that Manning spent the winter league season in the Dominican Republic after the NNL season although, again, no statistics for his time in that country are available.[16]

On the heels of his success in 1940, Manning ran afoul of Effa Manley – Abe's wife and the Eagles' co-owner who negotiated all salaries – when he held out for more money at the beginning of the 1941 season. Like most owners, Manley tried to sign her team's players for as little money as possible, and she often acted as though she had been betrayed when a player held out. Of his relationship with Effa Manley, Manning said, "She never cared too much for me as a person. We were both stubborn, [which] didn't help the situation."[17]

Manning deemed Manley's salary offer to be unsatisfactory and returned his unsigned contract to her. He included a letter with the contract in which he wrote, "A Negro baseball player's life is a hard one. He has to make money while he is still young and spend it wisely. Likewise he must obtain his salary however and where ever he can."[18] The "where ever" was an implied reference to the fact that Mexican League President Jorge Pasquel was luring away many Negro League players with higher salaries. Manley apparently got the hint as she acquiesced to Manning's salary demands.

Once the 1941 season commenced, Manning and the Eagles picked up where they had left off the previous season. In an instance of déjà vu, the team – this time under Mackey's guidance for the entire year – finished in third place with a 27-23-1 record in NNL play while Manning and Hill tied for the team lead in wins. The win total had fallen off to six for both pitchers, however, and Manning's final statistics show a 6-5 record, 50 strikeouts, and a 4.36 ERA in 109⅓ innings pitched.

In 1942 Manning may have thought that he was stuck in a time loop as Newark again finished in third place and he tied for the team lead in victories once more with seven (although Leon Day was the co-leader this year). The 1942 incarnation of the Eagles had six future Hall of Famers – Suttles, Wells, Day, Irvin, Ray Dandridge, and Larry Doby – but finished with a losing record of 28-30-3 in NNL play, although their overall record was 36-33-3. Mackey had departed, thus depriving the team of a seventh Hall of Famer, and Wells took over the managerial reins for the season. Manning showed vast improvement as he shaved more than 1½ runs off his ERA, lowering it from 4.36 in 1941 to 2.63 in 1942. He finished the campaign with a 7-5 record and 52 strikeouts in 99⅓ innings pitched. The 1942 Eagles team was another squad that Manning thought was better than the 1946 championship team; however, as had been the case with the 1939 Eagles, they did not achieve spectacular results.[19]

Manning's baseball career was put on hold when he was drafted and inducted into the US Army on September 1, 1942. He served for the duration of World War II plus another five months afterward, which caused him to miss the 1943 through 1945 seasons. He went through basic training in Fort Dix, New Jersey, and then was assigned to the Quartermaster Corps, serving with the 316th Air Squadron at Richland Airfield in Virginia. Unlike many baseball players, both black and white, Manning did not get to play on a baseball team at any point during his service. He did not completely forgo sports activities, though. In February 1944 it was reported that "Sergeant Max Manning, Newark, N.J., former pitcher of the Newark Eagles, professional baseball team, is now coach of the Owls basketball team of the 316th Aviation Squadron. ..."[20]

Manning did not coach basketball much longer because he was sent to France, where he arrived on July 6, 1944.[21] He became a truck driver on what was called the Red Ball Express, "hauling supplies to the frontlines for the Third Army."[22] After Germany surrendered, Manning was sent briefly to the Philippines and then to Japan.[23] In January 1946 he was sent back to Fort Dix, where he was discharged.

Manning was elated to be playing baseball again when the 1946 season began. He explained, "Being in the service and not playing ball for three years does something to you. It has an effect on you.

After getting home again, spring training was almost like therapy. There was a feeling of comfort and it let you kind of get back on track."[24] Manning was not the only military veteran who returned to the Eagles in time for the 1946 season. The press reported that Biz Mackey, who was back with Newark once more, "has whipped a host of ex-GIs into shape for the coming race and feels certain that the Newark club will be in the thick of the pennant battle."[25] In addition to Manning, the list of Newark's ex-GIs included Day, Doby, Irvin, Oscar Givens, Clarence "Pint" Isreal, Charles Parks, and Leon Ruffin. Playing with renewed vigor after their wartime experiences, they helped to take the Eagles to previously unattained heights.

The season began with a bang as Day pitched an Opening Day no-hitter on May 5 against the Philadelphia Stars. Manning recalled losing his first start but recovering quickly, saying, "Oh, Lord, it's going to be a bad season for me. That damn army ... and so on. Then I won 15 straight."[26] Mackey – with his fellow future Hall of Famers Day, Doby, and Irvin back in the fold – led the Eagles on a season-long tear through the NNL. Newark finished 50-20-2 in league play, and 56-24-3 against all competition, as the team won both the first- and second-half NNL titles. Manning was the winning pitcher on September 4 as the Eagles clinched the second-half title with a 17-5 annihilation of the New York Cubans at Newark's Ruppert Stadium. Newark scored nine runs in the first inning, Doby rapped out five consecutive hits in the game, and Manning supported his own cause with a home run in the eighth inning.[27] In light of the Eagles' dominance all year, it was a fitting way to clinch a trip to that year's Negro League World Series in which they faced the NAL's Kansas City Monarchs.

Kansas City had posted a 43-14 record in NAL play and, like Newark, had won its league's pennant without a playoff series. The Monarchs had their own stable full of future Hall of Famers, including outfielder Willard Brown, pitcher Hilton Smith, and the immortal Satchel Paige. Thus, the World Series ended up being a tight affair that required the full seven games to determine which team would be the champion of the Negro Leagues in 1946.

The Monarchs prevailed, 2-1, in Game One at New York's Polo Grounds on September 17. Two days later, boxer Joe Louis threw out the first pitch prior to Game Two in which Manning took the mound at Ruppert Stadium and pitched a complete game, striking out eight, as Newark evened the series with a 7-4 victory. The teams split the next two games before Manning made his second start in Game Five at Comiskey Park in Chicago. Manning again went the distance and struck out seven Monarchs batters, but he lost a 5-1 decision as the Monarchs took a three-games-to-two lead in the series. The Eagles then came back to win Games Six and Seven, 9-7 and 3-2, at Ruppert Stadium to claim the title.[28]

World Series Game Seven was played on September 29 and Manning joined a new team the very next day. On the heels of his outstanding 1946 season, Paige had selected Manning as one of the pitchers for his Satchel Paige's All-Stars team that barnstormed across the United States against major-leaguer Bob Feller's All-Stars from September 30 to October 26. In one game at Dayton, Ohio, Manning struck out 14 major-league hitters but took a tough 2-1 loss when he surrendered a homer in the ninth inning.[29]

Manning followed up his stint with Paige's All-Stars by traveling to Cuba to play for the Cienfuegos Elefantes. His initial foray into Cuba was not as successful as his season with the Eagles had been as he posted a 4-8 record with 29 strikeouts in 86⅓ innings pitched.[30] Cienfuegos finished the season at 25-41, which put them in a third-place tie with Marianao, 17 games behind first-place Almendares.

The lack of overall success in Cuba during the 1946-47 winter season did not mean that there were no highlights for Manning. On December 22 he outdueled St. Louis Cardinals pitcher Max Lanier, who was making his first start for Almendares, by a 1-0 score. Manning earned the win when player-manager Martin Dihigo – another future Hall of Famer – hit a game-winning ninth-inning single. It was "the last hit Dihigo recorded on a Cuban ballfield."[31]

On January 23, 1947, Manning shut out Marianao, 10-0. The game was reminiscent of Newark's second-half pennant clincher against the New York Cubans as Cienfuegos likewise scored nine runs in the first inning, allowing Manning to cruise through the game.[32] A month later, on February 18, Manning found himself in another pitchers' duel, this time against Cuban legend Agapito Mayor and the Almendares club. By all accounts, "Manning pitched superbly for Dihigo, giving up only two runs, but Almendares was hot and Mayor unbeatable."[33] The game ended as a 2-0 whitewash by Mayor.

Later in life, Manning rightfully summed up his 1946 season, saying that it "was probably my best year in baseball, in terms of things that I did and accomplishments that I managed to do."[34] From Newark to Paige's All-Stars and on to Cuba, Manning observed, "Everything happened that year" and laughingly asserted, "It was a good money year."[35]

When the 1947 season rolled around, Manning decided that he wanted to have a "good money year" with Newark as well and, for the second time, held out for higher pay. Once again, he sent his unsigned contract back to Effa Manley along with his salary demand. Manning was still holding out as spring training began, so Manley again acquiesced. As Manning recollected, "Finally, we made an agreement for $600 a month, almost double what I was getting before."[36]

Since Manning signed in time for the season's start, he was on hand for Opening Day at Ruppert Stadium on May 11. Prior to the game, the NNL president, Rev. John H. Johnson, presented watches to Irvin for winning the 1946 batting title and to Manning for having the best pitching record. Manning picked up where he had left off and began to earn his higher salary by pitching a five-hitter as Newark defeated the Philadelphia Stars, 10-2, in the first game of a doubleheader. Lennie Pearson and Doby both homered in support of Manning.[37] Doby soon was sold to the Cleveland Indians and integrated the American League that season. The Eagles also captured the nightcap, 4-0, and were off and running again.

The highlight of Manning's year – and no doubt a major reason that he desired higher pay – took place off the field: it was his marriage to Dorothy Winder, the daughter of James and Lucy (Boyd) Winder of Pleasantville, New Jersey. Manning told the story of how he won over his bride:

> I met her father first, he was a postman. ... I was always over at his house and Dorothy was always in the kitchen cleaning up. ... I went into the kitchen to talk to her. She didn't like me, but after 2 or 3 times I convinced her to go with me to a movie. We dated, her parents approved, and we were married in 1947.[38]

The couple remained married for 55 years, until Dorothy's death on December 29, 2002. They had four children, Max Jr., Belinda, Boyd Martin, and Joan.

On the field, Manning was earning every penny as he compiled a 12-5 record with 80 strikeouts and a 2.99 ERA in 132⅓ innings. He was impossible to overlook anymore and was selected to participate in his first East-West All-Star game. Two East-West games were played in 1947, but Manning played in only the first one, the annual showcase game at Chicago's Comiskey Park. In addition to 48,112 fans, several major-league scouts were present at the game on July 27. Unfortunately for Manning, who started the game for the East, this was one of his worst outings as he "gave up five hits in (2⅔) innings which were productive for the West in the sum of four runs which were enough to win the game."[39]

As for the Eagles, with Manning's 12 wins leading the staff, they finished 50-38-1 in the NNL, which left them in second place, six games behind the New York Cubans. Although there was no World Series for Manning this season, he did receive a compelling offer from the Cubans' owner, Alex Pompez, who was helping white teams to procure Negro League talent now that Jackie Robinson and Doby had begun the integration of the major leagues.[40]

Pompez asked Manning if he would like to play for the New York Giants. Manning recalled that, in the spring, "I had just had a big-time argument with (Effa Manley) about salary and I held out."[41] Although Manning and Effa Manley never got along well, he was an honorable man and – especially since Manley had granted his salary request and he was still under contract – he said that Pompez needed to negotiate with Manley. Pompez was taken aback and refused to do so. When Pompez asked Manning whether or not he wanted to play in the major leagues, Manning responded, "More than you could ever know, but if you don't have honor, what do you have?"[42] While most Negro League players freely jumped from one team to another and had no qualms about leaving the Negro Leagues for Organized Baseball, Manning was more than content to forgo his best opportunity to make the major leagues in order to keep his integrity intact.

With his conscience clear, Manning returned to Cienfuegos, Cuba, for the 1947-48 winter league season. While his team finished in third place again with a 35-37 record, Manning's second go-around in Cuba was much more successful individually. With a 10-8 record, he led the pitching staff in wins and had 69 strikeouts and a 3.13 ERA in 172⅓ innings.[43]

Manning attributed some of his success to a new pitch he learned from Carl Erskine, the soon-to-be Brooklyn Dodgers star. Manning always had trouble with one particular batter whom Erskine retired easily, so he asked, "What do you throw this guy to get him out? He told me it was a straight change and he showed me how to throw it. I picked it up real quick and I began to use it right away." Manning used his entire repertoire to great effect as he outdueled fellow Negro Leaguer Dave Barnhill of Marianao, 1-0 on October 24 and posted another shutout in a 2-0 triumph over Almendares on February 7.[44] Many players competed year-around, but all of this work soon contributed to the decline of Manning's career.

Manning admitted to being overconfident that he was already in shape during spring training in 1948 because he had played winter-league ball. Manager Biz Mackey wanted to bring Manning along slowly, but when Len Hooker was knocked out of a start after only one inning, Manning pitched the remainder of the game. He later confessed, "And I wasn't in condition and something went wrong."[45] Manning had a consultation with Dr. John Moore at Temple University Hospital who diagnosed a shoulder separation and told him there was nothing he could do other than to lift weights to try to thicken his muscles.[46] Weightlifting did not help much, so Manning had to alter his pitching style completely. As he put it, "I learned how to spot pitch – throw slow, slower, and then slower – and I managed to win ballgames."[47]

For the time being, the "new" Manning pitched as well as, or better than, the previous power pitcher had. He finished the season with a 10-4 record, 75 strikeouts, and a sparkling 1.62 ERA in 116⅓ innings pitched. His performance was rewarded with another selection to the East All-Star team. This time, Manning started the second East-West game, which was played before 17,928 fans at Yankee Stadium on August 24. He pitched three solid innings, allowing only one run and striking out two batters, as the East team claimed a 6-1 victory.[48]

Newark finished 29-28-1 in the NNL, which was only good enough for third place. The Homestead Grays won the last NNL pennant and the last Negro League World Series as the NNL disbanded at the end of the year. The continued influx of black players into the minor and major leagues had led to a dramatic decline in attendance at Negro League games that caused extreme financial hardships for team owners. Rather than simply disband the Eagles team, the Manleys sold the franchise to Dr. W.H. Young – a native Texan who had become a prominent Memphis dentist – and his business partner, Hugh Cherry. Young decided that they would move the team to Houston, Texas, for the 1949 season.

Manning looked back fondly on his time with the Manley-owned Eagles in Newark. He had developed a great relationship with Abe Manley, whom he and all the players called Cap [short for Captain]. Manning declared, "I had a lot of feeling for him. ... And he responded, too. He'd tell me things more than the other guys. ... His riding with the team [and] participating in the male companionship were the big part of getting to know him."[49] As for Effa Manley, Manning conceded, "Regardless of how you felt about her, you had to admire her abilities, what she was able to do. ... As I look back, I appreciate her more and more."[50] All of baseball eventually came to appreciate Effa Manley and, in 2006 she became the first – and as of 2019 the only – woman to be inducted into the Hall of Fame.

As the NNL was coming apart and the Eagles were being sold, Manning continued to pitch for Cienfuegos in the winter. In spite of the success he had managed to have with Newark, the toll that his shoulder injury was taking on him now began to show. He struggled to a 5-12 record and had a 4.24 ERA in 129⅓ innings; most tellingly, he struck out only 42 batters while walking 73 and his 12 losses were the most in the Cuban League that season.[51] One of his losses was a tough 1-0 game against Havana on December 5. Former Eagles teammate Rufus Lewis pitched a four-hitter for Havana while Lennie Pearson scored the winning run on a fly ball in the eighth inning.[52]

As spring training approached in 1949, Manning again held out for more money. Since he knew that his arm would not last much longer, it is likely that he wanted to maximize whatever earnings he had left in baseball. Although much of the Eagles' roster remained the same, some stars – most notably Leon Day and Ray Dandridge – had no interest in playing their home games in Texas and did not sign with the team. Young, the new owner, had hoped that the team would become financially viable again in Houston, which had an African-American population of over 80,000.[53] The Eagles were now part of the NAL's Western Division and played their home games at Buffalo Stadium – the home of the Texas League's Houston Buffaloes – when it was available. In order to keep expenses down, the NAL decided to play games only on weekends, and the Eagles played only at night in the hope that more fans would be able to attend.[54]

Nothing worked. The Houston fans had no idea who the Eagles players were – other than local hero Andrew "Pat" Patterson – and thus developed no rooting interest in the team. A spring-training article had reported, "Manager Ruben Jones ... stated that the Eagles will be one of the teams to beat for the championship," but that turned out not to be the case as the team finished in last place in both halves of the season.[55] The team was so wretched that Jones resigned after the first half, "citing old age," and was replaced by Red Parnell.[56] No doubt the Eagles' performance had aged Jones considerably in just a few months.

Manning did everything he could do, sore shoulder and all, once he joined the team in late May. In early August it was reported that he had a 5-2 record while second baseman Johnny Washington was among the NAL leaders with a .366 batting average; they were the lone bright spots on the team.[57] On August 11 he defeated the Monarchs, 7-4, in Omaha, Nebraska, retiring 16 consecutive batters at one point.[58] In perhaps his best performance of the season, he defeated the NAL Eastern Division's first-half champions, the Baltimore Elite Giants, by a 5-1 score at Baltimore's Bugle Field; his mound opponent that day was future Brooklyn Dodger Joe Black.[59] Complete statistics for the 1949 season are unavailable, but it is clear that Manning managed to thrive where others did not.

As his career started to wind down, Manning spent one last winter in Cuba, though he now played for the Havana Leones. His pitching line was better than in the previous year as he finished 8-5 with a 3.38 ERA in 130⅔ innings; however, he still struggled with control as a spot pitcher as was evidenced by the fact that his walks again outpaced his strikeouts, 53 to 27. Although he was with a different team, it finished in a familiar place – tied for third with Marianao, three games behind first-place Almendares.[60]

Manning had even fonder memories of the winters he spent in Cuba than he did of his seasons in Newark. The primary reason for his love of Cuba and other Latin American countries was the same as it was for most black players, namely that they were treated far better there than in their home country. Manning emphatically declared:

> I'm saying in terms of being somebody, when you went to Latin America, you were somebody and you were treated as somebody and the newspapers treated you as some-

body, and the people treated you as somebody. You had the best accommodations of all. ... It was just a marvelous experience and everywhere I went in Latin America it was the same thing.[61]

All of these circumstances stood in stark contrast to the racism and segregation that black players encountered in the United States.

When Manning returned from Cuba, he did not re-sign with the Houston Eagles for the 1950 season. Instead he pitched for Maracaibo in Venezuela's summer league. Manning said he was paid $1,000 per month plus expenses and that ex-Eagles Johnny Davis and Len Hooker played on the Maracaibo team as well.[62] The Maracaibo-based summer league did not receive the same level of fan support or press coverage as Venezuela's Caracas-based winter league and no statistics from the 1950 season are available. One certainty is that Manning's shoulder injury was getting worse. He said, "I remember going back to the hotel in Maracaibo after the game, putting hot towels, alcohol, wintergreen on my arm, trying to think what else I can use."[63]

In 1951 Manning became something of a baseball vagabond. He began the season with the Mexican League's Jalisco Charros, with whom he had limited success. In April he earned his first victory in Mexico, a 5-3 decision against Nuevo Laredo that completed a three-game series sweep.[64] Then, in late May, he defeated Torreon, 3-2, shortly before he left Mexico.[65] Manning finished his brief stint with Jalisco with a 2-4 record, 23 strikeouts and a 3.02 ERA in 59⅔ innings pitched.[66]

Manning's reason for leaving Jalisco in midseason was that he had one last shot at the major leagues, though he knew that his shoulder was too far gone for him to make it. The Philadelphia Athletics had offered him a tryout "by virtue of contact through Claude Larned, a scout in the St. Louis Cardinals organization."[67] The A's liked Manning, but all he ended up doing for the team was participating in exercises to try to get into better shape.

While he was in limbo in the Philadelphia Athletics organization, Manning's wife called to inform him of an offer to play in Canada. The Sherbrooke Athletics of the Class-C Quebec Provincial League offered Manning a two-month salary advance of $1,200 to play for them.[68] Manning honored his two-month commitment to Sherbrooke and then joined the Brantford Red Sox of Canada's Inter County League for the remainder of the season.[69] He continued to pitch in spite of the fact that he experienced constant shoulder pain. Just as he had resorted to various remedies while in Venezuela, Manning said of his time in Canada, "I can remember sitting on the bench up there in Sherbrooke and at that time they didn't have Tylenol and Excedrin and all these pain relievers. The only thing they had at that time was aspirin. I remember sitting on that bench, inning after inning, popping

aspirin, trying to reduce the pain."[70] Manning confessed that he put himself through such agony because "I didn't know how to do anything else but play ball."[71]

Manning soon sought to remedy that fact that all he knew was baseball. Once he returned home at the end of the 1951 season, he enrolled in the New Jersey State Teachers College at Glassboro with an eye toward finally finishing the studies that he had begun at Lincoln University 14 years earlier. Baseball was still in his blood, however, and he continued to pitch occasionally during the next few summers.

In August of 1952, Manning was in the Dominican Republic and ended up taking part in a game that devolved into chaos. *The Sporting News* reported that Luis Olmo, who had played for the Brooklyn Dodgers and Boston Braves, took umbrage when Cuban pitcher Wilfredo Salas sailed a pitch too close to his head. Olmo's reaction stemmed from the fact that a Salas beanball had put him in a hospital for a month when both players were in the Mexican League. On this occasion, Olmo went after Salas with a bat. According to the game report, "Marines, policemen, umpires, and players from both teams swarmed onto the diamond. When peace was restored, Olmo was hustled off to the local bastile [*sic*] by the gendarmes."[72] The game resumed and when Salas came to bat, he homered, "the wallop coming off the North American pitcher, Max Manning" who "eventually lost 8 to 1."[73] There are no further accounts of Manning in action in the Caribbean in 1952, and it is doubtful that he was there for long.

In similar fashion, Manning returned to Mexico in the summer of 1953 to play for Torreon. Whether he was simply trying to earn extra income in the summer the easiest way he knew how, or simply could not get baseball out of his system yet, Manning endured the shoulder pain and pitched on. In his limited time with Torreon he went 3-5 with 49 strikeouts and a 4.27 ERA in 71⅔ innings.[74] Manning related that his wife had tired of his baseball travels and wanted him to finish his education before the GI Bill of Rights benefits he had earned were set to expire. She may have been worried that her husband would succumb to the baseball bug full-time again before finishing his degree. Manning explained, "My wife wrote me and said, 'Look, fella, I don't want you to be a baseball bum.'"[75] Her missive had its intended effect as Manning told Torreon's management "I gotta go" and returned stateside to complete his education.[76]

Perhaps because Canada was a lot closer to home than Mexico, Manning did have one last stint with Brantford in the summer of 1954. He helped the Red Sox during the Inter County League's pennant race and on August 13 pitched a four-hit shutout against the Guelph-Waterloo Royals in the first game of a doubleheader; the Red Sox also won the nightcap and moved into first place.[77]

After this final hurrah, Manning finished his studies and graduated from Glassboro in the spring of 1955. During his time at the institution, he had played on the school's baseball and basketball teams – his professional baseball activities did not make him ineligible at that time – and he was inducted into the school's athletic Hall of Fame in 1986. The institution, now named Rowan University, noted that Manning "played for the baseball team from 1952-55, starting as a 33-year old freshman" while acknowledging that he "was a pitcher for the Newark Eagles in the Negro Leagues."[78] Given Manning's "Profesor" nickname, it was perfectly fitting that Glassboro's athletic teams were named the Profs.

After earning his degree, Manning taught sixth grade for 28 years in his hometown of Pleasantville, New Jersey, before he finally retired in 1983. Although he no longer worked at his profession, Manning was by no means inactive in retirement. In fact, a recap of his activities shows that he may have been busier than ever:

> Max Manning was a role model for children and a baseball mentor to many youngsters in the Pleasantville area. He became involved in civil rights activities and enjoyed gardening and writing sports stories.
>
> He served as president of the Pop Lloyd Foundation in Atlantic City for many years and was instrumental in securing funds for the restoration of the stadium that was named after the famous Negro League player. Max Manning's hometown renamed the Pleasantville Park Avenue recreation field in his honor.
>
> A Max Manning scholarship was established by the Pop Lloyd Committee honoring his career in the Negro Leagues and his 28 years in education. ... The award was designed to be granted to a student pursuing a career in education.[79]

On August 20, 1999, Manning received another honor during "Turn Back the Clock Night" at Atlantic City's Sandcastle Stadium. A large sculpture that included 12 players was unveiled to commemorate the Negro Leagues. Among the 12, Manning saw "his image as he was about to uncork a fastball to an unfortunate batter."[80] In a similar gesture, a mural depicting six Newark Eagles players, including Manning, was painted on Newark's Riverfront Stadium as a lasting tribute.[81]

Max Manning died on June 23, 2003, in Pleasantville after a lengthy illness. While many people call to mind the lanky, bespectacled Dr. Cyclops who starred for many years with the Newark Eagles, his daughter Belinda reminded everyone that there was much more to her father, saying, "I want him remembered as someone who had strength of character, not only in baseball but also in what he taught in the classroom and what he brought to the community."[82]

ACKNOWLEDGMENT

Many thanks to James Overmyer for providing a transcription of the interview he conducted with Max Manning in 1990 while in the process of gathering research for his book, *Queen of the Negro Leagues: Effa Manley and the Newark Eagles*. It provided invaluable information for this article.

SOURCE

Unless otherwise indicated, all Negro League player statistics and team records provided were taken from the Seamheads.com website. It should be noted that Negro League statistics often vary from source to source. Some variations are due to the fact that certain sources include both league and exhibition games, while other sources include only official league games in their tallies. Additionally, some sources do not include games for which only line scores – rather than full box scores – are available since appearances, starts, wins, and losses are the only statistics to be gleaned from them.

NOTES

1   Brent Kelley, *Voices From the Negro Leagues: Conversations With 52 Baseball Standouts* (Jefferson, North Carolina: McFarland & Company, 1998), 67.

2   James Overmyer, interview with Max Manning, August 23, 1990, Pleasantville, New Jersey.

3   Jorge S. Figueredo, *Who's Who in Cuban Baseball, 1878-1961* (Jefferson, North Carolina: McFarland & Company, 2003), 391.

4   U.S. Colored Troops Military Service Records, 1863-1865, ancestry.com, accessed January 5, 2019.

5   C. Maxwell Manning, "Negroes and Liberia: Why They Return," *Columbus* (Georgia) *Ledger*, September 6, 1903: 6.

6   Kelley, 68-69.

7   *Lynching in America: Confronting the Legacy of Racial Terror, Supplement: Lynchings by County, 2nd Edition*, eji.org/sites/default/files/lynching-in-america-second-edition-supplement-by-county.pdf.

8   Joseph DeLuca, "Max Manning – South Jersey's Pitching Ace," 1991, from the Max Manning file, National Baseball Hall of Fame, Cooperstown, New York.

9   Kelley, 69.

10   Ibid.

11   Overmyer interview.

12   Kelley, 67.

13   Overmyer Interview. Manning said that he started with the Eagles in 1938, which was the year that he signed with the Newark team; however, he did not pitch for them until the spring of 1939. Multiple sources list Manning with the Ponce team during the Puerto Rican winter league's inaugural 1938-39 season, but no statistics are available; for one such source, see William F. McNeil, *Black Baseball Out of Season* (Jefferson, North Carolina: McFarland & Company, 2007), 215.

14   Kelley, 70.

15   Overmyer interview.

16   There is a lack of documentation about this stint in the Dominican Republic, and it is possible that Manning once again played for Ponce in Puerto Rico rather than in the D.R., especially since the Manleys were known to send Newark personnel to play in Puerto Rico in the winter. Ships' passenger lists show only that Manning arrived in San Juan, Puerto Rico, on October 30, 1940, though he certainly could have traveled to the Dominican Republic from San Juan. All that can truly be ascertained at this time is that Manning did play winter-league ball again during this year.

17   Overmyer interview.

18   James Overmyer, *Queen of the Negro Leagues: Effa Manley and the Newark Eagles* (Lanham, Maryland: Scarecrow Press, 1998), 94-95.

19   Overmyer interview.

20   "Baseball Star Coaching Army Basketball," *Los Angeles Tribune*, February 14, 1944: 8.

21   DeLuca.

22   Brett Kiser, *Baseball's War Roster: A Biographical Dictionary of Major and Negro League Players Who Served, 1861 to the Present* (Jefferson, North Carolina: McFarland & Company, 2012), 152.

23   DeLuca.

24   Monte Irvin with James A. Riley, *Nice Guys Finish First: The Autobiography of Monte Irvin* (New York: Carroll & Graf Publishers, 1996), 97.

25   "Newark Eagles to Meet Stars," *Wilmington* (Delaware) *Morning News*, May 6, 1946: 15.

26   Kelley, 71. Manning may have won 15 games that year, although most sources list fewer wins. John B. Holway's *The Complete Book of Baseball's Negro Leagues: The Other Half of Baseball History* (Fern Park, Florida: Hastings House Publishers, 2001), 436, credits Manning with 13 wins that season while Seamheads.com shows Manning with an 11-3 record, 78 strikeouts, and a 3.06 ERA in 126⅔ innings pitched. See Source note for the reason for such discrepancies.

27   "Eagles Win, Take Flag," *Newark Star-Ledger*, September 5, 1946: 15.

28   The brief summaries of the World Series presented here were culled from Richard Puerzer's comprehensive account of the Series that appears in the present volume and from Kyle McNary, *Black Baseball: A History of African-Americans & the National Game* (New York: Sterling Publishing Company, 2003), 120-24.

29   Alfred M. Martin and Alfred T. Martin, *The Negro Leagues in New Jersey: A History* (Jefferson, North Carolina: McFarland & Company, 2008), 53.

30   Jorge S. Figueredo, *Cuban Baseball: A Statistical History, 1878-1961* (Jefferson, North Carolina: McFarland & Company, 2003), 281.

31   Lou Hernández, *The Rise of the Latin American Baseball Leagues, 1947-1961* (Jefferson, North Carolina: McFarland & Company, 2011), 96.

32   "Cubans Cheer Dolf and Mike in Battery Act Before Benefit," *The Sporting News*, February 5, 1947: 10.

33   Roberto González Echevarría, *The Pride of Havana: A History of Cuban Baseball* (New York: Oxford University Press, 1999), 37.

34   Kelley, 71.

35   Ibid.

36   Overmyer interview.

37   Bob Luke, *The Most Famous Woman in Baseball: Effa Manley and the Negro Leagues* (Lincoln: University of Nebraska Press, 2011), 135.

38   DeLuca.

39   Dan Burley, "Confidentially Yours: East-West Classic Replay," *New York Amsterdam News*, August 2, 1947: 10.

40   There are discrepancies among numerous sources as to whether this event occurred toward the end of the season in 1946, 1947, or 1948. The year 1946 is too soon for two reasons. The first is that even Jackie Robinson had not yet made it to the major leagues, so no offer to go directly to the Giants would have been forthcoming. The second reason is that Manning was not yet under contract for 1947; thus, if the offer had been made at that time, he would have felt no obligation to the Manleys and likely would have signed with the Giants. Manning's allusion to his holdout in the spring of 1947 and the higher salary it brought him also shows why he felt such an obligation to honor his contract with the Eagles at that time and make it clear that Pompez's offer came toward the end of the 1947 season. Additionally, the 1948 season is too late a date because the shoulder injury that Manning suffered early that year would have labeled him as "damaged goods" and it is unlikely that he would have received an offer to go to the majors at that point. According to DeLuca, when the Philadelphia Athletics contacted Manning in 1951, his integrity came to the fore again as he "tried to tell them that his arm was shot." It is most likely that he would have told the Giants the same thing if they had contacted him at the end of 1948.

41   Kelley, 72.

42   Martin and Martin, 55.

43   Figueredo, *Cuban Baseball: A Statistical History, 1878-1961*, 296.

44   Rene Canizares, "Player Battle May Force Cuban Loops Into Court," *The Sporting News*, November 5, 1947: 19; Pedro Galiana, "Gonzalez' Club in Spirited Bid for Cuban Flag," *The Sporting News*, February 18, 1948: 20.

45   Kelley, 72.

46   Overmyer interview.

47   Kelley, 72.

48   Larry Lester, *Black Baseball's National Showcase: The East-West All-Star Game, 1933-1953* (Lincoln: University of Nebraska Press, 2001), 321-22.

49   Overmyer interview.

50   Ibid.

51   Figueredo, *Cuban Baseball: A Statistical History, 1878-1961*, 312.

52   Pedro Galiana, "Gonzalez' Reds Creep Close to Almendares in Upsurge," *The Sporting News*, December 15, 1948: 23.

53   Rob Fink, *Playing in Shadows: Texas and Negro League Baseball* (Lubbock: Texas Tech University Press, 2010), 112.

54   Ibid.

55   "Pilot Jones Drills New Eagle Nine," *Pittsburgh Courier*, March 26, 1949: 29.

56   Fink, 115.

57   "A Pair With Houston: Eagles Meet Monarchs This Afternoon at Blues Stadium," *Kansas City Star*, August 7, 1949: 98.

58   "Monarchs Lose, 7-4," *Omaha World-Herald*, August 12, 1949: 29.

59   "Houston Eagles Trim Elite Giants by 5-1," *Baltimore Sun*, August 17, 1949: 16.

60   Figueredo, *Cuban Baseball: A Statistical History, 1878-1961*, 323, 329.

61   Kelley, 71.

62   Overmyer interview.

63   Ibid.

64   Jorge Alarcon, "Ramirez' Nifty Pitching Helps Jalisco Climb," *The Sporting News*, May 2, 1951: 22.

65   Jorge Alarcon, "Gonzalez' Bat in Spotlight for San Luis," *The Sporting News*, June 13, 1951: 34.

66   Pedro Treto Cisneros, *The Mexican League: Comprehensive Player Statistics, 1937-2001* (Jefferson, North Carolina: McFarland & Company, 2002), 386.

67   DeLuca.

68   Ibid.

69   Barry Swanton and Jay-Dell Mah, *Black Baseball Players in Canada: A Biographical Dictionary, 1881-1960* (Jefferson, North Carolina: McFarland and Company, 2009), 109.

70   Kelley, 72.

71   Ibid.

72   Alejandro Martinez, "Olmo Jugged in Dominican Diamond Row," *The Sporting News*, August 4, 1952: 32.

73   Ibid.

74   Cisneros, 386.

75   Kelley, 72.

76   Ibid.

77   Jay-Dell Mah, "1954 Ontario Game Reports," Western Canada Baseball, attheplate.com/wcbl/1954_90i.html, accessed January 8, 2019.

78   "Max Manning – Class of 1955 – Rowan University-Glassboro State College Hall of Fame," rowanathletics.com/hof.aspx?hof=8&path=&kiosk=, accessed January, 9, 2019.

79   Martin and Martin, 55.

80   Martin and Martin, 154.

81   Martin and Martin, 177.

82   "Negro League Star Manning Dead at 84," from the Max Manning file, National Baseball Hall of Fame, Cooperstown, New York.

CHARLES PARKS

BY JAY HURD

Catcher Charles Parks (at left) and pitcher Leon Day celebrate the ace hurler's Opening Day no-hitter against the Philadelphia Stars at Newark's Ruppert Stadium on May 5, 1946. *(Noir-Tech Research, Inc.)*

World War II ended when the Axis powers surrendered to the Allied powers in 1945. Men and women of the U.S. Armed Forces returned to an America deeply affected by years of war, and they sought to resume a simple, more pedestrian way of life. They looked to an America which embraced enterprise and entertainment, and which boasted a national pastime – baseball. While the game had retained its role as a diversion during the war, revitalization commenced with the return of players to the white

major leagues and the Negro Leagues. Alongside the many stars who picked up their careers again were lesser-known players such as Charlie Parks of the Newark Eagles.

Charles "Charlie" Ederson Parks was born on June 19, 1917 in Chester, South Carolina, approximately 60 miles north of Columbia.[1] He was the oldest of four children born to Sanders and Maggie [Woods] Parks, which included two brothers, George and Isiah, and one sister, Sadie Bell. Sanders' World War I draft registration card indicates his trade as farming, and his employer as Mr. Lee Carter.[2] Maggie, born in Chester, was one of eight children. By 1920, her name does not appear as a member of the family in that year's federal census; the exact year she married Sanders is not clear, but she did work as a homemaker.[3]

Chester, a one-time booming cotton and textile region, alternated between economic prosperity and desperate poverty. As the nation entered into the Great Depression, around 1929 when Charles was 12, the Parks family moved to Charlotte, North Carolina area 50 miles northeast of Chester where jobs were more plentiful. While other cities experienced little economic development at this time, Charlotte, as a railway system hub, presented employment opportunities and saw a 22% increase in population between 1930 and 1940.[4] Sanders found work as a laborer for the railroad system, and Charles and his siblings were raised there. They attended the Morgan School in the Cherry Neighborhood, Grier Heights/Griertown, of Charlotte. Grier Heights, named for well-respected funeral home director Arthur Samuel Grier, had been formed as a farm community in 1886 by former slaves.[5]

Neither the origins of Parks' involvement in baseball nor the beginnings of his professional career are known. He most likely played ball as a child in South Carolina and later as a young adult in one or more of North Carolina's baseball-rich communities:

"Years before the establishment of national baseball leagues for black competitors in the 1920s, African American men were playing baseball all over North Carolina, from Wilmington to Asheville. Black-owned ball clubs played at a high level, supported by a growing black business class…Baseball teams offered a means of extra income for players as young as 14. Many North Carolina boys left school around that age to work in fields and help support their families. Those who played well might earn the attention of bigger teams. In addition, teams such as the Negro National League's Newark Eagles and Schenectady Mohawk Giants spent spring training in North Carolina in the late 1930s and early 1940s. Their owners could scout the rosters of North Carolina semipro opponents and take the best players back north with them."[6]

It is possible he encountered or even played with men such as Tom Alston, Charlie Neal, and Buck Leonard and, by the age of 21, it must have been clear that Parks had a true talent for the game. He began a professional career in the Negro National League with the New York Black Yankees in 1938, who had Walter Cannady, a third baseman, as player-manager. Parks played in one game, had one plate appearance, and no hits; his name appears on the roster as a relief pitcher. He returned to the New York Black Yankees in 1939; however, this time, his position was designated as catcher. He appeared in two games, had eight plate appearances, and garnered one hit. His manager at this time was George Scales, who also played third base.

Entering the 1940 season, Parks played for the Baltimore Elite Giants. He shared catching duties with two other catchers, including Roy Campanella, who played the majority of the games. Parks and catcher Ziggy Marcell each appeared in one game, each had three plate appearances, and each had one hit while working under yet another player-manager/third baseman, Felton Snow. Parks did not stay with the Elite Giants the entire season as the next and most significant step in his career took him to the Newark Eagles. There he joined a star-studded cast that included Monte Irvin, Max Manning, Mule Suttles, and catcher Biz Mackey, who assumed the role as player-manager toward the end of the season, replacing manager Dick Lundy. This was certainly good fortune for Parks as he became Mackey's "understudy."[7] As the season progressed, it was reported that Biz Mackey "has been doing most of the catching for the Eagles this season, sharing the assignment with Charley Parks."[8] In 1940, Parks, who was then 23 years old, appeared in 14 games and had a .154 batting average in 30 plate appearances with the Eagles. Later that year, on October 16, he

registered for the military draft as the United States' entry into World War II seemed imminent.[9]

Prior to the start of the 1941 season, Parks and his siblings lost their mother, Maggie, at 40 years of age to ovarian cancer on January 15.[10] Nonetheless, he returned to Newark, where Biz Mackey, now 43 and still the player-manager, began to reduce his own playing time. Thus, Parks had more opportunity behind the plate; he appeared in 24 games, had 77 at-bats, and compiled a .246 batting average. He also earned recognition by exhibiting his throwing skill at the "John Borican Day" festivities at Newark's Ruppert Stadium on August 31, 1941; Borican was a "black track star from nearby Bridgeton, New Jersey who held six world records."[11] "Leon Day copped honors in the 100 yard dash… while Monte Irvin took honors in the outfielders' throwing test and Charlie Parks was adjudged winner of the catchers' accuracy contest throwing to second base."[12]

The 1942 season with the Eagles proved to be Parks' best as he caught in 41 games and hit .278 in 143 plate appearances. However, U.S. involvement in World War II had intensified, and Parks was called to military service on October 29, 1942. His tour of duty included training at Ft. Bragg, North Carolina and then active duty in European Theater Operations (ETO). He may have played baseball while in the military, either at Ft. Bragg or even abroad in Europe. According to his obituary in the *Charlotte Observer* of September 19, 1987, "While in the Army, he earned the rank of sergeant. He received the Bronze Star for bravery when his commander was wounded in a battle. Mr. Parks took command and led his company over open ground in the face of enemy automatic fire, capturing a number of the enemy."[13] James A. Riley, in *The Biographical Encyclopedia of the Negro Baseball Leagues,* states that "he served three years in the Army, winning three Bronze Stars and being discharged with the rank of sergeant."[14]

Both of Parks' brothers registered for the draft. Isiah, who was seven years younger than Charlie and was unmarried at the time, served in the Army for three years. George, who was five years younger than Charlie and had a wife named Verlee, did not enter into military service.[15] Sadly, George and Verlee lost their infant daughter, Alicia Maye, in October 1942. Parks' sister, Sadie Bell, apparently remained with their father Sanders in Charlotte, North Carolina. Isiah, as did Charlie, reached the rank of sergeant in the U.S. Army, and was awarded the Bronze Star.[16]

Charlie Parks was discharged from the U.S. Army on February 4, 1946, in time for that year's Negro National League season. Also discharged in February 1946 was teammate Leon Day, a star pitcher. On Opening Day – May 6 – the battery of Day and Parks led the Eagles to a no-hit shutout of the Philadelphia Stars. It was the start of an amazing season in which the Eagles, with an overall record of 56-25-3, won the Negro League World Series. Parks, age 29, completed that regular season with a .247 batting average in 100 plate appearances over 32 games. The Eagles defeated the Kansas City Monarchs in a tightly-contested seven-game World Series. Parks' role was restricted to two games and one hitless plate appearance. He played first base while 34-year-old Leon Ruffin assumed the catching responsibilities in each of the seven games. In 1947, Parks, who had earned nicknames "John" and "Hunkie" while playing for Newark, "ended his career with the Eagles as he had started, by sharing the catching duties with Biz Mackey, while batting .287 in his final year."[17]

With 1948 came the end of Charlie's career in the Negro National League. Tragically, that same year, he experienced another loss as his younger brother George, a "prize fighter," died at the age of 26 due to a cerebral hemorrhage cause by malignant hypertension.[18] George left behind his wife Verlee, his father, and his two siblings.

At some point, perhaps prior to his time in the Negro National League, Parks had married Clister Walker. He and Clister, who was eight years older, had a daughter, Virginia. Parks also raised a stepson, John Jackson, who was presumably from his wife's previous marriage.[19]

After his career in the Negro National League was over, Parks returned to North Carolina where he maintained his connection to baseball as a player and manager. In July 1948 the *Greensboro Daily News* reported, "Goshen's Redwings launch the second half of their season in the Negro American Association at Memorial Stadium tonight…The Redwings are playing under a new manager, Catcher Charlie Parks, who was secured from the Newark Eagles."[20] Later that season, the *Asbury Park Press* noted, "The Red Wings, managed by Charlie Parks, former Newark Eagle catcher, finished in the first division during the first half of the Southern association race…Parks will do the catching and will bat sixth…" His .333 average is second only to "center fielder David Sims, who is clipping the ball at a .342 gait."[21] Parks' team travelled outside of North Carolina as well as the *Hartford Courant* wrote, "The Greensboro, NC Red Wings, members of the Negro Southern American Association, will make an appearance at Bulkeley Stadium today to face the Hartford Indians…[the Red Wings] boast three .300 hitters…Centerfielder, David Sims at .342, Rightfielder Joe Siddle at .315, and Manager-catcher Charles Parks at .333."[22]

Parks extended his career in baseball in 1949. At the outset of the season, the *Asheville Citizen-Times* remarked, "One of the outstanding additions of the [Asheville] Blue's roster his season is Charles "Hunkie" Parks. Parks caught for Greensboro last season and was considered the best catcher in the league…Parks, who caught for the Newark Eagles for three years, is an aggressive type of player and is expected to add much to the offensive of the Blues

this season."[23] Shortly thereafter, the same newspaper noted that "Charles Parks, team captain will be in charge of the Blues until Manager [Robert] Bowman reports."[24]

Whether or not Parks participated in baseball on any level for his remaining years is not clear. However, by 1953, he had shifted from the baseball field to work as a machine operator for the Ray Construction Company in Charlotte, North Carolina. He remained in that company's employ for 20 years, until he retired in 1980. In 1955, he returned, with his wife, Clister, to the Griertown community, where the couple lived until his death on September 13, 1987, at the age of 70. Parks passed away at the Veterans Administration Medical Center in Salisbury, North Carolina. Clister said that he "was very well-liked in the community… [and] was a very loving hard-working person."[25] After a funeral service at the Little Rock African Methodist Episcopal (AME) Zion Church in Charlotte, Charles was interred at the Beatties Ford Memorial Garden Cemetery in Huntersville, which is part of the greater Charlotte metropolitan area. In addition to his wife, he was survived by "his daughter Virginia Gaston; his brother Issac [Isiah] Parks; sister, Mrs. Sadie Holley of Baltimore; foster son, John Jackson; one grandson; five great-grandchildren; and one great-great grandchild." Clister remained active in the Little Rock AME Zion Church and died 13 years later, at the age of 91, on February 1, 2001; she also was interred at the Beatties Ford Memorial Garden Cemetery.

In a career shortened by two years due to military service, Parks appeared in 117 games and compiled a .257 batting average. In addition to his NNL career with Newark, in 1943 he joined the NNL All Stars, one of four teams which made up the "Independent Clubs." Other teams included the Atlanta Black Crackers, the South All Stars, and the North All Stars. Parks shared catching duties with Bill "Ready" Cash, on this team managed by Goose Curry; in a series of three games, he appeared in one game and had two hits. Parks' obituary in the *Charlotte Observer* summed up his career by noting that he was "a catcher for the Newark Eagles in the Old Negro Baseball League," was "known for his strong throwing arm and powerful bat," and that he had "played with some of the greats who went on to break the color barrier in major-league baseball."[26]

SOURCES

For Negro League statistics, the author largely relied on the Seamheads database at www.seamheads.com.

NOTES

1   Parks' middle name also appears as Edison; however, his World War II draft card signature indicates Edison. Charles was also known as Charlie or Charley.

2   Sanders' name also appears as Saunders. Isiah Parks' name also appears as Isiah and Isaac. "U.S., World War I Draft Registration Cards, 1917-1918 for Sanders Parks. Ancestry. com. https://www.ancestry.com/interactive/6482/005152293_05332?pid=2415132 2&backurl=https://search.ancestry.com/cgi-bin/sse.dll?indiv%3D1%26dbid%3D64 82%26h%3D24151322%26tid%3D%26pid%3D%26usePUB%3Dtrue%26_phs-rc%3DROA234%26_phstart%3DsuccessSource&treeid=&personid=&hintid=&use-PUB=true&_phsrc=ROA234&_phstart=successSource&usePUBJs=true.

3   "George Woods in the 1920 United States Federal Census, Ancestry.com, https://search. ancestry.com/cgi-bin/sse.dll?indiv=1&dbid=6061&h=42988772&tid=&pid=&use-PUB=true&_phsrc=ROA253&_phstart=successSource.

4   Dr. Thomas W. Hanchett, "The Growth of Charlotte: A History." http://www.cmhpf. org/educhargrowth.htm.

5   http://www.charlotteobserver.com/news/special-reports/myers-park/article9087020. html.

6   Bijan C. Bayne, "Early Black Baseball in North Carolina," *Tar Heel Junior Historian*, 51:1 (fall 2011), https://www.nclor.org/nclorprod/file/edbef9bd-2dea-457d-8daf-25eb-1cfdc616/1/f11_black_baseball.pdf

7   Alfred M. Martin and Alfred J. Martin, *The Negro Leagues in New Jersey: A History* (Jefferson, North Carolina: McFarland & Company, Publishers, 2008), 62.

8   "Mackey Pilots Newark Eagles Veteran Catcher Replaces Lundy-Club Meets the Braves Tonight," *Asbury Park Press*, August 16, 1940.

9   "U.S., World War II Army Enlistment Records, Charles Parks," Ancestry.com, https:// search.ancestry.com/cgi-bin/sse.dll?ti=0&indiv=try&db=wwiienlist&h=64115. His draft registration card lists address as 1047 Brown Street, Precinct 2, Ward 2, Charlotte, North Carolina. He is noted as 5-foot-9 ½ and 189 pounds (these numbers vary somewhat with one military record showing him at 5-foot-8 and 188 pounds.)

10   "North Carolina, Death Certificates 1909-1976, Maggie Parks," Ancestry.com, https:// search.ancestry.com/cgi-bin/sse.dll?indiv=1&dbid=1121&h=1247753&tid=&pid=&use-PUB=true&_phsrc=ROA102&_phstart=successSource.

11   Jim Overmyer, "Something to Cheer About: The Negro Leagues at the Dawn of Integration," *The Cooperstown Symposium on Baseball and American Culture*, 1997 (Jackie Robinson) (Jefferson, North Carolina: McFarland & Company, Inc., Publishers, 2000), 66.

12   "Day and Irvin Star at 'Borican Day' in Newark Doubleheader," *New York Age*, September 6, 1941.

13   "Charles Parks Played With Baseball Greats," *Charlotte Observer*, September 19, 1987.

14   James J. Riley, *The Biographical Encyclopedia of the Negro Baseball Leagues* (New York: Carroll & Graf Publishers, 1994), 604.

15   Verlee Parks' name also appears as Veblee.

16   "Battle Tested Hero Awards to Forty in 761st Tank Outfit," *Pittsburgh Courier*, July 7, 1945.

17   James J. Riley, 604.   Seamheads.com Negro Leagues Data Base http://www.seam-heads.com/NegroLgs/team.php?yearID=1947&teamID=NE&LGOrd=1

18   North Carolina, Death Certificates, 1909-1976 for George S. Parks.

19   Records to confirm this information are difficult to locate. All names, however, do appear in his obituary. "Charles Parks Played With Baseball Greats," *Charlotte Observer*, September 19, 1987.

20   "Redwings To Battle Jacksonville Tonight," *Greensboro Daily News*, July 7, 1948.

21   "Greensboro Nine Foe Of Pelicans Tonight," *Asbury Park Press*, July 20, 1948.

22   "Greensboro Team At Stadium Today," *Hartford Courant*, August 8, 1948.

23   "Blues Open Spring Slate Here Today," *Asheville Times-Citizen*, March 27, 1949.

24   "Blues, Red Wings Clash In Opener Here Tonight," *Asheville Times Citizen*, April, 5, 1949.

25   "Charles Parks Played With Baseball Greats," Obituary, *Charlotte Observer*, September 19, 1987.

26   "Charles Parks Played With Baseball Greats," *Charlotte Observer*, September 19, 1987.

Andrew "Pat" Patterson

BY BILL JOHNSON

Andrew Lawrence Patterson was born on December 19, 1911, in Chicago.[1] Both of his parents died while he was extremely young, so the duty of raising the boy fell to his maternal grandparents.[2] Pat, as he became known, discovered athletics early on and augmented his classroom education as a multisport athlete at integrated Washington High School in East Chicago, Indiana, just across the state line from Chicago. There he starred in football, baseball, and basketball, as well as on the track oval.

After high school Patterson could have attended New York University to play football and baseball on scholarship, but he instead selected Wiley College in Marshall, Texas, just west of Shreveport, Louisiana, where he received a baseball scholarship and played all four sports as well. Patterson's choice to move from the Chicago area to staunchly segregated East Texas was not as odd a decision as it seems. According to Negro League historian Donn Rogosin, Patterson attended Wiley College "because of the cheap tuition and the chance to play serious baseball there. ... Patterson's decision was an indication of baseball's general preeminence at the time."[3]

By 1933, the 21-year-old Patterson was a player without a team, as the Great Depression forced Wiley to cancel the entire baseball program in order to save money. In the pre-NCAA days of institutional self-governance, the school did permit players to moonlight as professionals during the summer before returning in the fall. Patterson finagled a tryout with the independent Homestead Grays. After the tryout, he returned to college and graduated with a degree in education.[4]

The next year, 1934, the switch-hitting Patterson earned a spot with the still-independent Grays, and also played part of the season with the Cleveland Red Sox of the Negro National League. The team posted a 4-25 record before folding. Patterson, however, proved his mettle and enjoyed fan vote selection as the sole Cleveland representative in the annual East-West All Star Game in Chicago. There, in one of the "best pitching duels in East-West All Star game history," a game in which the sole run came in the top of the eighth inning when Jud Wilson drove in Cool Papa Bell, Patterson went 0-for-1 for the losing West squad as a late-game replacement for Sammy Hughes.[5]

In 1935, without a team but now with a professional reputation, Patterson caught on with Gus Greenlee's Pittsburgh Crawfords. There, playing alongside future Hall of Famers Josh Gibson, Oscar Charleston, Cool Papa Bell, and Judy Johnson on perhaps the finest Negro League team ever assembled, Patterson held his own. In the championship series against the New York Cubans, he was 7-for-27 at the plate, but his series highlight came in Game Six. With Pittsburgh trailing three games to two and with the game tied, 6-6, in the bottom of the ninth inning, Patterson doubled off Martin Dihigo and then scored on Judy Johnson's hit to win the game. The next day the Crawfords came all the way back in the series and won the title.

In 1935 Patterson left Pittsburgh in order to take up the nomadic baseball life with J.L. Wilkinson's Kansas City Monarchs. The statistics for the barnstorming teams of the day are notoriously unreliable, even more than normal league numbers, yet it is generally held that Patterson was one of the best hitters in the entire Midwest. He earned his second East-West Game bid, representing Kansas City in the August 23 game, and went 2-for-3 with a double, driving in a run in the West's 10-2 loss.[6]

The Monarchs often played against local white teams while on the road and, although conflict was rare during these interracial games, Patterson was involved in an unfortunate incident that presaged what black players would encounter once the integration of Organized Baseball began. In her history of the Monarchs franchise, Janet Bruce describes the incident involving Patterson:

> On a barnstorming tour in Texas, infielder Pat Patterson went up in the grandstand and punched a man because of his constant name-calling. Wilkinson fined Patterson $50. "He was right for fining me," Patterson recalled. "He explained to me, 'That's our policy – you just don't bite the hand that feeds you. Those people are coming out here and see you play ball.'" And for barnstorming black teams, the paying customer could say what he pleased.[7]

Patterson returned briefly to Negro League play, and Pittsburgh, in 1937, but like many of his contemporaries, he fell under the spell of the money bandied about by the Dominican Republic's dictator Rafael Trujillo and spent most of the season playing for Águilas Cibaeñas. After the Dominican season, Patterson returned to Kansas City for another round of barnstorming and joined the Monarchs in time for an exhibition slate against a team that featured Bob Feller, Lon Warneke, Mace Brown, and Johnny Mize. Patterson went 3-for-10 in the series, but the Monarchs lost three of the four games.[8]

Perhaps aware that he needed a more reliable livelihood should baseball not work out, Patterson began working in the offseason as a teacher and athletic coach at Jack Yates High School in his new home city of Houston, Texas.[9] As gifted Patterson was as an athlete, he was an even more talented and dedicated educator, and with the exception of three years in military service during World War II, he lived his life as an example to others of the area of the possible, even in a segregated America.

One example of Patterson's impact on black students in segregated Texas was his role in helping to shape the Prairie View Interscholastic League into a black sports league that would provide an organizational counterpart to the white schools' University Interscholastic League. Patterson created the organizational plan for high-school football, which he coached, and Yates principal William S. Holland met with E.B. Evans, the president of Prairie View A&M University, in the spring of 1939 in order to decide how to implement the plan the following year (1940).[10] Although the days of segregation were in the past, Patterson was honored as

Pat Patterson's early life was that of a baseball star. Later, he became a legendary football coach at Houston's Yates High School, where he led his teams to a 200-69-4 record and four championships. *(Noir-Tech Research, Inc.)*

a member of the inaugural class of the Prairie View Interscholastic Coaches Hall of Fame in 1980.[11]

Patterson spent the 1938-39 baseball seasons in Pennsylvania, this time with the Philadelphia Stars. After a pedestrian 1938 season, he returned the East-West game in 1939. Two East-West games were played that season, and Patterson appeared in both. He started at third base in the first iteration, on August 6 at Comiskey Park, and had a hit and stole a base in four at-bats in a 4-2 loss. In the second game, played at Yankee Stadium on August 27, Patterson went 0-for-5 but drove in a run in a 10-2 East victory.[12]

Patterson's speed and ability to make contact at the plate, along with a touch of pop in his bat, were his most valuable baseball gifts, but he had intangibles as well. He "had good speed on the bases," was considered a solid fielder, and he always hustled. While he could play every position except pitcher or catcher, he will forever be considered one of the finest third basemen in the Negro Leagues in the late 1930s and the 1940s.[13]

At age 28, Patterson again left the United States, this time to play with manger Ernesto Carmona's Mexico City Diablos Rojos (Red Devils) in 1940 and 1941. He hit .341 with six home runs in 60 games in 1940, and improved to a .362 mark in 1941.[14] Patterson was part of a large contingent of Negro League players who spent the season south of the border, as stars like Cool Papa Bell, Josh Gibson, and Burniss Wright filled out Mexican rosters as well. During his time in Mexico, Patterson wed Gladys Inez Clowe, from Texas. He was such a popular player that Carmona "declared a team holiday and threw 'a lovely party,' according to Gladys Patterson. 'I'd never seen a roast pig before,' she confessed."[15] Their union produced twin sons, Andrew Jr. and Patrick, and thrived until Patterson's death in 1984.

With his bride on his arm, Patterson rejoined the Philadelphia Stars for the 1941 Negro League season, and was the team's regular third baseman. The following season, 1942, he was moved to second base and was again selected to represent the East in both East-West games that year. Over the two contests he walked twice, stole two bases, drove in a run and scored one.[16] Those proved to be the final East-West opportunities for Patterson. In six all-star games he posted four hits, including a double, drove in three runs, and stole four bases. That latter mark tied Patterson for the lead in stolen bases in East-West Games.[17]

With the nation at war, Patterson stepped away from baseball for three years. On December 5, 1942, he returned to Houston and enlisted in the Army Air Corps.[18] Although he had earned his degree at Wiley College, he started his military career at the lowest station in the hierarchy, that of private. His official position was Athletic Instructor[19] and he administered physical training at several bases in the United States. According to his family records, Patterson was awarded the American Theater Ribbon, the Good Conduct Medal, and the World War II Victory Medal.

After his release from active duty in 1945, Patterson returned to the classroom at Yates High School and mulled over the possibility of returning to the baseball diamond as well. Philadelphia still owed Patterson's contract, but there was ongoing friction between Patterson and the team's manager. Never one to miss an opportunity, Abe Manley traded for Patterson to take over third base on his Newark Eagles. "The only reason I can get Patterson," Manley told his wife, Effa, "is because he's not getting along with the manager. He's one of those outstanding players that Philly wouldn't think of giving up otherwise."[20] During the Eagles' 1946 championship season, Patterson helped fill out an infield that included Larry Doby and Monte Irvin. In the 1946 Negro League World Series, despite leaving before the Series concluded in order to return to his primary career as a high-school teacher and coach,[21] Patterson had six hits in 23 at-bats on the Eagles' march to the title.

Patterson turned 35 in 1947 and played for three teams: Newark, the New York Black Yankees, and the Homestead Grays. His successes in baseball were coming further apart, and the demands of his persona as teacher and role model for many of Houston's black teenagers were becoming more strident. Patterson finally chose to leave baseball, although he gave it one last go in 1949 when the Eagles relocated from Newark to Houston. After a season in which he hit only .217, he knew it was time to hang up his spikes for good.

As successful as Patterson had been as a professional baseball player, he was even better in his real profession. In 1950 he completed graduate work and earned a master's degree in education from what was then called the Texas State University for Negroes (now Texas Southern University). In the classroom he touched countless lives, and as a coach he directly influenced several future professional athletes, including Expos outfielder Steve Henderson and Washington Redskins defensive end Leroy Brown Jr.[22] Patterson continued to coach and teach at Jack Yates High School until 1967, and in 1982 became the first black coach ever named to the Texas High School Coaches Association Hall of Honor.[23] After leaving Jack Yates, Patterson worked for a time as a stadium consultant for Houston's Jeppesen (now Robertson) Stadium, and then in 1971 was appointed assistant athletic director for the Houston Independent School District.

According to his family, Patterson loved to travel with his wife, Gladys, especially after he retired from the school district, and he often said, "I just wanted to be remembered as someone who tried to help young men."[24] He exceeded that noble goal by a long measure. In the early 1980s Patterson endured a heart-valve replacement, and finally succumbed to complications from that procedure on May 16, 1984.[25] He is buried alongside Gladys, who died on February 18, 2004, at the Paradise South Cemetery in Pearland, Texas, a suburb of Houston.

Limiting Patterson's biography to only his athletic achievements would be underselling the man. He was a husband, a father, a citizen, an educator, and a role model. By coincidence, he was also a pretty darn good ballplayer.

Newark co-owner Abe Manley obtained Andrew "Pat" Patterson in a trade with the Philadelphia Stars early in the 1946 season. Patterson took over the third base position and batted .288 on the season. (*National Baseball Hall of Fame*)

NOTES

1   Biographical data form for a reunion banquet of Negro League players, filled out by Andrew Patterson (available in the Patterson family archives).

2   Family memory; myheritage.com/person-1000001_53176192_53176192/andrew-l-patterson-sr. Accessed January 2015.

3   Donn Rogosin, *Invisible Men: Life in Baseball's Negro Leagues* (Lincoln: University of Nebraska Press, 1983), 48.

4   Ibid.

5   Larry Lester, *Black Baseball's National Showcase: The East-West All-Star Game, 1933-1953* (Lincoln: University of Nebraska Press, 2001), 61.

6   Ibid.

7   Janet Bruce, *The Kansas City Monarchs: Champions of Black Baseball* (Lawrence: University Press of Kansas, 1985), 60-61.

8   John B. Holway, *The Complete Book of Baseball's Negro Leagues: The Other Half of Baseball History* (Fern Park, Florida: Hastings House Publishers, 2001), 349.

9   Family memory; myheritage.com/person-1000001_53176192_53176192/andrew-l-patterson-sr.

10   "History of the Prairie View Interscholastic League," pvilca.org/history.html, accessed December 29, 2018.

11   Ibid.

12   Lester, 88

13   James Riley, *The Biographical Encyclopedia of the Negro Baseball Leagues* (New York: Carroll and Graf, 1994), 608-609.

14   Pedro Treto Cisneros, *The Mexican League: Comprehensive Play Statistics 1937-2001* (Jefferson, North Carolina: McFarland, 2011), 214.

15   Rogosin, 172.

16   Lester, 88.

17   According to Lester, 448, Patterson tied for career East-West Game steals (4) with Henry Kimbro, Artie Wilson, and Sam Jethroe. Patterson required six games to reach the mark (compared with 10 games for Kimbro, and seven for Wilson and Jethroe).

18   Army Enlistment record, online: Ancestry.com.

19   Family memory; myheritage.com/person-1000001_53176192_53176192/andrew-l-patterson-sr.

20   James Overmyer, *Queen of the Negro Leagues: Effa Manley and the Newark Eagles* (Lanham, Maryland: Scarecrow Press, 1993), 198.

21   Neil Lanctot, *Negro League Baseball: The Rise and Ruin of a Black Institution* (Philadelphia: University of Pennsylvania Press, 2004), 164; Brent Kelly, *Voices from the Negro Leagues: Conversations with 52 Baseball Standouts from the Period 1924-1960* (Jefferson, North Carolina: McFarland, 2005), 347.

22   northdallasgazette.com/2014/09/11/former-nfl-player-looks-back-on-college-and-professional-career/ Accessed January 2015.

23   Ibid.

24   Family memory; myheritage.com/person-1000001_53176192_53176192/andrew-l-patterson-sr.

25   *Yates Times* (Jack Yates High School), September 7, 1984. Article part of digital archive supplied by Andrew Patterson (son) online at: myheritage.com/search-records?action=person&siteId=53176192&indId=1000001&origin=profile.

WARREN PEACE

BY BILL NOWLIN

Warren Peace posted a 3-1 record with a stellar 2.59 ERA for the 1946 Negro League champions. His fondest baseball memory involved pitching a two-hitter against the New York Black Yankees. *(Courtesy of Hakes Auctions)*

William Warren Peace was born in Kittrell, North Carolina, on August 6, 1921. Kittrell is a village in Vance County, about 35 or 40 miles northeast of Durham. The population at the time of the 1920 census was 223. "It's a little one-horse town," Peace told interviewer Brent Kelley. "In fact, the horse died. [Laughs] I left there and went to Richmond when I was 20 years old."[1]

The Peace family had lived in Kittrell or nearby Granville for many generations, with Warren's great-grandfather Josephus Peace (1827-1915) coming from Granville.[2] Josephus is listed as a slave owner and farm owner in the "Slave Schedules" of the 1860 United States Census. Bill's paternal grandfather was a carpenter, Madison

Peace, listed as a "mulatto" with a Caucasian father (Josephus) and an African American mother, Martha Peace of Kittrell. One of Madison Peace's children was Warren's father, Thomas London Peace. Thomas was listed in the 1920 census as a "mulatto" living in Kittrell and working as a cook on the county road force. His skills appear to have offered him stable employment as in 1930 as "cook, highway camp." He later worked as a cook on the railroad.

Thomas Peace (1889-1959) and Kittie Wyche Peace (1889-1943) had several children – Thomas, George, Edwin, Albert, Walter, William (Warren), Margaret, and Payton. Margaret appears to have been the only girl born to the Peaces. Though their future baseball-playing son was given the first name of William, per the North Carolina Birth Index, he was listed as Warren in both the 1930 and 1940 censuses.

The 1940 census shows Kitty (as her name was rendered) as the head of the household, the same home they had lived in throughout the years of the Depression, with Albert working as a farm laborer and Walter working as a laborer in a plant, perhaps both of them in the tobacco industry. Information gleaned in researching the family shows Warren as having completed school only through the seventh grade. However, Peace himself reported attending Henderson Institute in Henderson, North Carolina, and completing two years at Kittrell College.[3] In fact, when asked who was the biggest influence on his baseball career, Peace wrote, "My high school math teacher gave me my first baseball shoes and that encouraged me to continue playing."[4]

By 1942, when he registered for the draft during World War II, Warren Peace had left home and was living in Richmond. He'd had asthma as a child, he said, but shook it off after leaving home. "I left for Richmond, Virginia, on December the fourth, 1941, and three days later the Japanese attacked Pearl Harbor and that whole winter I did just the opposite of what my mama told me to do. I took those long underwear off and threw 'em away and got me some boxer shorts and put 'em on and I went bare-headed all winter long and I didn't wear an overcoat. It would rain and sleet and I was walkin' around bare-headed, had icicles hangin' down from my hair, and I haven't had asthma since."[5]

Peace was of small stature, listed as 5-feet-8 and 135-140 pounds. He was right-handed, and became a pitcher in Negro Leagues baseball. At some point, he picked up the nickname "Father Divine" – at least in some circles. He told interviewer Larry Lester, "My teammates used to call me Father Divine[6] when I was with the Eagles, because my name was Peace. Len Hooker used to call me that. Father Divine had a church there in Newark."[7] His second wife, Janice Leonard-Peace, told the author in May 2018 that she had not heard of the nickname applied to him but allowed that it didn't surprise her in that he had "educated so many people in his family."[8]

Peace was not called to military service himself. He worked at print shops in Richmond, a trade at which he worked for 40 years.

He told Larry Lester, "I was mostly a relief pitcher, but could start, too." He added, "I was just a pitcher. I was a curveball pitcher. I could have played outfield or first base, but I couldn't hit. So I had to pitch. I would rather play first base or the outfield but you've got to be a hitter to play there."[9]

Peace's first year in professional baseball was 1945. He had an opportunity as a starting pitcher that season because so many players were in the service. He pitched for the Newark Eagles that year and reported putting up an enviable 15-5 record. The Seamheads database, however, shows him as 0-1. And the one game they show him as pitching was a disaster – eight innings, hitting one batter, walking five, and surrendering 14 base hits. He did strike out two, but was charged with 13 runs. How can such a discrepancy be reconciled? Negro Leagues researcher Gary Ashwill reports that Seamheads includes only statistics based on actual box scores. Needless to say, press coverage of Negro Leagues games is spotty under the best of conditions and the country was still embroiled in World War II for most of the 1945 season. He also notes, regarding the 15-5 record in 1945, that "the Eagles would certainly have played at least as many games against independent, semipro, and minor-league opponents as they did against Negro league teams, so there would have been plenty of opportunities for Peace to rack up wins against them. And it was typical for a team's second-line pitchers to soak up innings in those games."[10] Ashwill also opined that it's possible Peace exaggerated a bit in self-reporting the 15-5 mark.

Peace was almost certainly better than the 0-1 record reflected in the only box scores Ashwill has been able to find from 1945, in which two Harrisburg newspapers (the *Telegraph* and the *Evening News*) both reported on the July 7 game there when the Baltimore Elite Giants beat the Eagles, 13-6, with Peace going the distance and taking the loss.

Compounding the mystery somewhat, Peace was listed as one of the 1945 team's "dependable flingers" on a pitching staff led by Don Newcombe but also including Lenier (*sic*) Hooker, Charles Roberts, James Hill, and Sidney Williams.[11]

The Eagles finished in third place (25-24, 9½ games behind the Homestead Grays).

Peace recalled his salary as $200 a month to start with, with a top salary of $225. The most he ever made in baseball was $300 a month, he said.[12] It was more than he made at the print shop at the time, and in the offseasons.

It seems unlikely that Peace would have made the team in 1946, with all the returning veterans, if his only work was to have pitched that poorly in the one outing at Harrisburg.

Peace was indeed invited back. Responding to a letter from the Eagles, explaining that baseball equipment could be difficult to find in Jacksonville, where the team would begin spring training on April 1, and asking if there was any equipment they should bring for him, Peace wrote to co-owners Abe and Effa Manley on March 17, 1946, "I received my contract, and will meet you at the Elks Home March 30th. The only equipment I need is a pair of sliding pads. I will appreciate very much if you can get them for me."[13] The letter was signed "Warren Peace," thus removing any doubt as to whether he called himself "Bill" or "Warren" at the time.

"I called him Bill," said his widow in 2018. "His family that he was born into called him Warren, or Uncle Warren. With the Newark Eagles, he was also known as Warren."[14]

Looking ahead to the 1946 campaign, the *Newark Evening News* mentioned Peace as someone "who showed great promise last season."[15] Had his record truly been 15-5, the paper would have been more lavish in its praise, but had his record been 0-1, giving up 13 runs in Harrisburg, there would likely have been no praise at all.

He was certainly never seen in the same category as the 1946 team's other pitchers, as Peace himself readily agreed. In the Eagles' championship year of 1946, Peace explained, "I was relegated to relief 'cause the star pitchers were in the army and they came back out. I did most relief pitchin'. Like Leon Day and Max Manning came out of the service. And another guy, Rufus Lewis – he came out of the service."[16] In mid-July, Wendell Smith of the *Pittsburgh Courier* declared Day "the best pitcher in either league" and noted that Lewis had gone undefeated in the season's first half. "These two aces are backed up by Maxwell Manning, Leniel Hooker, Warren Peace, Cecil Cole and Jim Boyd. That is a staff capable of winning in any league."[17]

Peace pitched rather little, working a total of 24⅓ innings in seven games with a 2.59 ERA. He had two starts, including one complete game, a shutout, and posted a record of 3-1. He walked 8 and struck out 15. The game he remembered the most was at the end of the season, in Newark against the visiting Homestead Grays. "Leon Day was pitchin' for us. I don't remember who pitched for the Grays that day. … [T]he winner of this particular game would win the second half. We had already won the first half." It wasn't a game in which Peace pitched. He was coaching first base.

Day worked the entire game, all 15 innings, and the score was tied 3-3 when Day came up to bat in the bottom of the 15th. He hit a home run, to win the game. "When he came trottin' 'round to first base, I ran out on the field and trottin' along beside him. I'm trottin' around the bases with him, you know, and I'm pattin' him on his butt, congratulatin' him; I'm tickled to death 'cause we're goin' to the World Series – and he kept tellin' me, 'Get back! Get back!'

"And I ignored him. I kept trottin' along beside him. We got around to third base and he said to me, 'If that umpire calls me out, I'm gonna beat the stuffin's outta you!' Only he didn't say "stuffin's"; he used that other "S" word. [Laughs] So then I realized I shouldn't be on that field. I turned off and went into the dugout.

"(Day) kept on to home plate and when he got to home plate, half of the people in the stands had come out on the field and they were standin' there at home plate waitin' to greet him. *If* that umpire had called him out, he would've had a riot up there and I would still be runnin' from Leon."[18]

Thrilling as it no doubt was, Peace mischaracterized Day's 15-inning triumph as a clinching game. It took place on August 11, the first game of a doubleheader (the Eagles won the second game, 3-1), and "strengthened their grip on first place."[19]

In an exhibition game on August 6 against Satchel Page and the Kansas City Monarchs, some 8,720 fans came out to Ruppert Stadium. Paige lasted only three innings. The Eagles won 7-4 behind the "brilliant pitching of Leon Day and Warren Peace."[20] Day had pitched the first four innings.

The Eagles won the World Series; Warren Peace saw no action in the seven games, but he was standing by ready if called upon. "I was in the bullpen the whole time," he said.[21]

Peace worked out with the Eagles in Jacksonville for spring training in both 1947 and 1948.[22] His record for 1947 and for 1948 are equally as uncertain as for any other years. In the second game of a doubleheader against the Baltimore Elite Giants at Ebbets Field on July 27, Peace pitched a three-hit, 4-3 win. The Eagles won the first game, 10-9, after scoring seven runs in the last inning.[23]

Who were some of the toughest batters he faced? Larry Lester posed the question. "I would say Josh Gibson and Buck Leonard. Buck batted third and Josh batted fourth in the lineup. You couldn't walk one to get to the other one. Buck would say, 'If I don't get you, Josh will.' And they lived up to that. Luke Easter, he was a heck of a hitter, too. Henry Kimbrough could hit me, but the other pitchers on the team, they could get Kimbrough out. I couldn't get him out. I asked him, 'How can you whip me so well?' And he told me he knew what I was throwing."[24]

"That's the only team I played for in the Negro National League," Peace said. "I played in a semipro league down in Richmond, Virginia, after I left there. I hurt my arm. The Richmond Giants."[25] Indeed, the May 10, 1948, *Richmond Times-Dispatch* reported him pitching for the Richmond Giants in the second game of a Negro American Association doubleheader held at Richmond's CCA Park against the visiting Winston-Salem Pond Giants. Sonny Carroll won the first game, 3-1, with 11 strikeouts. Peace won the second game, 2-1, with nine strikeouts.[26] He won a 6-5 complete game, also against Winston-Salem, on July 16, and shut out Winston-Salem, 2-0, on September 4. On August 22, he held the Negro American Association All-Stars to three hits, beating them 9-3.[27]

In the spring of 1949, Peace was pitching for the Richmond Giants again in Palatka, Florida, earning a save with four innings of shutout relief, beating the Florida State League's Palatka Blue Caps, 7-5.[28]

Asked for his fondest memory of playing with the Eagles, Peace didn't hesitate. "I almost pitched a no-hitter against the Black Yankees once. I had a no-hitter going up to the eighth inning. We were playing in Trenton. I didn't realize I had a no-hitter going. No one on my bench would tell me. It's a superstition. You don't mention things like that. Hack Barker, he was the manager of the Black Yankee team. Nobody told me, so I didn't realize I had a no-hitter going. Hack Barker came up to bat against me and he yelled out to the pitcher's mound, "If you think you can pitch a no-hitter, you got another thought coming!" And he hit the first pitch for a base hit. I got the next three guys. In the ninth inning, somebody else got a hit but I pitched a two-hitter."[29]

Peace worked as a printing pressman for 40 years before retiring. His specialty was gold leaf printing. "I don't think anyone else in the shop could do it. My husband was very talented. He could do almost anything," said his widow Janice.[30] He was also quite successful with investments and, at the time he and Janice met, he was living in Paterson, New Jersey, where he had a number of rental properties. Janice said, "He was always being called to fix things, always being called to court to throw out people who didn't think they had to pay rent. All that stuff."

Peace was married twice. When he married his first wife, Queen Banister, he also welcomed her daughter into the family. His stepdaughter, Dr. Peggy Scurry, became an obstetrics doctor and gynecologist who graduated from Howard University College of Medicine and practiced for more than 35 years in the Silver Spring, Maryland, area. Peace lost Queen, sadly, the very day she and Bill moved into a new home. "They had bought a new home and the first day they were in the new home, she walked to the doctor's office and died. That was so sad. I think in retrospect they realized it was a heart attack."[31]

Janice was asked how she and Bill had later met. "My husband helped so many members of his family get their educations," she said. "One of them he helped through law school, his nephew Sylvester, was dating my best girlfriend – I called her my sister – and so of course we became friends. I was explaining to him that I didn't like to date younger men, because I was a single mom bringing up my son. I said I had to put my son first. He said, 'You know what? You have to meet my uncle. You sure you don't mind him being older?' And I said, 'I prefer older men.' We met by phone. There was a long time before I met him in person." They did meet and hit it off. She was teaching and living in Chester County, Pennsylvania, and he was living and overseeing the rental properties in Paterson. But, Janice said, "I owned my own condo in a really nice area with tennis courts, which was good for my son, with a swimming pool and a clubhouse and all." She frankly wasn't that interested in moving to Paterson. Ultimately, Bill decided to move to join Janice where she lived. They married in 1979 and soon had a daughter, Rimoini. Her name was a Liberian name. "He was so happy because he had never fathered a child before. He had reared a stepdaughter [Peggy]; he was the only father that she had known."[32]

For hobbies, Bill reported that he enjoyed both bowling and pinochle. His favorite two foods were shrimp and oysters.[33]

At one point, Bill and Janice moved to North Carolina. Janice's mother had end-stage renal disease and needed care. Janice's brother had died from a heart attack at age 38, so there was no one else to help out her mother. Bill Peace himself had come down with colon cancer. He'd had surgery to remove the cancer and Peggy said they had gotten it all, though he was still having chemotherapy. "He was doing wonderfully well," Janice said. She had noticed some changes, though. "Shortly before he died, I noticed that his writing had changed, that he was getting some letters backwards. The messages weren't clear, but he was doing OK."[34]

"It was a good marriage," Janice recalled. "It was really good. He loved his grandbaby so much. We have pictures of him with her from the day before he died. All he did was hold her."[35]

They were in the process of moving and had located a lot to build on – the strings were all laid out for the construction to begin. They had put their Pennsylvania house on the market and sold it, for the asking price, faster than they had expected. Janice was there in North Carolina and Bill was visiting his nephew and niece in Delaware when she got a call from Rimoini. "Daddy is not acting right. I'm going to call the rescue squad." He was taken to the Chester hospital. Janice rushed home, while the staff worked to keep him alive. She arrived just a little too late, but went in to say her goodbyes.

Warren Peace died on November 3, 2002, in Chester, Pennsylvania. He had suffered a hemorrhage, a "bleeding stroke."[36]

Asked about Warren's contact with fellow Negro Leaguers, Janice Leonard-Peace recalled that he had worked for some years in collaboration with some of the ballplayers from his past. "We went to Kansas City for the Negro League Baseball Museum. We were there. It was memorable because we shared a table with Blair Underwood. He was going to be in the movie about the Negro Leagues."[37]

"He had worked very hard to get the agreement that the national baseball organization owed something to the back players, the Negro League players. They had just gotten that settlement. They were only giving them $10,000 once a year, but it was a recognition of their role in baseball. I think he got it one year and then he died. He never really got the full benefit of something that he worked so hard on."[38] The recognition was nonetheless very meaningful.

Sources

Thanks to Amanda McKnight, Gary Ashwill, and Larry Lester for helping make this a better biography.

NOTES

1   Brent Kelley, "Warren Peace," *Voices from the Negro Leagues* (Jefferson, North Carolina: McFarland & Company, 1998), 174.

2   There was no attempt made at a deep genealogy but the Peace side of the family predates the founding of the United States. Bill Peace's great-great-grandfather John Peace was born in New Kent, Virginia, in 1742

3   Questionnaire completed by Bill Peace for Gregg Truitt of Wilmington, Delaware. A copy of the questionnaire was supplied by Larry Lester.

4   Truitt questionnaire.

5   Brent Kelley, 174.

6   Father Divine was an African American religious leader and civil-rights activist. The height of his popularity, especially with black Americans, came in the 1930s and '40s.

7   Larry Lester interview with Warren Peace on July 18, 1993.

8   Author interview with Janice Leonard-Peace on May 3, 2018.

9   Larry Lester interview.

10   Gary Ashwill email to author on April 25, 2018.

11   "Newark Eagles Face Lloyd in Tonight's Game," *Delaware County Daily Times* (Chester, Pennsylvania), August 29, 1945: 10.

12   Larry Lester interview.

13   Letter from Warren Peace dated March 15, 1946. Manley Papers, Newark Public Library.

14   Author interview with Janice Leonard-Peace on May 3, 2018. She agreed the name was amusing and that, even though she was a former English teacher herself, she had "hated reading that novel so much."

15   "Rookie Pitcher Impresses Eagles," *Newark Evening News*, April 13, 1946.

16   Brent Kelley, 170.

17   Wendell Smith, "The Sports Beat: Manley's Eagles Are Flying High," *Pittsburgh Courier*, July 13, 1946:16.

18   Brent Kelley, 173. The home run was hit off Homestead's Bob Thurman.

19   "Newark Eagles Defeat Grays, By 8-7 in 15th," *New York Amsterdam News*, August 17, 1946: 11.

20   Ibid. Attendance as reported in the August 7 *Newark Star-Ledger*.

21   Larry Lester interview.

22   "Eagles Open with Yanks," *Newark Star-Ledger*, April 6, 1947: 104. See also "Eagles Winging Way to Sunny Jacksonville Camp," *Pittsburgh Courier*, April 3, 1948: 15, and "Newark Opens Against the Grays," *New York Amsterdam News*, May 8, 1948: 26.

23   "Newark Eagles' Winning Streak," *New York Amsterdam News*, August 2, 1947: 15.

24   Larry Lester interview.

25   Ibid.

26   "Late Rallies Give Giants Two Decisions," *Richmond Times-Dispatch*, May 10, 1948: 16.

27   "Giants Divide Pair of Games with All-Stars," *Richmond Times-Dispatch*, August 23, 1948: 13.

28   "Richmond Giants Nip Palatka Nine, 7-5," *Richmond Times-Dispatch*, April 15, 1949: 33.

29   Larry Lester interview.

30   Interview with Janice Leonard-Peace.

31   Ibid.

32   Ibid.

33   Truitt questionnaire. Peace volunteered that he didn't like broccoli.

34   Interview with Janice Leonard-Peace.

35   Ibid.

36   Rimoini Peace herself was, in her mother's words, "a go-getter. She was beyond a social worker. She was a case manager for the City of Philadelphia. She flew all over the country reuniting kids with other relatives when their moms or dads were deemed unfit. This was the work she did." But the condition her father had was one she inherited, and she suffers from a cavernoma that has robbed her of her memory and she requires 24-hours-a-day care. The State of North Carolina does not provide adequate coverage for her condition and the heavy burden of paying for the care falls fully on her mother. "Every time I think about him, I think of how proud he was of her. Of course, she could wrap him around her finger! If it was raining outside and she told him the sun was shining, he would believe it." Interview with Janice Leonard-Peace.

37   Underwood starred in HBO's *Soul of the Game* (1996).

38   Interview with Janice Leonard-Peace.

LENNIE PEARSON

BY DAN D'ADDONA

First baseman Lennie Pearson was already a .300 hitter in 1946, but he took his game up another notch in the World Series as he banged out 11 hits for a .393 average. *(Noir-Tech Research, Inc.)*

Lennie Pearson was one of the mainstays of the Newark Eagles for more than a decade, but it wasn't until the 1946 Negro World Series that Pearson came out of the shadows. The first baseman batted an astounding .393 in the Series against the Kansas City Monarchs to help the Eagles put their stamp on their best season.

Pearson was born Leonard Curtis Pearson on May 23, 1918, in Akron, Ohio. His parents' names remain unknown, as do those of many African-Americans born in the 1800s. Pearson's family moved to East Orange, New Jersey, where he starred in football, basketball, and baseball. He and future Eagles teammate Monte Irvin played on the high-school baseball team together. Fittingly, they both became two of the key fixtures on the Negro National League championship Eagles team.

In high school Pearson's career path was forever altered. While playing football, he injured his arm and thereafter was no longer able to be a pitcher or catcher anymore – something he and Irvin had taken turns doing.[1] The arm injury forced Pearson to move to first base, a move that at the time was devastating, but in the long run turned out to be an important break in his career.

In his team rookie questionnaire publicized by the Eagles, Pearson stated, "I would like to express my desires in professional athletics. I hope someday to be chosen to play in the All Star game in Chicago, and stay in baseball at least 15 more year(s). Second is to play professional basketball with some famous team. … My favorite player or the one whom I understudy is George 'Mule' Suttles[,] especially his hitting and for fielding I understudy Jimmie Crutchfield."[2]

In 1937 Pearson dropped out of school and joined the semipro Orange Triangles. He then joined St. Louis of the Negro American League, and later that same year became a member of the Eagles. He batted .211 in 72 known plate appearances that season at age 19. His play picked up in 1938 as he hit .313 in 90 plate appearances for the Eagles. In 1939 he batted .232 in 141 plate appearances, and then surged to .347 in 163 appearances with 42 runs scored in 1940. In 1941 he batted. 273 in 118 plate appearances.[3]

Pearson spent 12 years in Newark and made six East-West All-Star Games with the Eagles and seven overall. Those East-West games could be pivotal to a player's salary. In 1941 Pearson made the team with Monte Irvin and Jimmie Hill. Each player's share from the game was $1,977.76, which was more than half of each of their salaries. Pearson made about $170 per month that season. His salary increased to $300 a month in 1946, after World War II when salaries began to climb again.[4] But Pearson was immensely valuable to the Eagles. When teammate Ray Dandridge, a future Hall of Fame third baseman, defected to the Mexican league, Pearson often found himself at third base during the 1939-41 seasons, making the East-West Game in the latter season.

In 1942, he hit .347 in 221 plate appearances with 43 runs scored in the last full season of his first stint with the Eagles. In 1943 he batted .263 in 171 PA's split between Newark and Philadelphia. He rejoined the Eagles in 1944, batting .266 in 137 PA's.

Being one of the mainstays in Newark, the 6-foot-2 Pearson was a favorite of Effa Manley, who along with her husband, Abe, owned the team. Effa Manley would become the first woman ever elected to the National Baseball Hall of Fame. She knew talent and knew how to keep her players happy. According to James A. Riley:

> Pearson, handsome and broad-shouldered, was one of owner Effa Manley's favorites, and she wanted to keep her paramour close to Newark during the offseason. Taking advantage of the relationship, he frequently borrowed money from the Eagles as an advance on his salary. [5]

In fact, Manley cared so much for Pearson that she interceded on his behalf when he was to be drafted into the military in World War II. "Once she did intercede on behalf of a player, when Pearson's draft board in East Orange called him up at the very end of the war. Besides pointing out that Pearson had previously been classified 4-F, or unacceptable for service because of a bad knee, she went on in her letter to argue that his presence on the club was important 'because of the big part the baseball team plays in the lives of the Negroes of New Jersey. It is about the only healthy outdoor recreational program they have.'"[6]

That winter Pearson, who loved playing basketball, chose not to play for the New York Rens basketball team as Manley had arranged and instead went to play winter ball in Puerto Rico. While playing there, Pearson wrote Manley a letter just as the United States entered World War II. "It's time everyone got in touch with their friends because you never know when you may have the chance again," he wrote. War in the Pacific "didn't mean as much but this is a small island and it wouldn't take too much to sink the whole island" –a reference to German submarines patrolling the US coast. [7]

Pearson sent Manley a Christmas card announcing his marriage in 1941, also asking about trade rumors. Effa replied: "I cannot understand why you or anyone else who had been connected with this club would feel that you're not going to be treated fairly." They then spoke on the phone and Pearson returned the four-month contract unsigned, saying he expected a five-month contract, threatening to play the season in Mexico instead. "But Manley's letter to Pearson's draft board, pointing out that she had advanced him $75 on his salary and that he had signed a contact, evidently dissuaded him. He played for the Eagles in 1942."[8]

Manley was helpful in landing Pearson and teammate Leon Day jobs with the Thomas Edison Company in West Orange, New Jersey, even writing them a letter of recommendation. "(Pearson) has always been most cooperative and helpful," she wrote. "… He is also a real team man. I am sure he will show the same spirit in any field of employment he finds himself in."[9]

Again, Pearson's name came up in the draft during the war, and again Manley went to bat for him. According to Luke, "Pearson received a call from Uncle Sam that would make him the thirteenth Eagle to be drafted. Just before Independence Day, however, Effa wrote a letter to Pearson's Selective Service Board asking that they delay his induction until the end of the season. She couched her request in terms of Pearson's value to the team, the 'big part that baseball plays in the lives of Negroes in New Jersey,' and the fact that he had previously been declared 4-F owing to a bad knee."[10]It worked. He would remain in Newark for the rest of the season.

It worked out in the long run for Pearson and the Eagles. He was a regular .300 hitter. In 1942 he doubled and scored in his only at-bat in the first of two All-Star games played that year. He had one at-bat in the second game and had an RBI. In 1943 Pearson had three at-bats in the East-West Game and went hitless. In 1945 he had one hitless at-bat. In 1946 he went 1-for-3 with an RBI.

Pearson seemed to come up big for the Eagles in the clutch. He hit .308 in 82 plate appearances in 1945, then .320 in 265 PA's in 1946.

That performance in 1946 was pivotal for the Eagles, who had big goals of winning a championship on a team with a strong blend of veterans and talented young players. The *Newark News* noted that "infield prospects are exceptionally bright with Pearson, Doby, Isreal and Watkins showing to advantage."[11] Pearson signed his contract for $300 per month.[12]

After seven games of the season, Pearson was leading the league with a .500 batting average.[13] On May 6 he had three hits, including a home run, as the Eagles defeated the Philadelphia Stars 14-6.

He had two hits on June 26 in a 12-8 win over the Homestead Grays to lead the Eagles to their ninth consecutive victory, breaking the club record. They would go on to break that record multiple times that season and during that stretch would win 14 of 15. On July 4 he hit a two-run homer against the New York Black Yankees, the decisive blow in a 3-1 Newark victory.[14]

Pearson continued his strong play all season. Perhaps his biggest game of the season was played on August 23 when his power hitting helped propel the Eagles to a 10-2 win over the Cuban Stars in the middle of the pennant race. The *Newark News* headlined the story: "Belting Spree by Pearson; Hits Two Homers and Double for Eagles." Playing first base, Pearson hit a 400-foot grand slam in the first inning to get the Eagles off to a fast start. "Pearson continued his timely slugging in the second inning when he banged a double to left to tally Monty (*sic*) Irvin. Again in the eighth Pearson slammed another home run after Monty Irvin had doubled against the centerfield bleachers to bring his runs-batted-in total to seven for the evening."[15]

On August 26 Pearson had three hits and three runs scored in a 12-5 win over the Homestead Grays.

On August 30, the Eagles played two games, one against the Grays, the second against the New York Cubans. Pearson hit a grand slam to help beat the Grays, 12-5, then hit another home run against the Cubans for a 10-2 win. "Len Pearson featured the offensive with a four-run homer in the first game and clouted another circuit with Monty [*sic*] Irvin on in the eighth."[16]

Pearson came up big in the clutch, especially in September for the Eagles. On September 3 he doubled, singled, and scored a run as the Eagles swept a doubleheader from the Philadelphia Stars to push a late-season winning streak to 14 games. On September 6 he homered to defeat the New York Black Yankees, 3-2, at Yankee Stadium. He played well at Yankee Stadium. "It was the third home run Pearson has hit in four Stadium games this season. He has made 10 hits in 24 trips to the plate in New York's big league parks."[17] It moved his season average to .322.

The Negro World Series opened on September 20 in New York. Newark's Leon Day faced Satchel Paige of the Kansas City Monarchs in one of the most anticipated head-to-head matchups in baseball history. It lived up to its billing with the Monarchs winning, 2-1.

Pearson nearly scored in the second inning. He was walked and Lassies Ruffin, according to one account, "bounced a ball over second which normally would have gone for a hit to score Pearson. However, Kansas City infielders were moving over to cover the

runners and Hamilton came up with the ball, touched second and rifled a peg to first for a double play."[18] Pearson came up in the eighth against Paige and grounded into a fielder's choice. In the next game, he hit a single off Paige, who came in as a relief pitcher in the seventh inning as the Eagles won 7-4.

The Eagles won the title on October 4, 1946, and Pearson, along with Monte Irvin, "made sparkling plays on infield drives in the fourth."[19] He was hitless in the game, but the Eagles held off the Monarchs, 3-2, to win the championship.

After the season Pearson traveled with the Jackie Robinson All-Stars on a barnstorming tour. (He also barnstormed on the Satchel Paige All-Stars against the Bob Feller All-Stars during his career.) He played two more full seasons in Newark, batting .279 in 236 PA's in 1947 and .294 in 218 PA's in 1948.

After the 1948 season the Eagles moved to Houston, but Pearson decided to stay closer to home and joined the Baltimore Elite Giants. He became the player-manager of the Elite Giants, batting a robust .332 and leading Baltimore to the 1949 championship of the Negro American League. It was Pearson's last year in the Negro Leagues, though his baseball career was not over. During his career in the Negro Leagues, Pearson also played a lot of winter ball. Like many of his teammates and other Negro League stars, he joined the Cuban winter league, finishing with a .262 career average. He also played in Puerto Rico. Pearson had watched several of his teammates help integrate the major leagues, including Newark teammates Larry Doby, Irvin, and Don Newcombe. He made his last appearance in the East-West Game in 1949 as a member of the Baltimore Elite Giants. He went hitless in five at-bats, finishing his East-West career with a .125 batting average in seven games.

In 1950 Pearson joined the Milwaukee Brewers of the American Association, his first time playing full-time on an integrated team. He responded by batting .305 for the season. The team finished in sixth place (68-85), 21½ games behind the champion Minneapolis Millers.

Pearson began 1951 in Milwaukee, but later moved to Hartford of the Eastern League. He batted .272. He finished his career with Drummondville of the Quebec Provincial League in 1953, batting .293 with 16 home runs and 58 RBIs. What Pearson did in 1952 is not currently known.

Pearson married Mae Justina Smith, who was born (date unknown) near Athens, Ohio, to parents Robert Lee Smith and Hattie Johnson. Lennie and Mae had a son, Allen Dodd.

After his career, Pearson never strayed far from his home in New Jersey. From 1952 to 1958, he operated the Club 111 Lounge in Newark, and then ran Len Pearson's Lounge before retiring in 1970.[20]

Pearson died on December 7, 1980, in East Orange, New Jersey, at age 62. Surviving relatives included his daughter, Valerie; two sisters, Rosa Lee Hunter and Mattie Joy Matthew; and two brothers, Ownsby and Hobie. He is buried in Rosedale Cemetery, in Orange.

SOURCES

In addition to the sources cited in the Notes, the author also consulted baseball-reference.com. Thanks to the staff at the East Orange Public Library.

NOTES

1   James A. Riley, *The Biographical Encyclopedia of the Negro Baseball Leagues* (New York: Carroll & Graf Publishers, 1994), 613.

2   Newark Eagles records, 1935-1946, Charles F. Cummings New Jersey Information Center, Newark Public Library, Box 10.

3   All batting statistics come from Seamheads.com, as of February 2019.

4   Salary information from James Overmyer, *Queen of the Negro Leagues: Effa Manley and the Newark Eagles* (Lanham, Maryland: The Scarecrow Press, Inc., 1998), 121.

5   Riley, 612-613.

6   Overmyer, 180.

7   Bob Luke, *The Most Famous Woman in Baseball: Effa Manley and the Negro Leagues* (Dulles, Virginia: Potomac Books, 2011), 68, 78.

8   Luke, 82.

9   Luke, 92.

10   Luke, 111.

11   *Newark News*, April 9, 1946.

12   Newark Eagles official contract to Leonard Pearson, Newark Eagles records, Box 10.

13   *New Jersey Afro American*, June 8, 1946.

14   *Newark News*, July 5, 1946.

15   *Newark News*, August 24, 1946.

16   *New Jersey Afro American*, August 31, 1946.

17   *New Jersey Afro American*, September 7, 1946.

18   *New Jersey Afro American*, September 21, 1946.

19   *New Jersey Afro American*, October 5, 1946.

20   "Leonard Pearson, Ex-Baseball Star," *Newark Star-Ledger*, December 9, 1980.

LEON RUFFIN

BY PAUL HOFMANN

Leon Ruffin, Newark's starting catcher in 1946, contributed greatly to the success of the Eagles' formidable pitching staff and earned a spot on the East All-Star team. (*Noir-Tech Research, Inc.*)

A superior defensive catcher, the well-traveled Leon Ruffin was a member of the 1946 Newark Eagles and a Negro League all-star that same year. Ruffin's defensive skills were legendary. He was noted for his ability to handle pitching staffs and to detect a batter's weakness. He had a strong throwing arm that was considered one of the best in the game. Cool Papa Bell

called him "one of the best catchers I ever saw," high praise from a man who played against Hall of Fame backstops Josh Gibson, Biz Mackey, and Roy Campanella.[1]

At the plate, the right-handed-hitting Ruffin was a light hitter with little power. He often finished the season under what is now known as the Mendoza line.[2] Despite his low batting average and lack of power, Ruffin was known for his patience at the plate and for his ability to handle the bat and play small ball. He often worked pitchers deep into the count and helped to move runners around the bases with a bunt or by hitting behind the runner. Sam Allen, who grew up in Norfolk and saw Ruffin play on the semipro circuit in and around Portsmouth after his Negro League career, said, "He was a heck of a bunter. He had the ability to place that ball wherever he wanted."[3]

Charles Leon Ruffin was born on February 11, 1912, in Portsmouth, Virginia. He was the third child and oldest son born to Thomas and Hattie (Holmes) Ruffin. Thomas was a laborer who worked on the dry docks of the Portsmouth-based Norfolk Naval Shipyard. Hattie was a laundress.[4] The couple and their six children were renting a home on 931 Seventh Street in Portsmouth at the time of Thomas's death on July 17, 1921, when Leon was 9 years old. Leon completed the ninth grade before going to work full-time.

Portsmouth, located on the western side of the Elizabeth River directly across from Norfolk, was booming in the early twentieth century. The population of Portsmouth more than tripled during the first 20 years of the century, largely due to the shipyard. Portsmouth became a popular destination among barnstorming Negro

League teams. Many of the greats of the game – players like Gibson, Satchel Paige, and Mule Suttles – made appearances at Sewanee Stadium.[5] The city soon became a hotbed of Negro League talent. Ruffin and Buster Haywood were two of the best players to come out of Portsmouth.[6]

By 1930, Ruffin was living with his mother, five siblings, and three nieces in a small rented house at 687 Nelson Street in Portsmouth. By this time, he had also followed in his father's footsteps and was working as a laborer at the Naval Shipyard.[7] When he wasn't working, Ruffin, who grew up playing baseball and football on the sandlots around Portsmouth, was making a name for himself as an athlete. According to Clay Shampoe and Thomas Garett, authors of *Baseball in Portsmouth, Virginia*, "Ruffin was an excellent athlete on diamonds and the gridiron for several Portsmouth and Norfolk semipro teams."[8] Sam Allen suggested that Ruffin's exploits on the football field were legendary among local residents. "He was a very good football player and would have had a good career in football had he had the opportunity to go to school," Allen said.[9]

Ruffin was built like a barrel. By this time the stocky catcher's 5-foot-11 frame had filled out to 175 pounds and his success at the semipro level in the early 1930s began to draw the attention of Negro League scouts. In 1935 Ruffin joined the Brooklyn Eagles of the Negro National League and stayed with the team after owner Abe Manley and his new wife, Effa, moved the team to Newark, New Jersey, for the 1936 season.

Ruffin's first two seasons with the Eagles foreshadowed most of his career. While Negro League statistics are incomplete and in some cases nonexistent, those that are available suggest that Ruffin struggled at the plate. According to *The Biographical Encyclopedia of the Negro Leagues*, during his first two seasons with the Eagles he hit a combined .171.[10] But despite his lack of productivity at the plate and his relative inexperience, Ruffin proved to be an above-average defensive catcher.

Ruffin married Daisy Brooks of Occupacia, Virginia, sometime in the mid-1930s. The couple moved into a small, rented home at 651 Fayette Street in Portsmouth and lived there with Daisy's younger brother, Richard. They eventually had one child, Leon Jr.

Ruffin was traded to the Pittsburgh Crawfords before the 1937 season. He served as the team's backup catcher to all-star Pepper Bassett in 1937 and became the starter in 1938. When Gus Greenlee, owner of the Crawfords, decided to move the team to Toledo, Ohio, in 1939, Ruffin sought any opportunity to avoid the transition. He wrote to Abe Manley, requesting that the Eagles reacquire him, offering to play for $140 a month.[11] Manley accommodated his request and in May of 1939 traded pitcher Bob Evans to the Crawfords for Ruffin.[12]

Ruffin's second stint with the Eagles was short-lived. By midseason he was traded to the Philadelphia Stars, who were in need of another catcher after Bill Perkins jumped the Stars to play in the Mexican League.[13]

Official Negro League seasons were short, at 40 to 60-plus games, only about a third or more the length of a 154-game major-league schedule.[14] However, that doesn't mean there weren't plenty of opportunities for Ruffin and other Negro League players to play. Barnstorming and engagements with semipro teams allowed Ruffin the opportunity to supplement his $740-a-year income as a presser at the dry cleaners in Portsmouth. And, of course, there were opportunities south of the border.

Ruffin returned to the Newark Eagles in 1942, his third time with the club. He batted .248 and was the batterymate of Day when the right-hander one-hit the Baltimore Elite Giants and struck out a Negro League-record 18 hitters, including the 20-year-old Campanella three times. Ruffin remained with the Eagles until, true to his Portsmouth roots, he enlisted in the US Navy during World War II. Ruffin served in the Navy from 1943 to 1945.[15]

With the exception of a few games in 1944, Ruffin missed nearly two full seasons to the war. After being discharged from the Navy, he returned to the Eagles for the fourth time in his career. However, this season would be like no other for Ruffin and the Eagles.

Despite his light hitting, Ruffin was the team's regular catcher in 1946. His work behind the plate more than compensated for any deficiencies with the bat. The Eagles were riding an eight-game winning streak in June when the *Newark Evening News* credited the team's success in part to the work of its seasoned catcher: "The great showing of the pitching reflects upon the skill that has been exhibited by Leon Ruffin behind the plate. Ruffin is a veteran receiver and his faultless handling of the hurlers has won much praise from veteran baseball fans and players."[16]

Ruffin enjoyed one of his better offensive seasons in 1946 and occasionally helped out with his bat. On June 30 he broke up a scoreless tie with a solo home run into the left-field bleachers at Ruppert Stadium in support of Day's five-hit, 3-0 victory over the Philadelphia Stars. Two months later, on August 27, he contributed four hits to the Eagles' 23-hit, 15-1 victory over the New York Black Yankees. Ruffin reportedly finished the 1946 season batting .250 (Seamheads shows him at .248).[17]

His efforts behind the plate and improved hitting earned Ruffin a spot on the Negro League's East All-Star squad along with teammates Larry Doby, Monte Irvin, Lennie Pearson, and Day. That year, the East (Negro National League) and West (Negro American League) played two all-star games, one in Washington and the East-West Classic in Chicago.

On August 15 there were 16,268 fans in attendance to watch the East All-Stars play the West All-Stars at Griffith Stadium. Under the rules of the games, no pitcher was allowed to throw more than three innings, which required the managers to utilize their benches.[18] Ruffin entered the game as a defensive replacement in the top of the fifth inning. He replaced Gibson behind the plate after the legendary catcher was lifted for a pinch-runner, the Philadelphia Stars' Murray Watkins, in the bottom of the fourth inning. Ruffin went 0-for-1 before being replaced by Louis Loudon of the New York Cubans in the East's 6-3 victory over the West.[19] The game was notable because it was the first East-West Game held in the nation's capital and the first with no extra-base hits.

On August 18 the 14th annual East-West Classic in Comiskey Park drew a crowd of 45,474, the second largest turnout in the event's history.[20] The West beat the East, 4-1, its fourth straight win and eighth victory overall in the series. Josh Gibson worked the entire game behind the plate for the East and Ruffin did not play.

The 1946 Negro League World Series was one for the ages. The high-flying Eagles, winners of the Negro National League pennant, were matched against the Negro American League champion Kansas City Monarchs. The Series was a back-and-forth affair as the Eagles rallied from a three-games-to-two deficit to capture the Series in seven games. Ruffin caught all seven games and went 7-for-25 (a respectable .280) with 4 RBIs against a strong Kansas City Monarchs pitching staff that included Paige and Hilton Smith.[21]

Ruffin and Day jumped to Mexico in 1947. He hit only .229 for the Mexico City Reds before returning to the United States and resuming his career in the Negro Leagues.

With the integration of baseball, the Negro Leagues experienced a dramatic decline in popularity. As a result, the Negro National League disbanded after the 1948 season and the Eagles joined the Negro American League. Effa Manley decided to combat the loss of revenue caused by integration by selling the team to W.H. Young, who relocated the Eagles to Houston in 1949.[22]

Ruffin returned to the Eagles in 1949 and played his final two professional seasons in Houston. At the time, the 37-year-old backstop was the longest-tenured Negro League catcher. He hit .174 in 1949 and .194 in 1950.[23] Low attendance was a common theme for all of the NAL teams, but the Eagles were also hurt by the fact that they finished in last place during both of their years in Houston.[24] Hoping to find a more supportive fan base, the Eagles moved to New Orleans.

With his professional career now behind him, Ruffin returned to Portsmouth for good. He was a fixture on local semipro teams, serving as manager and occasionally catching a few innings. Sam Allen, who grew up in Norfolk and played in the Negro Leagues during their waning years, played against teams managed by Ruffin.[25] "He was very knowledgeable," Allen recalled. "Like most catchers, he understood the whole game. He was an excellent manager for young ballplayers."[26]

When he wasn't managing and playing baseball on the semipro circuit, Ruffin worked as a presser at a local dry-cleaning store. On August 14, 1970, Ruffin suffered a stroke and died. He was 58 years old. Despite some family members' wishes that he not be buried in Portsmouth's Lincoln Cemetery, a poorly maintained graveyard that served the African-American community, Ruffin's widow, Daisy, insisted that he be interred there. She was buried there herself in March of 2010.

On September 29, 2010, a small ceremony attended by about 20 people, including Ruffin's son, Leon Ruffin Jr., was held to dedicate a marker that had been installed at the foot of Ruffin's grave earlier that year. The marker was part of a national movement, led by the Society for American Baseball Research's Negro Leagues Committee, to recognized long-forgotten Negro League players.

The Georgia gray granite marker is adorned with a pair of crossed bats, with a ball beneath, and a catcher's mitt.[27] The marker reads:

Charles Leon Ruffin

Negro League Legend

1935-1950

Catcher

1946 World Champion Newark Eagles

1946 East-West Negro League All-Star

Understanding where Leon Ruffin and many of his contemporaries fit into the landscape of Negro League baseball history is often difficult. As Lawrence Hogan, author of *Shades of Glory*, wrote, "There exists no official source of statistics … no compilations of scorecards. … Many gaps exist in the historical record."[28] Most of what we have to go on is anecdotal in nature. However, one thing is certain: In 1946 Leon Ruffin was the catcher for the greatest Negro League team in the world.

SOURCES

In addition to the sources cited in the Notes, the author also relied on Baseball-reference.com and Seamheads.com.

Sam Allen interviews with author, December 3 and 17, 2018. Recorded conversations in author's possession.

NOTES

1   Cool Papa Bell Oral History Interview, September 27, 1981. Retrieved from collection. baseballhall.org/PASTIME/cool-papa-bell-oral-history-interview-1981-september-27-3.

2   The Mendoza line is a baseball term for batting around or below .200 – mediocrity. The term was coined by George Brett after Mario Mendoza. The term has also crossed over into America's pop-culture lexicon and is frequently used to describe almost any type of subpar performance, from the performance of stocks and mutual funds to bad grades, and to quotas for salespeople.

3   Sam Allen, personal interview, December 3, 2018.

4   "United States Census, 1920," database with images, *FamilySearch* (familysearch.org/ark:/61903/1:1:MJF8-36V : accessed March 7, 2018), Leon Ruffin in household of Thomas Ruffin, Portsmouth Lee Ward, Portsmouth (Independent City), Virginia, United States; citing ED 235, sheet 4B, line 67, family 90, NARA microfilm publication T625 (Washington D.C.: National Archives and Records Administration, 1992), roll 1905; FHL microfilm 1,821,905.

5   Bill Leffler, "Hampton Roads Plays Host to Major Salute to Negro Leagues," *The Virginian-Pilot*, June 13, 2007. Retrieved from pilotonline.com/news/local/article_b0a08643-62ec-5659-b131-83a12fcd9a1e.html. Sewanee Stadium was the old baseball park near Washington and Lincoln streets in Portsmouth that frequently hosted local semipro and barnstorming games.

6   Buster Haywood was a catcher with the Indianapolis and Cincinnati Clowns, Birmingham Black Barons, and New York Cubans. Like Ruffin, Haywood became a semipro manager and is credited with helping discover Hank Aaron in 1951.

7   "United States Census, 1930," database with images, *FamilySearch* (familysearch.org/ark:/61903/1:1:CCDJ-YZM: accessed March 7, 2018), Leon Ruffin in household of Hattie Ruffin, Portsmouth, Portsmouth (Independent City), Virginia, United States; citing enumeration district (ED) ED 16, sheet 3A, line 3, family 51, NARA microfilm publication T626 (Washington: National Archives and Records Administration, 2002), roll 2473; FHL microfilm 2,342,207.

8   Clay Shampoe and Thomas Garett, *Baseball in Portsmouth, Virginia* (San Francisco: Arcadia Publishing, 2004).

9   Sam Allen, personal interview, December 17, 2018.

10 James Riley, *The Biographical Encyclopedia of the Negro Leagues* (Boston: DaCapo Press, 2002).

11 More recent Seamheads.com stats show him averaging .189 over the two seasons. Ibid.

12 Ibid.

13 Sam Allen said that Ruffin had played this second year in Mexico. Sam Allen, December 17, 2018. See also baseball-reference.com/bullpen/Leon_Ruffin.

14 Thomas Kern, "Leon Day," SABR BioProject.

15 Alfred M. Martin & Alfred T. Martin. *The Negro Leagues in New Jersey: A History* (Jefferson, North Carolina: McFarland & Company, Inc., 2008), 66.

16 "Eagles Riding Win Streak: Carry Eight-Game String Into Tilt Here with Grays Tonight." *Newark Evening News*, June 25, 1946: 26.

17 James Riley.

18 "Negro Nationals Beat Americans in All-Star Game," *Boston Globe*, August 16, 1946: 6.

19 Larry Lester, *Black Baseball's National Showcase: The East-West All-Star Game, 1933-1953* (Lincoln: University of Nebraska Press, 2001), 274.

20 James Segreti, "West Defeats East All-Star Negro Nine, 4-1: Gains 8th Victory Before 45,474," *Chicago Tribune*, August 19, 1946: 27.

21 Richard J. Puerzer, "The 1946 Negro League World Series: The Newark Eagles vs. the Kansas City Monarchs," in Rick Bush and Bill Nowlin, eds., *The Newark Eagles Take Flight: The Story of the 1946 Negro League Champions* (Phoenix: SABR, 2019).

22 Robert Fink, "Houston Eagles," *Handbook of Texas*, Retrieved from tshaonline.org/handbook/online/articles/xoh06.

23 James A. Riley.

24 Robert Fink.

25 Sam Allen played for the Kansas City Monarchs in 1957, the Raleigh Tigers in 1958, and the Memphis Red Sox in 1959.

26 Sam Allen, personal interview, December 17, 2018.

27 Ed Miller, "Baseball Fans Keep Negro League Player's Legend Alive," *Virginian-Pilot* [Norfolk], September 26, 2010. Retrieved from https://pilotonline.com/guides/african-american-today/article_8444af87-4abf-5cd3-9317-9b8b1f0bbd1b.html

28 Lawrence Hogan, *Shades of Glory: The Negro Leagues and the Story of African-American Baseball* (New York: National Baseball Hall of Fame and Museum, 2006), 380, quoted in Bill Johnson, "Josh Gibson," SABR BioProject.

Murray "Skeeter" Watkins

BY NIALL T. ADLER

Murray "Skeeter" Watkins was a baseball lifer. He was a Negro League all-star on the left side of the infield in the 1940s for the Cincinnati Clowns, Newark Eagles, and Philadelphia Stars, and when opportunities disappeared he played in the Canadian ManDak League in the early 1950s. He would continue to play baseball for local clubs well into the 1970s.

At 5-feet-4, Watkins was a sparkplug at the top of the lineup. He was described as "[a]n eagle-eyed leadoff batter who drew numerous walks (and) combined good speed and extra hustle. ... [H]e was a contact hitter with average power. The popular pepperpot was brilliant in the field."[1]

On the eve of the first Negro League All-Star Game in 1940, *Philadelphia Tribune* columnist Ed Harris wrote, "Unheralded and unsung they do their work day by day during the hot summer months ... whether we hear about them or not, they exist, (and) as long as they exist, baseball lives on."[2] Baseball existed because of unheralded lifers like Watkins, but he was realistic in his pursuits. "I was just too old when my chance (to play in the white majors) came," Watkins said years later.[3]

Maurice Clifton Watkins was born on October 16, 1915, in Towson, Maryland, to Thomas and Mary Watkins.[4] When Murray was 14 and playing the outfield, he dove for every ball hit to him," an article about him said. "I don't know why, but I had to fall down in order to make the catch." The article noted that unorthodox

Murray "Skeeter" Watkins started 1946 with Newark but was traded to Philadelphia in exchange for Pat Patterson early in the season. He is pictured here (at left) with Philadelphia Stars teammate Frank Austin. (*John W. Mosley Collection, Temple University*)

style of play led to a future on the infield, as he left the outfield for good in 1937.[5]

According to James Riley's *Biographical Encyclopedia*, Watkins began playing baseball with the Orangeburg Red Sox as a center fielder in 1932 along with two unknown brothers. He later played for Doc Thomas's Baltimore semipro Colts team.[6]

Watkins saw his first professional action with the 1941 Philadelphia Stars. Third baseman-shortstop Mahlon Duckett was one of the "freshmen" managers Oscar Charleston relied on.[7] Meanwhile, Watkins battled for playing time with infielders Duckett, David Campbell, and Larnie Jordan.[8] The Stars "limped" to the end of the season and finished 1941 with a record of 17-52.[9]

Watkins played for both the Cincinnati Clowns and Newark Eagles in 1942. The Clowns were a huge drawing card and featured the double-play combo of Ray Niel at second and Jim Oliver at short, who executed over 100 double plays in 1941.[10] Watkins was working in a steel mill at Sparrow's Point in Baltimore and chose to barnstorm with the Clowns for two weeks.[11] It is likely that the young backup infielder was discovered by the Newark Eagles while on tour with Cincinnati. The Clowns' nickname mirrored their clown-like antics. But they could play and draw a gate. Eagles owner Effa Manley said, "I didn't like the Ethiopian Clowns. I wanted baseball to be dignified." But one day in New York, she saw them "and I don't think anybody in the park laughed louder than I did. So after that, I stopped complaining."[12]

Watkins joined the Eagles in August 1942;[13] he was signed for $400 a month.[14] Newark featured Ray Dandridge, "the best third baseman in Negro Baseball"[15] and one of the "finest infields in Negro baseball" with shortstop Willie Wells and second baseman Pint Israel.[16] Watkins, at age 26, played in seven games and batted 3-for-24 (.125) with two RBIs and three walks. It was Wells, one of the "lauded stars (who) have seen their best days," whom Watkins looked to replace.[17]

According to Negro Leagues historian Jim Riley, the Eagles' owners were "diminutive, cigar-chomping Abe Manley, who made his fortune in the New Jersey numbers trade" and Harlem real estate, and his wife, Effa, a "feminist, businesswoman and a revelation (ahead of her time)."[18]

The Eagles played at Ruppert Stadium, home of the white Newark Bears of the International League. The venue was a "spacious ballpark on Wilson Avenue squeezed between warehouses, factories and rail yards. Billboards advertised Ballantine beer. Jocko Maxwell, one of the first African-American sportscasters, was the Eagles' public address announcer.[19] The Number 31 bus ran down South Orange Avenue and brought fans to the ballpark.[20] Although smoke and the smell from a nearby garbage dump were prevalent,[21] making for a less pleasant atmosphere when the wind blew in those scents, the Eagles still averaged 3,200 fans per game for 12 dates in 1942 and 2,500 for 11 dates in 1943.[22] Noxious odors aside, to black poet and Newark resident LeRoi Jones (later Amiri Baraka), the Eagles were "legitimate black heroes" and "extensions of us."[23]

According to batboy Ronald Murphy, "black kids, especially those who played baseball, 'idolized' the Eagles players.[24]

In 1943, after a monthlong spring training,[25] Watkins played shortstop and batted in the leadoff spot for manager Mule Suttles. According to box scores, Watkins played short and third and Larry Doby manned either second or short in 1943.[26] Watkins made $170 a month compared with future Hall of Famer Leon Day, who earned a team-high $300 a month in 1943. Watkins received pay raises to $225 a month in 1944, $250 a month in 1945, and $300 a month in 1946.[27]

Still regarded as a rookie in 1943, Watkins was considered "the best defensive third baseman in the league, but had only average range."[28] He performed well and became an all-star. Watkins went 1-for-5 as the starting third baseman for the North All-Stars at Griffith Stadium in Washington on September 9. The North was made up of players from the Eagles, New York Cubans, and New York Black Yankees. Marvin Barker of the Black Yankees was the shortstop.

The Eagles finished the 1943 season in the middle of the seven-team Negro National League with a 26-32 record. Watkins hit .230 in 33 games with 22 runs scored and 9 RBIs; the 22 runs ranked third on the team. On defense, he had a .908 fielding percentage at third base and .919 fielding percentage in five games at short.

Despite a light bat, Watkins claimed he got looks from the white major leagues. He told a reporter years later, "I could hit them all and I was a good fielder. At one time both the National and American League had representatives looking at me and talking to me, but by then I was already 29." With two years of minor-league seasoning, he would have been 31 (in 1946), too old, he thought, except for guys like Paige and Luke Easter.[29]

In 1944 Watkins hit .188 in 33 games with 18 runs, 3 extra-base hits (all doubles), and 8 RBIs. The Eagles finished the year at 32-35, well ahead of the last-place Black Yankees (8-33) but far behind the first-place Grays (47-24).

Watkins was one of the most popular Eagles in 1945. He received 1,275 votes in a popularity contest, with the two teammates who finished in second place garnering only 300 votes apiece.[30] Watkins earned $250 a month for the five-month season plus $20 per week during spring training. On April 19 Effa Manley told him that if she had a good year at the gate and Watkins played well, she'd give him an extra $100.[31] Watkins was fortunate to receive such an offer as Manley did not appreciate players asking for more money and "players who tried to wheel and deal during contract negotiations were met with an unbending resolve." The extra money could come in handy; Manley also expected her players to dress nicely off the field, with their attire including fedoras, long coats, and silk ties.[32]

According to the Eagles' publicist at the time, J.L. Kessler, "Watkins is a pint-sized individual with plenty of nerve. He is batting over .300 and gets in front of sizzlers that the average player would wave at and let go as a base hit. Has a steel arm that allows him to throw out speedsters after knocking down the ball down."[33] Watkins hit ninth at the 1945 East-West All-Star Game at Comiskey Park on July 29 as he and Black Yankees shortstop Willie Wells made up the left side of the infield.[34] Watkins was 2-for-2 with a walk in the East's 9-6 loss. In addition to playing in Negro League baseball's annual showcase game, Watkins also remembered the first time he faced Satchel Paige – in 1945, the "same day (World War II) ended. He never struck me out but I didn't get a hit off him. And I remember something else. He broke my bat off in my hand. You don't know how hard this man could throw."[35] For the 1945 season, Watkins hit .198 with 12 runs and 7 RBIs in 23 games for the third-place Eagles, who ended the campaign at 27-25.

After the season Watkins played for the Negro National League All-Stars in Brooklyn in a five-game series against Charley Dressen's All-National League All-Stars. The first games, a doubleheader on October 7, were played in front of 12,000 fans. In the nightcap, Watkins could not glove a ball off the bat of the Dodgers' Eddie Stanky, which allowed the winning run to score in the 2-1 loss.[36] After two more losses (10-0 and 4-1) and a 0-0 tie, Effa Manley noted that Watkins suddenly was error-prone, "seemed scared to death. In fact, all of the colored boys did."[37]

The 1946 Eagles saw the beginning of the end of the Negro Leagues, as players were scooped up by the white major leagues. Catcher Roy Campanella and pitcher Don Newcombe signed with Branch Rickey's Dodgers, and Effa Manley did not forget.[38] Upon seeing Rickey at a Black Yankees-Eagles game in July, she made the Dodgers owner "turn purple," stating, "I hope you're not going to grab any more of our players. ... Our contracts ... would stand up better in court than you have in the majors."[39]

Nevertheless, the 1946 Eagles assembled one of the top five teams in league history and finished 56-25-3.[40] The team featured five future Hall of Famers – Biz Mackey, Leon Day, Monte Irvin, Larry Doby, and Effa Manley, who helped to put together this formidable squad. The team would, however, be without Watkins before the end of the season.

In June the popular Watkins was traded for Philadelphia Stars third baseman Pat Patterson. In response to Effa's concerns about trading the popular Watkins, Abe Manley "just laughed and said that the fans would appreciate Patterson quick enough."[41] Effa Manley, who was ridiculed by the fans about the trade, said years later, "I don't think we would have won the pennant without (Patterson). He was magnificent."[42]

With the Stars, Watkins joined second baseman Mahlon Duckett and Frank Austin at shortstop and made a run at the first-half title. The *Philadelphia Tribune* wrote, "(T)he brilliant surge of the local nine has been attributed to the sparkling play of the new infield combination (which defensively is about the best in the Negro ranks)."[43] The Stars finished the first half in second place. Watkins, the "5 foot 4-inch firebrand," was a reserve for both East-West All-Star Games, on August 15 at Griffith Stadium and August 18 at Comiskey Park. He joined the East, which included a number of his former Eagles teammates, as one of six infielders on the team.[44] The Grays' Howard Easterling started at third for the East. Watkins ran for Josh Gibson in the first game and in the second game was hit by a pitch and scored the only run of a 4-1 loss. For all-star trivia purposes, Watkins, Lloyd "Ducky" Davenport, and Frank "Groundhog" Thompson were the game's all-time shortest players.[45]

Philadelphia was unable to keep up with the Eagles in the second half as "the Stars reverted to playing poorly ... and failed to challenge the Newark Eagles for the league championship."[46] The Stars finished fourth at 34-36-4. Watkins had his finest season yet as he batted .264 in 154 games with 28 runs and 15 RBIs.

The Stars played at Parkside Field at 44th and Parkside adjacent to the Pennsylvania Railroad roadhouse. The trains generated heavy smoke that showered coal dust on the fans.[47] Money and poor play became factors for the Stars as they finished fifth in 1947 and fourth in 1948. The integration of baseball also took a toll on the franchise. The Stars paid upward of $45,000 in ballpark rental and the Negro National League likely lost $100,000 in operating costs.[48] "Due to high salaries and dwindling gate receipts, nearly every Negro league team lost money (in 1947)," a local scholar wrote.[49] According to catcher Stanley Glenn, most of the travel for the Stars was confined to six cities – New York, Newark, Philadelphia, Baltimore, Pittsburgh, and Washington – and much of it was by train. Spring training was held in North Carolina and it was nothing to travel for 500 or 600 miles per day by bus, eat bologna sandwiches, and sleep on the bus or in someone's private home.[50]

In December 1947 manager Homer "Goose" Curry was replaced by Oscar Charleston. The 1948 team was old with the 31-year-old and "colorful" Panamanian Frank Austin at short and 32-year-old Watkins at third.[51] Four other players were over 35. The team also had financial problems and lost the use of Bolden Bowl; with both the Athletics and Phillies using Shibe Park, there was not space to use the major-league ballpark. The monthly payroll for each Negro League club also was reduced to $6,000.[52]

The Negro National League disbanded after the 1948 season. The Negro American League added the Stars, Cubans, and Baltimore Elite Giants and drafted players from the other disbanded clubs.

The Stars were considered the "dark horse in the race"[53] for the 1949 NAL pennant with a revamped and highly touted double-play combo of Bus Clarkson and Marv Williams.[54] Watkins remained at third. Struggles continued for the club. After Williams jumped to Venezuela, the Stars were left with 16 men and struggled for bodies in late July.[55] The team also embarked on a three-week road trip through Texas, Alabama, and Louisiana. In July it played at "home" Shibe Park for the first time in two months.[56]

In spite of the team's hardships, Watkins finished the 1949 season with a .959 fielding percentage at third base that was second only to Lou Brown's .975 for Chicago; he made just five errors. (Brown had two.) At the plate, Watkins hit .213 (51-for-240) with 32 runs and 7 RBIs in 62 games.[57] The Stars were 28-35, well behind Baltimore's 63 wins. The Elite Giants won both the first- and second-half Eastern Division crowns.

In October and November 1949, Watkins joined the Jackie Robinson All-Stars with Robinson, Campanella, Doby, Buck Leonard, and Don Newcombe.[58] Building off Robinson's popularity in the South, the All-Stars drew 75,000 in its first nine games; that number included 15,871 at Rickwood Field in Birmingham. A total of 148,561 spectators saw the team in its first 25 games, which far exceeded the 100,000 that its organizers had expected. Louisiana fans pushed through the turnstiles to the tune of 16,000 at Pelican Stadium in New Orleans and 8,000 "jubilant" fans attended at City Park Stadium in Baton Rouge.[59]

Watkins' final season in the Negro Leagues included time with the Stars and a brief stint with the Indianapolis Clowns. *Philadelphia Tribune* columnist Kimmie Debnam noted that Charley White took over at third base for the Stars,[60] but the same paper also listed Watkins as one of the players counted on for the Stars two weeks later.[61] He was listed in another box score at second base in late May.[62] *New York Amsterdam News* writer Joe Bostic wrote that Watkins was part of a Clowns team in June with Archie Ware, Verdes Drake, and Speed Merchant and that "a better than average degree of success is just about assured for your club (with those players)."[63] Later newspapers listed Honey Lott as the Clowns' third baseman in June and in October.[64]

The Clowns went 29-17-1 in the first half and 18-21-1 in the second half. Philadelphia was last in both halves, going a combined 15-28-1. The Negro Leagues had a "severe case of gate famine," and bad weather didn't help, but they trudged to the end of 1950.[65] With the Stars in 1950 Watkins hit .213 in 62 games with 32 runs and 21 RBIs; 51 of his 56 hits were singles.[66]

Many Negro Leaguers looked for better opportunities, and a number of players moved on to the ManDak League in Manitoba and North Dakota. At 35, Watkins joined the Brandon (Manitoba) Greys in 1950. He hit .222 in 42 games in 1950 (39-for-176);

.262 in 61 games (72-for-275) with 26 RBIs in 1951; and .225 (48-for-213) with 13 RBIs in 1952. In 1951 he led the league in steals with 19. In 1952, which was Watkins' final year in professional baseball, he led the league in fielding at .914. He also played for the Regina Caps in the Saskatchewan Baseball League in 1952.[67]

In addition to spending time in Canada in 1952, Watkins also played for the Orientales in the Dominican Summer League. He was one of several late-30s former all-stars on the roster, which included Cuban outfielder Pedro Formenthal and pitchers Robert Lee Griffith and Gready McKinnis.[68] The Orientales also featured 47-year-old Cuban star pitcher Cocaina Garcia; Julio Rojo, who debuted in pro ball when Watkins was one year old (1916) and spent 21 years in the Cuban League; and the "Dominican Deer" and father of Dominican baseball, Tetelo Vargas who one year later led the league in hitting at the age of 47.

A year later Watkins joined his brother Lin and played for the semipro Yokely Baltimore Stars. In a game against Willie Mays' Newport News Royals, Lin was doubled up on a fly ball to Mays to center and Murray was a part of a triple play turned on the infield.[69] It is likely Watkins continued to find a place on the diamond well into his 50s. At 58 he played twice a week for a semipro team in Baltimore, the Turner Station Red Wings.[70] The love of the game still tugged at him in his later years, even though he said, "Oh the legs aren't what they used to be. But I still got good reactions and my skills are still there." He also managed Turner Station and until the spring of 1973 he was a regular, batting leadoff.[71] When asked for the key to his longevity, Watkins replied, "Nothing much. Just don't drink whiskey and though I stay up late, I don't go chasing after women. That combination can rot a man's body."[72]

Watkins became a father of nine and a grandfather of 14. He worked as a custodian for the Baltimore Board of Education for 22 years.[73] His two older sons, Raymond and Lewis, were "both fine ballplayers," but they gave up the game. In 1973, his 12-year-old son Murray played Little League baseball.[74]

The final fastball came on March 26, 1987, as Watkins died in Bolton Hills, Maryland, at the age of 71. He had told a reporter in 1973, "I'd really stop playing even now but sometimes I stand on the sidelines and watch what some of the youngsters are doing wrong and I just have to get a glove and go out there." He did so despite the bus rides and a doubleheader in Philly followed by a night game in Baltimore (over 100 miles away), because he still missed the lifestyle. Murray Watkins was a true baseball lifer.[75]

NOTES

1   James A. Riley, *The Biographical Encyclopedia of the Negro Baseball Leagues* (New York: Carroll & Graf Publishers, 1994), 822.

2   Ed Harris, "Take Me Out to the Ball Game," *Philadelphia Tribune*, July 11, 1940: 11.

3   JD Berthea, "Grandpa Plays Third," *Evening Star* (Washington DC), June 22, 1973: E1, E4.

4   Maryland Bureau of Vital Statistics, Birth Record, Counties Index, 1910-19, W-Z, 76. msa.maryland.gov/megafile/msa/stagserm/sm1/sm27/000000/000011/pdf/msa_sm27_000011.pdf.

5   Associated Press, "At 58 Skeeter Still Is in the Infield," *Hanover* (Pennsylvania) *Evening Sun*, June 13, 1973: 41.

6   Riley, 822.

7   "Newcomers Sparkle for Philadelphia Stars," *Columbus* (Ohio) *Dispatch*, July 21, 1941: 13.

8   "Philadelphia Nine Here for Arc Game Tomorrow at 8:45," *Stamford* (Connecticut) *Daily Advocate*, September 3, 1941: 12. Duckett ended up being the last surviving member of the Stars when he died at 92 in 2015. John F. Morrison, "Mahlon Duckett, 92, Last Surviving Member of Philadelphia Stars," *Philadelphia Inquirer*, July 17, 2015. philly.com/philly/obituaries/20150717_Mahlon_Duckett__92__last_surviving_member_of_the_Philadelphia_Stars.html.

9   "Bolden's Stars Lose 4, Win 2 as 1941 Season Nears Climax," *Philadelphia Tribune*, September 6, 1941: 12.

10   Ibid.; "Caught on the Fly," *The Sporting News*, August 6, 1942: 7.

11   Riley, 822.

12   Effa Manley 1973 interview with John Holway, National Baseball Hall of Fame file on Manley, 6.

13   "Sullies Hits 3 Out of 4 ABs as Eagles Top Giants, 5-3," *New York Amsterdam Star-News*, August 22, 1942: 10.

14   Berthea.

15   Ibid.

16   "Star Negro Teams Play Here Sunday," *Richmond Times-Dispatch*, April 10, 1942: 24; "Grays Out to Clinch Second Half Title in Bargain Bill," *Washington Evening Star*, June 28, 1942: 35.

17   "Claim Negroes in Big Time Baseball Would Hurt Semi-Pros," *Kansas City* (Kansas) *Plaindealer*, November 27, 1942: 3.

18   Larry McShane (Associated Press), "Newark Eagles Join Hall of Fame," May 31, 1998, National Baseball Hall of Fame archives on Newark Eagles.

19   Ibid.

20   "The African-American Newark baseball team was a source of pride and identity in segregated times," NJ.com, February 12, 2009. blog.nj.com/ledgerarchives/2009/02/the_africanamerican_newark_bas.html.

21   Ibid.

22   Typewritten year-by-year attendance summaries at Ruppert Stadium, 1939-43, Hall of Fame archives, Newark Eagles.

23   Robert Cvornyek, *Baseball in Newark* (Charleston, South Carolina: Arcadia Publishing, 2003), 95.

24   NJ.com, February 12, 2009.

25   "Case Plans Charity Aid," *Trenton Evening News*, April 5, 1943, 13

26   Box scores at the time listed Watkins' spot in the order and where he played. Box score vs. Trenton, *Trenton Evening News*, May 3, 1943: 15; "Stars and Eagles Collide Tomorrow," *Trenton Evening News*, May 20, 1943: 20; Box score, *Trenton Evening News*, July 13, 1943: 12.

27   "Newark Eagle Monthly Salaries," handwritten, Hall of Fame archives, Newark Eagles.

28   Riley, 822.

29   Berthea.

30   "Murray Watkins Tops Club Poll," *Afro-American*, August 18, 1945: 22.

31   Effa Manley letter to Murray Watkins, March 24, 1945, Newark Public Library Archives.

32   Wil Haygood, "Woman of Summer," *Washington Post*, April 16, 2006: D01.

33   Cvornyek, 95.

34   "East-West Tilt in Chi Sunday," *New York Amsterdam News*, July 28, 1945: 8B.

35   Berthea.

36   "Dressens Cop Two from Negro Stars," *The Sporting News*, October 11, 1945: 131.

37   Neil Lanctot, *Negro League Baseball: The Rise and Ruin of a Black Institution* (Philadelphia: University of Pennsylvania Press, 2004), 278.

38   "Rickey Signs Two Other Negro Stars for Nashua," *The Sporting News*, April 11, 1946: 6.

39   Dan Parker, "Quotes," *The Sporting News*, July 17, 1946: 18.

40   Rob Neyer and Eddie Epstein, *Baseball Dynasties: The Greatest Teams of All-Time* (New York: W.W. Norton and Company, 2000), 226.

41   Blog quote from James Overmyer's *Queen of the Negro Leagues: Effa Manley and the Newark Eagles* (Metuchen, New Jersey: Scarecrow Press (1998). baseballthinkfactory.org/hall_of_merit/discussion/hall_of_fames_2006_negro_league_election/www.crookedbrook.com/www.crookedbrook.com/custom-embroidered-jackets.htm/P300.

42   William J. Marshall interview with Effa Manley, October 19, 1977, Louie B. Nunn Center for Oral History, University of Kentucky Libraries. nyx.uky.edu/oh/render.php?cachefile=1977oh079_chan041_manley_ohm.xml (36-minute mark).

43   Randy Dixon, "Phila. Stars Take Lead in NNL Race," *Philadelphia Tribune*, June 11, 1946: 11.

44   "West Favored Over East in Dream Game in DC," *Philadelphia Tribune*, August 13, 1946: 11.

45   Larry Lester, *Black Baseball's National Showcase* (Lincoln: University of Nebraska Press, 2001), 453.

46   Courtney Michelle Smith, "A Faced Memory: The Philadelphia Stars: 1933-53," Lehigh University, Theses and Dissertations, 64-65. preserve.lehigh.edu/cgi/viewcontent.cgi?article=1743&context=etd.

47   Neil Lanctot, "Baseball: Negro Leagues," Encyclopedia of Greater Philadelphia, 2014. philadelphiaencyclopedia.org/archive/baseball-negro-leagues/.

48   "Robinson's Success Sidetracks Interest from Negro League," *The Sporting News*, December 31, 1947: 4.

49   Courtney Michelle Smith.

50 Stars catcher Stanley Glenn as told to Brent Kelley, *Voices from the Negro Leagues: Conversations with 52 Baseball Standouts* (Jefferson, North Carolina: McFarland and Company, 1998), 159-160.

51 "Phila. Stars to Begin Spring Training April 1," *Philadelphia Tribune,* March 27, 1948: 10.

52 Courtney Michelle Smith.

53 "Stars-Monarchs Plan Season's Opener for Newark," *Philadelphia Tribune,* April 12, 1943: 10.

54 "Charleston Preps Stars for Week-End Series," *Philadelphia Tribune,* May 10, 1949: 10.

55 Kimmie Debnam, "Newcombe Hurls Eighth Triumph; Paige Checks Yanks," *Philadelphia Tribune,* July 30, 1949: 14.

56 "Stars Continue Tour of South; Return Home July 25th," *Philadelphia Tribune,* July 12, 1949: 10.

57 Personal communication from Carlos Bauer, March 2018.

58 Roster for Robinson All-Stars. docplayer.net/30613162-Rosters-of-barnstorming-and-independent-black-baseball-teams.html.

59 "Dixie Hails Jackie," *The Sporting News,* October 26, 1949: 17; "Jackie's Troupe Sets Gate Pace," *The Sporting News,* November 9, 1949: 13, 20; "Jackie Draws 16,000 in NO," *The Sporting News,* November 2, 1949: 18;

Michael Bielawa, Janice Bielawa, *Baseball in Baton Rouge* (Charleston, South Carolina: Arcadia Publishing, 2006), 52-53.

60 Kimmie Debnam, "Sports-I-View," *Philadelphia Tribune,* April 1, 1950: 11.

61 "Four N.A.L. Teams to Play in Virginia," *Philadelphia Tribune,* April 22, 1950: 10.

62 "2715 Watch Kaysee Win," *Omaha World-Herald,* May 24, 1950: 27.

63 Joe Bostic, "Visitors Home Team, The Scoreboard," *New York Amsterdam News,* June 3, 1950: 27.

64 "Negro Tilt Sunday at Bosse Field," *Evansville* (Indiana) *Courier and Press,* June 27, 1950: 18; "Robinson's Team Routs Local Club," *Raleigh News and Observer,* October 13, 1950: 18.

65 Kimmie Debnam, "Sports-I-View," *Philadelphia Tribune,* June 17, 1950: 11.

66 Personal communication from Carlos Bauer, March 2018. Watkins was listed having played for the Stars but was not listed among third basemen. White played in 30 games for Philadelphia at third.

67 1950, 1951, and 1952 League Statistics. attheplate.com/wcbl/1952_1j.html.

68 Negro Leaguers in the Dominican League. cnlbr.org/Portals/0/RL/Negro%20 Leaguers%20in%20the%20Dominican%20Republic.pdf.

69 "Mays Leads Newport News to Two Baltimore Wins," *Afro-American,* May 9, 1953: 15.

70 Berthea.

71 Ibid.

72 Ibid.

73 Associated Press, "At 58 Skeeter Still is in the Infield," *Hanover Evening Sun,* June 13, 1973: 41.

74 Ibid. We were otherwise unable to find information regarding his family.

75 Ibid.

JIMMY "SEABISCUIT" WILKES

BY BOB LEMOINE

Outfielder Jimmy Wilkes was so fleet of foot that he earned the nickname "Seabiscuit." *(Courtesy of Jay-Dell Mah/Western Canada Baseball)*

"They used to say Brantford could put its left-fielder five feet from the foul line, the right-fielder five feet from the other line and Jimmy Wilkes would cover the rest."

-- Bob McKillop[1]

"Riding the bus again!" Jimmy Wilkes said, his voice cracking with excitement. "I love it. Now, that brings back memories."[2] The 69-year-old Wilkes was on his way to Cooperstown, New York, to the Baseball Hall of Fame with about 20 other Negro League veterans. They had stayed in a hotel in Albany the night before and were on their way to honor their former teammate Leon Day, who was being inducted posthumously.

They reminisced about the days when they barnstormed the country, including the Jim Crow South, where they could not sleep in its hotels, use its bathrooms, or eat in its restaurants. They were segregated because of the color of their skin and could not play in the same game as white players until Jackie Robinson broke the color barrier. We will never know how great some of them were, and many stories have been silenced with the passage of time. "Their statistics were often lost, their glory obscured," wrote Sean Peter Kirst.[3] But on that July day in 1995, these former players were among baseball's honored guests who would exit the bus from another era, making sure we would always remember their stories. Jimmy Wilkes' life and career provide one such tale.

There was the game when Wilkes made a catch at the deepest part of Yankee Stadium. "Josh Gibson was batting, for the Homestead Grays," Wilkes recalled. "He hit a line drive to deep center field. That was in the old Yankee Stadium, where it went a long ways

back. I turned my back and started running. I reached up and stuck my mitt out and there was the ball. I was way back there. I turned around and there were the monuments for Babe Ruth and Lou Gehrig. It's been called one of the greatest catches ever in Yankee Stadium."[4] Perhaps the only difference between the legendary great catch Willie Mays made in the 1954 World Series and this catch by Wilkes is that Wilkes' games were not televised or followed by hordes of reporters, and its image has passed with those who saw it.

"If me and Willie were in the same outfield," Wilkes said, "they wouldn't need anybody else out there. We'd have caught everything that came out there."[5]

Wilkes was nicknamed Seabiscuit after the legendary racehorse and was the speedy leadoff hitter for the Newark Eagles. He was known for his electric speed in the outfield for nearly 20 years. He played in Canada for 10 years, where he remained for the rest of his life and umpired for another 26 years. Brantford, Ontario, became his adopted hometown, and "people who were too young to have seen him play, or who weren't even born then, looked up to this fun-loving guy whose ear-to-ear smile seemed to be permanent and whose laughter was infectious."[6]

James Eugene "Jimmy" Wilkes was born on October 1, 1925, in Philadelphia to Histron and Minnie (Gullick) Wilkes. The 1940 census lists the family living at 8509 Mornan Avenue in Philadelphia. Histron was a "laborer" for the "evening newspaper," but reported no income or weeks worked for 1939; however, there is a "yes" written in the box for "income from other sources." Mary Washington, listed as a widowed sister-in-law, also lived with them and worked as a housekeeper for a private family, earning $314 for the year. The family owned their home, which was valued at $2,000.

Wilkes graduated from John Bartram High School in Philadelphia, where he played on the baseball team. The Clippers won the Public High School Baseball Championship of 1943 and Wilkes went 3-for-3 with four RBIs in the championship game, two of them coming on a triple (the only extra-base hit of the game), which proved to be the deciding runs in the 5-3 win.[7]

After high school Wilkes served a brief stint in the US Navy during World War II but was discharged because of an injured back.[8] On July 25, 1944, Wilkes married Hattie M. Davis. The couple would have four children: James, Janice, Patricia, and Eugene.

Wilkes played in 1945 for the Brooklyn Brown Dodgers of the short-lived United States League. The USL, a third major Negro league that began play that year, was the brainchild of former Pittsburgh Crawfords owner Gus Greenlee. In order to lend credence to the endeavor, Greenlee struck a deal with Brooklyn Dodgers general manager Branch Rickey, who prompted the move of the USL's Hilldale franchise to Brooklyn. Oscar Charleston, Wilkes' manager and a scout with the Dodgers organization, brought Wilkes to the attention of Effa Manley, the owner of the Newark Eagles. She was impressed with Wilkes' speed and defense, and he remained on the team to finish the season and batted over .300.[9] "I used to tell the pitcher, keep the ball in the park and I'll catch it. If it goes out of the park, I can't catch it," Wilkes said.[10]

Wilkes' glove and his speed were major contributions to the 1946 Newark Eagles, the team that won the Negro League World Series. The season started magnificently, as Wilkes saw Day return from the military and throw a no-hitter against the Philadelphia Stars on Opening Day in May. That was an omen of things to come with Day on the mound and Wilkes darting around the outfield. Called a "hustling, never-give-up gang of young ballplayers from across the river," (in an unknown newspaper account), the Eagles swept the New York Cubans in a doubleheader at the Polo Grounds before 12,000 fans. The sweep pulled the Eagles into a first-place tie with the Philadelphia Stars. "Al [sic] Wilkes, purchased from the United States League last winter by the Manleys, came up with a sensational catch to snag a potential triple to centerfield."[11] Wilkes batted .272 during the season and .280 in the World Series, as Newark defeated the Kansas City Monarchs in seven games.[12]

In 1947 Wilkes "thrilled the fans last week with one of the greatest catches made a[t] Shibe Park this season."[13] His hitting tailed off to .234 in 1947.[14] The season is also synonymous with Jackie Robinson breaking baseball's color barrier, something Wilkes felt he himself could never have done. "The main reason Rickey signed him was because Jackie had been to UCLA," Wilkes said. "He'd mingled with the white people. A lot of us wouldn't have taken the crap Jackie took. Rickey knew Jackie would be a gentleman. What was it Rickey told him? If they smack you on your right cheek, turn your left cheek. I couldn't have done it."[15]

Wilkes played for Newark in 1948 and when the franchise moved to Houston, he played for this relocated Eagles team in 1949, batting .254.

Wilkes has been described this way: "A hustler, he was an excellent defensive player, with outstanding range and a good arm. He had a good eye at the plate, was a pretty good contact hitter, had excellent speed, and was a good base stealer, which made him a good leadoff batter."[16] Twice Wilkes led the Negro Leagues in stolen bases. "Fast, oh yeah," Wilkes said. "I'd get on first, you might as well put me on second. Just the same as a double."[17]

In 1950 Wilkes was invited to spring training with the major-league Dodgers, but they already had a great center fielder named Duke Snider. Wilkes never did make it onto a major-league roster, but he spent 1950-1951 with Dodgers farm teams. Early in 1950, the *Monroe* (Louisiana) *News-Star* reported that the new Eagles team in Houston "is captained by Jimmy Wilkes, regarded as the fastest center fielder in Negro baseball."[18] He batted .199 for the Eagles before joining the Elmira Pioneers of the Class-A Eastern League in the Brooklyn Dodgers' system. His arrival at Elmira was noteworthy, as "the *Elmira Star-Gazette reported that Wilkes and outfielder* Bob Wilson would be the first two blacks to wear the Pioneers uniform."[19] Wilkes batted .281 during his time with the Pioneers. Later that season, Wilkes also played for the Three

Rivers team in the Class-C Canadian American League, where he batted .180.

Wilkes played for Elmira again in 1951, and went 4-for-7 in his first regular-season game.[20] The surge of power "Little Jimmy Wilkes" showed surprised writer Jim Morse, who said "'Mighty Mite' doesn't appear to have enough power to hit the ball to the pitcher without the help of a strong wind."[21]

Over the course of the 1951 season, Wilkes batted .273 with Elmira in 10 games and .231 with the Lancaster (Pennsylvania) Red Roses of the Interstate League in 105 games. While still with Elmira, Wilkes came through in the clutch with a pinch-hit single with the bases loaded in the 10th inning to give the Pioneers a 4-3 win over Albany.[22] In a game for the Roses, Wilkes had a three-run homer and a triple with four RBIs in an 8-2 win over Wilmington.[23] On another occasion, Wilkes doubled in the 12th inning and scored the go-ahead run in a game at Allentown at which Connie Mack was present for an old-timers ceremony.[24]

In 1952 Wilkes played in nine games for the Great Falls (Montana) Electrics of the Class-C Pioneer League, batting .235.

The Dodgers wanted to send Wilkes to their Double-A affiliate in Birmingham, Alabama, but Wilkes refused to play in the South and asked for his release. Growing up in Philadelphia, Wilkes wasn't used to the segregation he encountered in the Jim Crow South. "I used to hate it when we went barnstorming to the South," he remembered. "We couldn't eat in restaurants, had to walk on the other side of the streets and use different water fountains. Being from Philadelphia I hadn't grown up with all that crap."

Wilkes continually had to tolerate racial slurs. "Call us black, or whatever, but that word would get everyone angry," he recalled. "What could you do? Say something and you'd get your head blowed off."[25] "We'd be down there in Mississippi. Oh, boy. Rough, rough. One time, I fouled a ball off my foot. It really hurt and I fell to my knees and someone in the crowd started yelling at me to get up and was using the 'N' word. I don't mind being called black or a Negro, but I don't like the word nigger. We also had to put up with walking on the other side of the street, back of the buses and crap like that. Even when I got signed with the Dodgers organization, they had to bring the food to me in the bus. We'd eat on the bus and sleep on the bus."[26]

After his brief stint with Great Falls, Wilkes returned to the Negro Leagues in 1952 and played for the Indianapolis Clowns of the Negro American League. Despite the name, the Clowns played their home games in Buffalo, New York. As suggested by their name, "[W]hat the Harlem Globetrotters are to basketball, the Clowns are to baseball," wrote the *Buffalo Criterion*.[27] The Clowns had moved to Buffalo in 1951 and were known for pulling pranks and wearing costumes to entertain the crowd, but they could also play ball with the best teams. "We'd get out there between innings and clown around, but then we had a team that could run you to death," Wilkes said. "We weren't clowning then."[28]

"We had a tough schedule," Wilkes remembered of his barnstorming days with the Clowns. "After the ballgame, each time, you'd go to the grocery store and buy some sardines and crackers and hit the bus for the road for the next game. Only time you had a bed was on the weekend, where you'd go into town the night before a doubleheader."[29]

While in the Offermann Stadium locker room in Buffalo on May 25, 1952, Milwaukee Braves scout Dewey Griggs asked Wilkes if anybody there could play in the majors. "That fellow sitting in the dugout," Wilkes responded. "If he doesn't go to the majors, my name ain't Jimmy Wilkes."[30]

That player was Hank Aaron, an 18-year-old infielder. "I guess you know how that turned out," Wilkes said almost 50 years later.[31]

Wilkes hit .325 with 49 stolen bases and 63 runs scored for the Clowns. He was the starting left fielder for the Eastern All-Star team at Comiskey Park in Chicago. Dr. John B. Martin, president of the Negro American League, in his column in the *Plaindealer of Kansas City*, said, "As a leadoff man, Wilkes is tops in the NAL. He leads the circuit in number of hits, and in stolen bases. He is second in runs scored. He is a fellow the West will have to watch."[32] Wilkes led off for the East team but went 0-for-3 in a 7-3 loss.[33]

"I could move, brother, they didn't call me Sea Biscuit for nothing," Wilkes said in 1997, remembering his days patrolling center field. "If I bunted a ball and it hopped twice, they might as well put the ball in their pocket."[34]

Wilkes saw the highs and lows of the Negro Leagues and its eventual demise after African-Americans left for opportunities in the major leagues. "The biggest crowd I ever played in front of was 70,000 people," he said. "Towards the end there were 1,000 or 1,500 fans in the stands. It was sad. Clubs just started folding because they weren't making money. It was like the bottom dropped out, like a bucket dropping into a well when you want to get water. But the bucket didn't come up no more."[35]

While on a barnstorming tour in Ontario, Wilkes was discovered by the management of the Brantford Red Sox in the Intercounty League. "I went 5-for-5. The local people liked me. I told them I was tired of riding around the country and if they were interested they should call me," Wilkes remembered. Team owner Larry Pennell offered Wilkes an immediate contract to come north. The Brantford team was able to lure Wilkes with the promise of a city public-works job during the day and $500 a month to play baseball at night and on weekends. Tired of the racism he faced in the Southern U.S., Wilkes saw Canada as a great opportunity. "They phoned over the winter and I came up in 1953. Opportunity only knocks once and if you don't take advantage it never comes again."[36]

Many African-American players left for Canada to play semipro baseball once the Negro Leagues began folding. Wilkes found both a job and a baseball team in Brantford, and while many players returned to the United States once their playing days were over, Wilkes became a Canadian citizen and spent the rest of his life there. "It was a new experience living here," he said. "It was God's country, that's all I can say. I didn't have any trouble like I had down in the States, no racial things. I was always surprised how well people liked us. They always treated me well."[37]

Wilkes' job with the city involved driving a street sweeper in the summer, and "in the winter I'd plow snow. One guy I had a beef with, I cleaned the whole street, parked down the street and saw him come out in the morning to see all the snow in his drive. I cleaned it out later."[38]

Wilkes played for the Brantford Red Sox from 1953 to 1963 and was a part of five straight titles from 1959 to 1963. "We had ballplayers that knew what to do," he said. "All our manager had to do was make up the lineup and say, 'Let's play ball.'"[39] The 1961 Brantford Red Sox went 30-4 with an .882 winning percentage.

Wilkes recalled, "I played until 1963 and when I retired they gave me a night. I was making money playing in Brantford but when the fans give you something you really appreciate it."[40]

During his seasons in Canada, Wilkes led the Intercounty League in hits, doubles, runs, and walks in 1956; runs scored in 1961 and 1963; and stolen bases in 1960. His impact on the team and its community was such that "he had his uniform number (5) retired and he was inducted into the City of Brantford's Hall of Fame."[41]

On March 24, 1979, Wilkes married Donna Newton in Brantford. It is unknown if his first wife was deceased, or if the couple had divorced.

Wilkes followed his playing career with a 26-year umpiring career, becoming one of the most respected and sought-after umpires in the league. "I loved being behind home plate," he said. "That's where all the action is."[42] He finally retired in 1988.

Wilkes worked in the Brantford Public Works Department for 34½ years. Kids would run outside when they heard his garbage truck or snowplow coming down the street and would shout and wave to him. The man once called Seabiscuit for his blazing speed was now called Yogi Bear by neighborhood children. Wilkes even had "Yogi" inscribed on his license plate."[43]

Wilkes also delivered prescriptions to area seniors for Shopper's Drug Mart in West Brant. "When they answered the doorbell they were always happy to see Jimmy standing there, ready to talk and to listen. His positive attitude and friendly smile probably did more for their general health than the pills he was delivering," wrote Ted Beare of the *Brantford Expositor,* noting that Wilkes' friendly chats often made him late for his next delivery.[44]

Wilkes also belonged to the Echo Lanes Seniors Monday Bowling League. When he wasn't bowling he loved to watch the Toronto Blue Jays on TV, or he would care for the birds around his house, even feeding chipmunks and squirrels out of his hand. He also spent time watching his stepsons and grandsons play baseball.[45]

Making at the most $500 a month in his playing days, Wilkes had trouble comprehending the baseball salaries of modern-day players. "We went hell for those guys playing today. They're making all that money," Wilkes said. "We played for the love of the game. I don't care who the player is, not one player is worth the money they earn."[46]

Wilkes remembered those days through the courtesy of old newspaper clippings he kept, which he shared with Michael Snyder of *Maclean's* magazine in 2001. *"There's* Paige," he pointed out. "Satchel struck me out three times in a row. He was tall. He'd step down on top of you and boom! The ball would be right there. And Josh. Josh Gibson. He was the Babe Ruth in our league. He could hit 'em a long way. If they would have broke the colour line earlier, he would have broke all kinds of records in home runs."[47] In his Hall of Fame questionnaire, Wilkes listed the greatest accomplishment of his career as getting four hits off Satchel Paige.[48]

Wilkes suffered with Alzheimer's disease in the last years of his life. He was interviewed by Tim Graham of the *Buffalo News,* "aided by a dog-eared scrapbook and gentle reminders from his proud wife. He had trouble recognizing a few photos, even of himself, without looking at the names written on the back."[49] While his memories faded, the scrapbook told an amazing story of his life and the people he knew from Philadelphia to Canada … the buses he rode … the bases he stole … and the children who waved … the man known as Seabiscuit.

Jimmy Wilkes died on August 11, 2008, in Brantford, Ontario, at the age of 82. He was cremated and a tree was planted in his memory at the Beckett-Glaves Memorial Forest.[50]

SOURCES

In addition to the sources cited in the Notes, the author also consulted:

Martin, Alfred M., and Alfred T. Martin. "James (Jimmy) Wilkes" in *The Negro Leagues in New Jersey: A History* (Jefferson, North Carolina: McFarland, 2008), 63-64.

NOTES

1   Bob Elliott, "Wilkes Has Seen It All," *Toronto Sun, April 20, 1997*. Story reprinted on the Western Canada website, retrieved August 14, 2015. attheplate.com/wcbl/profile_wilkes_jimmy.html.

2   Sean Peter Kirst, "Baseball Celebrates; Something's Missing," in *The Ashes of Lou Gehrig and Other Essays* (Jefferson, North Carolina: McFarland, 2003), 95.

3   Kirst, 96.

4   Kirst, 97.

5   Ted Beare, "Red Sox Star Loved City," *Brantford* (Ontario) *Expositor, August 11, 2008*. Story reprinted on the Western Canada website, retrieved August 14, 2015. attheplate.com/wcbl/profile_wilkes_jimmy.html.

6   Ibid.

7   Ken Hay, "Bartram Wins Public High Title," *The Jay-Bee* (Philadelphia), June 4, 1943. Article in Wilkes' Hall of Fame file.

8   Donna Wilkes, interview with the author, October 26, 2015.

9   Bob Luke, *The Most Famous Woman in Baseball: Effa Manley and the Negro Leagues* (Washington: Potomac Books, 2011), 112; Thom Loverro, "Brooklyn Brown Dodgers," in *The Encyclopedia of Negro League Baseball (New York: Facts On File, Inc., 2003)*. African-American History Online. Facts On File, fofweb.com/activelink2.asp?ItemID=WE01&iPin=ENLB0311&SingleRecord=True (accessed August 18, 2015).

10   "Remembering Jimmy 'Seabiscuit' Wilkes," published online August 16, 2008, from wire reports. blackathlete.net/2008/08/remembering-jimmy-seabiscuit-wilkes/, retrieved August 14, 2015.

11   "Newark Eagles Sweep Both Games With Cubans at PG," article of unknown origin in Wilkes' Hall of Fame file.

12   Later in life, Wilkes took credit for a game-saving catch in Game 7. "We were leading them," Wilkes recalled. "They had two men on, and Buck O'Neil was at bat. He hit a ball high, to left center, for sure it would have been a triple, and I went and got it. He said to me after, 'You little sonuvabitch. You won the World Series for them.' That's why they put me out there. If it was in the ball park, I'd get it." The story was told to Michael Snider for *Maclean's* magazine in 2001. The story was also recounted by O'Neil in a Wilkes obituary. Thanks to research provided by SABR member Frederick C. Bush, however, there are major gaps in this story. For one, O'Neil, in his autobiography, states that Leon Day made the catch to rob him of a hit. This detail is supported by Monte Irvin, who in his autobiography recalled that Day started Game 6 as the pitcher but later moved to the outfield. The *Pittsburgh Courier* also reported a much different ending to Game 7, stating that it was Kansas City's Herb Souell who flied out to Newark's Lennie Pearson to end the Eagles' 3-2 series-clinching victory after the Monarchs had put runners on first and second with two outs in the top of the ninth inning. In summary, the best research seems to show the catch would have occurred in Game 6, and it was made by Day, not Wilkes, Whether Wilkes intentionally took credit for the catch or, as O'Neil possibly did, confused this catch with another catch, is unknown. For Wilkes' version of the catch, see "Remembering Jimmy 'Seabiscuit' Wilkes," and Michael Snider, "God's Country: Former Negro League Players Found Their Fields of Dreams in Small Towns Across Canada," *Maclean's 114, no. 20 (2001): 37. Academic Search Complete, EBSCOhost (accessed August 17, 2015)*. For the various accounts that dispute Wilkes' version, see the following: Buck O'Neil, *I Was Right on Time* (New York: Simon & Schuster, 1996), 178-79; Monte Irvin, *Nice Guys Finish First* (New York: Carroll & Graf Publishers, Inc., 1996), 106; and "Newark Eagles New Diamond Champs: Win World Series from Kansas City," *Pittsburgh Courier*, October 5, 1946: 15.

13   "Larry Doby, New Home Run Sensation, Faces Stars Under Arcs Thursday," article of unknown origin in Wilkes' Hall of Fame file.

14   Numbers vary according to source. These were taken from the *Biographical Encyclopedia of the Negro Baseball Leagues*, coe.k-state.edu/annex/nlbemuseum/history/players/wilkes.html.

15   Bob Elliott, "Jackie Robinson Became the Major Leagues' First Black Player on This Day In 1947 and, for Jimmy Wilkes of Brantford, the Memories Remain Vivid," *Toronto Sun*, April 15, 1997.

16   "Jimmy Wilkes," in Negro League Baseball Museum website, coe.k-state.edu/annex/nlbemuseum/history/players/wilkes.html, retrieved August 17, 2015.

17   Snider, "God's Country,"

18   "Black Yanks Meet Houston Tomorrow," *Monroe* (Louisiana) *News-Star*, April 25, 1950: 10.

19   Barry Swanton and Jay-Dell Mah, *Black Baseball Players in Canada: A Biographical Dictionary, 1881-1960* (Jefferson, North Carolina: McFarland and Company, Inc., 2009), 178.

20   Jim Morse, "Fallon Relieves Mulleavy of Pilot's Duties Today," article of unknown origin in Wilkes' Hall of Fame file.

21   Jim Morse, unknown article in Wilkes' Hall of Fame file.

22   Jim Morse, "Jim Wilkes' Pinch Single Gives Stanek 3rd Win; Hugh Mulcahy to Pitch Tonight," article of unknown origin labeled May 21, 1951, in Wilkes' Hall of Fame file.

23   "Roses Home to Fight for Second," article of unknown origin in Wilkes' Hall of Fame file.

24   "Steen Hurls Roses to Win Over Cards," article of unknown origin in Wilkes' Hall of Fame file.

25   Elliott, "Jackie Robinson Became the Major Leagues' First Black Player."

26   Snider.

27   "Clowns, Memphis Red Sox Open Negro League Baseball Sun. May 25, 2 p.m.," *Buffalo Criterion*, May 10, 1952. Reprinted on the "Baseball Games" website, baseballgames.dreamhosters.com/NegroLeaguesBuffalo.htm. Retrieved August 16, 2015.

28   "Class Clowns."

29   Snider.

30   Elliott, "Wilkes Has Seen It All."

31   Tim Graham, "Class Clowns: The Indianapolis Clowns Have a Rich Place in Buffalo Baseball History; for Example Hank Aaron Was 'Discovered' at Offermann Stadium," *Buffalo News*, September 22, 2004. Story reprinted on "Baseball Games," website, baseballgames.dreamhosters.com/NegroLeaguesBuffalo.htm. Retrieved August 16, 2015.

32   Dr. J.B. Martin, "Dr Martin Says: East-West Classic Time Is Here," *Plaindealer* (Kansas City, Kansas), August 15, 1952: 5.

33   "West Nips East, 7-3, in Negro Game," *Chicago Tribune, August 18, 1952*.

34   Bob Elliott, "Jackie Robinson Became the Major Leagues' First Black Player."

35   "Class Clowns."

36   William Humber, *A Sporting Chance: Achievements of African-Canadian Athletes* (Toronto: Natural Heritage Books, 2004), 58.

37   Snider.

38   Elliott, "Jackie Robinson Became the Major Leagues' First Black Player."

39   Paul Ferguson, "Toronto Maple Leaf Baseball," *Toronto Sun*, August 4, 2001. Story reprinted on the Western Canada website, retrieved August 14, 2015. attheplate.com/wcbl/profile_wilkes_jimmy.html.

40   Humber, 58-59.

41   Swanton and Mah, 179.

42   Paul Patton, "Where Are They Now? Jim Wilkes Baseball," *Globe and Mail* (Toronto), March 5, 1988. search.proquest.com/docview/385954599?accountid=14612.

43   Beare, "Red Sox Star Loved City."

44   Ibid.

45   "James Wilkes," yourlifemoments.ca/sitepages/obituary.asp?oId=256573, retrieved August 18, 2015.

46   Elliott, "Jackie Robinson Became the Major Leagues' First Black Player."

47   Snider.

48   Jimmy Wilkes' Baseball Hall of Fame questionnaire.

49   "Class Clowns."

50   "James 'Jimmy' Eugene Wilkes Obituary," retrieved from obitsforlife.com/obituary/95253/Wilkes-James.php, August 5, 2015.

ROBERT "COTTON" WILLIAMS

BY RALPH CARHART

As is the case with so many of his Negro League brethren, the tale of the beginnings of Robert "Cotton" Williams has been shrouded by time. Even the most basic facts are in dispute. The Negro Leagues Database and Find A Grave list his birthday as January 18, 1917. The US Social Security Index claims it was June 18, 1917. Negro League researcher Larry Lester has discovered a third possible date, June 21, 1925. Lester also lists Williams's birthplace as Moncure, North Carolina,[1] despite virtually every other resource available claiming he was from Maryland. (No specific town is ever given.) To further thicken the plot, contemporary accounts from Williams's time claim he was from Philadelphia.[2]

Certainties for Cotton Williams do not begin until 1943, when he arrived in the training camp of the Newark Eagles. He was a promising young infielder with a powerful throwing arm. Teammates complained that his tosses were hurting their hands because he threw so hard. Manager Mule Suttles is credited as recognizing the potential in Williams's talent and began to experiment with turning him into a pitcher.[3]

Williams saw little action that first season. He split his playing time between backing up second base and shortstop for the teenage duo of Earl Richardson and Hall of Fame-bound Larry Doby. The Negro Leagues Database at Seamheads.com credits Williams with seven appearances in the field that season, batting .208, with five hits in 24 at-bats.[4] He struggled in the field as well, making four errors in 44 innings at shortstop.

(L-R) Rufus Lewis, Jimmy Wilkes and Robert "Cotton" Williams. Much of Williams' life remains shrouded in mystery, but he was a member of the Eagles' 1946 championship team. *(Noir-Tech Research, Inc.)*

Absent from the database is the fact that Williams appeared in another game that season. Suttles gave his experiment a try in a May 15 tilt against the Philadelphia Stars. It was, in fact, the opening game of the season at the Stars' 44th and Parkside Ballpark. Staff ace Leon Day had been scheduled to start,[5] but Suttles decided to save him for the home opener the following day. Instead, he put the rookie on the mound and Williams responded masterfully.

He pitched eight innings, surrendering only two runs in the sixth. With the game locked at 2-2 in the ninth, Williams was replaced by Len Hooker, who finished the contest with three scoreless frames. The Eagles won, 4-2, when Day and Johnny Davis were able to cross the plate in the top of the 11th.[6] Remarkably, despite this impressive debut, current research has not found another game that Williams pitched that year.

Williams disappears from the record entirely for the 1944 season. It is likely he spent the year strengthening his game while barnstorming, because when he returned to the Eagles in 1945, he was a much-improved player. He manned five different positions that season, including second base, third base, shortstop, and left field. His batting average soared to an impressive .304, and he played nine games at third base, making him the most-used third sacker on the club.

He hit his first Negro League home run in a July 7 contest against the Baltimore Elite Giants. It was a leadoff shot, coming off the first pitch of the game thrown by Elite Giants lefty Zack Morgan. The blast cleared the right-field fence, one of two balls hit out of the park in a game that was a veritable slugfest, with Baltimore ultimately clubbing the Eagles 13-6.[7]

Williams also took the mound for a single game in 1945, this time as a reliever. Newly installed manager Willie Wells must have agreed with his predecessor's assessment of Williams's pitching talent. Wells gave him one opportunity, in a May 13 contest against the Baltimore Elite Giants. Williams pitched 4⅓ innings, giving up a pair of runs. It will never be known if Wells would have given him another chance. After a spat with Eagles owner Abe Manley, Wells quit the club in early June.[8] His replacement, Biz Mackey, chose to keep Williams at third base and let Hooker and Don Newcombe handle the bulk of the season's pitching responsibilities.

After spending time playing in Jacksonville, Florida, at the start of the 1946 season,[9] Williams rejoined an already dominant Eagles squad in August. Having won the first-half crown, the team was on its way to capturing the second-half flag as well. The Eagles pitching rotation that year was the best in the Negro National League, and arguably in all of baseball. Day won anywhere from 11 to 14 games,[10] depending on the source, while Rufus Lewis and Max Manning had tremendous seasons, each posting sub-3.00 ERAs. Once an opponent got through these three top-line starters, they still had a very effective Len Hooker to face.

It was under these unlikely circumstances that manager Mackey decided to finally start committing the majority of Williams's playing time to the mound. His first three appearances for the year were as a reliever, including innings in both halves of a doubleheader on August 18. He did not fare well that day, surrendering five runs in a combined 5⅓ innings. Undeterred, Mackey tapped

Williams to pitch his first start of the year on August 26 against the New York Cubans.

The Cubans were the final threat to the Eagles' season of dominance and Mackey's choice of starting the relatively inexperienced hurler in such a high-pressure situation spoke volumes about his level of confidence. Williams began the game promisingly, taking a 6-2 lead into the eighth. Then the wheels fell off and he gave up three runs, managing to record only a single out before being relieved by Cecil Cole, who in turn surrendered another run, tying the score and costing Williams the victory. The Eagles rallied for two in the bottom of the eighth, aided in part by an error by Orestes "Minnie" Miñoso, and won the game, 8-6.[11] On September 4 Newark captured the second-half crown, and undisputed ownership of the Negro National League pennant, with a 17-5 trouncing of the Cubans.[12]

The victory earned them the right to face the Negro American League champions, the Kansas City Monarchs, in the 1946 Negro League World Series. The first game was played in the Polo Grounds, in front of 19,423 delighted fans,[13] many of whom were locals who had made the trip over the river to see the Eagles in action. Williams made an unsuccessful pinch-hitting appearance and otherwise spent the game on the bench, watching a tight contest that ultimately turned into the Satchel Paige show. Relieving Hilton Smith, Paige pitched four scoreless innings, striking out eight and scattering four hits. He also scored the winning run after getting on base with an infield hit, giving the Monarchs, and himself, a 2-1 victory.

The Eagles rebounded two nights later, scoring six runs in the seventh inning to claim a 7-4 Game Two victory at Ruppert Stadium in Newark. This time Paige faltered in relief and took the loss. Four days later the Series moved to Kansas City, and the Monarchs' home field, Blues Stadium. It was in this third game that Williams was given the most sustained playing time he would see in the Series. Unfortunately for Williams, the experience was one he likely would have preferred to forget.

The game was started by Hooker, who had a disastrous second inning, giving up four runs. Hoping Williams could stop the bleeding, Mackey pulled Hooker after the fourth and gave Cotton his big chance. But after pitching admirably for three innings, the still-inexperienced pitcher imploded. The Monarchs had a punishing seven-run eighth inning and dashed any hopes the Eagles had of digging their way out of the early hole. Williams's devastating final line was 3⅔ innings pitched, 11 hits surrendered, and nine runs allowed.[14] The final score of 15-5 made the Series look like a terrible mismatch.

It wasn't. Back in Newark the very next night, the Eagles evened the Series with an 8-1 victory over Ted Alexander. Four days later, after again exchanging victories with the Monarchs, the Series stood tied at 3-3. Newark starter Rufus Lewis outdueled Kansas City's Ford Smith in Game Seven, a tight, 3-2 contest, and secured the victory. For the first time in their history, the Newark Eagles were the champions of the Negro Leagues. Williams did not play in another game in that Series and would, in fact, never play in another World Series again.

The taste of victory may have inspired Williams, as he arrived at spring training in Jacksonville a determined and much-improved pitcher. By late April, sportswriters began to notice his development. The *New York Amsterdam News* reported, "One of the big surprises in training camp has been the great pitching of Cotton Williams, big right hander, who joined the Eagles in mid-season last year. Williams is a greatly improved pitcher and Manager Mackey has just about decided to make a regular starting pitcher out of him."[15] While this prediction did not come to pass, it was true that 1947, a seminal year in the game, would be Williams's best season on the mound.

By the end of May Williams was drawing (perhaps inflated) comparisons to Jackie Robinson,[16] who was electrifying crowds and shattering barriers in Brooklyn. With fellow young pitchers Warren Peace and Nelson Thomas, Williams was part of a core of hurlers who were not only filling the vacuum left behind by the departure of Leon Day, but were being credited with the early-season success of Newark.[17] The Eagles sat atop the standings in mid-June, but they had a number of teams nipping at their heels.

The Cubans were hungry and eager to atone for their near-miss the year before. The two teams had become bitter rivals, escalating into a brawl during an exhibition game at the Polo Grounds earlier that season.[18] They battled in a June 15 doubleheader at Ebbets Field with the league lead on the line. The Eagles lost the first contest, 7-5. Williams was tapped to pitch the second and hopefully to split the day's games. He gave a strong start, pitching a complete game and striking out six while surrendering three runs. But his teammates were unable to muster any offense. Williams took the loss and the Eagles ceded first place to the Cubans.[19]

After that loss, Williams ran off a string of four consecutive victories. The first two came from both ends of a June 22 doubleheader against the New York Black Yankees. Appearing in relief in both contests, he pitched a combined 7⅔ innings and did not allow an earned run. Late Eagles rallies in both games secured him a pair of victories on the day. He notched another win in his next appearance, on July 1, in a start against the Philadelphia Stars.[20]

That was followed by a July 15 start versus the Homestead Grays, a start that would turn out to be the best pitching performance in Williams's career. The game did not get off to a great beginning, when hits from the Grays' Luis Marquez and Luke Easter plated the first run. Easter was followed to the plate by legendary first baseman Buck Leonard, who promptly deposited the ball over the right-field wall for an early 3-0 lead.[21] After that early blow, Williams settled down and pitched into the ninth, scattering three more hits over the next 7⅓ innings. He walked only two and struck out nine, a career high, in the 4-3 victory.

Williams was also having his best year at the plate. He made one start at third base that year, on June 17, and had an incredible day, going 3-for-5 with two RBIs. He also made a handful of appearances as a pinch-hitter, including notching pinch hits in both games of a July 27 doubleheader against the Baltimore Elite Giants. By season's end, he finished with a .385 batting average, a career best, and an impressive 3.16 ERA.[22] Yet, despite the above-average performance of Williams at the plate and on the mound, as well as predictably fruitful contributions from Larry Doby (before he was sold to the Cleveland Indians in early July) and Monte Irvin, 1947 belonged to the Cubans. The team from New York defeated the Cleveland Buckeyes in the World Series, four games to one, securing them their only championship.

After his impressive showing in '47, Williams found himself earning even more playing time in 1948. New manager William Bell not only wanted him on the mound, but he wanted his bat in the lineup with more frequency. For the first time in his professional career, Williams found himself regularly playing left field, filling in for Irvin while the slugger battled illness that July.[23] Once again the Eagles began the season hot, perched atop the standings in mid-June, and again Williams and the pitching staff were credited with that success.[24]

As the season progressed, both Williams and the Eagles faded. After reaching his season-high batting average of .286 on August 15, Williams struggled at the plate over the next three weeks and ended the year with only a .241 mark. He tried to compensate on the mound, dropping his ERA from 4.65 to 4.03 over that same span,[25] but it was too late for the Eagles. The Homestead Grays became the NNL champs after they defeated the Elite Giants in the playoffs, and then they beat the Birmingham Black Barons in the final World Series in Negro League history.

The next year, 1949, proved to be one of tremendous change. The Negro Leagues suffered a great schism, as the National League folded. A handful of teams, including the Elite Giants, the Cubans, and the Stars, were absorbed into the newly expanded, two-division American League. Effa Manley sold Monte Irvin to the Giants for $5,000,[26] before selling the franchise itself to a Memphis businessman, Dr. W.H. Young. Young moved the team from Newark to Houston, where they joined the AL West Division. William Bell's tenure with the Eagles ended with Young's ownership and Ruben Jones took over as pilot of the club. It also marked the first time the team trained in Hot Springs, Arkansas. Cotton and most of the 1948 Eagles, but minus Irvin, Day, and Ray Dandridge, were on hand that spring.[27]

Williams also brought a little something new with him that season. Originally spotted by Mackey in 1943 because of his tremendous speed, by this point Williams was 32 years old and had lost a few miles per hour on his fastball. The 1949 season was the first time the press started to refer to him as a "curve ball specialist."[28] Even with the organizational shift, it was becoming clear to all that integration had put Negro League baseball in dire straits. It is likely Williams knew he was going to have to expand his arsenal if he were ever to have a chance to make the leap to the majors.

Fighting for economic survival, the new Houston Eagles played an increased number of exhibition games, including an August tilt against the Point Pleasant Pelicans. Williams had a solid start against the Pelicans, surrendering only two runs until the seventh inning, when he was pulled after three more crossed the plate. The Eagles offense was firing on all cylinders that night and Williams, despite his late struggles, walked away with a 16-5 victory.[29]

Lopsided victories like those were rare in league games. It was a tumultuous year for the Eagles, who went through three managers during their first season in Houston. Reuben Jones was replaced by Roy "Red" Parnell in mid-July. A short time later, catcher Leon Ruffin took over for Parnell for the final games of the season.[30] Unable to overcome the loss of their biggest stars, as well as all the internal conflict, the Eagles finished in last place. They watched the Elite Giants defeat the American Giants in the newly devised American League Championship Series for the season crown.

Approaching 33 (if he was indeed born in 1917), Williams, along with returning manager Parnell, began to concentrate on playing in the outfield. Still talked about as a part of the rotation in April 1950,[31] by July he was being referred to as a "former pitcher."[32] He responded well to the shift to the outfield, where he split time between left and center. In early June he was batting .333.[33] He was playing more often than he ever had in his career, and his hitting had become consistent enough that he was being eyed by major-league scouts.[34]

The Eagles, in fact, were hemorrhaging players to the majors. In July outfielders Bob Wilson and Jimmy Wilkes had their contracts sold to the Brooklyn Dodgers. Later that year, standout shortstop Curley Williams was sent to the Chicago White Sox. Desperate for cash, the club was not only selling its best players, but by July it was looking for a new home.[35] Disappointing attendance forced the team to play most of its home games in second half of the season in Nashville. Perhaps more disappointing to Williams, his final season average had sunk to a pedestrian .276[36] and he remained unsigned by a major-league team.

When the Negro League owners met in January, writer Wendell Smith referred to the theme of those meetings as "salvation,"[37] as they desperately scrambled to make the league viable. The previous season, only Kansas City and Birmingham had reported making a profit. The Eagles were particularly egregious financial failures and a former Memphis Red Sox owner, Dr. B.B. Martin, became a principal owner of the club in hopes of changing their fortunes. As part of that effort, it was decided at the January meeting that their new home field would be Pelicans Park in New Orleans, and that the club would adopt the name of their new hometown.[38]

Williams would not make that journey. For the first time in his professional career, he was not an Eagle. With the start of the 1951 campaign, he became a member of his hometown Philadelphia Stars. Sharing playing time with Al Henry, he regularly platooned in left field for the team. Helmed by Oscar Charleston, the Stars were still considered pennant contenders as late as August.[39] Williams was a consistent contributor to that effort, including saving some of his best stuff for when he faced his former team. In a June 21 tilt against the Eagles, he went 3-for-5 and knocked in the two winning runs in the ninth inning of a 9-7 Stars victory.[40]

After season's end Williams made an appearance with the Milford (Delaware) Yankees, an all-black squad, in a contest against the Mar-Del League All-Stars.[41] Months later, an item in the April 1952 Asheville Citizen-Times mentioned that Williams was still with the team the following season as it made a preseason trek to North Carolina. According to the article, he was still playing well enough at 35 years old that he was being scouted by the Boston Braves.[42] Despite these promising notes of a future career, no more records can currently be found of him setting foot on a baseball diamond. His long journey to reach the majors never came to pass.

The next time Williams appeared in the news was 33 years later, in 1985. While living in Philadelphia, he was one of 10 former Negro Leaguers honored by the Friends of Black Baseball Trailblazers at a ceremony held at the Afro American Historical and Cultural Museum in February.[43] He reappeared a year later at a presentation at the former Glassboro State College (now Rowan University) in Camden, New Jersey, just outside of Philadelphia. The evening presented an opportunity for old players to reminisce to an admiring crowd, including some one-on-one time as they signed baseballs for children of all ages. Fellow attendees included old teammates Leon Day and Max Manning, as well as the legendary Judy Johnson.[44]

That evening of memories is where Cotton Williams disappears from the public record. This may have been due in no small part to what could be perceived as a certain amount of modesty in the old ballplayer. Larry Lester once attempted to get Williams to fill out a player info questionnaire, but Williams declined. It is notable that many of the players at the February 1986 event spoke to the multiple newspapers that covered the event, providing quotes about their days on the diamond. Williams is not quoted in any of the articles.

Robert A. "Cotton" Williams died on December 28, 2000, at (presumably) the age of 83, in Philadelphia.

ACKNOWLEDGEMENT

The author would like to extend the deepest gratitude to Larry Lester, whose willingness to share his personal remembrances and statistical records of Cotton Williams were invaluable in the completion of this biography.

NOTES

1   Personal player files of Larry Lester.

2   "List Twin-Bill for Negro League Teams," *Philadelphia Inquirer*, May 14, 1948: 45. The Social Security Index reports that his SSN was issued in South Carolina before 1951. Given the inability to better pin down the details of his birth, we are unable to learn about his family or the days of his youth.

3   James A. Riley, *The Biographical Encyclopedia of the Negro Baseball Leagues* (New York: Carroll & Graf Publishers, Inc., 1994), 860.

4   seamheads.com/NegroLgs/.

5   "WAAC to Start Negro Leagues," *Philadelphia Inquirer*, May 15, 1943: 23.

6   "Newark Eagles Beat Stars 4-2," *Philadelphia Inquirer*, May 16, 1943: 45.

7   "Baltimore Trims Newark Eagles," *Harrisburg* (Pennsylvania) *Evening News*, July 9, 1945: 11.

8   Bob Luke, *The Most Famous Woman in Baseball* (Dulles, Virginia: Potomac Books, 2011), 110.

9   "Newark Eagles, Grays Clash Here Today," *Altoona* (Pennsylvania) *Tribune*, June 2, 1947: 10.

10   "Negro Leagues World Series," Center for Negro League Baseball Research. Retrieved January 24, 2018. cnlbr.org/Portals/0/RL/Negro%20League%20World%20Series.pdf.

11   "Eagles Nose Out Cubans, 8 to 6," *Wilmington* (Delaware) *Morning News*, August 27, 1946: B-16.

12   "Eagles Top Cubans to Clinch Flag; Josh Hits 410 Ft. Homer," *Pittsburgh Courier*, September 14, 1946: 17.

13   "Monarchs Triumph; 2 Players Hurt," *Philadelphia Inquirer*, September 18, 1946: 35.

14   Personal player files of Larry Lester.

15   "Eagles Shove Off for New York From Jacksonville," *New York Amsterdam News*, April 26, 1947: 12.

16   Os Figard, "Newark Eagles to Meet Grays Here Monday," *Altoona Tribune*, May 29, 1947: 8.

17   "Larry Doby Looms as Home Run King," *New York Amsterdam News*, May 31, 1947: 12.

18   "Eagles and Cubans in 3-Game Series At Ebbets Field," *New York Age*, June 14, 1947: 7.

19   "Colonels Meet Cubans Again," *Bridgewater* (New Jersey) *Courier-News*, June 21, 1947: 6.

20   Personal player files of Larry Lester.

21   "Newark Eagles Nose Out Homestead Grays, 4-3," *Wilmington Morning News*, July 16, 1947: 16.

22   The ERA figure comes from the Seamheads database.

23   "Newark Eagles Take to Road; Irvin Returns," *New York Amsterdam News*, July 24, 1948: 26.

24   "Newark Eagles Set Hot Pace for AL Nine," *New York Amsterdam News*, June 12, 1948: 27.

25   Personal player files of Larry Lester.

26   "The Demise of Negro League Baseball," Center for Negro League Baseball Research. Retrieved January 25, 2018. cnlbr.org/Portals/0/RL/Demise%20of%20the%20Negro%20Leagues.pdf.

27   "Pilot Jones Drills New Eagle Nine," *Pittsburgh Courier*, March 26, 1949: 29.

28   "Eagles, Stars Clash Tonight," *Wilmington News Journal*, May 30, 1949: 14.

29   "Pelicans Drop 16-11 Verdict in Night Fray," *Asbury Park* (New Jersey) *Press*, August 24, 1949: 25.

30   There are conflicting news reports about the Eagles' managerial changes in 1949 and why they were made. In his book about the Negro Leagues in Texas, author Rob Fink states that Reuben Jones resigned after the first half and that the team then hired local hero Roy "Red" Parnell, who had formerly managed the Houston Black Buffaloes. See Rob Fink, *Playing in Shadows: Texas and Negro League Baseball* (Lubbock: Texas Tech University Press, 2010), 115-116. Accordingly, the Pittsburgh Courier had two articles that heralded the hiring of Parnell to replace Jones. See "Roy Parnell New Pilot of Eagles," *Pittsburgh Courier*, July 23, 1949: 11, and J. Don Davis, "Lone Star Week," *Pittsburgh Courier*, July 23, 1949: 20. Oddly, a mere two weeks later, the *Courier* ran an article that stated Jones had been fired due to an on-field conflict with club secretary George Mitchell and had been replaced by catcher Leon Ruffin. See "Eagles Fire Jones, Ruffin Takes Helm," *Pittsburgh Courier*, August 6, 1949: 11. Fink, too, reports that Ruffin finished the season as Houston's manager, but states that he replaced a fired Roy Parnell, not Jones (Fink, 116). Fink's sources were the team's hometown African-American newspaper, the *Houston Informer*, and the *Dallas Express*; these two sources were obviously much closer to the team offices than the *Pittsburgh Courier*; thus, it is possible that the *Courier* misreported who was fired in its August 6 article. However, there is no information to be found in any source to explain why the Eagles ownership rehired Parnell to pilot the team in 1950 after firing him in 1949.

31   "Eagles Work Hard for Chi Giants Game," *Pittsburgh Courier*, April 15, 1950: 24.

32   "Red Sox Face Houston Negroes Here Tonight," *Journal and Courier* (Lafayette, Indiana), July 5, 1950: 14.

33   "Houston Eagles Tackle Bushwicks at Dexter Tonight," *Brooklyn Daily Eagle*, June 2, 1950: 17.

34   "Houston Eagles to Play Local Indians Friday," *Times Recorder* (Zanesville, Ohio), August 22, 1950: 7.

35   "Houston Eagles Seek New Hunting Grounds," *Pittsburgh Courier*, July 8, 1950: 23.

36   "Negro American League (1950) League Leaders," Center for Negro League Baseball Research. Retrieved January 26, 2018. cnlbr.org/Portals/0/Stats/NAL%201950/NAL1950.pdf.

37   Wendell Smith, "'Salvation' Theme of NAL Meeting This Week," *Pittsburgh Courier*, January 6, 1951: 14.

38   Leonard Lowery, "Sports: From a Ringside Seat," *Hattiesburg* (Mississippi) *American*, February 22, 1951: 8.

39   "Negro Teams Debut in Area May Preview Flag Winner," *Altoona Tribune*, August 17, 1951: 12.

40   "Philadelphia Stars Whip Eagles," *Tennessean* (Nashville), June 22, 1951: 39.

41   Pat Knight, "Clayton and Wyoming in Mar-Del Finals," *Denton* (Maryland) *Journal*, September 18, 1951: 1.

42   "Negro Pros Open NAL Season Tonight at McCormick Field," *Asheville* (North Carolina) *Citizen-Times*, April 24, 1952: 30.

43   Michael E. Ruane, "Honoring Stars of the Negro League," *Philadelphia Inquirer*, February 28, 1985: 7-B.

44   Ed Power, "Baseball Tales, Sweet and Bitter," *Philadelphia Inquirer*, February 27, 1986: 1-B.

ABE MANLEY

BY AMY ESSINGTON

Abraham Lincoln Manley was born on December 22, 1885, in Hertford, North Carolina, one of seven children of William and Rebecca (Faulk) Manley. The family owned land, raised and raced horses, and were practicing Quakers.[1] In high school, Abe worked in a sawmill, and lost the top of his left thumb while cutting a piece of wood.[2] After Hertford, Abe lived in Norfolk, Virginia; Brooklyn, New York; and Camden, New Jersey. He worked as a chauffeur, a laborer, and a barber.[3] He married Gertrude Stoves on December 2, 1914, in Brooklyn.[4] They lived in Brooklyn and later divorced.[5]

While living in Camden, Manley became part of numbers gambling, an illegal yet popular pastime in the African American community, as a "numbers banker." He developed his fortune at the prominent Rest-A-While Club in Camden. Manley owned the building that housed the club and he served as its treasurer. The club included "a private bar, a steward, sleeping apartments, a billiard and game room, and a piano valued at $8,000."[6] On September 12, 1932, an explosion damaged the front of the building. After the bombing, probably by a gambling competitor, the local district attorney, a friend, advised Manley to leave town. He did so, moving to New York City.[7]

Effa Manley later recounted meeting her second husband at the 1932 World Series.[8] If correct, the two met on either September 28 or 29, 1932, at one of the New York Yankees home games in the Series against the Chicago Cubs. They may have met earlier as evidenced by an event co-hosted by the Manleys on January 29, 1932, in Camden.[9] Whenever they met, Effa and Abe were

Abe and Effa Manley co-owned the Newark Eagles from their inception in 1936 through the 1948 season. Abe procured the on-field talent but was content to let Effa run all of the team's day-to-day operations. *(Noir-Tech Research, Inc.)*

married by the Manhattan city clerk on June 15, 1933. Their marriage lasted until Abe's death in 1952.

After the marriage the couple moved to 741 St. Nicholas Avenue in the Sugar Hill area of Harlem. Effa Manley received four mink coats, a seal coat, and a five-carat diamond ring from Tiffany's during their marriage. Abe drove a Lincoln Continental and furnished their house with Oriental rugs.[10] Effa claimed to never know how much money they had, but said, "Anything I wanted, I got."[11]

Abe Manley had enough money to purchase a Negro League baseball team. On November 13, 1934, the National Negro League owners awarded Manley the Brooklyn Eagles franchise.[12] The team spent spring training in Jacksonville, Florida, at the Richmond Hotel, and then played its home games at Ebbets Field, the home of the Brooklyn Dodgers. The Eagles celebrated Opening Day on Saturday, May 11, 1935. Effa brought in New York Mayor Fiorello LaGuardia to throw out the first pitch.[13] The Homestead Grays beat the Brooklyn Eagles, 21-7. The Eagles ended the season in sixth place in the eight-team NNL. In November 1935 the Manleys sent Brooklyn Eagles uniforms and some players to play in the Puerto Rico winter league and they won the championship.

Before the 1936 season the Manleys purchased the Newark Dodgers, combined the roster with that of the Eagles, and relocated the ballclub to Ruppert Stadium in Newark. While Effa began to take over more of the day-to-day operations, Abe was responsible for securing players. As a team owner, the players liked Abe Manley. They gave him the nickname of "Cap" for captain. He traveled to spring training and on the bus with the team during the season. He provided a daily $1 meal allowance. Abe also concerned himself with morality of the players. Fran Matthews, a Newark Eagle for five years, said, "[Abe] had an All-American boy idea about the ballplayers – no drinkin', no smokin', no women."[14]

The Manleys also became part of the management of the NNL. In March 1936 the owners elected Abe Manley vice president, and the following year he became the league's treasurer. Initially, Effa worked behind the scenes and completed much of Abe's work for the league. She moved into a more active and public role at the owners meeting at Philadelphia in January 1937 when she suggested changes for how to improve the league. Effa and Abe saw ways to improve the structure of the NNL. Abe wanted African-Americans to manage and control the operations of the league. Effa observed, "For the most part, Abe had been waging a one-man war against the booking agents from the first day he entered the picture as club owner. This served to make him highly unpopular (putting it mildly) with all the agents. … Abe always took the unwaverable position that the league teams should do their own booking of league games, and he fought constantly against the encroachment of private interests into the field."[15]

In 1938 the Manleys moved to an apartment at 55 Somerset Street and an office at 101 Montgomery Street in the Third Ward of Newark. In 1941 they purchased a three-story house at 71 Crawford Street.[16] During the 1940s, the teams grappled with the loss of players to the armed forces, restrictions on gasoline used by team buses, and players leaving for teams in Mexico or Latin America. As the number of jobs in local defense plants increased, by the end of World War II the Eagles saw a rise in attendance and profits. They ended each season between 1940 and 1945 in third place in the league, except for 1944, when they were fifth.

In 1946 the Eagles defeated the Kansas City Monarchs to become the Negro League champions. Managed by James Raleigh "Biz" Mackey, the team ended the season with a record of 56-24-3.[17] The home attendance was the club's best ever at 120,292 and the Manleys' profit for the season was $25,000.[18] Between 1935 and 1948, the team included seven future Hall of Famers, Ray Dandridge, Leon Day, Larry Doby, Monte Irvin, Biz Mackey, Mule Suttles, and Willie Wells, and one Hall of Fame executive, Effa Manley.

The 1946 season was the high point for the Manleys. That year Organized Baseball integrated when Jackie Robinson played with the Montreal Royals, the Dodgers top farm team. When Robinson joined Brooklyn in 1947, there was a major drop in attendance for the Eagles and a reduction in the Manleys' revenue. Fans were more interested in following the fates of black players in what was becoming integrated Organized Baseball rather than watch players in the segregated Negro Leagues.

After the 1948 season, the Manleys disbanded the Eagles and sold the club to W.H. Young, a dentist from Memphis, Tennessee.[19] That same year the Negro National League merged its remaining teams with those of the Negro American League. The last act the Manleys oversaw as owners of the Eagles included the sale of Monte Irvin's contract to the New York Giants.

Abe Manley died on December 9, 1952, at the home of his in-laws in Germantown, Pennsylvania. He had heart disease and had been suffering from prostate issues for several years. He suffered heart failure after surgery.[20] A funeral Mass was held at St. Madeleine Sophie Catholic Church in Germantown. Larry Doby and Monte Irvin were among the pallbearers. Manley was buried in Fairmount Cemetery in Newark.

NOTES

1   Bob Luke, *The Most Famous Woman in Baseball: Effa Manley and the Negro Leagues* (Dulles, Virginia: Potomac Books, 2011), 3

2   Luke, 4; World War I Registration Card.

3   Luke, 4.

4   Gertrude Stoves/Abraham Manley Marriage Certificate.

5   World War I Registration Card.

6   Luke, 4.

7   Luke, 5.

8   John Holway, *Voices from the Great Black Baseball Leagues* (New York: Dover Publications, 2012), 319.

9   Luke, 6.

10   Ibid.

11   James Overmyer, Queen of the Negro Leagues: Effa Manley and the Newark Eagles (Lanham, Maryland: Scarecrow Press, 1993), 13.

12   Overmyer, 33; Luke, 9.

13   Overmyer, 34.

14   Overmyer, 72-73.

15   Effa Manley and Leon Herbert Hardwick (Robert Cvornyek, editor), *Negro Baseball … Before Integration* (Haworth, New Jersey: St. Johann Press, 2006), 50.

16   Overmyer, 71.

17   seamheads.com/NegroLgs/organization.php?franchID=NE.

18   Overmyer, 202-203.

19   Overmyer, 241.

20   "Abe Manley, Baseball Founder, Buried," *Baltimore Afro-American*, December 20, 1952; Overmyer, 247.

EFFA MANLEY

BY AMY ESSINGTON

Effa Manley was "a businesswoman in primarily a man's world," yet "when she found a closed door, Manley kicked it open to improve her league and her team's playing conditions." *(Photo and quotations from the National Baseball Hall of Fame)*

Effa Manley co-owned the Newark Eagles with her husband, Abe. In 2006 the Special Committee on Negro Leagues elected her to the National Baseball Hall of Fame for her work as a baseball executive. As of 2019, she was the only woman inducted into the Hall of Fame.

On March 27, 1897, in Philadelphia, seamstress Bertha Brooks gave birth to a daughter, Effa Louise. The father was not Bertha's husband, John R. Brooks, a black man, but John Marcus Bishop, a wealthy white man who employed Bertha. In a 1977 interview,

Effa Manley said that Brooks successfully sued Bishop for alienating the affections of his wife and received damages in the amount of $10,000.[1] John Brooks and Bertha divorced after having four children together. Bertha later married Benjamin Cole and they had two daughters.

Sometime after high school, Effa Brooks revised her birth year to 1900. The census records from 1910 and 1920 list a birth year of 1897 as do high-school transcripts. With her marriage to Abe Manley in 1933, her birth year shifted to 1900. She claimed a birth year of 1900 in an 1977 interview and that was the year on her grave marker.

Throughout her life, most people who met Effa, including those in the Negro Leagues, believed she was African American. Effa grew up in a household with half-siblings who were of mixed parentage and lived in neighborhoods that had a majority black population so many assumed that she was African American. As a young adult, she would present herself as white when it suited her; she did so, for example, to secure better positions in employment. All four of Effa's husbands were black. She had no children. In a 1977 interview, Effa stated that her race was white. She recalled that Bertha clearly told her more than once that she was white. The 1870 census listed mulatto as race of both Bertha and her mother Agnes. The listing of mulatto for Bertha may have come from her father, who might have been black. The census listing for Agnes was probably related to the classification of her daughter as her parents were from Germany. The censuses of 1910 and 1920 noted the race of Bertha Brooks Cole as black. That determination made by the census taker may have been due to her parentage or her marriages to African-Americans. Despite her possible mixed maternal family heritage, Effa Manley argued later in her life that she was a white woman because she was the daughter of two white parents. Whatever the details of her genealogy may have been, Effa lived as part of the African American community all of her life.

Effa Brooks grew up in Philadelphia. She attended Newton Grammar School and graduated from William Penn Central High School in 1916. She then moved to New York City, where she lived in Harlem and worked at a millinery shop in Manhattan in a position she likely secured by presenting herself as white.[2] She continued to work in this industry until she began her career in baseball. By 1920, she and her first husband, George Bush, a chauffeur whom she had met in Atlantic City, lived on West 142nd Street in Manhattan.[3] They later divorced.

The year 1932 marked a major change in Effa Manley's life. A baseball fan who rooted for Babe Ruth and the New York Yankees, she recounted meeting her second husband, Abraham Manley, at the 1932 World Series.[4] If correct, the two met on either September 28 or 29, 1932, at one of the Yankees home games. They may have met earlier as evidenced by an event co-hosted by the Manleys on January 29, 1932, in Camden, New Jersey.[5] Whenever they met, they were married by the Manhattan city clerk on June 15, 1933. Their marriage would last until Abe's death in 1952.

After their marriage, the couple moved to 741 St. Nicholas Avenue in the Sugar Hill area of Harlem. On November 13, 1934, the National Negro League (NNL) owners awarded Abe a franchise, the Brooklyn Eagles. The team played at Ebbets Field, the home of the major-league Brooklyn Dodgers. Eagles players included Leon Day, Rap Dixon, and Ted "Double Duty" Radcliffe. Abe Manley may have owned the Eagles franchise, but it was Effa who would soon oversee the day-to-day management of the team.

On their first Opening Day as the Eagles' owners – Saturday, May 11, 1935 – Effa brought in New York Mayor Fiorello LaGuardia to throw out the first pitch. The Homestead Grays trounced the Eagles, 21-7, and Effa recounted, "I never saw so many home runs in my life. … I went home in the third inning and had my first drink of whiskey."[6] The team ended the season in sixth place of eight teams. The next season, the Manleys purchased the Newark Dodgers, combined the roster with that of the Brooklyn Eagles, and relocated to Ruppert Stadium in Newark.

The Manleys worked to improve the management of the NNL. In March 1936, the owners elected Abe Manley vice president and the next year as treasurer. Initially, Effa worked behind the scenes with Abe and completed much of his work for the league. She moved into a more active and public role at the owners meeting in January 1937 in Philadelphia when she suggested changes for how to improve the league. Like Abe, she suggested that the league operate more formally.[7]

In 1938 the Manleys moved to an apartment at 55 Somerset Street and an office at 101 Montgomery in the Third Ward of Newark. In 1941 they purchased a three-story house at 71 Crawford Street.[8] By this time, Effa was publicly overseeing the day-to-day operations, marketing, and fiscal management of the Newark Eagles. She also took over the task of press interviews from Abe. In addition to assuming those responsibilities, Effa arranged playing schedules, booked accommodations for the players on the road, publicized the games, purchased equipment, and negotiated contracts.[9] She also kept an eye on the behavior of the players. Pitcher James Walker said, "Mrs. Manley was the disciplinarian of the team. She would call you in and tell you how to dress, what to do, who to associate with. When you had your problems, if they were personal, you went to Mrs. Manley, and she was very understanding as long as you toed the line."[10]

In addition to her work in baseball, Effa actively worked in support of civil rights and supported numerous charitable endeavors. She organized boycotts against businesses owned by whites who would not hire black employees for any position other than that of elevator operator. She raised money for the Harlem Women's Club, which became the Citizens League for Fair Play. Effa pressured Blumstein Department Store in Harlem to not discriminate in their hiring. Those picketing the store carried signs that said, "We Won't Shop Where We Can't Work." Six weeks after efforts began, on July 26, 1934, the store owner agreed to hire black woman as sales clerks.[11] In 1937 Effa turned to raising funds for the victims of flooding in the Ohio and Mississippi River valleys.[12] She was also treasurer of the New Jersey National Association for the Advancement of Colored People (NAACP).[13] Her work for civil rights was also on the baseball diamond. She hosted an anti-lynching campaign at Ruppert Stadium during which the ushers wore sashes that read "Stop Lynching."[14]

The start of World War II saw many changes in professional baseball and American society. Teams replaced players who went into the service, managed bus travel restricted by gasoline rationing, and provided entertainment for war workers. Effa supported the war effort through her work as a local warden for the Newark Defense Council, for the Price Control Board, and by purchasing bonds offered by the Colored Women's Division of the Jersey City War Savings Committee. She often arranged for black entertainers to travel to Fort Dix, New Jersey, on the Eagles' team bus. She became secretary and treasurer of the Women's Volunteer War Service Committee.[15]

In 1946, it took seven games for the Newark Eagles to defeat the Kansas City Monarchs to become the Negro League champions.

Managed by James "Biz" Mackey for the second time, the 1946 team ended the season with a record of 56-24-3.[16] The home attendance for the Eagles was their best ever at 120,292 and the Manleys' profit for the season was $25,000.[17] The team that year had four future Hall of Fame players – Leon Day, Larry Doby, Monte Irvin, and Biz Mackey – and one future Hall of Fame executive, Effa Manley. Between 1935 and 1948, the team included three other future Hall of Famers, Ray Dandridge, Mule Suttles, and Willie Wells.

The 1946 season was the high point for the Manleys. That year Jackie Robinson integrated Organized Baseball when he played with the Montreal Royals, the Dodgers' Triple-A farm team. The 1947 season saw a major drop in attendance for the Eagles and a reduction in revenue for the Manleys. However, Effa set an important precedent for major-league teams that signed players from Negro League teams when Bill Veeck, owner of the Cleveland Indians, offered to purchase the contract of Larry Doby from the Eagles for $10,000.[18] The Manleys knew the offer undervalued Doby, but they did not want to appear to stand in the way of integration. Ever the businesswoman aware of issues of race, Effa Manley responded to the offer by saying, "Mr. Veeck, you know if Larry Doby were white and a free agent, you'd give him $100,000 to sign with you merely as a bonus. However, I realize I'm in no position to be bargaining with you. If you feel you're being fair by offering us $10,000, I suppose we should accept."[19] Veeck offered an additional $5,000 if Doby remained with the team for 30 days. Effa also insisted that Veeck offer Doby $5,000, which was more than the $4,000 salary he earned with the Eagles.[20] Veeck agreed and Doby integrated the American League when he joined the Indians on July 5, 1947.

After the 1948 season, the Manleys disbanded the Eagles and sold the club to W.H. Young, a dentist from Memphis, Tennessee.[21] That same year the Negro National League merged its remaining teams with the Negro American League. The last act the Manleys oversaw as owners of the Eagles include the sale of Monte Irvin's contract to the New York Giants. The Dodgers had released Irvin from a contract after Effa hired a lawyer and submitted a complaint with the offices of the commissioner of baseball, the head of the minor leagues, the National League, and the American Association. Members of the black press were concerned that she had prevented Irvin from signing with a major-league team.[22] But Irvin debuted with the New York Giants on July 8, 1949.

Abe Manley died in 1952. Effa married Henry Moton Clinton on December 25, 1953, in Washington DC. The marriage lasted until August 1954.[23] In 1955 Effa sold the house at 71 Crawford Street and moved to Philadelphia to be near her family.[24] She continued her social activism as a member of the Community Council for the

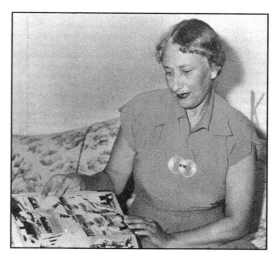

Effa Manley, the only woman to be inducted into the National Baseball Hall of Fame, is shown here looking through her scrapbook and reminiscing about her days as co-owner of the Newark Eagles. (*Noir-Tech Research, Inc.*)

Blind, the Junior Service League, the Concert Series Association, and the Friends of the Heritage House.[25]

Her final move was to Southern California. She married musician Charles Wesley Alexander on December 2, 1956, in Los Angeles. They lived at 4322 Kenwood Avenue. The marriage lasted only about a year and Effa said later than she regretted both marriages after her marriage to Abe.[26] She purchased a house at 451 North Occidental Blvd. in Los Angeles. She continued a relationship with baseball. In 1957 she wrote to Walter O'Malley, owner of the Los Angeles Dodgers, suggesting that the Dodgers pay each remaining Negro American League team for a first option on player contracts. O'Malley turned the letter over to general manager Buzzie Bavasi, who apparently did not respond.[27] In the 1970s, Effa participated in the effort to name a field after former Negro Leaguer Chet Brewer, who managed a local baseball program for boys.[28]

Effa worked to preserve the history of the Negro Leagues and to celebrate their best players. In 1976 she collaborated with Leon Herbert Hartwick to write *Negro Baseball … Before Integration*, which was one of the earliest publications about Negro League baseball. She pressured Fred Claire, the Dodgers publicity director, to recognize Negro League players, and also supported efforts to include them in the Hall of Fame.

In 1971 the Hall of Fame created the Special Committee on the Negro Leagues to elect Negro League players. The committee disbanded in 1977 after electing nine players. Effa began a letter-writing campaign with the goal of establishing a new committee to review all players from the Negro Leagues and to select those to have their names inscribed on a plaque. On June 20, 1977, *The Sporting News's* editor, C.C. Johnson Spink, penned a full column about the quest of a *"furious woman."*[29] In 1978, Manley attended the Second Annual Negro Baseball League Reunion as the special honoree. In 2006 the Hall of Fame established another committee on Negro Leagues, which elected 17 more Negro Leagues figures, including Effa Manley, who was the first woman to receive such recognition.[30]

Effa's health was in decline in the spring of 1981 and she moved into the Queen Ann Manor, a rest home managed by former Negro Leaguer Quincy Trouppe. Doctors diagnosed her with colon cancer and she developed peritonitis after surgery on April 8. In the early evening of April 16, Effa Manley suffered a heart attack and died at Queen of Angels Hospital in Los Angeles. A funeral Mass was held at Our Lady of Loretto Catholic Church and she was buried at Holy Cross Cemetery in Culver City, California. Her tombstone reads, "She Loved Baseball."[31]

NOTES

1   Effa Manley interview by William Marshall for the University of Kentucky Libraries A.B. Chandler Oral History Project, North Rutherford, New Jersey, October 26, 1977.

2   Bob Luke, *The Most Famous Woman in Baseball: Effa Manley and the Negro Leagues* (Dulles, Virginia: Potomac Books, 2011), 3.

3   1920 US Census.

4   John Holway, *Voices from the Great Black Baseball Leagues* (New York: Dover Publications, 2012), 319.

5   Luke, 6.

6   Holway, 320.

7   Luke, 25.

8   James Overmyer, *Queen of the Negro Leagues: Effa Manley and the Newark Eagles* (Lanham, Maryland: Scarecrow Press, 1993), 71.

9   Overmyer, 75-76.

10   Overmyer, 96.

11   Luke, 8.

12   Luke, 26-27.

13   Donn Rogosin, *Invisible Men: Life in Baseball's Negro Leagues* (New York: Atheneum, 1985), 94.

14   Gai Ingham Berlage, "Effa Manley: A Major Force in Negro Baseball in the 1930s and 1940s," in Bill Kirwin, ed., *Out of the Shadows: African American Baseball from the Cuban Giants to Jackie Robinson* (Lincoln: University of Nebraska Press, 2005), 129.

15   Overmyer, 167-168.

16   seamheads.com/NegroLgs/organization.php?franchID=NE.

17   Overmyer, 202-203.

18   The Brooklyn Dodgers did not compensate the Kansas City Monarchs for Jackie Robinson's contract.

19   Effa Manley and Leon Herbert Hardwick (Robert Cvornyek, editor), *Negro Baseball... Before Integration* (Haworth, New Jersey: St. Johann Press, 2006), 74-75.

20   Manley and Hardwick, 76-77.

21   Overmyer, 241.

22   Overmyer, 240-243.

23   Luke, 154.

24   Overmyer, 248.

25   Luke, 154.

26   Effa Manley interview by William Marshall.

27   Luke, 156.

28   Luke, 127.

29   Overmyer, 254-255.

30   Luke, 162.

31   Overmyer, 256.

Sherman "Jocko" Maxwell
Pioneer of Sports Radio

BY LESLIE HEAPHY

"Believed by many to be the first black sports broadcaster, he also was known as an unofficial historian of baseball's Negro Leagues, from his days as a sportswriter and sportscaster in Newark, N.J."[1]

Sportswriter Jerry Izenberg wrote on numerous occasions that one man gave us reports and box scores for the Negro Leagues and that man was Jocko Maxwell. He is not in the National Baseball Hall of Fame, but many of the men he spoke and wrote about are. Maxwell worked for over 40 years giving his fans the latest sports scores and news. He was a pioneer like Jackie Robinson, being the first African-American sportscaster on the radio. His writing also paved the wave for more well-known names like Sam Lacy, Red Barber, and Wendell Smith. Jocko Maxwell is a name anyone with an interest in baseball and sports history should know.

Sherman Leander Maxwell was born on December 18, 1907, in Newark, New Jersey. His father, William Maxwell, worked for many years in the journalism industry, primarily for the *Newark Star-Ledger*. Maxwell Sr. rose to work for the editorial staff, making him one of the few African-Americans to hold such a position at a white paper. In later life both Sherman Maxwell, his brother, Emerson, and his sister, Bernice, would also work for the *Star-Ledger*. His parents, Bessie and William, supported him in all his endeavors, encouraging him to pursue his dreams. Growing up in Newark,

Sherman "Jocko" Maxwell, the Eagles' P.A. announcer, had a lengthy broadcasting and writing career. He was elected to the Newark Athletic Hall of Fame in 1994. *(Noir-Tech Research, Inc.)*

Maxwell played baseball and graduated from Central High School. While in school he earned his nickname Jocko by climbing a tree to try to catch a ball. Jocko was the name of a popular monkey featured in seven films from the 1920s, highlighted by *The Lost World* (1925) and *Flat Broke* (1920). Maxwell loved baseball so much he even failed one year so he could keep playing.[2]

After finishing high school, Maxwell applied to go to college, but due to the racial attitudes of the time he was not accepted. He believed that because professional baseball was segregated, he could not make a career as a player. Maxwell wanted to stay involved in the game, so he applied to a variety of radio stations to host a sports show. He was turned down many times before finally getting a shot in 1929 at WNJ in Newark. There is some debate in the sources about this starting date; some claim he began in 1932. The preponderance of evidence supplied in newspapers points to 1929 and the fact that Maxwell was the first African-American sports announcer in the country. Maxwell had met the owner of WNJ, Herman Lubinsky, at a baseball game and Lubinsky was impressed enough that he offered Maxwell a start with a 10-minute weekly program on which he would announce scores. Maxwell began his radio career the way it would continue, reporting on sports and receiving no pay. The only occasional paycheck he got was from advertising and by endorsing products like Calvert drinks. In order to be able to work in radio, Maxwell took a job as a postal clerk in Newark. He worked there until he retired in 1967.[3]

After hosting his program at WNJ, Maxwell moved to WRNY around 1932 to host the show *Runs, Hits and Errors* three evenings a week. He was able to inform listeners around New York and New Jersey about the great Negro League play in their own backyard. In 1934 Maxwell moved to WHOM (Coytesville, New Jersey) to host a new program called *Sports Hi-Lites*. These shows all were typically 10 minutes long, so the focus was primarily on reporting scores. Maxwell obtained most of the scores by attending games himself or by collecting information from other people who saw games that he was unable to attend. These accounts became the basis for some of his later writing about the Negro Leagues.

By 1938 Maxwell was on the move again, taking his voice to WWRL (Long Island), where he stayed until he left to serve in World War II in the fall of 1942. He also started a sports interview program at WLTH (NYC) in 1939. At WWRL Maxwell was named sports director in April 1942, becoming the only African-American in such a radio position. While in the military, he served with the 375th Engineers and helped to entertain the troops in Europe. After serving his country, Maxwell returned to the post office and WWRL for his weekend shows until he left to join WNJR (Newark) in 1954.[4]

Maxwell was constantly pitching new shows and formats. A few examples are *The Sports Huddle*, *The College Football Scoreboard*, *Five Star Sports Final*, and *Sports with Maxwell*. While baseball was his first love, Maxwell also focused on football as well as sports news in general. He even set another precedent when he helped announce midget auto races at the Polo Grounds in 1948. He also was chosen to help pick a local football all-star team more than once.[5]

Maxwell liked to keep busy. In addition to his radio shows and his postal work, he also wrote. Maxwell sent in stories about the Newark Eagles and their competition to newspapers like the *Trenton Times*, the *Jersey Journal,* the *Star-Ledger* and the *Washington and Baltimore Afro-American*.[6] He also wrote for *Baseball Digest* and *The Sporting News*.

Jerry Izenberg, writing for the *Star-Ledger*, described the important role Maxwell played in keeping the Negro Leagues alive for fans, saying, "He let the world know what was going on in places like Ruppert Stadium and Forbes Field and Comiskey Park when the 'other' teams took over from regular tenants. And in his way, he made the part of America that would listen know all about these black knights of the open road."[7] When the Negro League teams came to town Maxwell was there to report on the games.

Maxwell wrote about the games but also became the announcer for Sunday games at Ruppert Stadium. When the Eagles played the Monarchs, Maxwell was there to report on the game. When the Eagles marched their way to win the Negro League World Series in 1946, Maxwell was there to tell fans about Larry Doby, Monte Irvin, and Leon Day. For example, he submitted one of his weekly articles after the Homestead Grays defeated the Eagles twice with Day the losing pitcher in the second game. Eagles owner Effa Manley sought out Maxwell and asked him to promote the Eagles games on the radio, which he did. She also asked him to try to encourage some of the white sportswriters he knew to write about the Negro Leagues.[8]

Maxwell eventually got to add to his weekly shows with sports interviews. By the 1940s his shows were generally 15 minutes in length and he used the extra time to interview local sports heroes. Some of his interviews included Sugar Ray Robinson, the boxer, Marty Glickman, the Olympic sprinter, Chicago Bears quarterback Sid Luckman, George Puccinelli of the Newark Bears, George "Mule" Haas of the Chicago White Sox, George Selkirk of the New York Yankees, Hank Greenberg of the Detroit Tigers, and sportswriter Dick Anderson. Later he turned these interviews into books. In 1940 Maxwell published *Thrills and Spills in Sports* and later published *Great Black Athletes*. The first review of *Thrills and Spills* was not positive. The published review said his book felt like his radio shows on paper. What the book really lacked was any editing to turn his interviews into a book. *Great Black Athletes* gave the readers short interviews with stars from all sports, including such well-known players as Willie Mays, Jim Brown, and Jackie Robinson.[9]

In addition to radio broadcasting and writing, Maxwell and his brother Emerson also played on and managed a semipro integrated baseball team. The Newark Starlings played around Newark for about 10 years in the 1930s and took on any team that challenged them. Emerson also umpired around the area when he was not working in the morgue for the *Star-Ledger*. His interest in all sports led Maxwell also to manage a local basketball team for two years, the Mercer Baths.[10]

As busy as he was, Maxwell was not all work. He married Mamie L. Bryant in 1943. After 20 years of marriage they adopted two Korean orphans, 10-year-old Bruce and 8-year-old Lisa. Mamie and Lisa preceded Jocko in death. He lived to 100, dying in July 2008 from complications related to pneumonia.[11]

When Maxwell died, all the obituaries brought him the recognition he rarely had received in life. They focused on his pioneering role as a sports announcer and his importance to remembering the Negro Leagues. Monte Irvin said Maxwell was a unique individual who helped people know about their leagues. One reporter in 1960 ranked Maxwell with Sam Lacy and A.S. "Doc" Young and another called him the "ace colored radio sports caster."[12]

One recognition Maxwell did receive was being elected to the Newark Athletic Hall of Fame in 1994. He also, at long last, had the opportunity to visit the Baseball Hall of Fame in 2001.[13] While there he finally met announcer Ernie Harwell, with whom he had corresponded early in Harwell's career, but the two had never met. Harwell said that he received a letter of encouragement from Maxwell when he first started. Maxwell later wrote about Harwell and called him "the sports voice of the South." In return, Harwell said that accolade meant so much coming from someone who was such a "sports authority." Maxwell's only presence in the Hall is a photo of him and Harwell from that 2001 visit.[14]

Never one to focus on himself, Maxwell revealed bits and pieces of his life over the years. His favorite athlete was Joe Louis. His favorite sport was baseball, with two favorite teams, the Yankees and the Cardinals. He thought Mel Allen was one of the best in his business. He loved hard work and he never really drank so that he could fill his evenings with his radio broadcasts. He did, however, smoke a pipe regularly. He loved scoring baseball games and telling people the stories and scores of all the games and matches he saw over the years. He also loved working in Newark, where he never really experienced any difficulty at the stadiums. He was always welcomed to sit with the white reporters. Maxwell's work opened the doors for many people, even if they were not always aware of

him. Much of what we know today about the Negro Leagues can be credited in part to the stories and records that Maxwell kept and shared for publication.[15]

NOTES

1. "A Pioneer Among Black Sportscasters," radioworld.com/news-and-business/a-pioneer-among-black-sportscasters, March 18, 2009.

2. IMDB; "Emerson Maxwell Rites Held Monday in Newark," *Afro-American*, March 24, 1962: 10; "Successful Negro Editor and Son Visit Portsmouth," *Portsmouth* (Virginia) *Herald*, August 8, 1940: 10.

3. *Baltimore Afro-American*, March 5, 1949; *Trenton Evening Times*, October 19, 1959.

4. Christopher H. Stirling and Cary O'Dell, eds., *Biographical Encyclopedia of American Radio* (New York: Routledge, 2010), 258-259; Mildred Jovien, "The Radio," *Washington Afro-American*, May 23, 1950: 11; "Name Maxwell Sports Director at WWKL," *Indianapolis Recorder*, April 4, 1942. (The station was actually WWRL); *Baltimore Afro-American*, August 29, 1942; *Kansas City Plain Dealer*, February 7, 1947.

5. "Sports Announcer Sets Precedent," *Baltimore Afro-American*, January 19, 1948: 13.

6. Jocko Maxwell, "Eagles Split," *Afro-American*, August 13, 1938: 23.

7. Bruce Weber, "Sherman L. Maxwell, 100, Sportscaster and Writer, Dies," *New York Times*, July 19, 2008. (https://www.nytimes.com/2008/07/19/sports/19maxwell.html)

8. Jocko Maxwell, "Homestead Grays Hog-Tie Eagles Twice, 9-2, 4-1," *Baltimore Afro-American*, June 11, 1938: 22; Laura T. Troiano, *Give Me a "Ball Park Figure": Creating Civic Narratives Through Stadium Building in Newark, N.J.* (Ph.D. Dissertation, Rutgers University, 2017), 83-85.

9. Jocko Maxwell, *Great Black Athletes* (Clearwater, Florida: Snibbe Publications, 1972, 3rd ed.); *The Sporting News*, September 12, 1935, March 5, 1936, and February 1, 1934; *Lexington Herald-Leader*, December 31, 1939.

10. Harold Lett, "Across the Color Line," in *Opportunity: Journal of Negro Life* (1939), 338-339; "Sports Announcer Sets Precedent," *Baltimore Afro-American*, January 19, 1948: 13.

11. *Newark Star-Ledger*, March 27, 1964.

12. "Along the Sports Trail," *Baltimore Afro-American*, July 23, 1938: 22.

13. Christina V. Baird, "Sportscasters Long Walk to Hall of Fame," October 27, 2001.

14. "Ernie Harwell: Praise Boosted this Novice Broadcaster," July 30, 2008. Maxwell file, National Baseball Hall of Fame, Cooperstown, New York, source not identified.

15. "Jocko Maxwell Tops as Sportscaster Over Air," *Baltimore Afro-American*, September 6, 1941: 47; "Jocko Maxwell, Sports Caster, Liked by Radio Fans," *Indianapolis Recorder*, May 10, 1941.

RUPPERT STADIUM

BY CURT SMITH

If "What's past is prologue," as Shakespeare wrote,[1] Ruppert Stadium's in Newark began with Charles A. Davids, a Bayside, New York, promoter.[2] To most of the public, though, it begins with the baseball original for whom the park was named, ultimately housing two teams so good that to some they seemed better than several teams in either major league.

In 1925 Davids bought the Reading, Pennsylvania, franchise in the Eastern League for a reported $80,000 and moved it to Newark.[3] He then paid $125,000 for the land to build a new park – the modestly named Davids Stadium – for his Newark Bears of the International League in the city's section now known as the Iron-bound[4] due to its numerous railroad tracks. For inspiration, Davids used the grandstand footprint of the wooden Wiedenmeyer's Park, home of the Newark Indians in the 1908-11 Eastern League and 1912-16 International League, which earlier that year accidentally burned to the ground and left only the playing field.[5] On one hand, Davids re-created its 12,000-seat single tier. On the other, lightly leveraged, he was soon missing bills.

By 1927, *Newark Star Eagle* publisher Paul Block bought Davids Stadium and the International League Newark Bears for $360,000 plus $160,040 in debts.[6] Ultimately, "with rumors flying like saucers that Block [too] was losing money," read an Associated Press story, "and that Brooklyn was going to take over," baseball's most famous owner thwarted the Dodgers by buying the Bears franchise for $360,000 in 1931.[7] The Yankees' Jacob Ruppert inherited Newark (a.k.a. Bears) Stadium, in 1932, renamed it

Ruppert Stadium was home to both the Triple-A International League's Newark Bears – a New York Yankees affiliate – and the Negro National League's Newark Eagles *(pictured here). (Noir-Tech Research, Inc.)*

Ruppert Stadium,[8] upped capacity to 19,000, and built "the golden era of Newark baseball and 18 years of perhaps the most successful farm club operation organized baseball ever will see," said the *New York Times*.[9]

From 1926 to 1949, Ruppert Stadium housed seven IL pennants, four Governor's Cups (a.k.a. playoff crowns), and three Junior World Series titles.[10] Before the Cubs bought and moved the team in 1950, Hall of Famers Yogi Berra and Joe Gordon played there – also Jerry Coleman, Tommy Henrich, and Red Rolfe.[11] Many deem the 1937 Bears the best minor-league nine of all time. Meantime, the ballpark's other regular, the 1936-48 Newark Eagles, became the Negro Leagues' gold standard with Class of Cooperstown Leon Day, Larry Doby, Monte Irvin, Raleigh "Biz" Mackey, and Effa Manley.[12] In 1946 they beat the Kansas City Monarchs of Satchel Paige and Buck O'Neil in likely the greatest Negro World Series. Like Jacob Ruppert, this Newark team's owner was gargantuan in her effect. Manley was called "The Queen of the Negro Leagues."[13]

"What symmetry!" said Jim Gates, 1995 librarian of the National Baseball Hall of Fame and Museum. "Jacob Ruppert and Effa Manley, both inducted at Cooperstown. The Bears dominate the International League the same 1930s decade [a poll also included the 1932, 1938, and 1941 clubs among the minors' 100 best-ever teams[14]] as Newark joins the Negro Leagues. An historic team rises in each league in the same city" – a nonpareil *urban twinning of the heart.* "You didn't need to go across the river to see Hall of Famers bloom in New York. Then both teams leave Newark at about the same time," the Bears moving to Springfield, Massachusetts; the Negro National League disbanding at about the same time as the Eagles left for Houston in late 1948. "You can look it up,"[15] Casey Stengel said, famously. In New Jersey, you don't need to.

Ruppert Stadium's odyssey starts with its namesake's Yankees dynasty and its Double-A club. (The Bears turned Triple A in 1946) Much of America's nineteenth-century immigrant populace was said to be figuratively born to beer. Ruppert was *literally* born – the second-oldest of six children of brewer Jacob Ruppert Sr.[16] and his wife, Anna, in the New York City of August 5, 1867. A second-generation American who spoke with a German accent all his life,[17] he grew up on Fifth Avenue, attended the Columbia Grammar School, and joined his dad's brewing business at age 20 in 1887 as a barrel washer working 12 hours a day for $10 a week[18] to become brewery VP and general manager. In 1886 Ruppert began a parallel military career, entering the Seventh Regiment of the New York National Guard. In 1890 he leapt to the rank of colonel, by which he was known the rest of his life. Ruppert then joined the staff of two governors of New York, David Hill and Roswell Flower. In 1898 he was elected as a Tammany Hall-backed Democrat to the US House from New York's 15th Congressional District.[19] The Colonel was re-elected in 1900.[20] He was then twice elected from the 16th District,[21] decided not to run again in 1906, and left office a year later.

In 1914 the politician/military man bought J&M Haffen Brewing Company for $700,000, hoping to close the brewery down and start a career of development in the Bronx.[22] On his father's 1915 death, Junior inherited the Jacob Ruppert Brewing Company and became president, decided to spend much of it on the boyhood love he had had little time to enjoy since grammar school. Several times Ruppert had vainly tried to buy John McGraw's New York Giants. In 1912 he had a chance to get the Cubs – but, thoroughly

New York in taste and fashion, cavalierly dismissed the Midwest as a time zone too far.[23] In early 1915, the Colonel barely had to leave the neighborhood to meet Frank J. Farrell and William S. Devery, owners of the recently redubbed American League New York Highlanders-turned-Yankees.

Today, given the Yankees' fame, it is hard to envision how they once suggested Ring Lardner's barb, in another context, as someone who "looked at me as if I were a side dish he hadn't ordered."[24] In 1903-12, the Highlanders had forgettably played in Hilltop Park, moving in 1913 to the Giants' Polo Grounds as a tenant. Even so, in 1915 Ruppert and his co-owner, the gloriously named Tillinghast L'Hommedieu Huston, a former US Army engineer and colonel, paid $460,000 and assumed another $20,000 in debt for the club.[25] On paper, the martial pair had made the big leagues, but they didn't stay matched for long. In late 1917, AL President Ban Johnson urged Ruppert to hire manager Miller Huggins. Huston, then in Europe, loathed Huggins, favoring a drinking pal, Brooklyn skipper Wilbert Robinson. Ruppert didn't care, giving Huggins a two-year contract before Huston got home.[26] The rough patch was never patched up, one colonel, Ruppert, buying the other out for $1.5 million in 1922.[27]

By then the Pinstripes had acquired a player who changed everything, so much that in the July 12, 1999, *Sports Illustrated,* Richard Hoffer likened Babe Ruth to "rock-and-roll and the Model T ... a seminal American invention. Be it his power at the plate, his popularity or his various appetites, the Babe was huge."[28] The Yankees won pennants in 1921-22 – their first of 40 through 2018, easily the most of any professional North American team. Furious, Giants owner Charles Stoneham raised the Yanks' rent for 1922 and, in effect, kicked the American Leaguers off Manhattan Isle. "They should move to some out-of-the-way place like Queens," huffed the 'Jints' McGraw, presuming no one would ever hear from them again.[29] Irate, Ruppert bought land across the Harlem River for $675,000 from the estate of William Waldorf Astor.[30]

That year construction of the first baseball field to be called a *stadium* – Yankee Stadium – rose in 284 working days one-quarter mile from the Polo Grounds.[31] The Bronx Bombers baptized it by winning the 1923 World Series and encoring in the 1927-28 fall classic – through 2018, their 27 World Series titles also a North American high. As sole owner, Ruppert pioneered team uniforms in 1929;[32] made Joe McCarthy skipper in 1931; swept the 1932 Series from Chicago; and forged a sublime farm system to give his dynasty near-perpetuity.[33] Newark was its hub. The ballpark named after him rose on a 15-acre plot of land near the Lehigh Valley Railroad in southeast Newark on 262 Wilson Avenue and Delancy Street in the vicinity of the Passaic River, Newark Bay, and the present Newark Liberty Airport.[34] For 13 years after 1935, Newark's two great baseball clubs shared it peaceably and memorably – indeed, to columnist Jerry Izenberg, "shared pieces of its [Newark's] heart and soul.

"These two teams wrote history of this town," Izenberg wrote movingly in the *Newark Star Ledger*. "They won the world championships of their social sets, and a dozen of baseball's Hall of Famers played for them. They were the kings of a city where every 8-year-old could explain the infield fly rule – where you could walk down the city's summer-night streets when the Bears played and through the open windows hear the radio voice of a man named Earl Harper – [and] where a remarkable reporter named Jocko Maxwell" observed Newark's "other players … great African-American players like Leon Day and Willie Wells and Ray Dandridge, whose only flaw in the eyes of Major Leagues Baseball was that they had been born too soon."[35]

Most of these players had begun to play in the 1920s, or before. By decade's end, with the majors segregated, the Negro League serviced America's roughly 10 percent black populace. Two verities existed: Black America loved baseball; and "colored" malaise had preceded 1929's Depression curve. The white-run Eastern Colored League had gone under the financial waves in 1928, a hint of things ahead. In 1931 the Negro National League (NNL) collapsed.[36] By 1933, Gus Greenlee, a black numbers shark involved in boxing, night clubbing, and gambling, "moved to revive the defunct Negro National League, this time with six clubs, all of them under the control of his fellow racketeers,"[37] including Newark, wrote Geoffrey C. Ward in his 1994 *Baseball: An Illustrated History,* based upon Ken Burns' PBS documentary. Before long, he wrote, the "numbers kings" owned most Negro League teams – "among the few members of the [black] community with enough money in the midst of the Great Depression to pay the bills."[38]

Ed [actually, James] "Soldier Boy" Semler, said Baseball magazine, was said to run the New York Black Yankees. In Harlem, Alex Pompez, gangster Dutch Schultz's muscle man, controlled the New York Cubans. Ed Bolden backed the Philadelphia Stars and Tom Wilson financed the Baltimore Elite Giants. If Abe Manley's gambling money kept the Eagles from going bankrupt, wrote Ward, his remarkable wife, Effa, kept them going each game, knowing the game as well as their manager, to "sometimes signal … her players to bunt or steal by crossing and uncrossing her legs."[39] The second Negro National (Eastern) League lasted for 16 years. All told, according to John Holway's *The Complete Book of Baseball's Negro Leagues: The Other Half of Baseball History,* 18 franchises competed at one time or another from 1933 to 1948.[40] In 1942-48, its champion played each Negro American (Western) League (NAL) leader in a Negro World Series. Prior to 1942, "titlist" meant winning the pennant; thereafter, the Series.

Ruppert Stadium in May 1953, five years after the Eagles' last opening day at the venue. The Newark Board of Education turned the stadium into a recreation center, but it was demolished in 1967. *(Courtesy of Newark Public Library)*

For a long time, redolent of their then-black second-class status, 1926-50 Negro League records were understandably incomplete. Across society, black and white, the Depression made people unconcerned with anything but a job. On his last day in office, President Herbert Hoover said, "We are at the end of our string. There is nothing more we can do."[41] Inaugurated on March 4, 1933, successor Franklin Roosevelt refused to accept defeat, asking and soon getting from Congress an array of powers to combat despair. All decade FDR fought unemployment, business monopoly, and wind and drought turning farms into sand.[42] The Negro Leagues would almost surely have not survived the 1930s without him. As things were, they suffered financially, much like Organized Baseball itself.

In the September 25, 1965, issue of *The Sporting News,* Bob Addie quotes Cleveland President Gabe Paul musing how then-Newark Stadium was built "without ticket windows. They had to use portable ticket booths when the park was opened."[43] Each pole stood 305 feet from the plate. Center field loomed 410 feet away. The left-center-field bleachers were far closer to the plate than right or center field, sans seats but "provid[ing] space for a larger crowd" by "roping off the area." In 1932 lights were added, the park used as a high-school field, leased for special events, and staging stock-car racing, midget racing, and boxing. The air evinced a next-door garbage dump, redolent of Brooklyn's nineteenth-century Washington Park III, near Gowanus Canal.[44] Play was often delayed by odor wafting from trash.[45] A deck wrapped the plate from pole to pole. A roof covered the top 70 percent of the seats from nearly third base to first. A General Electric Archives photo[46] shows players around the batting cage, the plate a stone's throw from the backstop. The joint was plain, and the fans were plainspoken.

As *The Negro Leagues in New Jersey* relates, on one hand "the many ballparks and playing fields" in the state made "fans … witnesses to a high caliber of baseball. [On the other,] (t)he Negro League teams had no ballparks of their own and had to settle for any arena that was available to them."[47] Ruppert was an exception – also, three other Negro League parks, extending this communal feel. In 1926, the Eastern Colored League Newark Stars attended Newark Schools Stadium. Builders evidently ran out of real estate, each line so abbreviated that a drive over the fence counted as a double. In 1933, the revived NNL arose. Its 1934-35 Newark Dodgers filled Meadowbrook Oval at South Orange Avenue and 12th Street – the outfield fence 12 feet high; center field 380 feet from the plate; each pole 300 away; its effect, baseball lighting Depression gloom. Each "Sunday [was] devoted to attending church and baseball games," read *The Negro Leagues*.[48] At morning service, ministers bade all "an enjoyable time" at the park, their flock then trekking there, "the men sporting their Sunday best. The women wore flowery dresses and hats placed over fancy hairdos." Everyone was "dress[ed] to the nines."[49]

Visiting teams stayed and home players boarded and met supporters at the Grand Hotel at West Market and Wickliffe Street. (The Bears lived at the Riviera Hotel on High Street.[50]) According to writers Alfred M. and Alfred T. Martin, it "was a haven for African Americans, especially during the days of segregation," jazz, dance, and other genres rocking to headliners Fletcher Anderson, Count Basie, Cab Calloway, Lionel Hampton, and Fats Waller – baseball with a beat.[51] Since no team owned a park, clubs needed the accessible and suitable. In 1936 the Brooklyn Eagles merged with the Newark Dodgers and began to share Ruppert with the Bears. Inexplicably, the Bears and Eagles never played despite sharing the same house through 1948, "players of both teams … willing."[52] As it was, Newark got an NNL home-field edge: sure facilities, sane scheduling, and steady cash. Admission cost 85 cents for a box, 65 cents a grandstand, 40 cents a bleacher seat. The Bears got 20 percent of the Eagles game's receipts.[53] Each team could plan but the Eagles gained a vital edge in a league whose Job One was finding a place to play.

Bears owner Ruppert died of phlebitis on January 13, 1939, his parent club aptly taking the World Series in each of the Eagles' first three years – 1936, '37, '38. Babe Ruth, whom Ruppert called *Root in* his German-inflected voice, addressing Babe by his last name, as he did everyone, even close friends, was among the last to see him alive. Before the Bears expired in 1950, the Yankees added Series titles in 1939, '41, '43, '47, and '49, dedicating a plaque in 1940 in Ruppert's memory to hang on the center-field wall at Yankee Stadium – "Jacob Ruppert: Gentleman, American, sportsman, through whose vision and courage this imposing edifice, destined to become the home of champions, was erected and dedicated to the American game of baseball." It rests in Monument Park at new Yankee Stadium.[54] Another plaque honors him at the Hall of Fame; Ruppert was inducted in 2013 by its new Pre-Integration Committee, which every three years evaluates managers, umpires, executives, and players of baseball prior to 1947.[55]

Before Ruppert's purchase, the unaligned Bears flunked the first division half of their first six years. There were exceptions: Lew Fonseca, baseball's future film director, once batted .381. Another year, Wally Pipp, his 1925 headache launching Lou Gehrig's games-played streak, averaged .312. Walter Johnson and Tris Speaker each managed, no longer able to regularly pitch or bat. Soon Ruppert's farm system, operated by general manager Ed Barrow and successor George Weiss, ran talent like the Passaic River through Newark. By 1932, New York's first year, the 109-59 Bears placed first, drew a Newark high 342,001, and had six regulars top .300, including comers Red Rolfe and Dixie Walker. The next year's 102-62ers led the league. At one end, future stars Johnny Murphy and Spud Chandler ended a collective 10-10; the other, Jim Weaver, a once and future big-league starter, 25-11. Bombers on the way down and up intersected. In 1934 Murderer's Row ex-pitcher and new hurler Bob Shawkey waved *another* flag. Twinkletoes Selkirk hit .357 for Newark, then .313 in the Bronx, but couldn't replace the Babe, as advertised. In 1936: Ossie Vitt succeeded Shawkey. In 1938, 1941, 1942, the Bears won the pennant, even as recession troubled FDR's second (1937-41) and early third term. None surpassed New Jersey's largest city's Greatest-Ever Team.

To Jerry Izenberg, "Joe Basile's 25-piece band was the centerpiece of the Bears' opening days just as Lena Horne, Joe Louis, and … Effa Manley … were the focal point of the Eagles' openers."[56] Save score, Basile had little to enjoy Opening Day 1937. "In a dull, dump and discouraging setting at Ruppert Stadium," wrote the *New York Times*, the Bears beat Montreal, 8-6. "The sun never showed up and neither did the anticipated crowd of 20,000. Only 5,000 showed,"[57] more returning. The 1937 Newark Bears won the pennant by 25½ games, finished 109-43, and savored Joe Beggs (21-4), Atley Donald (19-2), Vito Tamulis (18-6), and Steve Sundra (15-4). Newark hit 140 homers and batted .300. Charlie Keller, later a.k.a. "King Kong," debuted at .353, Babe Dahlgren batted .340, Buddy Rosar .332, George McQuinn .330, Willard Hershberger .325, and Frankie Kelleher .306. Bob Seeds, nicknamed Suitcase for his five big-league teams, added .305 with 20 homers, in one weekend going deep 10 times in 17 at-bats with 17 RBIs.[58] Joe Gordon, 22, hit .280 in his last minor-league year. Tommy Henrich, 24, played in seven games before joining the Yanks to stay. An italicized season ended with an exclamation point: Newark swept Syracuse and Baltimore in the IL playoff and Governor's Cup final, respectively, then erased a 0-3 deficit to nip Columbus in the Junior World Series.

Like the Eagles, the Bears – columnist Bill Newman recalled the "The Wonder Bears"[59] – knit Newark. In "Old Newark Memories," he evoked their eight-game five-cent "Knothole Ticket" for grade-school children – how after each game hundreds waited at the players exit. One day Newman gave his hero, pitcher Tamulis, a scorecard and pencil and asked for his autograph. Vito signed, held on to it, looked down at Newman, and said, "Hey kid, I bet I know something you don't." Bill: "What?" Tamulis: "You're standing on my foot." Heroes were closer then, dialogue more personal. On "Father & Son Night," some kids got in free with a father who bought a ticket, Dads finding they had never met.[60] In 1938 new skipper Johnny Neun evoked a favorite uncle, leading the Bears to a 104-48 first-place, postseason defeat of Rochester and Buffalo, then loss to Kansas City in the Junior World Series. Marius Russo joined the Bombers after going 17-8. A World War I tune asked, "How you gonna keep 'em down on the farm?" Newark couldn't. Keller left after stroking .365 to stay at The Stadium a decade. Tommy Holmes batted .339 and couldn't find a position. Dealt, he became a two-time NL hits titlist. How fertile was the Yanks' farm? Hank Borowy, 9-7 at Newark in 1939, didn't reach the bigs until going 15-4 in 1942.

By then, manager Neun owned *another* title from 1940, beating Jersey City, Baltimore, and Louisville in the postseason. In 1941's last summer of an uncertain peace, the 100-54 Bears beat Rochester in the playoff but lost a seven-game Governor's Cup final to Montreal. Their last wisp at the top aired versatility. That year, Newark's Johnny Lindell had a 23-4 W-L record and 2.05 ERA and batted .298. By 1943-44, he twice topped the AL in triples. Tommy Byrne was a 1940-42 Bears starter who once finished 17-4 and hit .328. A decade later he buoyed the Yanks staff –16-5 one year – and pinch-hit, too. In 1932 GM Barrow had hired Weiss as farm director. The system that Weiss built from four teams to 20 by 1947 survived Newark's IL demise. A decade-later film headlined *Winning with the Yankees*.[61] "What makes the Yankees tick?" narrator Mel Allen begins. Personae fuse: Billy Martin steals home. Skipper Casey Stengel tutors rookies and coaches Frank Crosetti, Bill Dickey, and Ralph Houk. "The scout's a nice guy, and tries to put you all at ease," Allen purrs. The numbers ran with Casey, like the Bears.

In July 1942, wartime US Navy member and famed pitcher Bob Feller fueled a Red Cross and Navy Relief Society benefit for the Norfolk Naval Training Station versus the Quantico Marines in a five-inning game at Ruppert. Babe Ruth, Larry MacPhail, Dolly Stark, and Gil Stratton Jr. umpired. Celebrities Lucille Manners and Gabriel Heatter appeared.[62] A Newark-Toronto IL set followed. In 1943 Newark drew only 983 per date. The bigs' future first relief ace, Joe Page, was 14-5 as a starter. Ghost of Yankees Past George Selkirk became manager. In 1947 Newark thudded to a 65-89 end. Gene Woodling's .289 was another '50s Yanks portent. Sherm Lollar hit 16 homers but found no room in the Bombers' tri-tiered inn: thus, dealt to Chicago, became a seven-time All-Star. Two other prospects, Yogi Berra and Bobby Brown, batted .314 and .341 respectively in 1946. Early in their Yanks tenure the roommates were reading at night – Berra a comic book and the future medical student, Dr. Brown, a journal. Finishing his comic, Yogi said, "So how is yours turning out?"[63] Such Bears alumni conjure almost any 1950s official World Series program as the Yanks captured eight pennants in that decade's 10 years.

In 1948 Newark's Bob Porterfield threw 20 complete games in 22 starts. He was again heard from when he went 22-10 for the Senators in 1953. The Bears' last year was 1949, Newark's 5.50 ERA earning last place on merit. Its last skipper was Buddy Hassett. A better choice might have been comic Buddy Hackett. The franchise's story had begun with the '26ers soaring (96-66) and drawing (3,322 a game). It ended with the '49ers breaking Newark's worst record (55-98) and peacetime gate (88,170). Most sat home to watch on the new kinetic tube the Dodgers, Giants, and Yankees as the racial line dissolved. In 1945 Jackie Robinson signed a contract with the Brooklyn Dodgers, a seismic act that precipitated other players leaving non-big-league black baseball. Historic and inevitable as their exodus was, Effa Manley knew what it foretold. Unable to survive the major leagues' at last *truly* national cachet, the Negro Leagues were doomed from the date Jackie inked his pact. Even so, Newark's greatest moment followed his arrival.

In 1935 the Brooklyn Eagles finished 32-30, the Manleys hoping that the merger with the Newark Dodgers would ensure next year's NLL's Eastern Division. Instead, the '36ers fell to 25-29-1. In 1937 Newark surged to 35-21-2 (second place), The decade closed at resolutely .500 (23-23) in 1938 and .638 percent second-half (37-21-1) in 1939, the latter's second-placers losing a first postseason to the Baltimore Elite Giants. (Most split-season records are not available.) Newark was 26-22-1 in 1940 and 30-25-1 in 1941, respectively. That December 7, Japan attacked the US naval base at Pearl Harbor in Hawaii, bringing America into World War II. Each Negro League and major-league team lost players via draft and/or enlistment. The Eagles sent a dozen men to the armed forces, including all branches of the military.[64] Ultimately, like players from other teams, they served their country in the European and Pacific Theaters and elsewhere. Much later Congress feted all-black divisions for their distinction – belatedly, but finally.

In 1942-44, Newark clung to mediocrity: 36-33-3, 26-32, and 32-35. As war ended and soldiers slowly returned, the 1945 Eagles, many players still at a front, plodded to a 27-25 .519 third-place finish. Few things suggested a championship. Still, advantages remained. Other NLL teams could not afford scouting. Geography was Manley's scout as many of the Eagles players were locals: Larry

Doby from Paterson, New Jersey; Monte Irvin, East Orange; Manning, Pleasantville. The Negro Leagues retraces a vagabond slate: 150 yearly games of spring training, regular season, exhibition, and post; a "grueling schedule" of two-week two-way travel from Newark to "Baltimore, Richmond, Bellefonte, Buffalo, Pittsburgh, and Indianapolis," return adding Altoona, Canton, Akron, and Columbus, including twin-bill and twilight that meant all night in a bus.[65] Only the Eagles' bus was air-conditioned. They returned to a stable homestead, Ruppert Stadium, which no other team possessed.

Home and away, a roster of great players preceded 1946's likely best-ever African-American club. Among them was the black press's vaunted "Million Dollar Infield." At first base – he also played the outfield – Mule Suttles swung a 50-ounce bat to hit a .317 Negro League average for eight teams, including the 1936-40 and 1942-44 Eagles. At second base, Dick Seay starred defensively for Newark from 1937 to 1940, making the double play so quickly that in the argot of a later age the ball seemed radioactive to his glove. He could even bat, using the bunt and hit-and-run to average as high as .267 in 1940. The infield's shortstop, Willie Wells – "The Devil" –was only demonic to the other side. Wells fortified 10 Negro League teams at least briefly from 1924 to 1948, including Newark in 1936-39 and 1942, batting as high as .363 and .355 for the Eagles. Third baseman Ray Dandridge played for the Newark Dodgers in 1933-34-35 – once batting .432 – and Eagles in 1936 through 1938. He left Newark "to play in Mexico for [several] years because he was offered a good salary," states The Negro Leagues in New Jersey, "paid all his expenses, and was provide with a family apartment."[66] Returning to Newark, he hit .341 in 1944. The Eagles' greatest third baseman made Cooperstown in 1987.

From 1920 to '47, Raleigh "Biz" Mackey was a black baseball icon, playing primarily for five teams. In 1939-41, he became the Eagles' star catcher. In 1945, rejoining Newark at 47 – his first of three final years – Biz hit .262 part-time. Cooperstown '06 retired having played in 998 games. Specific to this book, Mackey managed the '46ers to a world title,[67] his staff starring three torrid starters. A 1946-48 Eagle, Rufus Lewis used a medley of pitches to beat Kansas City twice in the 1946 World Series. Later, he thrived in the Mexican League and other winter-ball venues and pitched until injury forced him to leave the game in the early 1950s, by which time a mishap had forced second 1946 starter Max Manning out of baseball, too. Born in Georgia, Max had initially joined the semipro Johnson Stars before signing with Newark. The righty brought a high kick, fastball, glasses, and nickname – "Dr. Cyclops"[68] – his first Eagles game earning an A: consecutive strikeouts of Josh Gibson, Buck Leonard, Sam Bankhead, and Dave Whatley. Even healthy, Lewis and Manning had been bypassed by Mackey for Leon Day, who started on Opening Day 1946. Day had just returned from the war and had not pitched professionally in two years, but made up for lost time with a 2-0 no-hitter against the Philadelphia Stars. From 1934 to 1946, the 1995 inductee at the Hall of Fame played every position but catcher, usually second base or center field, if not forging a .687 pitching percentage. His winning percentage is second-best with Pedro Martinez at Cooperstown, behind only Whitey Ford.[69]

The glorious 1946 Eagles finished a pennant-winning 56-24-3 (.700 percentage), fueled largely by "The Big Four," as writers christened them – future Hall of Famers Larry Doby and Monte Irvin, plus Lennie Pearson and Johnny "Cherokee" Davis. Outfielder Davis was a 1940-48 Eagle, topping .300 yearly from 1942-46, as high as .343 and .341, and batting a lifetime .301. A 1937-48 Eagle, Pearson made five East-West All-Star Games, five times passed .300, peaked at .342 in 1940 and 1942, smacked 11 homers in 1942, and averaged .393 in the 1946 Series. Earlier integration would have made Lennie a big-league star. Instead, after Newark's baseball finis, Pearson became player-manager of the 1949 champion Baltimore Elite Giants and concluded with the 1950-51 Triple-A American Association Milwaukee Brewers.[70]

At the time and since, the Eagles' greatest victory was the 1946 World Series – by consensus the Negro Leagues' last moment in the sun. None helped like their two most noted players, each an adopted Jersey son. Larry Doby was born in 1923 in Camden, South Carolina,[71] a four-sport athlete in Paterson, New Jersey. Turning 17, he signed a 1942 contract for $300 with Newark stating that he would play till September before starting college. On October 23, 1945, Doby, only 21, heard on Armed Forces Radio of Brooklyn GM Branch Rickey signing Jackie Robinson to a contract with its Montreal Triple-A affiliate. Till now he had planned to coach or teach. Suddenly, Larry felt that he might crack the bigs, too.[72] Doby returned from war to play for the San Juan Senators in Puerto Rico, then rejoined Newark in 1946.[73] He made the All-Star roster, hit .329, had 52 RBIs, stole 8 bases, and led the team with 281 plate appearances, 62 runs, 80 hits, 8 homers, 8 triples, 14 doubles, and 37 walks – almost everything there was to lead. Among those watching was Cleveland Indians owner Bill Veeck. In late 1944 Kenesaw Mountain Landis, baseball's first commissioner and a segregationist, had died; successor A.B. "Happy" Chandler opened the big-league door. Veeck now plucked Larry from Newark to desegregate the American League. Doby debuted in Cleveland on July 5, 1947.

Like Doby, the Eagles' other Hall of Famer '73 left rural South Haleburg, Mississippi, for urban North Orange, New Jersey. After trying college, Monte began with Newark in 1938-39. Hitting .371 and .395 in 1940-41, Irvin asked for a raise. Refused, he won the 1942 Triple Crown at Veracruz in the Mexican League[74] -- and was assigned by the US Army to its Corps of Engineers in

Europe, historically in 1944-45's Battle of the Bulge. Back home, Irvin, solicited by Rickey, stayed in Newark. Prizing her players, Effa Manley had let Robinson and [pitcher] Don Newcombe leave her team [in 1945] without Rickey paying a cent. She wasn't about to forfeit rights to Irvin. "… Mrs. Manley felt that Branch Rickey was obligated to compensate her for my contract," Monte said. She "told Rickey that … she wasn't going to let him take me without compensation." If Rickey tried, Effa vowed to sue, whereupon Branch's interest ebbed. Monte's 1946 was as spectacular as the team's, hitting .374 and slugging .564.

In 1949, the four-time NNL All-Star signed with the Giants, ravaging the IL with Triple-A Jersey City. He spent most of 1950 with the parent 'Jints, then joined them for good next year, his sole dilemma time. In 1951, he was 32. Irvin had spent a decade fighting segregation and war – yet hit .312 as the Giants erased a 13½-game Brooklyn lead. Monte retired in 1957 after batting .293 in just 764 major-league matches. In 2006, Orange Park in Orange was renamed Monte Irvin Park. The pioneer died at 96, in 2016, the year his life-sized bronze statue was dedicated, 13 miles from Ruppert Stadium. Still alive at the end of 2018 was a man who pitched briefly there but later reigned at Ebbets Field. On May 20, 1949, Don Newcombe debuted for Brooklyn, that year among the first four black players named to a big-league All-Star team, with Cleveland's Doby and Dodgers teammates Roy Campanella and Jackie Robinson.

Born in Madison, raised in Elizabeth, Newcombe played integrated school and sandlot ball before joining the Eagles at 18: his two-year mark, 8-6. Newcombe and Baltimore's Campy then joined America's first racially integrated pro baseball team, the 1946 New England League's Nashua Dodgers. Don became the first pitcher to be Rookie of the Year, Most Valuable Player, and Cy Young Award honoree – in 1949, the first black pitcher to start a Series game.[75] In 1951, Newk was the first black to win 20 games in a year – and 1956, first of any race or either league as same-year Cy Younger and MVP.[76] He had a career .271 batting average and belted 15 homers. In 1956 a rival punctured his best (27-7) year, Yogi Berra making Don his piñata in the Series, slamming a Game Two grand slam and two seventh-game belts. Viewing on TV, President Eisenhower later wrote him: "I think I know how much you wanted to win a World Series game [he never did]. I for one was pulling for you," but "hard luck is something that no one in the world can explain." Ike suggested that "you think of the twenty-seven games you won that were so important in bringing Brooklyn into the World Series."[77]

In 1946, a Newark poster-turned-collector's-item read, "1945 [sic, 1946] Negro League World Series: Kansas City Monarchs Featuring Buck O'Neil, Satchel Paige, and Ted Strong vs. The Newark Eagles, Featuring Leon Day, Larry Doby, and Monte Irvin!"[78] The fifth

1942-48 postseason joust between the Negro Leagues' National and American League titlists became the most surpassing. In the Series opener at the Polo Grounds, Paige yielded one run and scored the Monarchs' 2-1 decider. Two days later, ex-heavyweight boxing titlist Joe Louis threw out the first pitch at Ruppert Stadium. Doby homering, the Eagles tied the Series, 7-4. In Game Three, Newark pitching dissolved in a 15-5, 21-hit KC rout. Next night Irvin's four hits and Rufus Lewis's complete game squared things, 8-1. Game Five shifted to Chicago's Comiskey Park, the Monarchs taking the Classic lead a third time, 5-1. The sixth set could have been staged at Fenway Park or Ebbets Field – drives clearing or careening around Ruppert Stadium. Irvin homered twice and Pearson once: Newark, 9-7. The September 29 final lured 19,000 to Ruppert. They saw Leon Day make a sprawling eighth-inning catch to save the Series with his glove; then, in the home half of the inning, Doby and Irvin walk and Johnny Davis lash a two-run double to give Newark a 3-2 victory.

The triumph was short-lived. After Rickey signed Robinson, the road ahead was clear, like a plunge in NNL attendance. Even at Ruppert Stadium, "The question of the day [became], 'How did Jackie do today?'" The 1947 Eagles finished 53-41-1 (.564) to finish second – yet drew just 57,000. Their final year, a 33-1-3 1948, barely made a scratch. Seeing the handwriting on the wall, Manley urged a firm relationship between the majors and the Negro Leagues. By contrast, the bigs wanted the *extinction* of the Negro Leagues: Less competition meant more profit. The 1948 season left the Manleys with a $25,000 deficit. They sold their interest in the Eagles for $15,000, including all assets, player contracts, and the team bus. The couple received $5,000 for Irvin's sale to the Giants. The NNL contracted and merged into the NAL, were sold, moved to Texas, and became the short-lived Houston Eagles.[79]

That November, Parke Carroll, Bears general manager, confirmed that the city's other trust, the Newark Baseball Club of the International League, "is for sale," noting that it had led the league in 1948 road attendance but ranked second-to-last at home.[80] The Bears blamed "inadequate transportation to and from Ruppert Stadium" and "a smoke nuisance" – in today's cant, pollution – for waning crowds. In truth, television and integration – the former, voluntary; the latter, necessary – destroyed the Bears and Eagles, respectively. In 1948, Ruppert staged another sport that TV overexposure would kill – boxing – hosting the Rocky Graziano-Tony Zale middleweight title bout.[81] Once a fight hotbed, Newark's revival didn't take. In 1950, its IL franchise moved to Pynchon Park in Springfield, Massachusetts. In 1959 Ruppert Stadium hosted a final year of the Newark Indians and the NAL.

On October 16, 1952, the Yankees gave up the ghost that baseball would return there, announcing, "The park will be torn down and the property offered for sale for real estate."[82] That November 25, the Newark Board of Education intervened, buying Ruppert Stadium for $275,000 and urging that another $50,000 be spent to make it a school sports center. In 1961 a 9-acre part of the 20-acre site was sold for $180,000 to developers of industrial property.[83] The stadium was leveled in 1967 and the land sold a year later. Where Ruppert stood is now "a landscape of chain-link fences and warehouses, factories and trucks."[84] Far more was demolished than earth and stone.

By 1981, Effa Manley's cancer of the colon regressed into peritonitis. She had a heart attack on April 16, at 84, four days after the death of her idol, Joe Louis.[85] Effa was buried in Holy Cross Cemetery at Culver City in Los Angeles, her tombstone reading, "She loved baseball." Newark loved it in 1999, debuting a $34 million taxpayer-financed 6,200-seat Riverfront Stadium. In baseball's once non-big-league capital, the new Bears of the independent Atlantic League hoped to recall a nonpareil baseball age. On May 8, 2001, hoping to draw on 5.4 million people within a 15-mile radius,[86] the ballpark was renamed "Bears and Eagles Riverfront Stadium." Two Newark alumni and Hall of Famers stood side-by-side at a ceremony to recall Newark's greatest teams of the Negro and International Leagues and "designed to right a historical wrong" – how, due to segregation, their two teams and leagues never met.[87]

Yogi Berra of the 1946 Bears evoked Newark drawing "great here. When we'd play the Jersey City Giants, we packed the place." Larry Doby of the 1940s Eagles recalled not thinking of "making 300, 400 dollars a month to play baseball [as] … work. We just loved to play." Even now, they wished they could have played each other. Sadly, the park once seen as the cornerstone of Newark's urban renewal failed to turn the corner. In 2008 the Bears folded, joined the Canadian American Association in 2011, and two years later died. In 2014 a liquidation auction was held. One headline read: "Game Over: Newark Bears Officially Out of Business, as Baseball Fades From City Again."[88] For the moment, F. Scott Fitzgerald sadly had been correct: "There are no second acts in American lives."[89]

SOURCES

My appreciation to the distinguished Negro Leagues historian and author Larry Lester, whose advice has been invaluable referencing events and players. I also want to thank longtime friend and colleague Ken Samelson for his great help. Unless otherwise indicated, individual, team, and league Negro League batting, fielding, and pitching statistics are courtesy of the Seamheads Negro Leagues Database from seamheads.com/NegroLgs/ powered by the Baseball Gauge. In addition to sources cited in the Notes, most especially the Society for American Baseball Research, the author also derived major- and minor-league baseball statistics from

baseball-reference.com and retrosheet.org and relevant websites for box scores, player, season, and team pages, batting and pitching logs, and other material relevant to this history. FanGraphs.com provided statistical information. In addition to the sources cited in the Notes, the author also consulted:

Books

Benson, Michael. *Ballparks of North America: A Comprehensive Historical Encyclopedia of Baseball Grounds, Yards and Stadiums, 1845 to 1988* (Jefferson, North Carolina: McFarland, 1989).

Lester, Larry. *Black Baseball In New York City: An Illustrated History, 1885-1959* (Jefferson City, North Carolina: McFarland, 2017).

Shannon, Bill, and George Kalinsky. *The Ballparks* (New York: Hawthorn, 1975).

Smith, Ron. *The Ballpark Book: A Journey Through the Fields of Baseball Magic* (St. Louis: The Sporting News Co., 2000).

Newspapers

The *New York Times* has been a primary source of information about Ruppert Stadium. Another key source has been the Newark Star-Ledger. Other sources include the Associated Press, *The Sporting News, Washington Post,* and *USA Today.*

Interviews

Larry Lester, with author, November 2018.

Harold Rosenthal, with author, March 1982.

NOTES

1   enotes.com/Shakespeare-quotes/whats-past-prologue.

2   digitalballparks.com/International/Ruppert_640_2.html.

3   "Ruppert Stadium to Be Torn Down: Newark Property of Yankees Will Go for Real Estate," *New York Times*, October 17, 1952: 37.

4   revolvy.com/page/Newark-Bears-(International-League).

5   newarksports.net/buildings/ruppert.php. "Newark Sports Old Newark"

6   milb.com/milb/history/top100.jsp?idx=53.

7   "Ruppert Stadium to Be Torn Down."

8   "Ruppert Stadium Is New Name of Baseball Park in Newark," *New York Times*, January 9, 1932: 23.

9   "Ruppert Stadium to Be Torn Down."

10   Ibid.

11   baseballhall.org. National Baseball Hall of Fame and Museum.

12   Ibid.

13   Alfred M. Martin and Alfred T. Martin, *The Negro Leagues in New Jersey: A History* (Jefferson, North Carolina: McFarland, 2008), 67.

14   milb.com/milb/history/top111.jsp "Top 100 Teams." MilB.com. 2001.

15   baseballreflections.com/2018/03/18/look-casey-stengel/.

16   Jay Maeder, "Jacob Ruppert: The Old Ball Game," *New York Daily News*, March 2, 1999: 2.

17   Jay Brooks, "Historic Beer Birthday: Jacob Ruppert, Jr.," August 5, 2018. brookstonbeerbulletin.com/tag/baseball

18   Pat Gannon, "Col. Ruppert's Typical 'Burgher': Won Battle with Ban Johnson," *Milwaukee Journal*, January 15, 1939: 12.

19   "From Tweet to Crocker: Do the Changes in Men and Methods Show That Parties in Great Municipalities are Growing Better or Worse?" *Deseret News* (Salt Lake City), January 6, 1906: 24.

20   "New York City – Bryan Carries It by About 28,000 – Belmont Elected; Ruppert Wins; McClellan and Cummings Re-elected," *New York Times*, November 7, 1900: 1.

21   "Democrats for Congress – Belmont Turned Down for Sullivan and Hearst. Goldfogle, Sulzer, McClellan, Rider, Shober, and Ruppert Named in Other Districts – Several Conventions Adjourned," *New York Times*, October 3, 1902.

22   "Col. Ruppert Buys Haffen Brewery: Sale Involving $700,000 Is One of the Largest Made in the Bronx; To Discontinue Business; Land on Which Brewery Stands Will Be Used as a Site for Modern Office Buildings," *New York Times*, January 20, 1914.

23   Maeder, "Jacob Ruppert."

24   brainyquote.com/quotes/ring_lardner_137685.

25   Daniel R. Levitt, "Jacob Ruppert," sabr.org/bioproj/person/b96b262d.

26   "Miller Huggins to Pilot Yankees: Signed for Two Years to Succeed Wild Bill Donovan. Tom Connery Will Scout for Yankees," *Hartford Courant*, October 26, 1917: 14.

27   "Col. Ruppert buys out Col. Huston for $1.5 Million," *Yankees Timeline*. Major League Baseball: May 21, 1922. newyork.yankees.mlb.com/nyy/history/timeline.jsp.

28   Richard Hoffer, "Our Favorite Athletes. It's Not Nice to Play Favorites But We're Making An Exception Here Celebrating Not Necessarily the Greatest but Those Who Brought Us the Greatest Joy," *Sports Illustrated*, July 12, 1999.

29   baseball-injury-report.com/new-york-yankees/.

30   Harvey Frommer, "Colonel Jacob Ruppert: The Man Who Build the Yankee Empire (Part II), August 8, 2013. theepochtimes.com/colonel-jacob-ruppert-the-man-who-built-the-yankee-empire-part-ii_237122.html.

31   newyork.yankees.mlb.com/nyy/ballpark/stadium_history.jsp.

32   Dick Heller, "Going by the Numbers," *Washington Times*, January 19, 2009.

33   Daniel R. Levitt, "Jacob Ruppert," sabr.org/bioproj/person/b96b262d.

34   Martin and Martin, *The Negro Leagues in New Jersey*, 20.

35   Jerry Izenberg. "Berra, Doby Hoping New Name Is a Sign an Old Rift Is Healed," *Star Ledger* (Newark), May 9, 2001.

36   Geoffrey C. Ward, *Baseball: An Illustrated History* (New York: Alfred A. Knopf, 1994), 198.

37   Ward, 203.

38   Ibid.

39   Ibid.

40   John B. Holway, *The Complete Book of Baseball's Negro Leagues: The Other Half of Baseball History* (Fern Park, Florida: Hastings House, 2001).

41   brainly.com/questions/9370338.

42   Samuel I. Rosenman, *Working with Roosevelt* (New York: Da Capo Press, 1972), 92-96.

43   Bob Addie, "ADDIE'S ATOMS: The Stadium They Built Without Ticket Windows," *The Sporting News*, September 25, 1965.

44   Philip J. Lowry, *Green Cathedrals: The Ultimate Celebration of All 271 Major League and Negro League Ballparks Past and Present* (Reading, Massachusetts: Addison-Wesley, 1992), 118.

45   Lowry, 288.

46   Schenectady (New York) Science Museum.

47   Martin and Martin, *The Negro Leagues in New Jersey*, 17.

48   Martin and Martin, *The Negro Leagues in New Jersey*, 10.

49   Ibid.

50   Izenberg. "Berra, Doby Hoping New Name Is a Sign an Old Rift Is Healed."

51   Martin and Martin, *The Negro Leagues in New Jersey*, 71.

52   Martin and Martin, 20.

53   Ibid.

54   Richard Sandomir, "Everyone Agrees Steinbrenner's Plaque Is Big," *New York Times*, September 21, 2010.

55   Dave Anderson, "No Longer Overlooked," *New York Times*, December 8, 2012.

56   Izenberg, "Berra, Doby Hoping New Name Is a Sign an Old Rift Is Healed."

57   Louis Effrat, "Newark Celebrates Inaugural With 8-5 Victory Over Royals," *New York Times*, April 23, 1937: 26.

58   Russell Roberts, *Discover the Hidden New Jersey* (Rutgers, New Jersey: Rutgers University Press, 1995), 75.

59   Bill Newman, "Old Newark Memories." oldnewark.com/memories/sports/newman-bears,htm.

60   Ibid.

61   *Winning with the Yankees*, Mel Allen narrator (Frankenmuth, Michigan: Encore Entertainment, Inc., 1956).

62   "Celebrities Listed for Newark Program," *New York Times*, July 24, 1942: 14.

63   jworld.com/news/2015/oct/10/your-turn-berra-was-one-kind/.

64   Martin and Martin, *The Negro Leagues in New Jersey*, 76.

65   Martin and Martin, 78.

66   Martin and Martin, 95.

67   Martin and Martin, 50.

68   Martin and Martin, 53.

69   baseballhall.org. National Baseball Hall of Fame and Museum.

70   Martin and Martin, 62.

71   sabr.org/bioproj/person/4e985e86.

72   Martin and Martin, *The Negro Leagues in New Jersey*, 31.

73   John McMurray, "Larry Doby." sabr.org/bioproj/person/4e985e86.

74   Richard Justice and Chris Haft, "Trailblazer Irwin Dies at 96," MLB.com, January 12, 2016.

75   David Nemec and Scott Flatow, *Great Baseball Feats, Facts, and Firsts*, 2008 Edition (New York: Signet, 2008), 198.

76   Nemec and Flatow, 152.

77   "Eisenhower Advises Newcombe To Remember His 27 Triumphs; In Letter, President Says He Was Pulling for Don, Routed Twice in World Series," *New York Times*, November 10, 1956: 233.

78   newarksportsnnet/photos/displayimage.php?pid=33. Poster from Rich Olohan.

79   Martin and Martin, 72.

80   "Bears Up For Sale, Yankees Confirm," *New York Times*, November 12, 1948: 37.

81   "Jersey Tries Comeback as Fight Center, *Washington Post*, June 8, 1948: 19.

82   "Ruppert Stadium to Be Torn Down."

83   "Newark Plot Sold for Industrial Plant," *New York Times*, August 25, 1961: 37.

84   Kevin Coyne.

85   peoplesworld.org/article/today-in-women-s-history-birth-of-effa-manley-baseball-hall-hall-of-famer/.

86   Ronald Smothers, "Newark Hails Baseball's Return, but the High Cost of a New Stadium Raises Doubts," *New York Times*, July 4, 1999: 21.

87   Associated Press, "Newark Rights Baseball Wrong," *The Record* (Hackensack, New Jersey), May 9, 2001.

88   Mark Di Ionno, "Game Over: Newark Bears Officially Out of Business as Baseball Fades From City Again," *Newark Star-Ledger*, April 28, 2014.

89   brainyquote.com/quotes/f_scott_fitzgerald 166303.

1946 NEWARK EAGLES TIMELINE

BY BILL NOWLIN

For this 1946 season timeline, we have tried to be as complete as we can. It is frustrating to see a game announced in one newspaper's columns, or even see the game advertised it its pages, but then never be able to determine whether the game was ever played.

Some of the game accounts here have rather skimpy details, but that is because the details provided are all we could find. As with all the works that SABR publishes, if there are corrections or additions, please let us hear from you and we will adjust the information we provide.

SPRING TRAINING

The Eagles planned to "make the jaunt to pep up" in Jacksonville, Florida, starting on April 1.[1]

In mid-March Effa Manley announced that the Eagles had re-signed Biz Mackey to manage the team. He had taken over for Willie Wells in 1945 and helped lead the Eagles to a second-place finish. Johnny Davis had played in Puerto Rico over the winter and had been thinking over an offer to play in Mexico for the 1946 season but signed again with Newark.

Mexican League raiders didn't make the inroads they had made in years past; over the years, they had enticed Ray Dandridge, Len Hooker, Monte Irvin, Terry McDuffie, and Willie Wells — at least for a period of time.

REGULATIONS

1. The Club's playing season for each year covered by this contract and all renewals hereof shall be as fixed by the Negro National League of Professional Baseball Clubs.

2. The Player must keep himself in first-class physical condition and must at all times conform his personal conduct to standards of good citizenship and good sportsmanship.

3. The Player, when requested by the Club, must submit to a complete physical examination at the expense of the Club and, if necessary, to treatment by a regular physician or dentist in good standing at the Player's expense. For refusal of the player to submit to a complete medical or dental examination the club may consider such refusal as a violation of this regulation and may take such action as it deems advisable under regulation 6 of this contract. Disability directly resulting from injuries sustained while rendering service under this contract shall not impair the right of the Player to receive his full salary for a period not exceeding two weeks from the date of his injury, at the termination of which he may be released or continued on the salary roll. Any other disability or misconduct may be ground for suspending or terminating this contract at the discretion of the Club. A Player who sustains an injury while playing baseball for his club must serve written notice upon his club of such injury, giving time, place, cause and nature of the injury within ten days of the sustaining of such injury.

4. The Club will furnish the Player with uniform, exclusive of shoes. Upon the termination of the playing season or release of the player the player agrees to surrender the uniform or uniforms to the Club.

5. The Club will provide and furnish the Player while "abroad," or traveling with the Club in other cities, with proper board, lodging, and pay all proper and necessary traveling expenses and meals en route.

6. For violation by the Player of any regulation, the Club may impose a reasonable fine and deduct the amount thereof from the Player's salary or may suspend the Player without salary for a period not exceeding thirty days, or both, at the discretion of the Club.

7. In order to enable the Player to fit himself for his duties under this contract, the Club may require the Player to report for practice at such places as the Club may designate and to participate in such exhibition contests as may be arranged by the Club for a period of .... days prior to the playing season without any other compensation than that herein elsewhere provided, the Club, however, to pay the necessary traveling expenses and meals en route of the Player from his home city to the training place of the Club, whether he be ordered to go there direct or by way of the home city of the Club. In the event of the failure of the Player to report for practice or to participate in the exhibition games, as provided for, he shall be required to get in playing condition to the satisfaction of the Club's team manager, and at the Player's own expense, before his salary shall commence.

This contract page outlines the regulations by which the players and team agreed to abide for the 1946 season. *(Courtesy of Newark Public Library)*

Monte Irvin had also played winter ball in Puerto Rico, winning the batting title and the MVP, and helping San Juan win the championship. Abe and Effa Manley were reported to have outbid the Mexican League's Jorge Pasquel for Irvin's services and the March 30 issue of the *New Jersey Afro-American* reported his signing. Already having played for Veracruz in 1942, he had Mexican League experience under his belt (and knew the money was good). One of the reasons he wanted to stay was to see more of his young daughter.[2] He may also have had his eye on the possibility of following Jackie Robinson in signing with a major-league organization.

Irvin had served in England and France during the war. Leon Day had taken part in the invasion at Normandy with the 818th Amphibious Truck Company and later served in Germany.

Clarence "Pint" Isreal was one of 11 war veterans who joined the Eagles in Jacksonville, in his case coming straight from Alaska's Aleutian Islands, where he had been stationed. Other returning veterans in Eagles spring training included James Brown, Cecil Cole, Larry Doby, Rufus Lewis, Charles Parks, Pat Patterson, and Leon Ruffin.[3]

Don Newcombe didn't make the Eagles team bus as it headed south; it was soon learned that he had signed with the Brooklyn Dodgers and been placed with their farm team in Nashua, New Hampshire. Effa Manley was more than ticked. "If [Branch] Rickey wanted to employ a player from a major league chain, I believe he would first negotiate with the player's club. … I believe the same courtesy is warranted where a colored league is concerned."[4] She added, "What will become of colored baseball leagues if players are picked out by major league owners without consulting the team management?"

Abe Manley said he had been impressed with the team spirit shown in Jacksonville and suggested that a tire blowout on the team bus as it headed south was about the only adversity the team had yet faced.[5]

Back at Newark's Ruppert Stadium, new signs reading "No Gambling" had been painted and a new system of lighting used to indicate plays on the scoreboard. Hot dogs were still to be 15 cents and cokes remained a dime. Readers were reminded that "[a]n attractive gin mill provides the heartier lushie with drinks from soda pop to the finer liquors."[6]

In Jacksonville the team stayed at the Bellview Hotel at 708½ Davis Street. In a letter dated January 28, the cost was set at $2.00 per person per day for board and $35.00 for 20 men per week, for a total cost of $315.00 per week for 20 players.

The *Newark Evening News* published four reports from spring training. Unfortunately, there does not seem to have been an African-American publication in Jacksonville. The April 9 issue said

the team was "rapidly rounding into form" and working the kinks out. Manager Mackey was said to be satisfied with the progress. The paper declared, "The pitching staff is the strongest in the history of the club. Leon Day looms as the big start in this department."

Four days later, the *Evening News* offered an update. The Newark team had beaten the Jacksonville Eagles, 8-3, in their first exhibition game. "Impressive in his first Eagles trial was Rufus Lewis, an elongated right-hander from Mississippi. Lewis showed a blazing fast ball, a sharp breaking curve and a knuckle ball that baffled the opposing batsmen." Mackey was "elated" to welcome back Leon Day from the Army, and Max Manning. The other pitchers named in the article were Robert Cheeks of Bayonne, "who was recommended by Day" and Cecil Cole, Len Hooker – "mainstay of the staff last year" – and Vernon [*sic*] Peace, "who showed great promise last season."[7]

The April 16 issue featured Monte Irvin. "That boy will cause opposing pitchers many heartaches this year," said Biz Mackey of Irvin, the MVP of the Puerto Rican winter league. The newspaper said of Irvin, "He led in batting and was rated one of the best players to ever perform on the island."

On April 21 the Eagles beat the Pepsi Cola Giants, 19-7. The Eagles' win broke a 24-game winning streak by the Giants. Lewis and Day pitched for Newark. The two teams were reported to be playing a 2:30 P.M. doubleheader on April 22 at Port Tampa.[8]

The April 24 *Tampa Times* reported on a scheduled game at 8:15 P.M. that evening at Tampa's Plant Field against the Tampa Grandstanders. The newspaper noted: "A special section of the stands will be reserved for white spectators."[9]

The April 27 issue of the *New York Amsterdam News* provided details on two preseason exhibition games played against the Jacksonville Eagles. The scores were 16-8 and 7-2, both in favor of the Eagles. Rufus Lewis started the first game, before an overflow crowd, "and showed he was ready for NNL ball by hurling effective ball and showing a blazing fast ball, sharp breaking curve, fine control and a good knuckler."[10] Parks hit both a double and a triple in the first of the games, with Watkins and Doby both doubling. Lennie Pearson was 4-for 5 in the Tuesday game. Harvey homered over the right-field fence. Leon Day and Max Manning both got in some work, with reassuring results: "Both hurlers have been in service but the absence from league ball is not noticeable."[11] Day allowed just two singles in four innings of work.

The final report was published on April 30, simply reporting that, "after undergoing four weeks of strenuous Spring training," the team had broken camp and was heading home to Newark. "Mr. Mackey is well pleased with the progress of his charges and expressed the belief that his team will get off to a winning start."

Abe Manley proclaimed it the most successful spring training the team had had.[12] Columnist Dan Burley wrote, "Mrs. Manley and her husband, Abe, who live, sleep and eat baseball, went all the way to get a winner this year."[13] There were to be games played in Tampa and Richmond as the team headed north.

Uniform Numbers of the 1946 Newark Eagles

1	James Wilkes, u
2	--
3	William Felder, ss
4	Maxwell Manning, p
5	Leniel Hooker, p
6	Larry Doby, 2b
7	Leon Day, p
8	Clarence Isreal, u
9	Leon Ruffin, c
10	Pat Patterson, 3b
11	Oscar Givens, u
12	Rufus Lewis, p
13	--
14	--
15	--
16	Monte Irvin, cf
17	Johnny Davis, lf
18	Bob Harvey, rf
22	Leonard Pearson, 1b
36	Charles Parks, c
40	Biz Mackey, mgr.

--*Philadelphia Tribune*, August 6, 1946: 10.

THE REGULAR SEASON

The original first-half schedule had the Eagles opening the season in Wilmington playing the Stars on May 4 in a doubleheader that also featured the Baltimore Elite Giants playing the Homestead

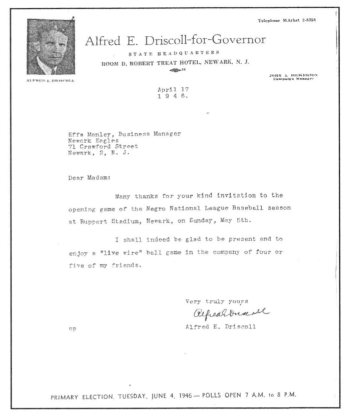

Co-owner Effa Manley made every effort to ensure that a Who's Who of New Jersey would be in attendance for Opening Day, including gubernatorial candidate Alfred E. Driscoll. *(Courtesy of Newark Public Library)*

Grays. The New York Black Yankees were to play the New York Cubans at Trenton. None of the teams were to play on their own home field.[14]

Newark Mayor Vincent J. Murphy designated Sunday, May 5, as "Newark Eagles Day" in Newark. With the mayor out of the city at the time, Deputy Mayor Barney Koplin threw out the first ball. Game time was 1:30 P.M.

May 5, 1946: Newark Eagles 2, Philadelphia Stars 0, at Ruppert Stadium, Newark

"Fireworks at Eagles Game" was the headline in the May 6 *Newark Evening News*, as Leon Day threw a 2-0 no-hitter against the visiting Philadelphia Stars. Barney Brown of the Stars had held the Eagles to five hits, but Newark had put across two runs in the bottom of the sixth. Catcher Bill Cash of the Stars challenged a decision by umpire Pete Strauch allowing Larry Doby to score with Newark's second run of the inning. Cash struck Strauch and both men fell to the ground fighting, setting off a brawl that involved both teams. Day faced only 29 batters. He walked one, and three reached on errors. At game's end, once the no-hitter was announced, a "near riot" of celebration ensued among the fans. A full game story is provided elsewhere in this book.

May 6, 1946: Newark Eagles 14, Philadelphia Stars 6, at Wilmington Park, Wilmington, Delaware (neutral site)

After the president of the Wilmington City Council threw out the first pitch, Philadelphia scored four runs in the bottom of the second for a 4-1 lead. Stars starter Joe Fillmore was heavily pounded by Eagles batters and Newark scored seven runs in the top of the third; he'd walked himself into trouble, granting the first three batters free passes. He was relieved by Harris, off whom all the runs were scored, the first three charged to Fillmore, of course, the last three on a homer over the left-field wall by Johnny Davis.

Max Manning was touched up for two more Stars runs in the bottom of the third, and it was 8-6 in Newark's favor, but Newark kept scoring and Philadelphia was shut out the rest of the way. Curry tripled for the Stars to lead off the fifth, but Manning struck out the next two batters and then induced a grounder to third base. Fourteen Eagles runs scored in the game, off four Philadelphia pitchers, with Monte Irvin, Lennie Pearson, and Johnny Davis all hitting homers.

May 12, 1946: Newark Eagles 8, New York Black Yankees 2, at Ruppert Stadium, Newark

Leon Day started again for Newark and Alex Newkirk pitched for the New York Black Yankees. With the third of three hits against Day, Newkirk drove in the first run of the game in the top of the second. Newark came right back with a walk to Pearson, a stolen base, and Pearson advancing to third and then scoring on successive infield hits by Bob Harvey and Johnny Davis. In the third inning, each team scored another run, New York's Willie Wells doubling in Harry Williams, and then doubles by Charles Parks and Benny Felder tied it back up. Day shut New York down the rest of the day. In the bottom of the fifth, Parks broke the 2-2 tie with a 370-foot two-run homer into the center-field bleachers. David drove in two more runs later in the game, and doubles by Doby, Pearson, and Harvey brought in the final two runs in the bottom of the eighth.

This was to have been a doubleheader, and the Eagles held a 3-0 lead in the second game – Rufus Lewis pitching for Newark – but it was halted in the fourth inning by rain. The May 13 game was also rained out.

May 14, 1946: Newark Eagles 3, Homestead Grays 3 (tie), at Ruppert Stadium, Newark

In a twilight game, Rufus Lewis pitched for the Eagles and got himself in a hole right away. The Grays got all their runs in the top of the first inning thanks to Buck Leonard's three-run homer

into the right-field bleachers. In the fourth inning, Larry Doby led off for Newark with a home run into the center-field stands, a 380-foot drive. Pearson then singled and took second on a fielding flub. Irvin singled, and Pearson scored. After Davis walked, Harvey sacrificed the both unners to second and third. With the pitcher on deck, Parks was walked intentionally. Manager Biz Mackey had Jimmy Wilkes pinch-hit for Lewis. Wilkes worked a walk and the game was tied. Lewis had struck out seven in his four innings, including twice striking out Josh Gibson. Max Manning pitched the fifth and sixth for the Eagles. After six innings, the game was called on account of rain, standing as a 3-3 tie.

May 19, 1946: Baltimore Elite Giants 4, Newark 3 (first game); Baltimore Elite Giants 5, Newark 3 (second game, seven innings), at Ruppert Stadium

"Eagles Flop in Clutches." The still-undefeated Eagles dropped two games to the visiting Elite Giants, much to the disappointment of about 6,000 fans. Len Hooker started game one "and for six innings completely baffled his opponents," allowing just two hits.[15] Newark had scored once in the second off Baltimore's Bill Byrd and once in the fifth. Both runs were driven in by Bob Harvey, one on a solo homer. Things were looking good. In the seventh, however, Baltimore banged out four hits. With one out, Bill Hoskins singled and Henry Kimbro doubled. Pinch-hitter Tito Figueroa singled them both in to tie the game. A walk and Doby's error set things up for Byrd to single in the go-ahead run. A fourth run followed on a sacrifice fly.

Leon Day started the nightcap for Newark and Ruffin for Baltimore. The Eagles committed five errors behind Day and the poor support cost him the game. Baltimore scored three times in the first. Newark came back with two, but saw the Elites add runs in the fifth and seventh. Doby hit a home run and Newark got one run back in the bottom of the seventh, but that was the final inning of the shortened second game.

May 20, 1946: Philadelphia Stars 7, Newark Eagles 1, at Norfolk (probably Tar Field), neutral site

The Stars, wrote the *New Journal and Guide*, "took advantage of the weak offerings of a rookie pitcher, Cole." Joe "Fireball" Fillmore was pitching for Philly. The Eagles got to him for one run in the first inning, but then failed to score again, as he "showed masterful control throughout and his mixture of pitches stymied the Newark batsmen."[16] Cecil Cole gave up four runs in the second inning and the Stars never looked back. One of the runs in the inning came when Philly first baseman Doc Dennis hit a solo home run high over the left-field fence. There were several defensive plays of note during the course of the game, on both sides.

May 22, 1946: Newark Eagles 5, Philadelphia Stars 2, at Norfolk (probably Tar Field), neutral site

A game scheduled for Tuesday night, May 21, was rained out. It was the second time that "recently acquired war vet" Rufus Lewis had been slated to pitch. Both times, the games had been postponed. He got his shot this Wednesday night, and won the game. The Norfolk newspaper noted that the game started slowly, taking an hour and 20 minutes to play the first three innings, but that the next six required just 1:15.

The Eagles might have scored more than they did, considering that right-hander Wilmer Harris "couldn't find the plate and filled the bases in the second and third innings."[17] Indeed, in the second inning, the Eagles scored one run on four walks and no hits. Eddie Jefferson took over in relief. Larry Doby homered off Jefferson in the seventh, a 320-foot drive over the right-field wall. He hit a ball even farther in the eighth inning, all the way to the center-field fence. It stayed in the ballpark, but he got a triple and drove in Jimmy Wilkes.

The two Stars runs scored on a walk to Murray Watkins in the second inning. He took third on a single by shortstop Frank Austin, then scored on a groundout by center fielder Gene Benson. Bus Clarkson hit a solo homer for the Stars later in the game. Lennie Pearson and Johnny David each drove in runs for Newark. Watkins also played for the Eagles in 1946.

May 24, 1946: Philadelphia Stars 8, Newark 1, at Trenton, New Jersey

There was a day game at Ruppert Stadium on May 24; the International League's Newark Bears played at Ruppert, beating the Jersey City Giants, 4-3. The Negro National League's Newark Eagles played the Philadelphia Stars that evening in Trenton. Max Manning started the game for the Eagles but the Stars jumped on him and scored five runs in the top of the first inning. They added another run in the second inning and two more in the fourth. Len Hooker relieved Manning at some point during the game. Stars starter Bill Ricks held the Eagles to five hits and one run (scored by Leon Ruffin in the seventh). He was relieved by Henry McHenry in the ninth inning, after Eagles manager Biz Mackey inserted himself as a pinch-hitter – and got a base hit. The box score in the next day's *Philadelphia Inquirer* shows a catcher named Fox appearing in the game for Newark, but apparently only briefly since he has no outs, assists, errors, hits, or runs.[18]

May 26, 1946: New York Black Yankees 3, Newark Eagles 1, at Yankee Stadium, the Bronx (second game)

Although the Eagles outhit the Yanks, six hits to three, they came up short in runs. Leon Day pitched for Newark. Lennie Pearson's 430-foot second-inning home run into the left-field stands provided their only run. The game was tied 1-1 after six innings, but New York scored once in the seventh and once in the eighth. The go-ahead run came on a walk, a sacrifice, and a single. The eighth-inning run came on a home run. Coming off a five-game slump, Biz Mackey talked about shaking things up, maybe benching a struggling Monte Irvin and Bob Harvey.[19] The Homestead Grays had won four straight and claimed first place. Newark was in fourth. The day's first game, in the three-team doubleheader, had seen the Grays shut out the Black Yankees, 7-0.

The *Philadelphia Tribune* declared, "The failure of Monty Irvin to hit the ball up to expectations has been the talk of the league. Monty is rated as the greatest prospect in Negro baseball but he seems unable to get going and has looked very weak against pitchers who in former years he would bat in corners of the park." It was suggested he might be benched in favor of Jimmy Wilkes and that a brief stay on the bench might be salutary. "He has the ability to carry the team to the pennant and may stage a comeback and live up to pre-season predictions."[20] Irvin clearly did just that.

The *Tribune* also called out Bob Harvey as "overweight" and said he "may be forced to undergo a serious siege of reducing by Manager Mackey." The paper wrote of the second-best hitter in the league in 1945, "Bob has been woefully weak at the plate and may be benched in an effort to get more punch in the lineup."[21]

May 28 – The game against the Cubans at Ruppert was rained out.

**May 30, 1946: Philadelphia Stars 7, Newark 4 (first game);
Newark 6, Philadelphia Stars 3 (second game),
at Ruppert Stadium**

Rufus Lewis started the first game and was treated to two Eagles runs in the second on a Wilkes home run with Doby on base, and a third run in the third inning. The Stars tied the game with three runs on four hits in the top of the fifth, though. Newark again took the lead, scoring once in the bottom of the eighth when Bob Harvey tripled and Biz Mackey pinch-hit for Lewis and knocked him in. Getting three outs in the ninth proved difficult, however. Cecil Cole was on in relief, working in his first game for Newark. He got two outs but then Stars pitcher McHenry homered into the left-field stands. This tied the game but also seemingly opened the gate. The next four Stars hit safely and scored three more runs to win the game.

In the second game, Len Hooker allowed four hits and two bases on balls in the top of the third, giving Philadelphia a 6-3 lead. He was bailed out big-time in the bottom of the fifth when the Eagles scored six times. The two big outbursts were the sum total of the scoring in the seven-inning game.

**May 31, 1946: Newark 9, Philadelphia Stars 2,
at Shibe Park, Philadelphia (second game)**

The three-team doubleheader at Shibe Park drew 11,990 fans. After a first game in which the Stars beat the New York Black Yankees, 7-2, the Eagles took on the Stars. The Eagles collected 15 hits off three Philadelphia pitchers. Harvey had three hits, while Wilkes, Isreal, Doby, Davis, and pitcher Leon Day each had two. Larry Doby had homered into the left-field bleachers in the first inning. Two batters later, Johnny Davis hit one that landed just a few feet away from where Doby's had.

Leon Day threw a seven-hitter and Newark won, 9-2. It was "something of a moral victory" for Philadelphia, though, since the seven hits were seven more than they had gotten off Day in the Opening Day no-hitter.

June 1: Rain interfered once more, again washing out a game against the Cubans.

**June 2, 1946: Newark Eagles vs. Brooklyn Bushwicks,
exhibition doubleheader, Dexter Park, Queens**

An article in the June 2 *Brooklyn Daily Eagle* announced a 2:00 P.M. doubleheader between the two teams. Earlier in the season, both the Philadelphia Stars and New York Cubans had played the noted Bushwicks semipro team. Rain hit the area on June 2, canceling a local golf tournament and, we assume, these games.

**June 3, 1946: Newark 4, Baltimore Elite Giants 2,
at Tar Park, Norfolk, Virginia (neutral site)**

The very brief summary in the *Newark Evening News* simply said, "Rufus Lewis pitched brilliant ball." He threw a four-hitter and Larry Doby was the "big gun" with a homer, reported the *Atlanta Daily World.* Lewis beat Bill Byrd.

**June 5, 1946: Baltimore Elite Giants 13, Newark 2,
at Memorial Field, Salisbury, Maryland (neutral site)**

Four Eagles pitchers couldn't stem the tide and Baltimore easily won the night game at Salisbury's Memorial Field behind the four-hit pitching of Bill Barnes. Pitching for the Eagles was a player named Butts, who gave up seven runs in the second inning. The next day's *Salisbury Daily Times* said the game was witnessed by an estimated 500 fans. See June 12; the pitcher was almost certainly Harry Butts.

**June 6, 1946: Baltimore Elite Giants 9, Newark 4,
at Municipal Stadium, Hagerstown, Maryland (neutral site)**

"The game was well played and a fair crowd was on hand," wrote the *Hagerstown Daily Mail.* The 8:30 P.M. game at Municipal Stadium saw Baltimore collect eight hits to Newark's six. Baltimore committed two errors, and Newark one, but the Elite Giants came out on top with runs to spare.

**June 7, 1946: Baltimore Elite Giants 3, Newark 2 (first game);
Newark 5, Baltimore Elite Giants 3 (second game, 10 innings),
at Bugle Field, Baltimore**

Newark scored twice in the second inning but Baltimore's Jonas Gaines two-hit the Eagles, with only Patterson and Pearson getting hits. Baltimore scored one run each in the fourth, sixth, and seventh innings, beating Len Hooker. It was a seven-inning game. The second game was tied 3-3 after seven, and ran on till the 10th, when Newark scored twice (Pearson driving in the winning run) and Baltimore failed to score at all. Max Manning got the win over Baltimore's Joe Black. Black struck out 10; he gave up 10 hits to Black's eight. Newark didn't have an extra-base hit in either game.

At this point in the season, the Eagles added two players, Pat Patterson to take over at third base replacing Clarence Isreal, and Oscar "Givvy" Givens to play shortstop.[22]

**June 8, 1946: Newark 7, Homestead Grays 5,
at Wilmington Park, Wilmington, Delaware (neutral site)**

Eugene Smith started for the Grays and weathered a three-run top of the third. Johnny Davis was the starting pitcher for the Eagles. He gave up one run to Homestead in the bottom of the fourth. Newark made it 4-1 in the seventh inning, but then Josh Gibson hit a three-run homer and Homestead scored a total of four runs in the bottom of the seventh to take a 5-4 lead. In the top of the ninth, a base on balls, an error by Marquez, and three Eagles hits drove Smith from the box, leaving it to Red Fields to get the final two outs. Newark scored three times and won the game, 7-5. Marquez did get two RBIs. Davis drove in two for the Eagles.

The end result is not in question, but the *Wilmington Journal* box score leaves us with some questions. It claims that Day "ran for Day in ninth" and then indicates that he played second base. This appears to indicate that Day ran for Doby, perhaps due to a minor injury. (Doby played the next day).[23] The box score also informs us that Max Manning and "Harvel" (presumably Bob Harvey) both pinch-hit, for Felder and Givens respectively, but that both made outs. Hooker may have been the one who shut down Homestead in the bottom of the ninth.

Len Pearson also homered in the game. Davis walked eight Grays. Smith walked nine Eagles. Both teams left 12 men on base. The game drew 2,702. It was a very long game, reported at 3:00.

**June 9, 1946: Newark 7, New York Cubans 1 (first game);
Newark 6, New York Cubans 2 (second game),
at the Polo Grounds, New York**

The Eagles moved back into first place, taking two from the Cuban Stars, punctuating both games with sizable ninth-inning scoring. Day threw a four-hitter in the first game, and Lewis a seven-hitter in the second game. Day was also 3-for-3 at the plate in the opener. The Eagles scored once in the top of the second and the Cubans tied it with one in the bottom of the third. So it stood, 1-1, until the top of the seventh. With Day on second and Wilkes on first, Pat Patterson tripled and made it 3-1. In the top of the ninth, Newark iced it with four insurance runs. Day led off with a single to left field, and then ran all the way to third on an infield hit by Wilkes. He scored on a groundout. Doby singled and Len Pearson doubled, driving in Wilkes and Doby. Then Pearson scored when Johnny Davis singled. Barnet Morris and Pat Scantlebury pitched for the Cubans.

Lewis didn't allow a hit for the first four innings of the second game. The Eagles scored twice in the first and added one in the seventh. The Cubans pressed back with their first hit – a solo homer by Rogelio Linares in the fifth into the upper deck in left field –

and added one more run in the seventh. In the top of the ninth, the Eagles once again piled up the runs. Oscar "Gibby" Givens walked, and then five singles followed (Leon Ruffin, Lewis, Isreal , Wilkes, and Patterson), with three runs scoring.

The *New York Amsterdam News* enthused about the "hustling, never-give-up gang of young ballplayers from across the river" – the Newark Eagles. About 12,000 fans at the Polo Grounds saw the Eagles do "about everything right" and "how important it is to have team spirit, cooperation and youth."

**June 10, 1946: New York Cubans 4, Newark 1,
at Dexter Park, Queens**

Cecil Cole (six innings), James Boyd (the seventh inning), and Warren Peace (the eighth inning) all pitched for Newark. Impo Barnhill threw a complete game for the Cubans. The Cubans scored first, in the second inning on singles by Harry Williams and Linares and then a wild pitch uncorked by Cole. The Eagles scored their only run – it tied the game at the time – in the top of the sixth when Len Pearson singled, stole second, and ran home on Monte Irvin's single. The New Yorkers struck back right away with two runs in the bottom of the sixth. Cole walked Lou Louden, who wound up on third base after Charles Parks tried to throw him out stealing but instead sent the ball sailing into center field. Williams walked, putting runners on the corners. Silvio Garcia singled in Williams. Linares grounded out, 4-3, but Garcia streaked for the plate and was safe when Pearson's throw home went wild. The Cubans added a run in the seventh. Cole had allowed only three hits, but he walked six and there were three Eagles errors.

**June 12, 1946: Newark Eagles 7, Lloyd A.C. 2,
at Lloyd Field, Chester, Pennsylvania**

On June 12, the Eagles played a 6:30 P.M. exhibition game against the Lloyd A.C. in Chester, Pennsylvania. Somewhat sadly, more information is available about this exhibition game than about many of the championship-season games (thanks to good coverage in the June 13 *Delaware County Daily Times* of Chester, Pennsylvania).

Newark scored twice in the first and twice in both the third and the fourth.

Jim Wilkes led off with a double off Kime. After Clarence Isreal walked, Patterson reached on a fielder's choice. Irvin doubled and both Wilkes and Patterson had scored. The pitcher for the Eagles was listed as Harvey Butts, but is almost certainly Harry T. Butts, who later pitched in 1949-51 for the Indianapolis Clowns. The newspaper account says that Butts singled to lead off the fourth. Wilkes walked. And Isreal "cleared the right field screen for a double," which sounds like a ground rule for a short right field. He drove both baserunners in. That knocked starter Jack Kime out of the box. Jack "Lefty" McGillen (employed by the Eddystone Fire Department), came in as "fireman" with one out in the top of the fourth inning; he held the Eagles to just four hits and one more run for the rest of the game.

The Lloyd team only had four hits in the game, and all four came in the bottom of the fifth inning, scoring both of their two runs. McGillen doubled to drive in the first run and scored on a single to account for the second.

June 13, 1946: Homestead Grays 10, Newark 8, at Griffith Stadium, Washington

Josh Gibson ruled during this night game at Griffith, banging out a single, a double, and a home run and driving in four runs while scoring three times. Len Hooker started the game and gave up three runs to the Grays in the first inning. Leon Day was "chased … with a six-run barrage in the sixth." (*Newark Star-Ledger*) R.T. Walker started for Homestead and Double Duty Radcliffe relieved in the final two frames.

June 15, 1946: Newark 7, Baltimore Elite Giants 4, at Dunn Field, Trenton (neutral site)

Monte Irvin's seventh-inning grand slam was the big blow in the game. Johnny Davis had homered earlier, in the fifth, with no one aboard.

The June 15 *Newark Evening News* noted that the team had won five of its last six games and jumped from fourth place to first place, adding, "Eagles' hurlers have turned in sparkling performances and are now living up to pre-season predictions. Leon Day, Max Manning, Len Hooker and Rufus Lewis have all proven effective in recent game and seem ready for a tough pennant drive."

June 16, 1946: Newark 5, Baltimore Elite Giants 2 (first game); Newark 2, New York Black Yankees 1 (second game), at Ruppert Stadium

Given that it was a scheduled three-team doubleheader, the plan was to ensure that both games ran the full nine innings. It saved a little time that in neither game did Newark need to bat in the bottom of the ninth. Both games were "sensational pitching battles," pitting Rufus Lewis against Baltimore's Joe Black and Max Manning against Newkirk in the nightcap. "Home runs decided the first game," wrote the *Newark Evening News*. With Givens on base in the bottom of the second, Lewis homered into the

right-field stands. Baltimore tied it with solo homers by Kimbro in the third and Johnny Washington in the eighth, both of those into right field as well. In the bottom of the eighth, Johnny Davis hit a three-run homer to left field. Lewis allowed only four hits.

The second game saw no scoring for either side through the first five. In the bottom of the sixth, "Monty Irving" (as both the *Evening News* and *New Jersey Afro-American* sometimes called him) singled. Pinch-hitter Bob Harvey walked. Leon Ruffin singled in Irvin. An inning later the Eagles added another run on a base on balls to Benny Felder, a sacrifice by Pat Patterson, and a single by Larry Doby. The Black Yankees spoiled the shutout when they put together two of their four hits to score one run. Mimicking Lewis, Max Manning likewise allowed only four hits.

June 18, 1946: Newark 16, Homestead Grays 2, at Ruppert Stadium

"Hitting Orgy for Eagles." The game against the Grays was held under the lights. Frank Williams and Cool Papa Bell both singled in the first and an error by Doby allowed Homestead to take an early 1-0 lead. The Eagles obliterated that by sending 16 batters to the plate in the bottom of the third. They scored 11 runs on nine hits, with Patterson, Doby, and Irvin (the 2, 3, and 4 men in the batting order) each collecting two hits in the inning. Leon Day could cruise from that time on; he allowed one more run in the top of the seventh. The Grays got to Day for six hits, but suffered 11 strikeouts.

Newark had added one run in the fourth, three more in the fifth on Johnny Davis's three-run homer, and another one in the seventh on a solo home run by Larry Doby, his fourth hit of the game.

June 21, 1946: Newark 6, New York Black Yankees 5 (first game); Newark 11, New York Black Yankees 0 (second game) at Ruppert Stadium

It was a twilight/night twin bill with the first game starting at 6:30 P.M. In the reversal of the usual pattern, the first game was scheduled to be seven innings long and the second game the regulation nine. The Eagles kept taking the lead, and kept losing it – three times – with one run in the first, giving up two in the top of the second, tying it with another run in the bottom of the second and scoring two more in the third. The Black Yankees scored twice in the fourth, and the Eagles then ran it to 5-4 in the fourth. In the top of the seventh (and scheduled final inning), New York tied it, 5-5. In the bottom of the seventh, the Eagles loaded the bases. Mackey had Leon Day pinch-hit for Len Hooker and Day won the game with a single.

The second game saw Cecil Cole throw a two-hit shutout, yielding a single in the second and a single in the sixth. The Eagles scored early and often – three in the first, two in the fourth, four in the seventh (with Patterson on board, Doby hit a two-run homer), and two more in the eighth.

June 23, 1946: Newark 6, New York Cubans 1 (first game); Newark 3, New York Cubans 1 (second game), at Ruppert Stadium

Rufus Lewis and Leon Day each allowed the Cubans one run, and only one run, in two games in Newark. Monte Irvin hit two homers in the first game in successive at-bats in the third and fifth innings. The Eagles already had a 1-0 lead on a first-inning walk to Wilkes, a double by Patterson, and a fly ball. Patterson walked in the third, Doby tripled him in, and then Irvin hit the first of the two homers. The second was a solo shot. In the sixth, successive singles by Lewis, Wilkes, and Patterson scored the sixth run. The one run the Cubans got was on a home run by Silvio Garcia who, in fact, was Cuban.

So was Minnie Miñoso, who hit a solo home run in the fourth inning of the second game, giving New York a 1-0 lead. It was one of only four hits Leon Day allowed. Newark's Johnny Davis singled in Pearson to tie the game in the bottom of the fifth. With Irvin and Doby on board in the bottom of the sixth, Pearson hit a ball to Miñoso at third base, the ball took a bad hop, and both baserunners scored. The seven-inning game ended with the score still 3-1.

The Eagles were rising an eight-game win streak, noted the June 25 *Newark Evening News*, and the paper gave credit to the team's catcher: "The great showing of the pitching reflects upon the skill that has been exhibited by Leon Ruffin behind the plate. Ruffin is a veteran receiver and his faultless handling of the hurlers has won much praise from veteran baseball fans and players."

June 25, 1946: Newark 12, Homestead Grays 8, at Ruppert Stadium

"Eagles Streak Is New Record" The Eagles won their club-record ninth in a row beating the Homestead Grays, 12-6, on June 25. Max Manning had a rough game, giving up the eight runs on 13 hits including two homers by Buck Leonard, but he went the distance and got the win. Leonard singled in the second run of the game, in the first inning. With a two-run homer in the third and a three-run homer in the eighth, Leonard collected six RBIs in the game. Newark scored in every one of the first six innings – 1, 2, 3, 2, 3, 1 – before putting up goose eggs in the seventh and eighth. Jerry Benjamin tripled twice in the game for Homestead.

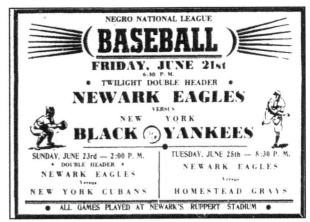

Between Leonard and Benjamin, they cornered the market in both home runs and triples. Doby had two doubles. Pearson's three RBIs were tops for the Eagles. Bob Thurman had started for the Grays; in all, three Grays pitchers gave up 17 base hits.

June 26, 1946: Newark 8, Homestead Grays 4, at Dunn Field, Trenton (neutral site)

Mackey's Eagles won their 10th game in a row and stretched their lead over the second-place Stars to 2½ games. The *Trenton Evening Times* reported that 1,555 fans saw Homestead's Howard Easterling hit a solo home run off Leon Day and the Grays thus take a 1-0 lead in the first inning, but then saw the Eagles score four runs in the second inning on three singles and a costly error by pitcher Gene Smith. The Grays came back with two in the fourth inning. Rufus Lewis took over pitching duties in the sixth inning. When the Eagles batted in the sixth, Johnny Davis hit a bases-loaded double and three more runs were added to Newark's tally. Irvin was 3-for-3 while Easterling had a big 4-for-5 day. Day was given the win, improving to 6-2. He struck out only one, while Gene Smith struck out eight – but Smith also walked six of the Eagles.

June 27, 1946: Homestead Grays 13, Newark 11, at Griffith Stadium, Washington

It was a "slam-bang affair" with Newark outhitting Homestead – but the Grays came out on top. Josh Gibson's home run "paced the 12-hit attack off Hooker, [James] Boyd and [Warren] Peace. Doubleduty Radcliff and [Frank] Thompson scattered 18 hits made by the Newarkers." [*Newark Evening News*, June 28]

June 28, 1946: Newark 11, Homestead Grays 10, at Ruppert Stadium

"Eagles Win Slugging Bee." There was no shortage of either base hits or runs when the two teams contended again at Ruppert

Stadium the very next night. Cecil Cole started for Newark and was hammered for four runs in the top of the first. Josh Gibson was up with the bases loaded and hit a ball to Monte Irvin in right field. Irvin slipped and by the time he got the ball back in, three runs had scored and Gibson was on second base. Bob Thurman tripled in Gibson. The Eagles promptly evened the score with four of their own in the bottom of the first. Patterson doubled, Irvin walked, and Len Pearson doubled. A walk and an error by Josh Gibson followed. The Eagles added two in the third, three in the fifth, and single runs in the sixth and seventh.

Homestead scored four in the sixth. Mackey replaced Cole with Max Manning, who came in with the bases loaded. Both teams had 11 hits. The Grays scored four times, but Manning got credit for the win, since the Eagles scored one more run. The Eagles remained three games ahead of the Stars in league standings.

June 30, 1946: Newark 3, Philadelphia Stars 0 (first game); Newark 6, Philadelphia Stars 0 (second game), at Ruppert Stadium

"Eagles Clinch Midway Title." The Newark Eagles swept an afternoon doubleheader and clinched the first-half Negro National League title with a double whitewash of the Philadelphia Stars that pleased the 5,000 Eagles fans at Ruppert Stadium. Leon Day battled with Bill Ricks in the first game and neither team scored through the first six innings. In the bottom of the seventh, Leon Ruffin homered into the left-field bleachers. That one run was all that was needed, it turned out, though, that a Pat Patterson double, a Larry Doby triple, and Monte Irvin's single gave the Eagles a couple of insurance runs in the eighth. The Stars got two men on base in the top of the ninth, but Day buckled down and struck out a pinch-hitter called Farn to end the game. Farn does not appear in any of the Negro Leagues databases. Day threw a five-hitter.

In the second game, Pat Patterson bunted to third base and ended up on third base when Murray Watkins threw the ball into right field. Doby singled him in. Another Stars error in the third inning led to another run on a throwing error by the catcher when Doby stole second. The wild throw allowed Doby to reach third base and come in on a groundout. A triple by Bob Harvey, a single by Charlie Parks, and a home run by the pitcher, Rufus Lewis, gave the Eagles three more runs. Lewis had thrown a three-hitter. The game was called after six because of rain.

The *New York Amsterdam News* wrote, "In winning the first half the Eagles staged one of the most sensational drives in the history of the Negro National League. Starting out in fourth place, the team began a winning streak that saw them win 11 of their last 12 league games. During this pennant drive the club displayed a terrific batting punch, airtight defense and brilliant pitching."

July 2, 1946: Newark 7, New York Black Yankees 1, at Ruppert Stadium

The *Newark Star-Ledger* box score shows only eight men playing for Newark, eighth in the order being the pitcher Boyd and ninth being the pitcher Hooker. We're not really sure what to make of this. It may be the one game that James Boyd pitched for the Eagles in 1946; he did win the one game he pitched. The box score fails to reflect a first baseman, and it is unlikely Newark played without one. No doubt it was Lennie Pearson, as he doubled and scored a run in the game.

We don't know how the Yanks scored their run, but the text explains how the Eagles scored theirs. Alex Newkirk pitched the full game for the Black Yankees. With one out in the first inning, Pat Patterson walked and stole second. Larry Doby singled him in. In the third inning Ben Felder reached first on an infield error. Patterson singled. Doby hit a three-run homer into the right-field bleachers. The inning wasn't over yet. Len Pearson doubled, the ball bouncing up and off the left-field wall. Johnny Davis then hit one in the other direction, a single down the first-base line that scored Pearson. In the eighth, Monte Irvin and Bob Harvey singled and Johnny Davis doubled them both in.

July 3, 1946: Brooklyn Bushwicks 6, Newark Eagles 3, at Dexter Park, Queens (exhibition game)

An exhibition night game in Queens saw the Bushwicks' Emil Moscowitz hold off the Eagles, allowing nine hits but striking out nine. Warren Peace started for Newark. Though the Eagles scored first with one run in the top of the first, the Bushwicks scored twice in the second and twice in the fourth. Peace left the game after 3⅔, relieved by Cecil Cole. He had been wild, giving up four hits but walking five batters and hitting one. He also threw a wild pitch. Cole also walked five. Newark scored two runs in the top of the sixth, but never quite caught up. Brooklyn added an insurance run in the seventh and another in the eighth. Peace bore the loss. Tony Cuccinello was 3-for-5 for Brooklyn and his brother Al was 1-for-2. Between them they accounted for four of the Bushwicks' seven hits. Cal Irvin, Patterson, and Harvey each had a pair of hits for the Eagles. Monte Irvin, Harvey, and Davis each drove in one run. Harvey had a double and both Johnny Davis and Charles Parks tripled. Some 5,700 spectators took in the game.

July 4, 1946: Newark 3, New York Black Yankees 1, at Yankee Stadium, the Bronx

The first half of the season officially ended with the July Fourth afternoon game at Yankee Stadium. Newark won its 14th of 15 games, atop the standings. Max Manning struck out nine, allowed five hits, and was "the master of the situation throughout the battle." Slim Johnson kept Newark scoreless through the first six innings. In the top of the seventh, Pat Patterson hit a ball to deep center field that Felix McLaurin "failed to hold." Patterson reached second base. He tagged up and took third on a deep Doby fly ball to McLaurin. Irvin pushed a single over the infield, scoring Patterson. Len Pearson homered to left to make it 3-0. The Yanks scored one run in the bottom of the eighth.

July 4, 1946: Newark 31, Industrial League All-Stars 4, at Dunn Field, Trenton (exhibition game)

Apparently the Eagles scooted over to Trenton from the Bronx for night baseball at Dunn Field and played an exhibition game against an Industrial League All-Stars team. "Adding machines, comptometers, and various other devices were required to compute the score last night," wrote the *Trenton Evening Times*, noting that it was an "absurd score." Len Hooker pitched the full nine innings for Newark, allowing 10 hits.

Doby, Patterson, and Davis each had four hits. Pearson, Harvey, and Davis each hit home runs. The first pitcher for the All-Stars, Lonnie Heisler, did well to hold the Eagles scoreless for the first three innings and with one run in the first and another in the third, the Industrial League team held a 2-0 lead after the first third of the game. As other pitchers rotated in, the Eagles began to pile up the runs. In the final six innings, they scored 2, 5, 6, 1, 3, and finally 14 runs in the top of the ninth.

July 5, 1946: Lloyd A.C. 6, Newark Eagles 5, at Lloyd Field, Chester, Pennsylvania

On Friday night, July 5, the Eagles played another game in Chester. They went down in the twi-night game, 6-5, in seven innings when the Lloyd team scored four runs in the fourth and, with two outs in the bottom of the seventh, pinch-hitter Remo Ciccone homered over the right-field screen. Warren Peace started for the Eagles, relieved by Davis. The *Philadelphia Tribune* reported, "A large crowd witnessed the melee."[24]

Fred Wilson of the *Chester Times* observed in his July 12 Sports Shorts column "[C]rowds at Lloyd Field are developing major league habits. They are keeping the balls which are hit into the stands, something they didn't do in the past. In the game last week with the Newark Eagles, three dozen baseballs disappeared. This represents $54, which isn't exactly peanuts. …What they are worried about is not the cost, but the scarcity. It's mighty tough to get baseballs."

July 7, 1946: Newark 9, Homestead Grays 5 (first game); Newark 8, Homestead Grays 5 (second game, six innings), at Forbes Field, Pittsburgh

The *Pittsburgh Courier* was impressed with the Eagles. On July 6 the paper wrote, "Newark's youngsters of yesterday are Newark's 'Mad Eagles' today. The kids have grown up. They learned baseball right while growing up. Manager Bizz Mackey taught it that way. The faith that Abe Manley and his wife, Effa, had in young baseball players has been justified. The patience of Mackey in teaching baseball the right way is paying off. Newark is the hottest thing in baseball."[25] They were, the paper said, setting attendance records all over.

The Grays scored five runs in games pitched in Pittsburgh by Day and Lewis, but in both games the Eagles scored more. The second game was "stopped by the Sunday law" after six innings.[26]

July 8 – a planned game between the Eagles and the Baltimore Elite Giants was canceled due to rain.

July 10, 1946: Newark 7, New York Black Yankees 3, at Ruppert Stadium

Manning improved his record to 7-1, striking out six but allowing nine hits. Patterson homered to right field in the bottom of the first. The Eagles added two more in the second when Davis doubled, Harvey and Wilkes both singled, and Ruffin brought home the second run with a sacrifice. Pearson and Davis singled and Leon Ruffin doubled and they got two more in the third. The "Manleymen" added single runs in the sixth and the eighth. It might have been a 7-1 game but Clyde Parris hit a two-run homer in the eighth for New York.

July 12, 1946: Newark 5, New York Cubans 0, at Ruppert Stadium

Len Hooker shut out the Cubans, 5-0, the first time they'd been shut out all year, on a five-hitter. Only one Cuban baserunner reached third base. Harvey singled three times, Doby tripled twice, and – with Len Pearson on base in the fourth inning – Johnny Davis hit a 330-foot home run into Ruppert Stadium's left-field stands. That was the game-winning hit. Newark added one run each in the fifth, sixth, and eight innings. It was the Eagles' ninth win in a row, and they'd won 19 of their last 20 games.

July 13, 1946: Newark 12, New York Black Yankees 11, at Trenton (likely Dunn Field, in any event a neutral site)

Warren Peace got the win in the game at Trenton, though he was named as Jim Peace in one of the very few newspaper mentions of this game.[27] We lack other information about this game.

At some point in July, Givens left the team "to attend summer school at Morgan College" (today's Morgan State University), according to the July 20 *New York Amsterdam News*. It was expected he would rejoin the team in August after they returned from a trip to play several games in Ohio and Pennsylvania.

July 14, 1946: Philadelphia Stars 7, Newark 5 (first game); Philadelphia Stars 6, Newark 3 (second game), at Ruppert Stadium

"Stars Scissor Eagles' Spurt." Eagles fans hoping to see their team continue its almost uninterrupted winning ways were rudely surprised when the visiting Philadelphia Stars swept Newark, beating both Leon Day and Rufus Lewis. The Eagles held a 3-1 lead through the first five innings of game one but the Stars got three runs on three base hits, a walk, and a two-run error in the seventh when Monte Irvin let a ball skitter between his legs. In the eighth, Clarence Isreal misjudged a line drive hit by Bus Clarkson that drove in two more.

Newark also held a lead in the second game, 2-0 after five. But a double, a single, and Clarkson's home run gave the Stars three runs. It was 3-3 after six innings in the seven-inning game, but the Eagles committed three errors in the seventh which, combined with two hits, gave Philadelphia three more runs and left Lewis with his first loss of the season.

July 16, 1946: Newark 6, Kansas City Monarchs 3, at Ruppert Stadium

It was an interleague game, the Eagles against the Kansas City Monarchs, in effect an exhibition game that didn't count in the standings. And it was a night game, with the lights playing a role in the first inning as Monarchs fielders lost Pat Patterson's ball in the lights (it went for a double) and then Larry Doby's inside-the-park home run, likewise lost in the lights. Newark's Cal Irvin led off the bottom of the fifth with a walk. Manning sacrificed him to second. Patterson singled and Doby walked. Cal's brother

Monte was up with the bases loaded, and on a 3-and-2 count he hit a grand slam some 385 feet to left field. The Monarchs got one in the sixth and two in the seventh. The Monarchs outhit the Eagles, 10 to 6, but scored only half as many runs. The *Star-Ledger* reported an attendance of 4,387, declaring it the largest home crowd of the season.

July 18, 1946: Cleveland Buckeyes 11, Newark 4, at Red Wing Stadium, Rochester, New York – interleague play (neutral site)

The *Philadelphia Tribune* wrote, "General Patton's Third Army Tank corp [*sic*] could not have been more devastating than the World champion Cleveland Buckeyes were when they invaded the city of Rochester, N.Y. Thursday night and let loose their big guns on the Newark Eagles."[28] Cecil Cole was the losing pitcher for Newark, when the Buckeyes jumped on him in the third inning for two walks and five hits for seven runs. Warren Peace pitched in relief of Cole and "stopped the avalanche," in the words of the *Rochester Democrat and Chronicle*. Newark scored three runs in the fifth, sending Cleveland starter Eugene Bremer to the showers. The Eagles may have been a bit fatigued, having left Newark at 7 A.M. That was Effa Manley's explanation, quoted in the August 3 *New York Amsterdam News*. The Eagles committed six or seven errors in the game (accounts differ.)

The game featured what appears to be the one and perhaps only appearance of first baseman George Dusphy or Dusphyn (his name was spelled the first way in the *New York Amsterdam News* game story but the second way in the accompanying box score).[29]

July 20 – Newark Eagle 13, Local Team 4, at Warren, Ohio

This was an exhibition game against a local team from Warren.[30]

July 21, 1946: Newark 6, Cleveland Buckeyes 5 (first game); Newark 1, Cleveland Buckeyes 1 (tie, second game – though the actual score may have been Buckeyes 9, Eagles 0), at League Park, Cleveland – interleague play

The first game of two saw the Eagles score twice in the second and twice in the fifth. It was 4-0, but then Patterson walked and Doby hit an inside-the-park home run. That made it 6-0. After six innings, the Buckeyes got to Leon Day and scored three times in the bottom of the seventh. Rookie center fielder John Miner doubled off the right-field wall, driving in two. He himself scored all the way from second when Carswell laid down a bunt and Newark's third baseman threw the ball into right field. Sam Jethroe led off the bottom of the eighth with a single to center. An error by Larry Doby put runners on first and second; a single and a fielder's choice brought them both home. But the Buckeyes couldn't get themselves a sixth run and so came up one short.

Leon Day won the first game, but Len Hooker pitched better ball in the second. Chet Brewer pitched for Cleveland. He held the Eagles to one run on two hits through the first seven innings. It was Brewer's fifth-inning fly ball that drove in third baseman Alphonso Smith – who had tripled – with the one Buckeyes run.

The game ended either in a 1-1 tie in one of the more controversial games of the season, or as a 9-0 forfeit win assigned to the Buckeyes. It's unclear what really occurred. The August 3 *Pittsburgh Courier* ran a column headlined "What Happens When a Team Quits?…" It said that in the second game "the Newark Eagles walked off the field during a game with the Cleveland Buckeyes because they did not like the decision handed down by the umpire on a close play." The *Courier* expressed surprise that neither the NNL nor the NAL president took any disciplinary action, taking the position that Newark should at least be fined, and saying that this kind of inaction was harmful to the fans and to taking Negro League baseball seriously.

That same day (August 3), Dan Burley's column in the *New York Amsterdam News* was devoted to the subject. Effa Manley had responded to a press release that had been issued by the Buckeyes. Burley said that Mrs. Manley had "pounced on me" at a ballgame. She told Burley that the second game had been called due to local curfew laws.

Mrs. Manley wrote to the *Courier* and her response was printed in the August 10 edition. In it she detailed what she had been told by both manager Mackey and her husband, Abe, after they had returned to Newark:

"The score was tied, 1-1, in an extra inning game. Hooker came to bat and got a hit. Mackey sent Isreal to run for him. The next man to come to bat was pitched one ball by the Cleveland pitcher and Isreal was called out, due to the fact Isreal did not tell the umpire he was running for Hooker. Now, there is no question the umpire should have been told that Isreal was pinch-running, and the Eagles were at fault in not doing it; but the penalty in the rule book for such an offense is a fine for the captain or manager of the team at fault. Under no condition is the runner to be called out by the umpire for this offense. I do not like the team to squabble on the field, but I am sure no one would expect a manager to take a decision like that without arguing.

"Mackey also said the umpire did not tell him to stop arguing, or give him any kind of warning that he planned to call the game. Mackey also said after the game the officials in the press box showed Cleveland the rule in the book. One of the Cleveland players – the manager, to be exact – said he knew the decision was wrong, but did not say anything at the time."

This account makes no mention of either team leaving the field, which the *Courier* still believed had occurred. There was no mention of a local curfew. And the game remained reported as a tie. Normally, if a team simply left the field, the game would have been forfeited to the other team. Two Cleveland newspapers mentioned the forfeit. The *Plain Dealer* said it was "Calbin Irvin" who had been the substitute runner. The *Cleveland Call and Post* wrote that umpire Jimmy Johnson had declared a forfeit in favor of the Buckeyes not because the Eagles left the field but because they "failed to resume play after a called intermission." The fans didn't appear to take affront the way they might had the Eagles stalked off the field. The paper wrote, "A rumble of anger and irritation arose from the fans who decried Umpire Johnson's decision as the fumble-bumble actions of an inefficient umpire." Indeed, "Reviewing the major league baseball rules, it was found that Johnson was wrong in calling a substitute runner out, because he failed to report to a game official before taking the base. Therefore Johnson's decision to forfeit the game because the Newark team continued to protest the original ruling appears to be a hasty generalization under the existing circumstances."[31]

The whole story remains a mystery.

July 22, 1946: Newark 8, Cleveland Buckeyes 5, at Hudson Field, Dayton, Ohio (neutral site) - interleague play

Rufus Lewis won the 8:30 P.M, ballgame, but only in the top of the 10th inning when Newark scored three times in the "Negro tilt at the west side emporium" when "Pat Patterson's big bat spelled doom for the Bucks in the extra frame, his long two-bagger driving in two tallies." (*Dayton Herald*)

July 23, 1946: Cleveland Buckeyes 8, Newark 5, at Ainsworth Stadium, Erie, Pennsylvania (neutral site) - interleague play

Max Manning was the complete-game loser in this one, in the rubber game of the series. Sam Jethroe had his number. Jethroe hit a two-run homer in the first inning, a double in the second (again scoring Archie Ware), and a triple in the seventh. All he lacked for a cycle was the single. Jethroe drove in four of the Buckeyes' eight runs. The date differs from one other source that cited July 24, but both newspaper mentions and Effa Manley's comments to Dan Burley cite July 23.

July 26, 1946: Newark 17, Homestead Grays 3, at Wilmington Park, Wilmington, Delaware (neutral site)

The Eagles pretty much slaughtered the Grays. Leon Day was the winning pitcher with a complete-game effort. Bob Thurman started for the Grays. He gave up three runs in the first inning, and was replaced by Dave Hoskins during Newark's crushing seven-run third inning. For good measure, the Eagles added four more runs in the fourth inning. It was 14-0 after four. Day struggled a bit in the fifth inning, saw the bases get loaded, and then saw them get cleared by Howie Easterling's double to left field. That was the only scoring for the Grays all night. The Eagles added three more runs in the top of the ninth.

Leon Day not only won the game, but was 5-for-5 at the plate with a double, triple, and three singles. Monte Irvin and Johnny Davis homered. Irvin had five RBIs. Wilkes had three, while Davis, Day, and Pearson each had two.

Even with the 17 Eagles base hits and the 10 by the Grays, and all the other plays, the game took only 2:25 to complete.

July 27, 1946: Newark 6, Philadelphia Stars 5, at 44th Street and Parkside Avenue, Philadelphia

Lewis, Cole, and Peace pitched for Newark, with Will Harris and Henry McHenry pitching for the Stars. Newark scored four runs in the top of the third. It wasn't until the bottom of the seventh that the Stars got on board, but it was with just one run. The Eagles scored twice more in the top of the eighth, giving them a 6-1 lead. They needed every one of those runs, though; Philadelphia scored four times in the bottom of the eighth. Just one run short, the Stars held the Eagles scoreless in the ninth. Despite throwing up two pinch-hitters, they failed to score themselves and it was another Newark victory. Wilkes and Irvin each had two hits for the Eagles. Gene Benson had three for Philadelphia.

July 28, 1946: Homestead Grays 3, Newark 0 (first game); Newark 4, Homestead Grays 3 (second game, eight innings), at Griffith Stadium, Washington

The Grays and Eagles split a 2:00 P.M. twin bill at Washington's Griffith Stadium, one of the two home parks of the Grays, the other being Forbes Field. Homestead's Wilmer Fields shut out Newark on six hits in the first game, Len Hooker bearing the loss. Cecil Cole, Warren Peace, and Max Manning pitched Newark to a 4-3 win in the second game. It had been 3-0 in Newark's favor but the Grays rallied for three runs to tie it in the bottom of the seventh. Charley Parks led off the top of the eighth with a double and Len Pearson singled to center. There was no scoring in the game from then on.

Both games were played under protest because of the "non-appearance" of the official umpire.[32]

July 29 – The *Richmond Times-Dispatch* advertised an 8:15 P.M. game between the Eagles and the Philadelphia Stars. We have not yet determined whether the game took place.

July 30, 1946: Newark Eagles 7, Philadelphia Stars 4, at Tar Park, Norfolk, Virginia

The Eagles and the Philadelphia Stars squared off on Tuesday night in Norfolk. It was the biggest crowd of the year in Norfolk. The local newspaper noted, "Order has really improved since ABC forced beer out of the stands, but many people still bring the brew in." A large "No Gambling" sign in the back of the grandstand was seemingly ignored with a lot of talk such as "Show me your denomination," which the paper acknowledged was not about religion.[33]

Johnny "Cherokee" Davis, as the Norfolk paper called him, pitched for Newark. The first run scored off him in the top of the fourth on a walk and a single, followed by 10 consecutive balls. In the bottom of the fourth, Larry Doby walked. Monte Irvin was hit by a pitch, and an infield ball resulted in an error, loading the bases. Harvey drove in one run and Thomas drove in another. In the sixth, Irvin and Pearson both singled, and Harvey hit a three-run homer over the right-field fence.

August 2, 1946: Newark 9, Baltimore Elite Giants 7, at Bugle Field, Baltimore

Joe Black started for Baltimore, but "the Birds" chased him this Friday night "in the second inning under a six-run onslaught." (*Baltimore Afro-American*)

Tito Figueroa came on in relief, but too much damage had been done. Leon Day pitched a complete game for Newark.

August 4, 1946: Newark 3, Cleveland Buckeyes 2, at Yankee Stadium (first game of doubleheader) – interleague play (neutral site)

Once again the Buckeyes and Eagles linked up, as two teams in a four-team doubleheader at Yankee Stadium that drew 13,000 fans. Cleveland's Chet Brewer held Newark to six hits; Len Hooker held the Buckeyes to seven. In the second inning, Johnny Davis hit a two-run homer into the left-field seats to give Newark a quick lead. In the third, Pat Patterson tripled to right field to lead off and Larry Doby doubled to left. In the fifth, two Buckeyes got on base thanks to a fielder's choice and an error, then Archie Ware smashed a line drive over Larry Doby's glove, which only barely grazed the ball. Both baserunners scored.

A feature in the August 4 *Newark Sunday Call* quoted Effa Manley as enthusing about "Mr. Second Base" – Larry Doby – and calling him "the best prospect in baseball" who could "do all the things Jackie Robinson has done." She noted that Branch Rickey had come to Yankee Stadium the last time the Eagles had been there, to join the scouts checking out Doby.[34]

Indeed, there were apparently some Mexican League scouts at Yankee Stadium this day, and when Effa Manley spotted a couple of them talking to Johnny Davis and Len Pearson, she hustled down and spoke up forcefully: "Davis, you and Pearson are in uniform and playing a game. You go back to the dugout. I'll see both of you later." To the "foreign-looking hombres" she said, "Now, you fellows should be ashamed of yourselves trying to steal my ballplayers right under my eyes. This is awful. I never heard of such a thing. Aren't you ashamed of yourselves, you-you-you chili con carners?"[35]

August 5, 1946: Newark 16, New York Black Yankees 0, at Dexter Park, Queens

Jimmy Wilkes hit a leadoff home run off Yanks starter Walter Barbee in the top of the first. With one out, Larry Doby tripled. After Irvin walked, he and Doby executed a double steal and Doby scored. David walked and Bob Harvey singled to left field for a quick three-run lead before the Black Yankees got up to bat. Rufus Lewis put down New York. When it was his turn to bat in the top of the second, Benny Felder pinch-hit for him, and Max Manning worked the rest of the game as Newark's pitcher.

The Eagles didn't score in the second, but they did add two runs in the third, three more runs in the fourth, five more runs in the sixth, then added a pair in the eighth and a final one in the top of the ninth. Wilkes's smash was the only home run; there were five other extra-base hits in the game, all by Eagles. Three of the Eagles drove in three runs apiece: Harvey, Pearson, and Manning.

Johnny Johnson replaced Barbee in the fourth, and Barbee went to play first base. Manning got the win.

August 6, 1946: Newark 7, Kansas City Monarchs 4, at Ruppert Stadium – interleague play

"Eagles Treat Paige Harshly." This was a game that was understood to perhaps be a forerunner to the 1946 World Series. It was billed

as a duel between Satchel Paige vs. Leon Day. The *New Jersey Afro-American* ran artwork billing it as "King Meets King!!" and proclaiming "Class vs. C-L-A-S-S."

Day had beaten Paige once before when Day was a member of the Homestead Grays, and beat Paige, 4-1. Paige was said to welcome the chance to turn the tables. The Monarchs and Eagles had each won the first half of their championship season, and both teams were playing well, the Eagles boasting seven hitters with averages over .300 going into the game. An announced crowd of 8,763 turned out to see "Ol' Satch." Day was leading the league with 65 strikeouts.

"Paige didn't disappoint his admirers," wrote the *Newark Evening News*. "Whipping his throwing arm around his head in the old familiar manner which drew a chorus of 'ah's' from feminine fans which would have made Frank Sinatra envious, then the hesitation while he lazily scanned the bags, he scorched the plate with his fast one. Satch drew applause after every pitch." That said, the Eagles were not cowed. Monte Irvin hit a ball hard to center field and scored after a rundown between third and home. The Monarchs scored two in the top of the third, but three singles to right field by Day, Patterson, and Irvin retied the game, 2-2.

Paige left the game after three innings, and the Eagles greeted Steve Wylie by scoring three more times in the fourth. Tex Alexander relieved Wylie and got out of the inning. Both Bob Harvey and Johnny Davis made spectacular plays in the outfield. After four innings, Day left the game and Warren Peace pitched the rest of the way, holding the Monarchs to two hits.

August 7, 1946: Newark 17, New York Black Yankees 1, at Ruppert Stadium

No details have yet been found for this game.

August 8, 1946: Memphis Red Sox 11, Newark 4, at Ruppert Stadium – interleague play

"Error Binge Ruins Eagles." It was indeed a "comedy of errors" which was "coupled with a sensational bunting attack by Memphis" that cost the Eagles this game. Charles England, recently discharged from military service, started the game for Newark but had to be relieved by Cole in the fourth inning. England had given up one run in the second, but the Red Sox started bunting and bunting in the fourth and got six hits, and saw the Eagles commit three errors. Memphis scored eight runs. England was charged with the loss. The Eagles scored once in the fourth off Red Sox starter Frank Pearson, and twice more in the fifth. Dan Bankhead relieved Pearson in the sixth and gave up one run while striking out seven.

August 9, 1946: Newark 21, Cleveland Buckeyes 3, at Ruppert Stadium – interleague play

The very next night, it was baseball with the Buckeyes again and the Eagles produced the most lopsided score of their season. Rufus Lewis held Cleveland scoreless through five innings, while Newark scored two runs in the first inning, eight runs in the third inning, six runs in the fourth inning (including a three-run homer by Monte Irvin into the center-field bleachers), and another run in the fifth. A pitcher named Cotton is shown in the box score as taking over for Lewis and working the final four innings. This was Robert "Cotton" Williams.

August 11, 1946: Newark 8, Homestead Grays 7 (first game); Newark 3, Homestead Grays 1 (second game), at Ruppert Stadium

Newark swept the Homestead Grays, and patrons got "bonus baseball" to boot. The Eagles scored one in the first and four in the fourth, while the Grays got two in the third and then one in the eighth. It stood 5-3 through eight, and it looked as though Leon Day would get the win. But he weakened in the top of the ninth and gave up three singles and then a home run to Howard Easterling. It was 7-5, Homestead.

Day was up first in the bottom of the ninth and he walked. Wilbur Fields took over pitching duties from Eugene Smith and he retired Jimmy Wilkes. But then Patterson hit a two-run homer into the right-field bleachers and the game went into extra innings. Day kept pitching. And pitching. Neither team scored for the next five innings. Day himself put an end to the game in the bottom of the 15th with a solo home run into the left-field bleachers.

In the first inning of the seven-inning second game, Doby and Len Pearson singled and Monte Irvin doubled for a 2-0 Eagles lead. In the fourth inning, Irvin hit a 450-foot home run to left-center. Len Hooker got the win, giving up just one run in the sixth.

August 12, 1946: Newark 6, Philadelphia Stars 2, at Shibe Park (first game of three-team doubleheader)

The Stars played a doubleheader at home, drawing a big crowd reported as 11,570. They lost the first game to Newark, 6-2, and then battled the Indianapolis Clowns to a 7-7 tie that was only halted due to curfew when the clock struck midnight. The Eagles scored all six of their runs in the third inning, driving Wilmer Harris from the game. Bill Ricks came on and one-hit Newark for the rest of the game. Patterson drove in two runs. Patterson, Doby, Irvin, and Harvey each had doubles.

August 15 – Negro National League 6, Negro American League 3, at Griffith Stadium, Washington

Two picked teams squared off at 8:30 P.M. in what Sam Lacy called an "Eastern version of the East-West extravaganza."[36] The NNL team (the "East" team) won the game, 6-3. Larry Doby singled to center in the first inning, driving Henry Kimbro to third base. Doby advanced to third and scored on an infield groundout. Doby scored two runs in all. Monte Irvin drove in a run later in the game, and then Pearson drove in Irvin. Day and Ruffin each appeared in the game.

August 16 – That afternoon's Newark newspaper said the Eagles would be hosting the Indianapolis Clowns for a game that evening. The historical record available to us included no clippings from August 17 through 22.

August 18, 1946: Baltimore Elite Giants 7, Newark 3 (first game); Baltimore Elite Giants 7, Newark 1 (second game), at Bugle Field, Baltimore

The games were played with "the big guns" out of the city, given the All-Star Games in Washington and Chicago.

Twenty-four soldiers from the rehabilitation center at the Veterans Administration Hospital north of Baltimore at Perry Point, Maryland, were guests at the twin bill. After the games, they were treated to a banquet at the Club Barbecue. The USO and VA collaborated on the event.

August 20, 1946: The *Buffalo Evening News* announced an 8:30 game for that evening at Offermann Stadium between the Eagles and the New York Cubans. As in some other cases, we were unable to determine whether the game was played.

**August 23, 1946: Newark 10, New York Cubans 2,
at Ruppert Stadium**

"Belting Spree by Pearson." Len Pearson's first-inning grand slam provided four of the six runs the Eagles scored in their first time at bat. In the second inning, he doubled in Monte Irvin to make it 7-1, Eagles. The Cubans scored one more run in the game, in the fifth, but Max Manning held them to eight hits and just two unearned runs. In the bottom of the eighth, the Eagles added three more runs, two of them when Pearson homered after Irvin doubled off the center-field bleachers.

The August 24 *Baltimore Afro-American* offered the observation that five of the top 10 batters in the NNL were Newark Eagles and that four of the top 10 batters in the Negro American League were on the Kansas City Monarchs.

Each team had won first-half honors and was well-positioned to do the same in the second half, thus avoiding the need for playoffs between the first-half and second-half teams in each league prior to the World Series.

**August 25, 1946: Newark 12, Homestead Grays 5,
at Ruppert Stadium (second game of
a three-team doubleheader)**

After a first game between Philadelphia Stars and the Homestead Grays that saw Wilbur Fields beat the Stars, 7-1, the Eagles played the Grays. The plan for the day was that the winner of the first game would play the Newark Eagles. Hence it was Grays vs. Eagles.

Though he gave up 11 hits and was tagged for three in the sixth inning, Rufus Lewis improved to 8-1 for the season. The Eagles had 16 hits, with a double by Lewis their only extra-base hit of the game. A three-run second and a seven-run fifth were their two big innings. Jimmy Wilkes, Len Pearson, and Johnny Davis each had three hits.

**August 26, 1946: Newark 8, New York Cubans 6,
at Wilmington, Delaware (neutral site)**

The Eagles were deemed the home team for this game, played before about 1,200 fans in 2 hours 15 minutes. Their starting pitcher was reported as "Cotten" – Robert "Cotton" Williams. Bill Anderson started for the Cubans and gave up two runs to Newark in the bottom of the first. The Cubans tied it right back up with two in the top of the second. Newark added three more in the third, and another (giving them a 6-2 lead) in the fourth. In the eighth inning, however, the New Yorkers put four runs across and tied the game. Cole had taken over for Cotton Williams after

one out in the eighth. When Newark came to bat in the bottom of the eighth, neither of its two pinch-hitters produced – but the Eagles nonetheless scored two runs and held on in the ninth (with Johnny Davis on the mound) for the 8-6 win.

Lou Louden had a double and a triple and five RBIs for the Cubans. Wiggins pitched 7⅓ innings, walking five and striking out one, giving up nine of the Cubans' 10 hits. Cecil Cole got the final two outs of the eighth, and, as the pitcher of record when the Eagles broke the tie, he got the win.

**August 27, 1946: Newark 15, New York Black Yankees 1,
at Ruppert Stadium**

There was worry that the Black Yankees could produce an upset, but Len Hooker threw a two-hitter, the first just a scratch hit with two outs in the top of the seventh and the second with two outs in the ninth. Both hits came after errors; there should have been three outs both times (though the second one followed an error by Hooker himself.) He walked two and struck out five. He had plenty of cushion to work with, after a five-run second inning by the Eagles. Newark batters had 23 hits, including four apiece by Doby, Davis, and Ruffin. Two of Doby's were triples. Davis hit the only homer. The Eagles also scored twice in the fifth, twice in the sixth, and six times in the seventh.

**August 28, 1946: Newark 2, Baltimore Elite Giants 0,
at Ruppert Stadium**

Leon Day improved his record to 11-4 with a shutout of Baltimore, allowing just two hits, one in the first and one in the ninth. He struck out 11. Bill Barnes of the Elite Giants pitched exceptionally well, too, allowing only four hits. Doby singled in the first inning, then as Irvin's drive got by shortstop Pee Wee Butts, it seemed that no one had backed up Butts. Doby rounded the bases from first to home as "the visitors stood dumbfounded by his daring base running." The only other run of the game also followed an error by Butts. Irvin doubled in the bottom of the third. Pearson got on base after Butts made an error, while Irvin moved up to third. The run scored on a double steal.

**August 30, 1946: Newark 2,
Baltimore Elite Giants 2 (tie, 11 innings),
at Bugle Field, Baltimore**

Max Manning and Baltimore's Joe Black each went the distance in a game ending in an 11-inning tie at 2-2. The Giants got eight hits,

the Eagles only four (one a triple by Patterson and one a double by Doby). Newark scored once in the top of the first inning and once in the sixth; Larry Doby drove in both of the runs. Baltimore scored two runs in the bottom of the third inning, both runs knocked in by Henry Kimbro.

September 1, 1946: Newark 3, New York Black Yankees 2, at Yankee Stadium, the Bronx (second game of doubleheader)

Rufus Lewis struck out 11 and allowed only seven hits, all singles. The only two runs scored by the Black Yanks came as a result of errors. Newark was nonetheless trailing, 2-1, until the eighth when Pat Patterson got on base and Len Pearson hit a two-run home run. It was his third homer in four Yankee Stadium games, and he was 10-for-24 in New York City big-league ballparks.

September 2, 1946: Newark 11, Philadelphia Stars 10 (first game); Newark 7, Philadelphia Stars 0 (second game), at Ruppert Stadium

"Eagle Streak Reaches 14." The Stars scored twice in the top of the first off the starter, Hooker, but the Eagles scored three times. The Stars added three more in the second; the Eagles added one on a home run by Charley Parks. It was still 5-4, Stars, through four, but then the Stars seemingly put the game out of sight, scoring five runs in the top of the fifth. Cotton Williams took over pitching for the Eagles. Pat Patterson hit a solo home run in the sixth to make it Stars 10, Eagles 5. But the Eagles rallied for five runs in the eighth, with doubles by Doby and Pearson being key hits.

The game went into extra innings, with left fielder Johnny Davis taking over pitching duties for Newark. It's not clear who played left field. Davis kept the Stars scoreless for three innings. In the bottom of the 12th, Jimmy Wilkes led off with a single. Patterson sacrificed him to second, and Wilkes scored when Larry Doby hit a single over second base. Davis got the win, reported as the second win of the year for the Eagles left fielder.

In the second game, Warren Peace shut out the Stars on four hits while Monte Irvin hit two home runs. The game was called on account of darkness after Philadelphia had batted in the top of the sixth. Apparently no one wanted to turn on the Ruppert Stadium lights.

September 3, 1946: Philadelphia Stars 12, Newark 7, at Shibe Park, Philadelphia (second game)

In a four-team twin bill that drew 7,183 patrons, the New York Cubans beat the Baltimore Elite Giants in the first game, 6-4. The second game saw the Stars beat four Newark pitchers, 12-7. Pearson drove in three runs. Doby hit a solo home run off the Stars' McHenry in the fifth. The four pitchers used were Hooker, Cole, Lewis, and manager Biz Mackey himself. Mackey pitched two innings, giving up two hits. He struck out one and didn't walk anyone. It was Hooker who got the loss.

September 4, 1946: Newark 17, New York Cubans 5, at Ruppert Stadium

"It was an inspired and determined Eagles team that took the field for this important clash with the title at stake." By virtue of beating the second-place New York Cubans, the Eagles clinched the Negro National League pennant. Given that Kansas City had already won the Negro American League title, this day's lopsided win for Newark set up an Eagles-Monarchs World Series.

Max Manning started for the Eagles and got off to a bad start when Silvio Garcia hit a two-run homer off him in the top of the first. But Newark wasted no time striking back, getting to starter Lefty Crue right away and scoring nine times in the bottom of the first. The Eagles added two more in the second, one in the third, and two more in the fourth, then tacked on one in the sixth and two in the eighth. Manning improved his record to 12-1 and even hit a home run in the eighth inning. He was 3-for-5 at the plate. Only two of the Cubans' five runs were earned.

Larry Doby was 5-for-6 with two doubles and a triple. Clarence Isreal had two doubles, too.

September 6, 1946: Newark 11, New York Cubans 7, at Dunn Field, Trenton (neutral site)

Details were skimpy in the *Trenton Evening Times*, but readers were told that Monte Irvin had been 4-for-5 and that the Cubans' Garcia got two doubles. The Cubans got nine hits off Cecil Cole, and seven of them were for extra bases. Cole got the win. Bill Anderson got the loss. The game drew 1,427 spectators.

September 8, 1946: New York Cubans 1, Newark 0, at the Polo Grounds (second game of doubleheader)

The Eagles were shut out for only the second time all season. Rufus Lewis pitched valiantly for Newark and held the Cubans to just one run. Lefty Luis Tiant held the Eagles to six hits, and protected the one-run lead he was given in the fourth inning when Harry Williams reached first on Clarence Isreal's error. A base on balls moved Williams to second, and he took third on a sacrifice, then scored on a fielder's choice. Pearson had doubled in the second inning, but Tiant got out of it. Likewise, he buckled down after Johnny Davis tripled to lead off the fifth, and after Isreal and Irvin both singled in the sixth – and then pulled off a double steal. He walked Pearson intentionally and then got Davis to ground out. And Tiant escaped from a bases-loaded, two-out situation in the ninth when he induced Lewis to pop out.

The September 8 *Richmond Times-Dispatch* announced 8:15 P.M. games for September 9 and September 14 at Mooers Field. We do not know if the games were played.

September 10, 1946: Newark Eagles 9, Homestead Grays 8, at Tar Park, Norfolk

Norfolk hosted a night game between the Eagles and the Homestead Grays. The Eagles outhit the Grays, 11 to 10, and outscored them 9-8. The Eagles scored scoring five runs in the first inning, but the Grays offense came right back with three runs in Homestead's second inning. Newark added three more runs in the fifth, but – thanks to a couple of Eagles errors, the Grays scored four more runs in the sixth. The game entered the ninth inning 8-7 in Newark's favor. In the top of the ninth, Grays pitcher Bob Thurman threw one to Johnny Davis, who hammered it over the left-field scoreboard for a home run. Len Hooker, pitching for the Eagles, surrendered a solo home run to Thurman himself in the bottom of the ninth. Leading off, the Grays pitcher hit the ball over the center-field fence. With one out, Cool Papa Bell reached first base on an infield hit. Buck Leonard came to bat, but popped up to second baseman Larry Doby. Bell had taken off when Leonard hit the ball and was easily doubled off first base, ending the game.

September 11 – City Stadium in Portsmouth, Virginia, was to host a night game between the Eagles and Grays. We do not know if the game occurred.

September 15, 1946: Baltimore Elite Giants 13, Newark 12 (first game); Baltimore Elite Giants 6, Newark 3 (second game), at Bugle Field, Baltimore

These two games were more crucial for Baltimore than for Newark. The doubleheader win clinched them third place in the standings. Our friend Cotton Williams showed up again, pitching the first game for the Eagles. He was replaced by Hooker in the third; Baltimore had scored once in the first and scored five more times in the third and another two off Hooker in the fourth. It was 8-0 in favor of the Giants after four. Newark scored once in the top of the fifth, but Baltimore added one more in the bottom of the fifth. Both teams scored once in the seventh, so it stood 10-2 in favor of Baltimore with but two innings to play.

This was a game with a lot of base hits. Newark really poured it on, scoring four times in the top of the eighth. The Eagles then scored six times in the top of the ninth and took a 12-10 lead. But Baltimore wasn't done yet. The Elite Giants came back with three runs in the bottom of the ninth to win the game, 13-12.

There were no home runs in the game. Baltimore had 18 hits, with four of them doubles and one a triple. Newark had 17 hits, one a double and one a triple. Willie Wells drove in three runs for Baltimore and Johnny Washington drove in two. The only Eagle to drive in more than one run was Wilkes, with two. There were six bases on balls (combined) and six errors.

Baltimore won the second game, 6-3. No box score or game account has yet been located.

September 16, 1946 – a *Times-Dispatch* newspaper announcement mentioned an exhibition game at Richmond's Mooers Field, with

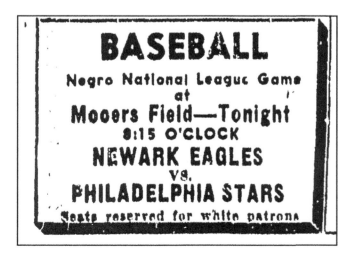

"Seats Reserved for White Patrons." We do not know whether the game was played.

At season's end, the Eagles had five batters who had hit over .300 – Monte Irvin led the NNL with a .395 batting average. Larry Doby was fifth with .348. Pat Patterson was sixth with .337. Johnny Davis was seventh with a .335 batting average, tied with Benson of the Philadelphia Stars. Len Pearson hit over .300, too.

Rufus Lewis (9-1) was the rookie of the year. Max Manning was 12-1. Warren Peace (3-0) had a 1.000 winning percentage. Leon Day was 11-4.[37]

World Series [see separate article by Rich Puerzer]

9/17/1946

9/19/1946

9/23/1946

9/24/1946

9/25/1946

9/27/1946

9/29/1946

After the Negro World Series concluded, a series of five exhibition games was held in which the Jackie Robinson All-Stars played Honus Wagner's All-Stars, a group made up of players from the Pittsburgh Pirates and Cincinnati Reds. Playing for the Robinson All-Stars were pitcher John Wright, Roy Campanella, and three members of the Newark Eagles: Larry Doby, Monte Irvin, and Lennie Pearson.

The first game was on October 6 in Cincinnati and the "major stars" won, 10-4.[38]

The game held at Youngstown, Ohio, on October 7 was a 5-5 tie through seven (Robinson and Marvin Rackley had both homered in the seventh to tie it), but the Wagners pushed over a run in the ninth for an 8-7 win. Robinson was 4-for-5 in the game.[39]

The two teams played at Forbes Field, Pittsburgh, on October 8. Robinson had three hits. The score was tied, 4-4, after six innings. In the bottom of the seventh, Robinson and Monte Irvin were on base, and Lennie Pearson drove them both in with a triple to right-center field. The final score was 6-4.[40]

On October 13 the Robinson All-Stars won a game at Comiskey Park in Chicago, 10-5. John Wright started the game for Robinson. He was relieved by Mike Nozinski, who finished up. This was an integrated team. Nozinski was white, as were Rackley and shortstop Al Campanis. Robinson had two hits as did Campan-

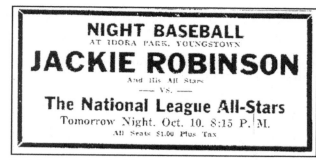

ella.[41] It was said to be "the first time a mixed club had played in Comiskey park."[42]

Cleveland Municipal Stadium was the venue on October 14. The rubber game was an 8-0 shutout for the Robinson team, giving them three out of five games. Irvin and Robinson were the batting stars.

The Robinson All-Stars then flew to Omaha for a game against Rex Barney's All-Stars, and then planned to fly to San Francisco to play Bob Feller's American League team.[43] The Newark Eagles players were not involved in the West Coast games.

An article in the September 28 *New York Amsterdam News* outlined games to be held on October 1 at the Polo Grounds, October 2 at Ebbets Field, and games to follow in Harrisburg, Pittsburgh, Dayton, and Columbus, with ones envisioned for Chicago and Cleveland, and possibly St. Louis. As it happens, Robinson had to play for Montreal against Louisville in the Little World Series through October 4.

SOURCES

In preparing this timeline of the 1946 Eagles season, we are deeply indebted to the efforts of SABR member Bob Golon for numerous visits to the Newark Public Library in February, March, and April 2018. Bob researched Newark newspapers and other holdings of the library and downloaded hundreds of articles, documents, and graphics that were not only essential for the writing of this timeline but were made available for the other SABR researchers who worked on this book.

The *Newark Evening News* was the newspaper that was initially consulted, as it provided the most complete daily coverage of Eagles games throughout the season. All unattributed information and headlines sprinkled throughout come from *Evening News*.

As with almost every SABR article, this was a collaborative effort with Gary Ashwill and Rick Bush each supplying a number of additional game stories and box scores, ones that helped fill in some gaps and made for more complete coverage. Thanks to Rich Bogovich for discovering several games, including spring training and exhibition games, and locating both "Fox" and "Dusphy" in box scores.

NOTES

1   "Eagles to Alight in Fla. April 1," *New Jersey Afro-American*, March 9, 1946.

2   Fred Bailey, "Monte Irvin, Back from Puerto Rico Loop, Off on Another Baseball Trip," *Newark Sunday Call,* March 31, 1946.

3   Fred Bailey, Leon Day, ETO Star, Back to Newark," *Newark Sunday Call*, March 24, 1946.

4   "Eagles Boss Raps Rickey Method of Signing Hurler," *New Jersey Afro-American*, April 20, 1946.

5   John Robinson, New Jersey Sportlight," *New Jersey Afro-American*, April 20, 1946.

6   John Robinson, "New Jersey," *New Jersey Afro-American*, May 3, 1946.

7   "Rookie Pitcher Impresses Eagles," *Newark Evening News*, April 13, 1946.

8   "Newark Breaks Giants' Streak," *Tampa Tribune*, April 22, 1946: 8.

9   *Tampa Times*, April 24, 1946: 10.

10   "Newark Eagles Sweep 2-Game Series in Jax," *New York Amsterdam News*, April 27, 1946: 12.

11   Ibid.

12   Associated Press, "Eagles Will Leave Camp," *Newark Sunday Call*, April 21, 1946.

13   Dan Burley, "Confidentially Yours," *New York Amsterdam News*, August 3, 1946: 11. Burley's column was written after the Eagles had secured the first-half championship.

14   "Negro National League 1st Half Schedule 1946 Season" document in the Effa Manley Papers at the Newark Public Library.

15   "Eagles Flop in Clutches," *Newark News*, May 20, 1946.

16   "Eagles, Philly Split 2 Games, 7-1, 5-2," *New Journal and Guide* (Norfolk, Virginia), May 25, 1946: B19.

17   Ibid.

18   "Phila. Stars Beat Newark, 8-1," *Philadelphia Inquirer*, May 25, 1946: 13.

19   "Newark Outhits Yankees, but Bow, 3-1, in New York," *New Jersey Afro-American*, June 1, 1946.

20   "Biz Mackey Irked Over Slump; Cracks Whip Over Newark Eagles," *Philadelphia Tribune*, June 1, 1946: 11.

21   Ibid.

22   "Eagles Add Two Players, Hit Road for Eight Days," *New Jersey Afro-American*, June 8, 1946.

23   "Eagles Top Grays, 7-5, With 3 Runs in Ninth," *Wilmington Journal*, July 10, 1946.

24   "Lloyds Score Over Newark Eagles, 6 to 5," *Philadelphia Tribune*, July 9, 1946:11.

25   "Newark Here on Sunday for Twin Bill at Forbes Field," *Pittsburgh Courier*, July 6, 1946: 25.

26   "Newark Defeats Grays in Two League Games," *Pittsburgh Post-Gazette*, July 8, 1946: 18.

27   See *New York Amsterdam News*, July 20, 1946: 10.

28   "Buckeyes Submerge Newark Eagles, 11 to 4," *Philadelphia Tribune*, July 23,1946: 11.

29   "Cleveland Bucks Batter Newark," *New York Amsterdam News*, July 27, 1946: 11.

30   Effa Manley notes this game in comments made to sports columnist Dan Burley. See "Cleveland Buckeye-Newark Eagle Series Lowdown," *New York Amsterdam News*, August 3, 1946: 11.

31   Buckeyes Gain Split with Eagles, 5-6, 9-0 as Umpire Forfeits 2nd Fray," *Cleveland Call and Post*, July 27, 1946: 9B. The much briefer account in the *Plain Dealer* said the umpire was named Jim Thompson.

32   "Baseball Data," *Philadelphia Tribune*, August 3, 1946: 11.

33   John T. Mitchell, "Eagles Trim Philly Stars 7-4; Harvey Hits Homer," *New Journal and Guide* (Norfolk, Virginia), August 3, 1946: 17.

34   "Paterson Boy One of Best in Baseball, Says Mrs. Manley," *Newark Sunday Call*, August 4, 1946.

35   Dan Burley, "The Senors Get in Mrs. Manley's Hair," *New York Amsterdam News*, August 10, 1946: 12. Whether the quotes were accurate is unknown, as is the story that the men slunk off under the eyes of approaching policemen "stuffing the handful of greenbacks they had been waving under Davis' and Pearson's noses into their pockets as they fled."

36   Sam Lacy, "16000 See East Top West in AllStar Diamond Tilt," *Baltimore Afro-American*, August 17, 1946: 26.

37   All figures came from John Robinson in the September 14, 1946, *New Jersey Afro-American*.

38   "Robinson's Stars Split in Openers," *The Sporting News*, October 16, 1946: 23.

39   Associated Press, "Wagner All-Stars Top Jack Robinson's Negro Stars 6 to 5," *Boston Globe*, October 8,1946: 7.

40   "Big Leaguers Put Okay on Robinson," *Pittsburgh Courier*, October 12, 1946: 26.

41   "Jackie's All-Stars Drub Major Leaguers," *New Jersey Afro-American*, October 18, 1946.

42   Fay Young, "Through the Years," *Chicago Defender*, October 19, 1946: 11.

43   "Robinson's All-Stars Win 3 Out of 5 Games," *Pittsburgh Courier*, October 19, 1946: 24.

Leon Day and Baseball's Other Opening Day No-Hitter

BY FREDERICK C. BUSH

On May 5, 1946, Leon Day pitched the only Opening Day no-hitter in Negro League history. The feat was all the more remarkable since it was Day's first game after two years of military service. *(Noir-Tech Research, Inc.)*

It is common knowledge that Cleveland Indians Hall of Famer Bob Feller tossed the only Opening Day no-hitter in major-league history against the Chicago White Sox at Comiskey Park on April 16, 1940. On the 75th anniversary of the event, Major League Baseball's official website touted it as "the first – and to this day – the only Opening Day no-hitter in modern baseball history."[1] The fact that Rapid Robert accomplished the feat first is not in dispute, but the assertion that he is the only pitcher to do so is entirely in error. Six years after Feller's accomplishment, Newark Eagles right-hander Leon Day no-hit the Philadelphia Stars on May 5, 1946, which was Opening Day for the Negro National League.

Feller's no-hitter did not lack for thrills as he had to protect a 1-0 lead in the ninth inning. Chicago's Luke Appling, batting with two outs, fouled off several pitches, so Feller decided to walk him in order to face the next batter in the White Sox lineup. The strategy almost backfired when Taft Wright smacked a hard grounder that "necessitated a diving play by second baseman Ray Mack, who knocked it down, whirled and made a perfect throw" to end the game.[2]

In spite of the thrilling conclusion to Feller's gem, Day's no-hitter was so filled with excitement that it made Feller's game seem almost mundane. The fact that Newark's tilt with Philadelphia ended with a close 2-0 score actually turned out to be only half of the action in this contest. Though it was a shining moment for Day on the mound, a near-riot in the sixth inning – precipitated by a controversial call at home plate – and the concern about the impact that the event might have on the progress of Organized Baseball's integration received equal attention. In light of these circumstances, it is surprising that the only other Opening Day no-hitter in professional baseball history remains little remembered, even by many baseball aficionados.

The 1946 opener between the Eagles and the Stars at Newark's Ruppert Stadium was a highly anticipated event. The *Wilmington Morning News* previewed Newark's season by reporting that Eagles manager Raleigh "Biz" Mackey "has whipped a host of ex-GIs into shape for the coming race and feels certain that the Newark club will be in the thick of the pennant battle."[3] Day was one of those ex-GIs, a group that included Larry Doby, Oscar Givens, Monte Irvin, Clarence "Pint" Isreal, Max Manning, Charles Parks, and Leon Ruffin. The Army had drafted Day on September 1, 1943, and he had served in the 818th Amphibian Battalion – with which he had landed at Utah Beach on D-Day – before being discharged in February 1946.[4] The big question surrounding Day now was whether he could resume his stellar pitching career where he had left off prior to his military service.

In addition to the Eagles' high hopes for their pennant chances and Day's return to the mound, the *Newark Star-Ledger* noted:

> A crowd of about 15,000 is expected to watch the two National Negro League combinations launch the season. The usual pre-game ceremonies and parade will attend the occasion. Mayor Vincent J. Murphy has proclaimed today as "Newark Eagles" Day by proclamation issued earlier this week.[5]

Effa Manley, who co-owned the Eagles with her husband, Abe, often solicited funds for various organizations during the team's home games, and she had volunteers out in force to collect donations for the NAACP on this occasion.[6] Before the start of the action, Deputy Mayor Barney Koplin tossed out the first pitch.[7] Thus, although the crowd of 8,514 constituted little more than half the anticipated throng, the day was still a hallmark occasion.

Once the game began, the fans in attendance were not disappointed. Day admitted, "I was a little nervous, like I always was at the beginning of a game, but after I got started, everything was all right."[8] He overcame his jitters and pitched every bit as well as he had in his last all-star season of 1942. The *Baltimore Afro-American* enthused, "[T]he crack Bird flinger virtually handcuffed the opposition."[9] However, Day was locked in a mound duel with Philadelphia southpaw Barney Brown, who matched him zero-for-zero on the scoreboard through the first five innings.

Although Day was pitching brilliantly, the umpires and official scorer did make some questionable calls in the game. Bill "Ready" Cash, the Stars' catcher, years later went so far as to declare about home-plate umpire Peter Strauch, "I knew he was really screwing us during the game. Nobody can tell me that Eagles owner Effa Manley didn't offer him a little something extra to cheat us."[10] Though Cash is the only player to have engaged in a conspiracy theory about the umpiring, the game was contentious enough that the *Trenton Evening Times* noted it "was almost called several times due to arguments with the umpires."[11] As for the scorer's calls, Newark shortstop Benny Felder was charged with two errors, one of which was controversial. On the questionable play, Felder fielded a grounder cleanly but hesitated on his throw and then unleashed a wild one to first as he tried to nail the runner in time. Cash was irked that the play was scored as an error, and even Day graciously conceded, "(Felder) should have had him out, but they probably should have given the man a hit."[12]

Day's no-hit bid provided the excitement through the top of the sixth inning, but the poor play-calling took center stage in the bottom of the same frame as Newark broke through with the only runs of the game. Isreal led off with a line-drive triple to right-center field and scored the first run on Doby's single up the middle. Doby stole second base and then, after Irvin flied out, the most notorious play of the game occurred. Lennie Pearson hit a slow dribbler to Philly second baseman Mahlon Duckett, who threw to first baseman Wesley "Doc" Dennis for the out.[13] In the meantime, Doby was attempting to score on the play. Cash remarked in his autobiography, "I mean, what was he thinking? Most players with good sense would've held at third. But Doby wasn't *most* players."[14]

As Doby steamed around third base, Cash received the relay throw from Dennis. Doby slid into home plate head first as Cash

Philadelphia Stars catcher Bill "Ready" Cash applies the tag to Larry Doby. When umpire Peter Strauch called Doby safe, Cash went berserk and an on-field riot ensued. *(National Baseball Hall of Fame)*

stretched forward and applied the tag. Although it appeared to most observers that Doby was clearly out on the play – a photo in the *New York Amsterdam News's* May 11 edition later confirmed as much – Strauch called him safe.[15] In the heat of the moment, Cash jumped up to dispute the call, wildly waving his arms around, and ended up hitting Strauch with his glove hand and knocking him to the ground.

Accounts of Cash's exact action, as well as speculation as to whether or not he intended to hit Strauch, vary. The *Afro-American* wrote that Cash "jumped Struack [sic], nailing him to the ground."[16] Similarly, the *Amsterdam News* reported that Cash "hit the umpire in the left eye."[17] Cash asserted that he had accidentally hit Strauch "under his chin, knocking him to the ground," and was adamant that he had not attacked the umpire.[18] Irvin later provided the most germane observation, writing, "[R]egardless of whether it was intentional or not, the ump went down."[19]

Homer "Goose" Curry, Philadelphia's player-manager, escalated the situation when he ran from his position in right field and delivered a few kicks to Strauch as he was down. The fact that Strauch was a white man turned this baseball fracas into a potential race riot as there were also white fans in attendance. Both benches emptied as players tried to separate Cash and Curry from Strauch. Fans also spilled onto the field, and a general melee ensued. The police were called in, and it took mounted officers and foot patrolmen 30 minutes to restore order in the ballpark.

Before play resumed, Cash was ejected and was replaced at catcher by Pete Jones. Curry also was expelled, but he refused to go quietly. The *Amsterdam News* tried to inject some humor into its account of the action, stating that "'Goose' refused to vamoose after Ump Strauch had pulled the watch on him, but the Law took matters in their hand and out went the 'Goose.'"[20] After Curry had been removed, he was replaced in right field by Harry "Suitcase" Simpson.

The Stars continued the game under protest, but later withdrew their complaint because Isreal's run, which provided the winning margin, was not contested. Irvin was struck by something other than the on-field fisticuffs, as he noted, "I guess the most interesting thing about that incident was that Leon Day just sat calmly in the dugout watching the whole thing until it was over. Then he went back out and finished his no-hitter."[21]

Day put an exclamation point on his effort by striking out Henry McHenry, who was pinch-hitting for Brown, on "three lightning-sharp pitches" to end the game.[22] He recalled that before he faced McHenry, one of his teammates told him, "Don't throw him anything but fastballs, he's a slow swinger."[23] Day heeded the advice, saying, "Every pitch I raised it a little. The last one was up around his eyes."[24]

A final round of chaos ensued when some fans decided to celebrate the announcement of Day's feat by throwing seat cushions into the crowds that were heading for the stadium exits. Just as umpire Strauch had been struck during the in-game insurrection, a woman was hit by one of these flying projectiles in the post-game pandemonium and was knocked off her feet. The *Newark News* reported, "She was knocked unconscious after her head struck the concrete floor of the grandstand, but was revived without medical attention."[25]

The action of certain overzealous fans notwithstanding, there was ample reason to celebrate Day's accomplishment. He had faced only 29 batters, striking out six and allowing three baserunners on a walk and the two errors by Felder; none of the baserunners reached second base. Effa Manley extolled her starting pitcher's heroics in a letter to an acquaintance, relating the fact that the no-hitter had ended when McHenry "[w]ent down swinging" and exclaiming, "Can you imagine what a thrill that was?"[26] However, she was also concerned about the on-field incident with Strauch, especially since controversies with umpires had become quite frequent in the Negro Leagues. In 1946 all eyes were not only on Jackie Robinson, who had just begun his first and only season in the minor leagues with the Montreal Royals, but also on the Negro Leagues' players. In particular, some members of the African-American press were concerned that any perceived misbehavior on the part of black ballplayers would bring black baseball into disrepute and would affect how Organized Baseball chose to deal with the Negro Leagues or, worse yet, that it might stall or quash the game's integration altogether.[27]

In an effort to prevent future flare-ups, Effa Manley wrote to Ed Gottlieb, the white promoter who assigned the umpires for Eagles games at Ruppert Stadium, and questioned whether Strauch should continue to work games for the team.[28] She expressed concern that "[t]he Negro men are as prejudiced against the white umpires as the white people are against the colored."[29] Manley's request to keep Strauch out of future Newark games, and thus to keep the races separate, was consistent with her long-held desire that Negro League baseball should be exclusively in the hands of African-Americans. Effa objected to white ownership of some of the NNL clubs, and she and Abe had fought losing battles to try to wrest away control of nonleague games, which were essential to the team's financial survival, from powerful white promoters like Gottlieb. However, in spite of her separatist outlook on black baseball, she did not stand in any player's way when a major-league team offered an opportunity, though she did fight to receive compensation from the teams that signed the Eagles players.

On May 13 the NNL office handed Cash a three-game suspension and levied a $50 fine while also announcing, "In the future any player striking an umpire will be fined $100 and will be suspended for ten days."[30] Oddly, Curry incurred no punishment for his actions even though they clearly had been deliberate and he had been forced from the field by the police. He may have escaped further repercussions because "[b]laming his conduct on the excitement of the game, Curry after the game apologized to Struack [*sic*] for himself and Cash."[31] In contrast to his manager, Cash remained unapologetic, asserting decades later, "And to this day, some people think the reason I didn't make it to the majors was because I smacked a white umpire. Shoot, as bad as that call was, I should've stomped him."[32]

As for Day, he began his comeback campaign with a flourish, but he also injured his arm during the game when he fielded a bunt and slipped while trying to throw to first for the out. According to Day, "When I threw it, I could feel something pull. ... That was opening day and I never was no good the whole season."[33] He nevertheless finished the 1946 NNL season with a 14-4 record, a 2.53 ERA, and a league-leading 65 strikeouts in 174 innings pitched.[34] His injury did worsen as the season progressed, though, and he was less effective in the two games he pitched against the Kansas City Monarchs in the World Series. He still was a major contributor to Newark's championship as he made a sparkling, game-saving catch in Game Six after he had moved from the mound, where he had started the game, to the outfield.

Leon Day was elected to the National Baseball Hall of Fame on March 7, 1995, just six days before he died of heart failure in Baltimore at the age of 78. Four other members of the 1946 Newark Eagles keep company with him in Cooperstown, New York – Doby, Irvin, Mackey, and Effa Manley – demonstrating that both the team and its feats, including Day's Opening Day no-hitter, are as worthy of commemoration as Feller and his accomplishments.

NOTES

1   Alyson Footer, "#TBT: Feller Tosses the One and Only Opening Day No-Hitter," mlb.com/news/tbt-bob-feller-tosses-the-one-and-only-opening-day-no-hitter/c-118626392, accessed January 24, 2018.

2   Ibid.

3   "Newark Eagles to Meet Stars," *Morning News* (Wilmington, Delaware), May 6, 1946: 15.

4   Gary Bedingfield, "Baseball in Wartime: Leon Day," baseballinwartime.com/player_biographies/day_leon.htm, accessed January 24, 2018.

5   "Eagles Make Bow Today," *Newark Star-Ledger*, May 5, 1946: 27.

6   James Overmyer, *Queen of the Negro Leagues: Effa Manley and the Newark Eagles* (Lanham, Maryland: Scarecrow Press, 1998), 59.

7   "No-Hit Bow: Day, Eagles Ace, Throttles Stars 2-0 in Opener," *Newark Star-Ledger*, May 6, 1946: 11.

8   James A. Riley, *Of Monarchs and Black Barons: Essays on Baseball's Negro Leagues* (Jefferson, North Carolina: McFarland & Company, 2012), 154-55.

9   "Day Hurls No-Hitter as Eagles Cop Opener, 2-0," *Baltimore Afro-American*, May 11, 1946: 29.

10   Bill "Ready" Cash and Al Hunter Jr., *Thou Shalt Not Steal: The Baseball Life and Times of a Rifle-Armed Negro League Catcher* (Philadelphia: Love Eagle Books, 2012), 73.

11   "Eagles, Stars Clash Tonight," *Trenton Evening Times*, May 8, 1946: 25.

12   James A. Riley, *Dandy, Day, and the Devil* (Cocoa, Florida: TK Publishers, 1987), 69.

13   Cash remembered the play somewhat differently in his autobiography, which was written more than 60 years after the game in question. He claimed that Irvin had hit the slow grounder to Stars shortstop Frank Austin rather than Pearson hitting it to the second baseman, Duckett. An examination of the box score shows that Cash's memory was faulty after the long interval, his protestations to the contrary notwithstanding. Cash remembered correctly that Isreal tripled, Doby singled, and that there then was a fly out before the grounder on which Doby tried to score. An examination of the game's box score shows that Irvin batted between Doby and Pearson in Newark's lineup that day; thus, he had to have been the batter who flied out, and Pearson had to have been the batter who hit the grounder. Additionally, Pearson must have hit the ball to Duckett, as was reported at the time; if the ball had been hit to Austin at short, it is doubtful that Doby would have tried to advance even to third base, let alone to attempt to score on the play. (For Cash's account, see Cash, 75).

14   Cash and Hunter, 5.

15   "Play That Caused Near Riot in Newark Eagle's No Hit Win From Philly," *New York Amsterdam News*, May 11, 1946: 12.

16   "Day Hurls No-Hitter as Eagles Cop Opener, 2-0."

17   "Play That Caused Near Riot in Newark Eagle's No Hit Win From Philly."

18   Cash and Hunter, 6, 74-75.

19   Monte Irvin with James A. Riley, *Nice Guys Finish First: The Autobiography of Monte Irvin* (New York: Carroll & Graf Publishers, Inc., 1996), 74.

20   "Police Halt Philadelphia Stars-Newark Eagles Riot," *New York Amsterdam News*, May 11, 1946: 1.

21   Irvin with Riley, 74.

22   "Play That Caused Near Riot in Newark Eagle's No Hit Win From Philly."

23   Riley, *Dandy, Day, and the Devil*, 70.

24   Ibid.

25   Jim Ryall, "Fireworks at Eagles Game/Fists Fly as Leon Day Hurls No-Hitter," *Newark News*, May 6, 1946.

26   Bob Luke, *The Most Famous Woman in Baseball: Effa Manley and the Negro Leagues* (Lincoln: University of Nebraska Press, 2011), 124.

27   *Pittsburgh Courier* sportswriter Wendell Smith took Newark and both the NNL and NAL league offices to task after the Eagles walked out on a July 21, 1946, exhibition game against the NAL's Cleveland Buckeyes because a controversial call went against them. When it became apparent that neither league office intended to penalize Newark, Smith wrote a scathing column in which he admonished:

"This attitude simply substantiates Branch Rickey's charge that 'Negro leagues do not actually exist.' When the presidents of the two leagues refuse to step in and crack down on teams that take the baseball law into their own hands, it simply means that the rules and regulations governing the game mean absolutely nothing.

Consequently, the fans never can be sure that they're going to get what they pay for. ..." (See Wendell Smith, "The Sports Beat: What Happens When a Team Quits?" *Pittsburgh Courier*, August 3, 1946: 16.)

Upon reading Smith's article, Effa Manley responded with a letter in which she attempted to explain why manager Biz Mackey had led the Eagles off the field without completing the game. She concluded her missive to Smith, which was printed in his next column, by asserting, "I will never condone any unsportsmanlike conduct from the Eagles. On the other hand, I do not expect them to accept decisions like this one without protesting." (See Wendell Smith, "The Sports Beat: Mrs. Manley Has Her Say," *Pittsburgh Courier*, August 10, 1946: 16.)

Manley's justifications for her team's actions notwithstanding, Smith's column reflected the concerns of most observers who wanted to ensure that Negro League players did not behave in a manner that would give Organized Baseball's leagues a convenient excuse to discontinue the integration of the game.

28   Luke, 124. Ed Gottlieb, in addition to being one of the prominent white promoters of black baseball games, was also a part-owner of the Philadelphia Stars. In light of

this fact, Cash's accusation that Effa Manley had paid off Strauch to call the opener in Newark's favor has little credence, if it ever had any at all. Strauch stood to lose more money by showing bias against the Stars and displeasing Gottlieb, who had the power not to assign him to work future games, than he had to gain by accepting a one-time bribe from Manley.

29   Ibid.

30   "8 Players Get 5-Year Suspensions, Elites Lose Star to Grays in NNL Action at Philly," *Baltimore Afro-American*, May 18, 1946: 30. In his autobiography, Cash gives the fine as $25 (See Cash, 6 and 76), but the contemporary newspaper account reported a $50 fine.

31   "Day Hurls No-Hitter as Eagles Cop Opener, 2-0."

32   Cash and Hunter, 6.

33   Riley, *Dandy, Day, and the Devil*, 70.

34   John Holway, *The Complete Book of Baseball's Negro Leagues: The Other Half of Baseball History* (Fern Park, Florida: Hastings House Publishers, 2001), 436. It should be noted that – as is often the case with Negro League ballplayers – different sources list different statistics for Day in 1946. Often the discrepancy results from the fact that one source includes both league and exhibition games while another source includes only league statistics. In other instances, more recent research that has been able to make use of newly available source material, such as digitized newspaper archives, may have turned up additional games that have been added to the statistical record.

"Leon's Terrific, Wonderful, Magnificent, Very Good Day"

August 11, 1946: Newark Eagles 8, Homestead Grays 7 [15 innings], at Ruppert Stadium, Newark

BY BOB LEMOINE

It was a cool, sunny day at Ruppert Stadium, home of the Newark Eagles, on Sunday, August 11, 1946, a beautiful day for a Negro League doubleheader. The Homestead Grays, the dominant team of the Negro National League in the 1940s, were in town to take on the surprising Eagles. The times were indeed changing in Negro League baseball. The soaring Eagles were on their way to their only Negro World Series championship. Jackie Robinson was in Montreal, playing in the Brooklyn Dodgers minor-league system. In less than a year, he would integrate the national pastime, and the Negro Leagues would begin to fade into baseball history. While Robinson opened up opportunities for young stars of color, other great players never had those opportunities. One such player was Leon Day, and this game was a glimpse of what a great player he was. The *Pittsburgh Courier* called this game a "thrill-packed, fifteen-inning contest."[1]

While Satchel Paige is by far the most notable name among pitchers in the Negro Leagues, Day was no slouch in pitching greatness. Larry Doby, his teammate who would one day break the color barrier in the American League, thought Day was even better than Paige. Day certainly didn't have Paige's flare for the dramatic; he just went quietly about his business, including a simple no-wind-

Leon Day (here in a Winnipeg uniform) excelled at long games. On September 14, 1950, he pitched all 17 innings of Winnipeg's 1-0 victory over Brandon that gave the Buffaloes the first ManDak League championship. *(Courtesy of Jay-Dell Mah/Western Canada Baseball)*

up delivery. Lost to history but fresh in Day's memories in later life were his historic matchups with Paige. Day was believed to have beaten the icon three of four times. Justifiably, both men are celebrated as Baseball Hall of Famers today.

Day had returned in 1946 from serving his country in World War II. Rejoining the Eagles, he threw a no-hitter in his return game on May 5, which was Opening Day for the Negro National League. That was just one of the great memories Newark fans would have of this championship season.

On August 11 the Grays sent Eugene Smith to the mound to oppose Day. Phil Cockrell umpired the contest along with two other umpires, one by the last name of Moore and Peter Strauch, whose controversial call as the home-plate umpire for Day's no-hitter had precipitated a riot at Ruppert Stadium.[2]

The Eagles jumped to a 1-0 lead in the first inning. The Grays countered with two runs in the third, but the Eagles put four more on the board in the fourth, grabbing a 5-2 lead. The Grays got a run back on the eighth, and the score was 5-3 in favor of Newark heading into the ninth. Smith, Jerry Benjamin, and Sam Bankhead each singled to load the bases for the Grays. Howard Easterling crushed a grand slam to propel the Grays into the lead, 7-5. But the game was far from over.[3]

In the bottom of the ninth, Day drew a walk, and when Smith threw another ball to Jimmy Wilkes, his wildness forced his removal in favor of Wilmer Fields. Wilkes flied out to left. Pat Patterson, however, sent the game into extra frames when he clubbed a home run to right, tying the score, 7-7.

Day had new life on the mound and the workhorse threw an additional six scoreless innings. The Eagles finally broke through when Day decided it was time to call it a day … well, at least until Game Two. He clubbed a 350-foot home run to left field off reliever Bob Thurman, who initially had entered the game as a pinch-hitter in the bottom of the 11th, to seal the Eagles' 8-7 win as the "Newark fans went wild with glee."[4]

Day finished his long outing with 10 strikeouts while surrendering 14 hits. Benjamin and Easterling led the way with three hits each for Homestead. Lennie Pearson and Leon Ruffin had three hits each to spark the Eagles. The Grays used hurler Bob Thurman, who would have a five-year span as a utility outfielder and pinch-hitter for the Cincinnati Reds late in his career, in addition to Smith and Fields. The trio allowed 12 hits between them.[5]

The Grays swept the doubleheader with a 3-1 victory in the nightcap behind the strong pitching of Leniel Hooker and a 450-foot home run by Monte Irvin. The standings posted in the *Courier* through August 11 showed Newark in first place in the Negro National League with a 12-3 record, 1½ games over the New York Cubans, while the Grays occupied the basement at 3-8. The Grays would rally to finish second by season's end, but they were far behind the Eagles.

SOURCES

"Fair Weather: Continued Moderate Temperatures Loom," *Newark Star-Ledger*, August 12, 1946: 1.

Kern, Thomas. "Leon Day," SABR BioProject. sabr.org/bioproj/person/f6e24f41 Retrieved January 11, 2019.

NOTES

1   "Newark Tops Grays in 15 Inning Tilt; Increase Lead in Negro Nat'l Loop," *Pittsburgh Courier*, August 17, 1946: 16.

2   "Police Halt Philadelphia Stars-Newark Eagles Riot," *New York Amsterdam News*, May 11, 1946: 1.

3   "Day Eagles' Hero in Twin Victory," *Newark News*, August 12, 1946.

4   Ibid.

5   "Newark Eagles Defeat Grays, By 8-7 in 15th," *New York Amsterdam News*, August 17, 1946: 11.

THE 1946 EAST-WEST
ALL-STAR, GAME ONE

AUGUST 15, 1946: EAST 6, WEST 3, AT GRIFFITH STADIUM

BY MARK S. STERNMAN AND FREDERICK C. BUSH

The first East-West All-Star Game of 1946 took place before 16,268 fans at Griffith Stadium in Washington, D.C. This was the first time the East game would be played in the nation's capital, inspiring sportswriter Sam Lacy to hope it also would be "the first time to put on an Eastern version of the East-West extravaganza, held annually in Chicago."[1] The low turnout for the game was disappointing, however, as the *Pittsburgh Courier* had enthused on August 3 that the sluggers of the East team were likely "to scalp the West and lure a record crowd of sports history, probably 30,000 fans to the stadium."[2] The low attendance was attributable in part to the absence of Satchel Paige, who initially had been expected to start for the West team but who did not participate in the game. Without Paige, the *Courier's* anticipated matchup of "the exceptional pitching of the NAL [West] against the power hitters of the NNL [East]" did not materialize.[3]

The *Courier's* prediction of an East-team victory proved to be correct as a quartet of high-flying Newark Eagles – Leon Day, Larry Doby, Monte Irvin, and Lennie Pearson – sparked the East to a 6-3 win over the West. Batting second and playing second

base, Doby had two hits, two runs scored, and a stolen base, Irvin scored one run and knocked in another, while Pearson added an RBI of his own. On the mound, Day, described by Irvin as "cat-quick and a great pitcher,"[4] picked up the save with one inning of one-hit ball. Newark catcher Leon Ruffin also played but went hitless in his lone plate appearance.

Before the Eagles' stars could soar, they first had to wait out a delay of the game as "Players of the West squad … held up the all-star game for 15 minutes … in a baseball version of the sit-down strike. The group left the field en masse at the conclusion of the pregame practice and refused to go through with the contest until an understanding was reached under which they would get more money."[5] Dr. J.B. Martin, president of the Negro American League, which composed the West team, later explained that the West players had been guaranteed $50 each for their participation in the game, but they had demanded $100. The *Baltimore Afro-American* pointed out that a similar strike had been staged by the East team's players before the 1944 all-star game in Chicago. New York Cubans owner Alex Pompez pointed to this strike while castigating the West players, telling them, "This sort of thing every time we have an all-star game has got to stop. You're doing nothing but sending your own baseball to ruin."[6] The matter was settled in a locker-room negotiation session, but neither side would reveal the outcome of the deal.

Once the action finally got underway, the East grabbed a quick lead by scoring a pair of runs in the bottom of the first inning off the "fireball pitching"[7] of "Dan Bankhead, ace of the Memphis Red Sox … [who in regular-season play had] four wins and no losses, with 50 strikeouts in 36 innings, and 11 walks."[8] On this day, however, Bankhead walked the leadoff batter, Baltimore's Henry Kimbro, and surrendered back-to-back singles to Doby and Howard Easterling (of the Homestead Grays) that resulted in a 1-0 deficit. Easterling tried to stretch his hit into a double and was retired in a rundown, but Doby advanced to third on the play and scored the second run of the inning on a groundout by Homestead's Buck Leonard.

Philadelphia Stars lefty Barney Brown was the East team's starter and, according to reporter Sam Lacy, "the American League [West] bats were woefully impotent before the offerings of Brown."[9] After pitching three scoreless innings, Brown gave way to Pat Scantlebury of the New York Cubans.[10] Scantlebury faced just five batters, retiring only one and giving up three hits and an error by shortstop Sam Bankhead of the Homestead Grays.

In the top of the fourth, Birmingham's Artie Wilson led off with a single. Scantlebury then retired the Cleveland Buckeyes' Archie Ware before inducing what should have been a double-play grounder by Cleveland's Sammy Jethroe to Bankhead, "who came up with one of his rare bobbles," leaving both runners safe.[11] Now in a bind, Scantlebury faced Birmingham's Piper Davis, who "shot a sizzler down the left-field foul line that Monte Irvin of Newark held to a single by some fast fielding."[12] Wilson scored and Jethroe went to second. Yet another Buckeye, Willie Grace, lashed a single that scored his teammate Jethroe to tie the game. Baltimore's Bill Byrd relieved Scantlebury, but the East fell behind when Byrd "watched Davis cross the plate as he was vainly trying to throw out Cowan [Bubba] Hyde, Memphis, at first."[13]

The West's lead was short-lived. The East scored two runs in the bottom of the fourth off Cleveland's Vibert Clarke to retake the lead, 4-3. Easterling led off the inning with a bunt single and moved to second on a sacrifice by Leonard. Irvin smacked a single that plated Easterling and tied the game once more. After a basehit by Josh Gibson (Homestead), Pearson batted for Philadelphia's Gene Benson and drove in Irvin, his Newark teammate, with the go-ahead run.

Another Newark player, Doby, was at the forefront of the East's next rally, in the bottom of the fifth inning, when the East scored the final two tallies of the game. Kimbro led off with a bunt and reached safely after he "dived on his stomach and eluded [West first baseman] Ware's outstretched hand. At the finish of his slide, Kimbro was resting on first base while Ware was looking around with unbelieving eyes."[14] Kimbro's derring-do went for naught when he was erased from the basepaths on Doby's fielder's-choice grounder. Doby stole second base, advanced to third on an Easterling hit, and scored on a wild pitch by Gentry Jessup of the Chicago American Giants. Easterling scored on another Leonard RBI groundout. Leonard's second RBI of the game produced the sixth and final run, and was the last of his record 14 RBIs in Negro League All-Star Games.[15]

Day pitched a scoreless ninth inning to pick up the save in support of Byrd, the winning pitcher. Clarke took the loss for the West. The majority of these players would meet again for the second East-West All-Star Game three days later at Chicago's Comiskey Park, the traditional venue for the annual highlight of the Negro League season.

NOTES

1   Sam Lacy, "16,000 See East Top West in All Star Diamond Tilt," *Baltimore Afro-American*, August 17, 1946: 26. The 1946 season was not the first time two East-West Games were played, but the previous East games had not been nearly as successful as the annual showcase game at Chicago's Comiskey Park. In 1939 an estimated crowd of 20,000 attended the game at Yankee Stadium in New York, which was only half of the estimated 40,000 that attended the Comiskey Park game. The disparity in attendance was even greater in 1942 when only 10,791 spectators showed up for the game at Cleveland's Municipal Stadium, compared with the 45,179 who packed Comiskey Park that year.

2   "Top Stars to Clash Before Record Throng in Washington All-Star Tilt," *Pittsburgh Courier*, August 3, 1946: 17.

3   Ibid.

4   Monte Irvin, "Introduction," Mark Chiarello and Jack Morelli, *Heroes of the Negro Leagues* (New York: Abrams, 2007), 6.

5   Sam Lacy, "All-Star Classic Delayed by West's Pay Demands," *Baltimore Afro-American*, August 17, 1946: 1.

6   Sam Lacy, "All Star Classic (Continued From Page One)," *Baltimore Afro-American*, August 17, 1946: 27.

7   "Negro All-Star Teams Tangle at Griffith Stadium Tonight," *Washington Post*, August 15, 1946: 19.

8   "Negro All-Stars Play Thursday," *Washington Post*, August 10, 1946: 11.

9   Lacy, "16,000 See East Top West in All Star Diamond Tilt."

10   "The last black player who stepped directly from a Negro team into a major-league uniform was veteran … Pat Scantlebury, who pitched in eight games for the Cincinnati Reds in 1956." Robert Peterson, *Only the Ball Was White* (New York: McGraw-Hill Book Company, 1984), 203.

11   Lacy, "16,000 See East Top West in All Star Diamond Tilt."

12   Ibid.

13   Ibid.

14   Ibid.

15   Larry Lester, *Black Baseball's National Showcase: The East-West All-Star Game, 1933-1953* (Lincoln: University of Nebraska Press, 2001), 426, 448.

THE 1946 EAST-WEST
ALL-STAR CLASSIC, GAME TWO

AUGUST 18, 1946: WEST 4, EAST 1, AT COMISKEY PARK

BY MARK S. STERNMAN AND FREDERICK C. BUSH

After the East defeated the West, 6-3, in Washington, D.C., on August 15, the two All-Star squads went west to Chicago for the annual game that had originated in 1933 and had been played at Comiskey Park every season since then.[1] The *Pittsburgh Courier*'s Wendell Smith reported that, since its inception, "spectators have paid out $383,000 and 434,000 have witnessed the classics" and asserted, "No other sports event attracts such a crowd. Not even a Joe Louis fight has more magnetism than the East-West Game."[2] The 1946 contest followed suit with expectations that "the 'dream game' will attract a throng of at least 35,000 fans … from all over the United States … to watch the 'million dollar gems' of Negro baseball tangle in the biggest and most spectacular game of the season."[3]

The West held a 7-to-6 edge in the previous classics, and a crowd of 45,474 packed the ballpark to see if the East team could even the ledger.[4] After winning the first of two All-Star Games in 1946 and "[w]ith an announced starting lineup of hitters averaging close to .333 in Negro National league completion, the East rules [as] the favorite. … The presence of the 'home run twins of Negro baseball' – Catcher Josh Gibson and First Baseman Buck Leonard of the Homestead Grays – apparently gives the East the offensive edge."[5] Once anticipation gave way to action, Birmingham Black Barons shortstop Artie Wilson turned in a star performance that

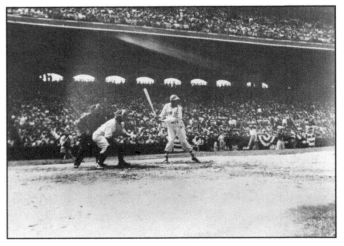

Action from the annual East-West Game at Chicago's Comiskey Park on August 18, 1946. The West won this game, 4-1, in front of 45,474 fans. *(National Baseball Hall of Fame)*

helped lead the West to its fourth consecutive triumph over the East at Comiskey Park.

Philadelphia Stars pitcher Barney Brown started for the East and, just as he had done on August 15, hurled three scoreless innings. The difference between this game and the first clash in D.C., however, was that the West's Felix Evans accomplished what his

Memphis Red Sox teammate Dan Bankhead had been unable to do in Washington, match Brown zero for zero.

This time Bankhead took the mound in the fourth inning and had better success as he kept the East off the scoreboard for an additional three frames. Meanwhile, the West batters broke through against Baltimore's Bill Byrd, beginning in the bottom of the fourth inning. Byrd's troubles began when, after retiring leadoff hitter Sam Jethroe of the Cleveland Buckeyes, he walked Birmingham's Lorenzo "Piper" Davis. Cleveland's Willie Grace knocked a base hit to right field that Philadelphia's Gene Benson bobbled for an error that allowed Davis to advance to third and Grace to second. Benson's error was uncharacteristic for someone considered to be "a truly great defensive outfielder."[6] A sacrifice bunt by Memphis's Alec Radcliffe enabled Davis to score the game's first run, and then fellow Red Sox Cowan "Bubba" Hyde singled to drive in Grace for a 2-0 West lead.

In the bottom of the fifth, the West added two more runs against Byrd. Wilson singled to lead off the inning and advanced to second on a sacrifice by Cleveland's Archie Ware. Jethroe reached first safely when he hit a grounder that New York Cubans shortstop Silvio Garcia misplayed for an error. The lead grew when the "West worked that double steal like a clock. Sammy Jethroe broke for second and stopped halfway down the line. Gibson threw to Garcia at second and Wilson came charging home from third. Garcia tried to peg him out, but Art slid in safely and Jethroe took second."[7] Davis followed with a single to center that scored Jethroe to double the West's lead to 4-0. Baltimore Elite Giants lefty Jonas Gaines relieved Byrd at this point and retired the side.

The East, which had tallied six runs at Griffith Stadium, managed only one run at Comiskey. The score came against Johnny "Nature Boy" Williams of the Indianapolis Clowns in the top of the eighth inning. Williams hit the leadoff batter, Philadelphia's Murray Watkins, and then surrendered a single to the Cubans' Pat Scantlebury, who was pinch-hitting for Gaines, with Watkins advancing to third on the play. Baltimore's Tom Butts ran for Scantlebury but was erased on a fielder's choice by his Elite Giants teammate Henry Kimbro as Watkins had to hold at third. Newark's Larry Doby flied out to left field, which allowed Watkins to score, but Hyde, the left fielder, got the third out by gunning down Kimbro attempting to advance to second base.

While Wilson's steal of home highlighted the game, the West took the rematch 4-1 because "Chin Evans and Dan Bankhead, both of the Memphis Red Sox, and John Williams of the Indianapolis Clowns, subdued the eastern stars of the Negro National League with four hits."[8] Bankhead "got the win for the West with three scoreless innings. He finished the year with a 7-3 record that far

outshone his team's 24-36 mark."[9] Williams got the save for his three innings of one-run ball.

In a game that featured no extra-base hits, Gibson and Leonard had but one single and one walk between them in eight plate appearances. Leonard's was "a corking blow to right center [but he was] out trying to stretch it into a two-base hit. With none out, fans believed Buck should have been stopped at first."[10]

Two of the four hits registered by the East team belonged to Doby and Monte Irvin of the Newark Eagles, who each singled once. Their Newark teammate Leon Day closed the game for the East, giving up one hit and fanning a batter in his lone inning of work.

The West had used just 11 players – eight fielders and three pitchers. Although a newspaper report places pitcher Gentry Jessup, third baseman Clyde Nelson, and manager Jim Taylor (who served as a coach) of the Chicago American Giants on the West squad,[11] neither Jessup nor Nelson played in front of their hometown fans.

The two 1946 All-Star Games had settled nothing. Both the East and the West had won one game, with each squad scoring seven runs. A rubber match did not take place that year, but a third All-Star game did occur. This contest split the West into North and South teams, and this time Jessup not only played, but starred as he "pitched and batted the North Negro All-Stars to an 8 to 2 victory over the South All-Stars at Comiskey Park on September 22. He drove in four runs with two singles and restricted the losers to five hits. The North team was selected from the Chicago American Giants and Cleveland Buckeyes, with the South being chosen from the Memphis Red Sox and Birmingham Black Barons."[12]

SOURCES

The play-by-play recap contained here was reconstructed primarily from the game account found in the following article:

Segreti, James. "West Defeats East All-Star Negro Nine, 4-1: Gains 8th Victory Before 45,474," *Chicago Tribune*, August 19, 1946: 27.

NOTES

1   In some seasons, two East-West Games were played – such was the case in 1946, with the first game having been played at Griffith Stadium – but the true showcase game was always the one held in the West at Comiskey Park.

2   Wendell Smith, "The Sports Beat," *Pittsburgh Courier*, August 17, 1946: 16.

3   "Rosters Set for 'Dream Games' in D.C. and Chicago: East-West Classic in Chicago on August 18," *Pittsburgh Courier*, August 10, 1946: 16.

4   The record for the East-West Games given here is for the games played at Comiskey Park games; the August 15, 1946, game played at Griffith Stadium is not included in this tally.

5   "Negro All-Star Nines Assemble for 14th Game," *Chicago Tribune*, August 17, 1946: 17.

6   Mark Chiarello and Jack Morelli, *Heroes of the Negro Leagues* (New York: Abrams, 2007), 124.

7   Wendell Smith, "The Sports Beat: Dream Game Star Dust …" *Pittsburgh Courier*, August 24, 1946, as reprinted in Larry Lester, *Black Baseball's National Showcase: The East-West All-Star Game, 1933-1953* (Lincoln: University of Nebraska Press, 2001), 277.

8   "Negro West Stars Win," *The Sporting News*, August 28, 1946: 32.

9   Rory Costello, "Dan Bankhead," sabr.org/bioproj/person/62db6502 (accessed July 14, 2015). An online source lists Bankhead's 1946 record at 5-3. baseball-reference.com/nlb/player.cgi?id=bankhe001dan. (accessed July 16, 2015).

10   Fay Young, "Ace West Hurlers Beat East, 4-1," *Chicago Defender*, August 24, 1946, as reprinted in Larry Lester, *Black Baseball's National Showcase*, 275.

11   "Name West Nine for 14th Negro All-Star Game," *Chicago Tribune*, August 11, 1946: A5. A follow-up article asserted, "Gentry Jessup, right handed pitching star of the Chicago American Giants, who starred in the East-West game the last two years, has been named as the West's starter on the mound. …" "East vs. West Today in 14th Negro Game," *Chicago Tribune*, August 18, 1946: A2.

12   "Negro North All-Stars Win," *The Sporting News*, October 2, 1946: 33.

THE 1946 NEGRO LEAGUE WORLD SERIES:
NEWARK EAGLES VS.
KANSAS CITY MONARCHS

BY RICHARD J. PUERZER

The 1946 Negro League World Series played between the Negro National League's Newark Eagles and the Negro American League's Kansas City Monarchs was one of the great postseason series in the history of professional baseball. The Series was closely contested, going the full seven games, and is one of the most interesting focal points in the history of the Negro Leagues. In many ways it represented in microcosm the later, transitional, history of the Negro Leagues. Attendance varied wildly, depending on where and when the games were played. Often the distances between venues were so far that the Eagles and Monarchs traveled between cities by airplane instead of by train. The series featured future Hall of Famers and a number of others who went on to play in the major leagues. However, the talent pool in the Negro Leagues was already being diminished as former Monarch Jackie Robinson was now playing with the Montreal Royals and would move to the Brooklyn Dodgers in 1947. Don Newcombe, who pitched as a 19-year-old for the Eagles in 1945, had been signed away to the Dodgers organizations as well. Although there was solid coverage of the Series in the African-American press, the games were often overshadowed by minor-league games in which Robinson played. Less than three seasons later, the Newark

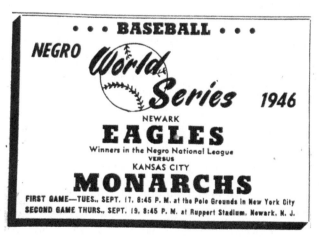

Newspaper advertisement for the first two games of the 1946 Negro World Series between the NNL's Newark Eagles and the NAL's Kansas City Monarchs. (*New York Afro American,* September 14, 1946)

Eagles relocated to Houston before their, and the Negro Leagues', inevitable demise.

In 1946 both the Eagles and Monarchs were powerhouse teams that won their respective leagues to earn the right to play in the World Series. The Monarchs were owned by J.L. Wilkinson and managed by Frank Duncan. They featured a number of star players including Hank Thompson at second base and often hitting in the leadoff spot, Ted Strong in right field, Willard Brown in the outfield and batting cleanup, and Buck O'Neil at first base. The Monarchs had a great pitching staff, with future Hall of Famer Hilton Smith, Connie Johnson, Jim LaMarque, and the one and only Satchel Paige. Including team owners, managers, players, and an umpire, 10 future Hall of Fame members were directly involved in the Series.[1]

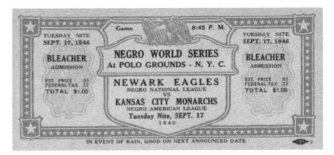

Bleacher-seat ticket for Game One of the 1946 Negro League World Series between the Newark Eagles and Kansas City Monarchs. (*Noir-Tech Research, Inc.*)

Game One

September 17, 1946: Kansas City Monarchs 2, Newark Eagles 1, at the Polo Grounds, New York

The opening game of the World Series was played on Tuesday night, September 17, at the Polo Grounds in New York City. The pitching matchup featured a pair of future Hall of Famers, with Hilton Smith starting for the Monarchs and Leon Day for the Eagles.

The game got off to a fast start as Hank Thompson led off with a single to right field that went through the legs of Bob Harvey, allowing Thompson to advance to third base. He scored on a single to right by Herb Souell. Ted Strong followed with another single, advancing Souell to third. Leon Day was able to strike out Willard Brown, but loaded the bases when he walked Buck O'Neil. However, Day was able to pitch out of the jam, striking out John Scott and inducing a weak groundout from Jim Hamilton. The Eagles threatened in the bottom of the first frame when, with two outs, Larry Doby used his speed to first beat out a bunt for a hit and then steal second. Monte Irvin followed, but popped out to short to end the inning. The Eagles had another scoring opportunity in the second inning when Lenny Pearson and Johnny Davis reached base to lead off, but Bob Harvey fouled out to third. Leon Ruffin, on a hit-and-run play, knocked the ball up the middle to Monarchs shortstop Hamilton, who was covering second base on the play and was able to field the ball, touch second, and throw to first to convert the hard-hit ball into a double play that ended the inning.

Leon Day pitched in and out of trouble through the first five innings of the game, allowing four walks and five hits. Aided by two double plays turned by his fine infield, Day was able to keep the Monarchs from scoring any further runs until he left the game in the bottom of the fifth. Rufus Lewis pitched the remainder of the game for the Eagles.

In the top of the sixth, the Eagles tallied their first run. Larry Doby led off the inning with a walk, which led Monarchs manager Frank Duncan to bring in Satchel Paige in relief. It was reported that Paige was met with "mingled cheers and boos" from the Polo Grounds crowd when he entered the game. Paige proceeded to strike out

Irvin and Pearson, but he allowed Doby to swipe second. Doby then scored when Johnny Davis banged a single off the right-field wall.

In the top of the seventh, Paige hit the ball up the middle off pitcher Lewis's glove. Doby made a play on the ball, but threw it past first, allowing Paige to advance to second. Herb Souell singled to left, driving in Satchel for the second Monarchs run of the game. In his only appearance in the series, Eagles manager Biz Mackey pinch-hit in the eighth inning but failed to reach base. Paige was able to shut down the Eagles for the remainder of the game, striking out eight batters in four innings, and was awarded the win. The game was played in 3 hours and 5 minutes and drew 19,423 fans.

The game was marred by two serious injuries. Eagles third baseman Clarence "Pint" Isreal dislocated his knee when he fell into the box seats chasing a fly ball. Isreal would return later in the Series. A more serious injury befell Monarchs rookie shortstop Jim Hamilton. In the fifth inning, Hamilton was attempting to turn a double play when Bob Harvey took him out in what *Afro-American* sportswriter Sam Lacy described as a "play-smearing slide." The 24-year-old Hamilton suffered a broken right leg in what was essentially a career-ending injury.[2]

| Monarchs | 1 | 0 | 0 | 0 | 0 | 0 | 1 | 0 | 0 | 2 | 8 | 0 |
| Eagles | 0 | 0 | 0 | 0 | 0 | 1 | 0 | 0 | 0 | 1 | 9 | 2 |

Game Two

September 19, 1946: Newark Eagles 7, Kansas City Monarchs 4, at Ruppert Stadium, Newark

Game two of the World Series was played at Ruppert Stadium in Newark, New Jersey, on the night of Thursday, September 19, before a crowd of 9,787. In a pregame ceremony, heavyweight boxing champion Joe Louis threw out the first pitch. The pitching matchup featured Ford Smith for the Monarchs against Max Manning of the Eagles. Both pitchers started strong, with Smith allowing a run in the third inning but otherwise holding the Eagles in check over the first six innings. The Monarchs scored once in the fourth, and then extended their lead to 4-1 on Willard Brown's three-run homer in the top of the fifth.

In the bottom of the seventh, Larry Doby hit a two-run home run off Smith to bring the Eagles within a run. The Monarchs went to their bullpen and brought in Satchel Paige, hoping he would replicate his fine performance from the previous game. However, after Monte Irvin singled, Lennie Pearson drove a ball well over the left-field fence, only to have the blast called foul by umpire Bullet Rogan. After an extended argument over the foul-ball call, Pearson drove the ball to left, where it was bobbled by Johnny Scott, allowing Irvin to score and tie the game. Paige then gave up successive hits to Davis, Ruffin, and Manning, and when the inning finally ended, the Eagles had scored six runs and won the game, 7-4. Max Manning pitched a complete game, striking out eight for the win, with Paige taking the loss.

| Eagles | 0 | 0 | 0 | 0 | 1 | 3 | 0 | 0 | 0 | 4 | 2 | 2 |
| Monarchs | 0 | 0 | 1 | 0 | 0 | 0 | 6 | 0 | X | 7 | 12 | 2 |

Game Three

September 22, 1946: Kansas City Monarchs 15, Newark Eagles 5, at Blues Stadium, Kansas City

The third game of the World Series was scheduled for Sunday, September 22, but was rained out, taking away a big Sunday crowd and payday for the teams. The series resumed instead on Monday, September 23, at Blues Stadium in Kansas City. Jim LaMarque toed the slab for the Monarchs while Len Hooker started for the Eagles.

The game quickly became a blowout for the hometown Monarchs, who scored runs in six of the eight innings in which they batted. They tagged Len Hooker for nine hits and six runs before chasing him after the fourth inning. Suffering worse was Eagles reliever Cotton Williams, who gave up 11 hits and 9 runs in 3⅔ innings of work. Chico Renfroe, Herb Souell, and Hank Thompson each had four hits, and Ted Strong hit a 360-foot home run to right field in the Monarchs' seven-run barrage in the eighth inning. LaMarque benefited from the run support, as he gave up five runs to the Eagles but struck out eight in going the distance for the win.[3]

| Eagles | 0 | 2 | 0 | 0 | 0 | 1 | 2 | 0 | 0 | 5 | 7 | 3 |
| Monarchs | 1 | 4 | 0 | 1 | 1 | 1 | 0 | 7 | X | 15 | 21 | 1 |

Game Four

Newark Eagles 8, Kansas City Monarchs 1, at Blues Stadium, Kansas City

Game Four of the Series was played on Tuesday, September 24. It was again a night game played at Blues Stadium. A sparse crowd of 3,836 was in attendance. Rufus Lewis started the game for the Eagles against Ted Alexander for the home-team Monarchs. The Monarchs struck first, scoring a run in the second inning. The run came when Willard Brown singled, stole second, advanced to third on an infield out, and scored on Buck O'Neil fly ball to center field.

After that run, the remainder of the offense belonged to the Eagles. Newark scored two runs in the third and again in the fifth, chasing Alexander from the game. Satchel Paige came on in relief once more and again was ineffective, giving up three runs to the Eagles in the sixth and a soaring home run over the right-field fence to Monte Irvin in the seventh. Larry Doby also slugged the ball, collecting a double and triple along with a stolen base. But the offensive star of the game for the Eagles was leadoff hitter Jimmy Wilkes, who went 4-for-5 with two doubles and four runs scored. The overall star of the game, however, had to be Eagles hurler Rufus Lewis. Lewis dominated the Monarchs in pitching a complete game, scattering four hits and walking none while striking out six.

With their victory, the Eagles tied the series at two games apiece as the teams now moved on to Chicago for Game Five.[4]

| Eagles | 0 | 0 | 2 | 0 | 2 | 3 | 1 | 0 | 0 | 8 | 14 | 0 |
| Monarchs | 0 | 1 | 0 | 0 | 0 | 0 | 0 | 0 | 0 | 1 | 4 | 3 |

Game Five

Kansas City Monarchs 5, Newark Eagles 1, at Comiskey Park, Chicago

The fifth game of the series was played on the evening of Wednesday, September 25, before 4,000 fans at Comiskey Park in Chicago. The Monarchs played as the home team and sent Hilton Smith to the mound to start the game against the Eagles' Max Manning. Both pitchers started strong, blanking their opponents over the first three innings.

In the fourth, Hank Thompson walked, stole second, and then advanced to third on a hot shot to short that was knocked down by Monte Irvin. Ford Smith then singled to drive Thompson home. Smith was playing right field in place of Ted Strong, who had left the team after the fourth game of the Series to play in the Puerto Rican Winter League.

In the sixth inning, Thompson again got things started for the Monarchs, this time with a double. He advanced to third on a groundout by Willard Brown and then scored on a squeeze bunt executed by Buck O'Neil. Then John Scott tripled and scored on a wild pitch by Manning to give the Monarchs a 3-1 lead. In the

Banner honoring the 1946 Newark Eagles who captured that season's Negro World Series championship by defeating the Kansas City Monarchs in a seven-game series. *(Courtesy of Texas State Historical Association)*

seventh the Monarchs scored two more. Hilton Smith and Chico Renfroe both singled and were then driven home on a two-run double by Willard Brown.

Although they had 10 hits in the game, the Eagles were limited to one run. They scored in the eighth inning when Monte Irvin singled and scored on a double by Lennie Pearson. Despite giving up 10 hits, Hilton Smith walked only one and struck out eight to earn the complete-game win. Max Manning struck out seven and took the loss. The Monarchs now led three games to two and needed but one more win to take the Series.[5]

| Eagles | 0 | 0 | 0 | 0 | 0 | 0 | 0 | 1 | 0 | | 1 | 10 | 1 |
| Monarchs | 0 | 0 | 0 | 1 | 0 | 2 | 2 | 0 | X | | 5 | 9 | 0 |

Game Six

September 27, 1946: Newark Eagles 9, Kansas City Monarchs 7, at Ruppert Stadium, Newark

For Game Six of the World Series, the teams traveled back to Newark, where they played on Friday night, September 27, at Ruppert Stadium. Leon Day, who had been given extra rest after his Game One start, pitched for the Eagles against Jim LaMarque, who had started Game Three for the Monarchs. However, neither pitcher went beyond the first inning.

The Monarchs started hot, scoring five runs in the first inning, including a three-run clout over the center-field fence by Willard Brown. After the Monarchs' first-inning offensive explosion, Leon Day was relieved by Len Hooker. Day, however, did not leave the game. He moved to center field, which he manned for the rest of the game. In the Eagles' half of the first, LaMarque walked the first three batters. Len Pearson and Leon Ruffin followed with singles

to score a total of four runs, and bring the score to 5-4 after the raucous first inning.

Steve Wylie relieved LaMarque, and gave up two more runs to the Eagles on Monte Irvin's home run in the bottom of the second. The Eagles scored two more runs in the fourth on Pearson's home run, to make the score 8-5. Wylie was relieved by Ted Alexander in the fifth. The Eagles tacked on one more run in the sixth on Monte Irvin's second home run of the game, making the score 9-5.

The Monarchs tried to come back once more in the seventh, on a single by Willard Brown and a home run by Buck O'Neil, his first round-tripper of the season. However, Len Hooker was able to otherwise shut down the Monarchs and get the win for the Eagles, thanks to the support he received from his fellow moundsman Day, who was now manning center field. Monte Irvin recalled that "Buck O'Neil hit a deep line drive to right center field and Leon made a great over-the-shoulder catch to save the game."

As for Irvin, he scored four runs in the game as the Eagles staved off elimination and forced a seventh and final game for the Series.[6]

| Monarchs | 5 | 0 | 0 | 0 | 0 | 0 | 2 | 0 | 0 | | 7 | 11 | 2 |
| Eagles | 4 | 2 | 0 | 2 | 0 | 1 | 0 | 0 | X | | 9 | 10 | 3 |

Game Seven

September 29, 1946: Newark Eagles 3, Kansas City Monarchs 2, at Ruppert Stadium

The seventh and deciding game of the 1946 Negro League World Series was played on Sunday afternoon, September 29, at Ruppert Stadium. A total of 7,200 fans were in attendance for the game to see who would be crowned the champions of the Negro Leagues for 1946. Among those in attendance were scouts from the New York Giants and Brooklyn Dodgers. The pitching matchup featured

Ford Smith, starting his second game of the Series for Kansas City, against Newark's Rufus Lewis, also starting his second game after his dominant performance in Game Four.

An intriguing twist to this game was the absence of both Willard Brown and Satchel Paige, who failed to appear at the ballpark for the game. Brown apparently missed the game because he was in New York City signing a contract to play winter ball in Puerto Rico. Paige likely was making plans for the barnstorming tour that he was soon going to lead, going up against a team led by Bob Feller. Buck O'Neil, in his autobiography *I Was Right on Time*, said, that Paige had been slated to start the game. However, he also opined that Ford Smith was pitching better in the series than Paige and believed that Paige's absence might not have made any difference.[7]

The Eagles got things started right away, scoring a run in the first inning. Pat Patterson reached on an error by Monarchs second sacker Hank Thompson, moved to second on a walk to Larry Doby, and scored on a single by Monte Irvin. After this tally, both starters held the other team in check until the sixth inning.

In the top of the sixth, Buck O'Neil hit a solo home run, his second round-tripper of the Series, to tie the game. In the bottom of the sixth, Ford Smith lost his control for a time, walking Larry Doby and Monte Irvin on eight straight pitches. Johnny Davis then drove both men home on a double, giving the Eagles a 3-1 lead. The Eagles collected only three hits in the game, but they made the most of their opportunities.

In the top of the seventh, Jim Green, Ford Smith, and Herb Souell each singled, but the Monarchs were able to score only one run, leaving the Eagles ahead, 3-2. The Monarchs tried to rally in the ninth. Leading off the inning, Monarchs catcher Earl Taborn singled to right but was thrown out trying to stretch the hit into a double. The Monarchs put two more men on base, but Rufus Lewis was able to battle through and prevent the Monarchs from scoring, giving the Eagles the 3-2 victory in the game and a four-games-to-three victory in the Series.[8]

| Monarchs | 0 | 0 | 0 | 0 | 0 | 1 | 1 | 0 | 0 | | 2 | 8 | 2 |
| Eagles | 1 | 0 | 0 | 0 | 0 | 2 | 0 | 0 | X | | 3 | 3 | 1 |

Series Postscript

Monte Irvin led the Eagles in the series, batting .462 with 3 home runs and 8 RBIs. Rufus Lewis pitched two complete-game victories and had an ERA of 1.23 in 22 innings. On the Monarchs' side, Willard Brown hit three home runs and Buck O'Neil hit two. It was reported by Monte Irvin that each Eagles player received $600 for winning the Series and that Eagles co-owner Effa Manley was the happiest woman in Newark.[9] Many of the Eagles, along with a number of the Monarchs, joined the Satchel Paige All-Stars immediately after the Series. The players on the All-Stars included Eagles Monte Irvin, Rufus Lewis, Max Manning, and Lennie Pearson; the Monarchs were Frank Duncan, Willard Brown, Hank Thompson, Hilton Smith, and Buck O'Neil (in addition to Paige himself). Their barnstorming tour started in Pittsburgh on September 30, just one day after the end of the World Series.

SOURCES

Clark, Dick, and Larry Lester, eds. *The Negro Leagues Book* (Cleveland: Society for American Baseball Research, 1994).

Moore, Joseph Thomas. *Pride Against Prejudice: The Biography of Larry Doby* (New York: Praeger, 1988).

Overmyer, James. *Queen of the Negro Leagues: Effa Manley and the Newark Eagles* (Lanham, Maryland: Scarecrow Press, 1998).

Riley, James A. *The Biographical Encyclopedia of the Negro Baseball Leagues* (New York: Carroll & Graf Publishers, Inc., 1994).

seamheads.com.

NOTES

1   This list includes, from the Monarchs: Willard Brown, Satchel Paige, Hilton Smith, and J.L. Wilkinson; and from the Eagles: Leon Day, Larry Doby, Monte Irvin, Biz Mackey, and Effa Manley. Wilber "Bullet" Rogan, former Monarchs pitcher, served as an umpire for several of the games in the Series as well.

2   For Game One, the following references were used: "Eagles Bow," *Newark News*, September 18, 1946; Sam Lacy, "19,423 Fans See Paige in Brilliant Performance," *Afro-American*, September 21, 1946: 13.

3   For Game Three, the following references were used: "Eagles Beaten at Kansas City," *Newark News*, September 24, 1946; "Monarchs Take Lead in Series," *Afro-American*, September 24, 1946: 17.

4   For Game Four, the following references were used: "Series Is Tied as Eagles Win," *Newark News*, September 25, 1946; "Monarchs Take 3-2 World Series Lead," *Afro-American*, September 26, 1946: 31. (Note that this article combines the stories for Games Four and Five for the series).

5   For Game Five, the following references were used: "Eagles Returning Here, Trailing 3-2," *Newark News*, September 26, 1946; "Monarchs Take 3-2 World Series Lead," *Afro-American*, September 26, 1946: 31; "Monarchs Take Lead," *The Call* (Kansas City), September 26, 1946; Frank Young, "Monarchs Win 5th Game of World Series Played in Chicago, 5-1," *The Call,* September 27, 1946.

6   For Game Six, the following references were used: "Eagle Homers Knot Series," *Newark News*, September 28, 1946; "Eagles Beat Monarchs, Square Negro Series," *News Journal* (Wilmington, Delaware), September 28, 1946: 10; Monte Irvin with James A. Riley, *Nice Guys Finish First: The Autobiography of Monte Irvin* (New York: Carroll & Graf, 1996), 106.

7   Buck O'Neil with Steve Wulf and David Conrads, *I Was Right on Time* (New York: Simon & Schuster, 1996), 176-179.

8   For Game Seven, the following references were used: "Eagles Hit in Clutches," *Newark News*, September 30, 1946; "Newark Eagles Win World Series Crown: Whip Monarchs, 3-2, Before 7,200," *Afro-American*, October 5, 1946: 17.

9   Irvin with James A. Riley, 107.

THE NEWARK EAGLES:
SWINGING AWAY DURING
NEWARK'S HEYDAY

BY BOB GOLON

During the first half of the twentieth century, Newark, New Jersey, thrived as a city of commerce and culture. Its waterfront location and transportation facilities established Newark as an industrial center, providing jobs for its diverse citizenry. By the 1930s and '40s, Downtown Newark was home to major retailers like Hahne's, Bamberger's, S. Klein on the Square, and Kresge's, attracting shoppers from miles around. There was easy rail access to New York City and beyond as Newark was a major stop on the busy Northeast Corridor line. Newark Airport, opened in 1928, was the largest commercial airport in the country and the only airport to serve New York City until the opening of LaGuardia Airport in 1939. Bus and streetcar transportation extended through the city to its suburbs. Newark was a cultural and entertainment center with live shows and first-run movies at its many theaters and concert halls. Night life was rich as the big bands and jazz performers of the day made Newark nightclubs a stopping point on their show tours. The Mosque Theater, later known as Newark Symphony Hall, was home to classical, opera, and symphony stage performances. There was something for everyone in Newark.

Newark was a melting pot of nationalities dominated by immigrants from Europe. German and Irish settlers arrived first and were joined later by Eastern Europeans. Together, they filled Newark's

Newark Deputy Mayor Barney Koplin tosses out the first pitch for the Eagles' opening day game against the Philadelphia Stars at Ruppert Stadium on May 5, 1946. *(National Baseball Hall of Fame)*

tight-knit wards along ethnic lines, with each community having its own unique culture. African-Americans were attracted to Newark during their migration from the South in pursuit of the many manufacturing jobs that became available, particularly during World Wars I and II. They, too, brought their unique culture to the overall Newark experience.

Newark fans wait eagerly for the opening day game against the Philadelphia Stars to begin. Eagles hurler Leon Day pitched a no-hitter that created post-game pandemonium and sent the fans home happy. *(National Baseball Hall of Fame)*

Newark was also a baseball town. It was home to minor-league clubs beginning in the 1880s, most notably the famed Newark Bears team that, in Newark's heyday, was the top affiliate of the New York Yankees. The 1937 Bears are considered to be one of the greatest minor-league clubs of all time. The Newark Peppers of the Federal League played across the Passaic River in neighboring Harrison and gave Newark one season of major-league status in 1915. Built in 1926, venerable Ruppert Stadium in Newark's Ironbound section became home to baseball and other major sporting events. Every baseball season, thousands of fans from Newark and its surrounding towns came by bus and streetcar to the spacious, 19,000-seat concrete and steel ballpark on Wilson Avenue. From 1936 through 1948, Newark's African-American community also flocked to Ruppert Stadium to rally around a team of its own, the legendary Newark Eagles of the Negro National League. The history of the Eagles parallels that of blacks in America who struggled through the segregation era to break down color barriers in baseball as well as life.

BASEBALL'S COLOR BARRIER
AND THE NEWARK CONNECTION

Unfortunately, Newark was also the place of the launching of a racial injustice that lasted 70 years – the "gentlemen's agreement" that resulted in the banning of blacks from the highest levels of professional white baseball. Prior to the Newark incident, the drums of prejudice were already being sounded. On July 11, 1887, *The Sporting News,* an influential voice for the game of baseball, editorialized against "certain baseball associations [which have] done more damage to the International League than to any other we know of. We refer to the importation of colored players into the ranks of that body."[1]

That summer, pitcher George Stovey and catcher Moses "Fleetwood" Walker, both black, played for the Newark Little Giants of the International League. Stovey had a record of 33-14 while Walker batted .236. On July 19, 1887, the Chicago White Stockings (later the Cubs) of the National League arrived in Newark to play the Little Giants in an exhibition game. Chicago manager Adrian "Cap" Anson refused to allow the White Stockings onto the field if Stovey and Walker played. Fearing the loss of a lucrative gate, the Little Giants complied.[2] By the 1888 season, the unwritten but unyielding segregation agreement was in place, not to be broken until Jackie Robinson took the field for the Montreal Royals at Jersey City's Roosevelt Stadium in April 1946.

EARLY SEGREGATED BASEBALL –
SETTING THE STAGE FOR THE EAGLES

In the late nineteenth century, all-black barnstorming teams formed, which competed mostly against white teams in the minor leagues. A notable New Jersey entry was the Cuban Giants, a squad that played in the Mid-States League and called Trenton its home. In 1920 Rube Foster formed the original Negro National League, eventually a 10-team circuit which played through 1931. In the Northeast, the Eastern Colored League began play in 1923,[3] and during its run, the Atlantic City Bacharachs brought organized Negro league baseball to New Jersey.

The Bacharachs, named because of the backing of Atlantic City Mayor Harry Bacharach, played in the 1926 Negro League World Series, losing to the Chicago American Giants, five games to three. They were led by shortstop John Henry "Pop" Lloyd, also known as "the black Honus Wagner."[4] They disbanded in the 1930s, during the period in which black baseball was establishing itself in Newark.[5]

The Negro National League re-formed in 1933. In 1934 the Newark Dodgers joined the league, and in 1935 they were joined by the Brooklyn Eagles, owned by Abe and Effa Manley, who recently had relocated from Philadelphia. Playing at Ebbets Field when the white Brooklyn Dodgers were away, the Manleys sought to take advantage of the growing black population in the Bedford-Stuyvesant section of Brooklyn for fan support.[6] However, they found this was not enough as the competition for the Depression-era entertainment dollar in Brooklyn was fierce. The Eagles' attendance was poor, and the Manleys, determined to succeed in Negro baseball, looked across Newark Bay for greener pastures.

THE MANLEYS' EAGLES COME TO NEWARK

The Negro National League's Newark Dodgers, a last-place club in 1935, had little success drawing fans. The Manleys purchased the

THE STORY OF THE 1946 NEGRO LEAGUE CHAMPIONS

club from Charles Tyler, merged rosters with the Eagles, and left Brooklyn for Newark in 1936. The combined roster included two young players who would eventually be enshrined in the National Baseball Hall of Fame in Cooperstown, the Eagles pitcher Leon Day and the Dodgers third baseman Ray Dandridge. These two players formed the backbone of the Newark Eagles into the 1940s.[7]

The Manleys met at Yankee Stadium during the 1932 World Series and married in 1935.[8] Prior to moving to New York, Abe made a considerable amount of money running a numbers game in Camden, New Jersey, as well as in real estate. Even though wealthy, he mostly shunned black high society and focused on his life as a "sportsman," enjoying his wealth in a man's world. Owning a baseball club was a natural match for Abe, and his percentage of investment in his team was one of the highest among all Negro league owners.[9]

Abe Manley is frequently overshadowed by his wife Effa's ownership accomplishments, but he himself was an important presence with the Eagles and the league. He was named treasurer of the NNL in 1937 and was a league officer for most of his ownership tenure.[10] While Effa ran the business management of the Eagles, Abe was chiefly responsible for the on-field aspects. There were no elaborate scouting operations in Negro baseball, and Abe functioned as the talent evaluator for up-and-coming players. He did establish working agreements with feeder teams in the Southern Negro League, the Winston-Salem Eagles and the Asheville Blues.[11] Between this and his scouting New Jersey for local talent, Abe managed to build a consistently competitive club for Newark.

THE EARLY EAGLES: 1936-1940

In a league that was dominated by the powerful Homestead Grays, the Eagles finished in second place in three out of the five years preceding World War II. The 1937-38 Eagles infield was thought to be the best in the league. At first base was the power-hitting George "Mule" Suttles, who led the league in home runs in both seasons.[12] Slick-fielding Dick Seay and Willie Wells held down second base and shortstop respectively. Ray Dandridge was a mainstay at third base. The 1930's outfield usually consisted of Jimmie Crutchfield, 1939 NNL batting leader Ed Stone (.439), and 1940 league leader Lennie Pearson (.389).[13] Catching duties were shared by Johnny Hayes and Leon Ruffin. Ruffin was traded in 1939 for catcher Raleigh "Biz" Mackey, who would become manager of the club in 1941.[14] The pitching staff was anchored by Leon Day (14-7 in 1939), Jimmie Hill, Terris "The Great" McDuffie, and Bob Evans. Pleasantville, New Jersey's Max Manning became an Eagle in 1938, and Len Hooker joined the club in 1940.

Manley found one of his best players in Orange, New Jersey, adjacent to Newark. In 1938 Monte Irvin joined the club as a shortstop. A four-sport star in high school, Irvin decided on baseball over a career in football. With shortstop in the capable hands of Willie Wells, Irvin was moved to the outfield, and alternated between there and the infield throughout his Eagles career. He hit .324 lifetime for the Eagles, and went on to a Hall of Fame career with the New York Giants in the National League from 1949 through 1956.[15]

EFFA MANLEY, WORLD WAR II, NEWARK, AND ITS EAGLES

By 1941, the Eagles were firmly established in black Newark. Attendance rose to an average of 2,696 per game, but Sunday games averaged 4,293.[16] In 2009, writer Peter Genovese, in the *Star Ledger,* stated that "Sunday games were quite the event. They started at 2 PM to allow churchgoers time to reach the ballpark. Fans came dressed in the Sunday best – women with fashionable flowery hats, men in jackets and ties."[17] Genovese added that at Ruppert Stadium in 1939, "admission was 85 cents for box seats, 65 cents for grandstand seats and 40 cents for bleachers. ... A local band performed the national anthem before each game and played between innings. Jocko Maxwell, often called the first African-American sportscaster, was the Eagles PA announcer." *Star Ledger* columnist Jerry Izenberg called Maxwell the "Eagles' Lord High Chancellor of Communications."[18] Maxwell was an evening sportscaster on radio stations in Newark and Jersey City and had a strong local following while also writing for the *Newark Afro-American.* He frequently coordinated Eagles public-relations activities with Effa Manley.

Numerous dignitaries were among the crowd of 8,514 fans who were on hand for opening day at Ruppert Stadium in 1946. *(National Baseball Hall of Fame)*

When the owners of other Negro National League clubs and Negro league players and fans thought of the Eagles, the first person who came to mind was Effa Manley. It was not known until many years later that the "Queen of the Negro Leagues" was white. She was born in 1897 to a white mother, Bertha Ford Brooks, who was married to an African-American and lived in a black neighborhood in Philadelphia. During the marriage, Brooks had an affair with a white man, and Effa was their daughter. According to columnist Amy Ellis Nutt in the *Star Ledger,* "Blond and hazel-eyed, Effa grew up in a black neighborhood, played with black children and for all intents and purposes was treated as being black. In fact, being black was exactly what she thought she was."[19] Effa lived in a black world, traveled in black high society, championed black causes, and, chief among all, became a team owner of epic proportions in a black man's world.

Before the term "marketing" was fashionable, Effa was doing just that. She became the Eagles' best public-relations person through her relationships with the press, Newark's black community, her volunteerism and her tireless charitable efforts. She raised funds for the Booker T. Washington Community Hospital, of which Effa stated, "This hospital is the only one in the state offering an opportunity for colored physicians and nurses to get hospital training. This is a civic responsibility."[20] She promoted fundraising for the NAACP at Eagles games, organized and bought equipment and uniforms for a black youth baseball club, the Newark Cubs, and started a "knothole gang" organization for black kids to attend Eagles games.[21] As the Eagles' business manager, she did everything from making sure the uniforms were clean to scheduling games and organizing the team's off-field staff and planned entertainment at Ruppert Stadium. Effa was also responsible for making sure that her players were provided for. Paychecks were always on time (a rarity in the Negro leagues) and Effa was the first to provide an air-conditioned bus for team travel during the grueling 150-game schedule, which included many single-game stops. She was the face of the franchise, and her adept management in a tight financial environment was so renowned that in 2006 she became the first and as of 2019 the only woman to be elected to the National Baseball Hall of Fame.

In 1940 Newark's black population was nearly 46,000. Their contribution to the World War II industrial effort increased the economic status of the black community as black war production jobs increased from 7,990 in 1940 to 27,000 in 1945.[22] Effa Manley's volunteerism during the war had a positive influence on the growing image of Newark's black patriotism. She was awarded four annual service stripes as a local warden for the Newark Defense Council. She volunteered for the wartime Office of Price Administration, making decisions on food and gasoline rations for the Price Control Board in Newark. She organized bus trips of black entertainers to travel to Fort Dix to entertain black troops.[23] The war had negative effects on baseball in general, as players, black and white, left for the service. Travel restrictions made scheduling difficult, particularly for the Negro leagues, as clubs relied on revenue from their numerous barnstorming exhibition games to help supplement their regular league income. Yet, there was also a positive effect for the Eagles, as black Newarkers used some of their increased war income to seek entertainment options, helping attendance at Eagles games. By 1943 the Eagles were making a profit for the first time.[24]

As the Eagles grew in popularity, they became a major presence in the Newark black experience. Max Manning was once quoted as saying, "The Eagles were to [black] Newark what the Dodgers were to Brooklyn."[25] Newark's white mayors, realizing the impact of this community, never missed an Eagles Opening Day. Black celebrities like boxing champion Joe Louis and singer-actress Lena Horne threw out first pitches. The now-demolished Grand Hotel in downtown Newark was the place where Eagles players gathered after games to rub elbows with black high society. Activist, author, and poet Amiri Baraka (LeRoi Jones), in his *Autobiography of LeRoi Jones*, explained, "At the Grand Hotel, the ballplayers and slick people could meet. … [The Eagles were] legitimate black heroes … pure love … in the laughter and noise and colors and easy hot dogs, there was something of us celebrating ourselves … in the flying around the bases and sliding and home runs and arguments and triumphs there was more of ourselves in celebration than we were normally ever permitted. It was ours."[26]

In 1942 Abe Manley found another jewel on the fields of New Jersey – Paterson's Larry Doby. A second baseman, Doby was one of the best athletes who ever attended Paterson Eastside High School. Like Monte Irvin, Doby was a multisport athlete but eventually chose to concentrate on baseball.[27] As World War II ended, important players like Doby, Leon Day, Max Manning, and Monte Irvin began returning from the service, setting the stage for the greatest season ever of Newark Eagles baseball.

THE CHAMPIONSHIP 1946 SEASON

With World War II over, the Eagles and the Negro leagues settled back to business in 1946, but there was a glaring change in the plight of the black ballplayer that caused both joy for players yet consternation for team management. Branch Rickey's signing of Jackie Robinson of the Negro American League's Kansas City Monarchs to a minor-league contract with the white Brooklyn Dodgers was an affirmation of changing attitudes toward blacks. Besides the contributions that blacks made to the war effort at home, many also served in the military. Although still in segregated units, they nevertheless fought side by side with their white counterparts

The 1946 Newark Eagles championship team included Hall of Fame player Leon Day, Larry Doby, Monte Irvin, and Biz Mackey and Hall of Fame co-owner Effa Manley. (National Baseball Hall of Fame)

to defeat the Axis powers. The question immediately surfaced: If blacks could fight for the country in war, why couldn't they play major-league baseball? The answer was obvious, but only Branch Rickey had the courage to address the issue and the wisdom to pick Jackie Robinson because of the challenges that Rickey knew he would face. Rickey signed other blacks for the 1946 season, among them another of Abe Manley's young players found in New Jersey. Pitcher Don Newcombe of Elizabeth, at age 19, won eight games against four losses for the 1945 Eagles, and was depended upon to anchor the Eagles pitching staff for 1946 and hopefully for years to come.[28] Even though happy to see Newcombe get a chance in white baseball, Effa Manley was quick to realize how the signing of Negro league players without compensation to their clubs was a concern for the future. She "expressed elation" for Newcombe, but also said, "What will become of colored baseball leagues if players are picked out by major league owners without consulting the team management? … If Rickey wanted to employ a player from a major league chain, I believe he would first negotiate with the player's club. … I believe the same courtesy is warranted where a colored league is concerned."[29] She would confront Rickey directly over this issue in the future, and her fears for the long-term viability of her business were genuine.

The 1946 season opened impressively for the Eagles. On May 5, with 8,500 fans in attendance at Ruppert Stadium, pitcher Leon Day no-hit the Philadelphia Stars, 2-0. Day walked one batter, and two others reached base on errors by shortstop Billy Felder.[30] The team started the season with a 5-5 record, causing Abe Manley and manager Biz Mackey to make a crucial change. In early June they obtained third baseman Andrew "Pat" Patterson from Philadelphia, and moved Monte Irvin from the outfield to shortstop. This move enabled Bob Harvey to play the outfield on a regular basis.[31] The infield defense tightened up and the batting order strengthened. Larry Doby and Irvin were a dependable double-play combination. Besides Patterson at third, Lennie Pearson played first base. Joining Harvey in the outfield were Jimmy Wilkes and Johnny Davis. Leon Ruffin and Biz Mackey shared the catching duties. Leon Day was joined on the strong pitching staff by Max Manning, Rufus Lewis, and Len Hooker.[32] The Eagles were locked and loaded.

Black fans, while keeping one eye on the daily exploits of Jackie Robinson for the Triple-A Montreal Royals, were noticing a new resolve by the Negro league players. Up to 1946, Negro baseball was marked by a relaxed looseness. Robinson's signing changed that. Effa Manley, in a letter to Dan Parker of the *New York Mirror* in mid-July, wrote that "Negro ballplayers are taking the work seriously for the first time. Up to now their work has been a lot of fun. Now they all think they have a chance to enter White Major League baseball, and that is the thing they would love to do."[33]

The 1946 Eagles steamrolled through the Negro National League, with a first-half record of 25-9 and an equally impressive second half of 22-7. They batted .304 as a team. Monte Irvin led the league with a .395 average. Larry Doby batted .348, Pat Patterson .337, Johnny Davis .335, and Lennie Pearson .300. On the mound, Max Manning finished the season at 12-1, Leon Day won 11 while losing 4, and rookie-of-the-year Rufus Lewis was 9-1.[34]

The Kansas City Monarchs won the pennant of the Negro American League. Led by the legendary pitcher Satchel Paige, their formidable lineup included league batting champion Buck O'Neil (.350), home-run leader Willard Brown (13),[35] and Hank Thompson, who would play with Monte Irvin on the New York Giants from 1949 through 1956. The Negro World Series promised to be a good one, and in order to help maximize revenue and profits, Game One was scheduled for New York's Polo Grounds and Game Five at Chicago's Comiskey Park, with all other games scheduled for the team's home parks. Nearly 19,500 were in the Polo Grounds on September 17 to see the Eagles lose to Paige, 2-1. The series moved to Ruppert Stadium on September 19. To mark the occasion, Effa Manley spent nearly $700 to outfit the Eagles in new white home uniforms. Nearly 10,000 attended to see Joe Louis throw out the first pitch and Max Manning defeat the Monarchs, 7-4.[36] After splitting Games Three and Four in Kansas City, the Eagles were defeated in Chicago and returned to Ruppert Stadium behind three games to two, and in danger of elimination.

Game Six did not begin well for the Eagles as the Monarchs scored five runs in the first inning off Leon Day. Len Hooker relieved Day and stopped the Monarchs. Monte Irvin led the Eagles with four hits, including two home runs, to help defeat the Monarchs, 9-7, forcing a deciding seventh game.[37] In Game Seven, Rufus Lewis scattered eight hits and outpitched Ford Smith to defeat the Monarchs, 3-2. Key RBIs by Monte Irvin and Johnny Davis led the Eagles.[38]

Effa and Abe Manley had their long-sought-after championship. The club drew over 120,000 fans to Ruppert Stadium in 1946 and recorded a profit of $25,000.[39] The Eagles were revered in black Newark – they were swinging away in Newark's heyday. The future looked bright for both the Eagles and Newark. Or so it seemed.

THE QUICK DEMISE OF THE NEWARK EAGLES

Effa Manley had an unwitting part in sowing the seeds of the Newark Eagles' destruction. In 1942 she took on the honorable cause of integrating white baseball. She joined over 70 prominent blacks, social and labor leaders, and politicians in the Congress of Industrial Organizations' (CIO) Citizen's Committee to End Jim Crow in Baseball. She proposed the Negro leagues sending the finest player they had, one who could perform at the highest level while withstanding the pressure, to the major leagues. Branch Rickey, who became her adversary, followed her advice with the signing of Jackie Robinson.[40] More black players signed to play in white baseball in 1947. Bill Veeck, owner of the Cleveland Indians of the American League, signed Larry Doby away from the Eagles. After receiving no compensation for Don Newcombe, Effa Manley received $15,000 from Veeck for Doby, who played his final game in Newark on July 4, 1947. The Eagles fell from first place, losing the pennant to the New York Cubans.[41] Monte Irvin was signed by Branch Rickey but relented when Manley threatened legal action. Irvin then signed with the New York Giants in 1948. By then, it did not matter. The Newark Eagles and the Negro National League were essentially put out of business.

Black attendance at Brooklyn Dodgers games increased by 400 percent from 1946 to 1947. Meanwhile, the Eagles' attendance dipped to 57,000 in 1947 and dropped even more in 1948. The Manleys lost $50,000 during these two seasons. They sold the club and it was moved to Houston for the 1949 season.[42] All but three clubs from the Negro National League survived, but the league itself did not. The remaining clubs, including the Houston Eagles, were merged into the Negro American League.

They heyday of the city of Newark was also ending. James Overmyer quoted Newark historian John Cunningham as writing, "After the economic euphoria of the wartime defense industry ended … its aged industrial sections were losing tenants and jobs to areas outside its crowded urban setting, slum housing was still prevalent for the lower classes, and the city's tax base, from which could come the money to cure some of these ills, had shrunk dramatically."[43] Newark became a city of urban blight. It experienced a tragic week of civil disobedience in 1967. The big retailers left. Ironically, Ruppert Stadium was also demolished in 1967. Since then, Newark has been fighting its way back, with economic progress being gained from downtown redevelopment. It still has a long way to go.

The *Star Ledger,* in an article remembering the Newark Eagles in 1996, stated, "After 10 years of hard times, the Eagles seemed to be on the way to real economic stability … but, in keeping with the irony that had so often haunted this league, they would be remembered as the team that remained only to turn out the lights on a world that seemed to have reached its finest hour only to find it was also its final hurrah."[44] Jerry Izenberg has been writing sports for the *Star Ledger* since 1951. Prior to that, he spent much time at Ruppert Stadium, watching the Eagles and the Bears play. In 2006, Izenberg reminisced, "I am thinking … of the Eagles I used to watch in Ruppert Stadium as a young kid … of their 1946 championship season with Larry Doby and Monte Irvin … with Day and Manning … with Biz Mackey and Lennie Pearson. …

It was great for this city that has precious little to root for these days. It's important that the joy of what that team was live on in memory."[45]

NOTES

1   Bob Golon, *No Minor Accomplishment: The Revival of New Jersey Professional Baseball* (New Brunswick, New Jersey: Rutgers University Press/Rivergate Books, 2008), 10.

2   James M. DiClerico and Barry J. Pavelec, *The Jersey Game* (New Brunswick, New Jersey: Rutgers University Press, 1991), 136-137.

3   Merl F. Kleinknecht, "The Negro Leagues: A Brief History," in Dick Clark and Larry Lester, eds., *The Negro Leagues Book* (Cleveland: Society for American Baseball Research, 1994), 15.

4   DiClerico, 140-141.

5   Golon, 17, 18.

6   James Overmyer, *Queen of the Negro Leagues: Effa Manley and the Newark Eagles* (Lanham, Maryland: Scarecrow Press, 1998), 32.

7   Overmyer, 40.

8   DiClerico, 153.

9   Overmyer, 71.

10   Ibid.

11   Overmyer, 85.

12   Dick Clark and Larry Lester, "Negro Baseball Register," in *The Negro Leagues Book,* 240.

13   Ibid.

14   Overmyer, 55-56.

15   Ibid.

16   Overmyer, 106.

17   Peter Genovese, "Where the Eagles Soared: The African-American Newark Baseball Team Was Regarded as a Source of Pride and Identity in Segregated Times," *Star Ledger* (Newark, New Jersey), February 13, 2009: 27.

18   Jerry Izenberg, "Unfortunately, the Hall Missed This Call," *Star Ledger* (Newark, New Jersey), July 17, 2008: 23.

19   Amy Ellis Nutt, "Baseball's 'Black' Trailblazer: The Peculiar Story of Effa Manley and Her Negro League Team," *Star Ledger* (Newark, New Jersey), February 22, 2008: 8.

20   Ibid.

21   Overmyer, 60-61.

22   Overmyer, 176.

23   Overmyer, 167-169.

24   Overmyer, 177.

25   Overmyer, 58.

26   Genovese, 27.

27   DiClerico, 151.

28   "Organized Baseball Records," in *The Negro Leagues Book,* 327.

29   "Eagles Boss Raps Rickey Method of Signing Hurler," *New Jersey Afro-American,* April 20, 1946.

30   Jim Ryall, "Fireworks at Eagles Game," *Newark Evening News,* May 6, 1946.

31   Overmyer, 200.

32   DiClerico, 156.

33   Effa Manley, letter to Dan Parker, July 19, 1946.

34   John Robinson, "New Jersey Spotlight," *New Jersey Afro-American,* September 14, 1946.

35   "Seasonal Leaders," in *The Negro Leagues Book,* 238-239.

36   Overmyer, 204.

37   "Eagle Homers Knot Series," *Newark Evening News,* September 28, 1946.

38   "Eagles Hit in Clutches," *Newark Evening News,* September 30, 1946.

39   Overmyer, 203

40   Overmyer, 216.

41   Overmyer, 239.

42   Golon, 19.

43   Overmyer, 210.

44   "Newark Baseball's Finest Hour: The Eagles' Championship in 1946," *Star Ledger* (Newark, New Jersey), May 19, 1996.

45   Jerry Izenberg, "Baseball's Chance to Right a Wrong," *Star Ledger* (Newark, New Jersey), February 26, 2006.

CONTRIBUTORS

Niall Adler has spent much of his career in sports PR. He has worked baseball games on four continents, which has included USA Baseball, Australian Baseball, Stanford, and Long Beach State Baseball.

Richard Applegate serves as a SABR publications volunteer following his career retirement as a church pastor and professor in the fields of leadership and ethics. He holds a Masters in Management Science from Friends University. He and his wife Ida live in the St. Louis community and have six grandchildren and two great grandchildren. He was introduced to the game of baseball via the *Mutual Game of the Day* in the late 40's and early 50's while growing up on a wheat farm in NW Kansas. The Brooklyn Dodgers became his favorite team and Jackie Robinson was his boyhood hero.

Richard Bogovich is the author of *Kid Nichols: A Biography of the Hall of Fame Pitcher* and *The Who: A Who's Who,* both published by McFarland & Co. He has contributed to such SABR books as *Bittersweet Goodbye: The Black Barons, the Grays, and the 1948 Negro League World Series* and wrote SABR's biography of an early member of the Pittsburgh Crawfords, Charlie Hughes. He works for the Wendland Utz law firm in Rochester, Minnesota.

Frederick C. (Rick) Bush joined SABR in March 2014. Since that time he has written articles for numerous SABR books and the Biography and Games Project websites. In addition to the current volume about the Newark Eagles, Rick and Bill Nowlin also co-edited *Bittersweet Goodbye: The Black Barons, the Grays, and the 1948 Negro League World Series* and are already at work on another Negro Leagues book about the 1935 Pittsburgh Crawfords.

Rick lives with his wife, Michelle, and their three sons – Michael, Andrew, and Daniel – in the greater Houston area, and he teaches English at Wharton County Junior College in Sugar Land.

Ralph Carhart is a theatre director and manager, and a baseball historian. He is the head of SABR's 19th Century Baseball Grave Marker Project, an endeavor that placed its fifth stone, for Hicks Hayhurst, in Philadelphia in spring of 2019. He has contributed to the SABR books *The 1986 New York Mets: There Was More Than Game Six, Bittersweet Goodbye: The Black Barons, the Grays and the 1948 Negro League World Series,* and an as-yet untitled volume on players from the Dominican Republic. Ralph is the creator of The Hall Ball, a project that aimed to photograph a single baseball with all of the members of the Hall of Fame, living and deceased. His book about the journey of The Hall Ball is scheduled to be published by McFarland & Company, Inc. later in 2019.

Dan D'Addona is the author of *In Cobb's Shadow: The Hall of Fame Careers of Sam Crawford, Harry Heilmann and Heinie Manush,* published by McFarland & Co. He is an award-winning journalist as sports editor at *The Holland Sentinel* in Holland, Michigan, where he lives with his wife Corene and daughters Lena and Mara. He also writes for *Swimming World Magazine* and interned at the National Baseball Hall of Fame in Cooperstown. He is a member of SABR's Negro Leagues Committee and Deadball Era Committee.

Amy Essington is a lecturer in the history departments at California State University, Fullerton, and Cal Poly Pomona. She is the Executive Director of the Historical Society of Southern California. She completed a Ph.D. at Claremont Graduate University and is the author of *The Integration of the Pacific Coast League: Race,*

Baseball, and the West (University of Nebraska Press, 2018). Amy was an intern at the National Baseball Hall of Fame Library and the Smithsonian's National American History Museum.

Bob Golon is a retired manuscript librarian and archivist at Princeton Theological Seminary Library, Special Collections, Princeton, New Jersey. He also spent three years as Labor Archivist at Rutgers University Special Collections and University Archives. Bob is Past-President of the New Jersey Library Association History and Preservation section and a member of the Mid-Atlantic Regional Archives Conference. Prior to getting his MLIS from Rutgers University in 2004, Bob worked 18 years in sales and marketing for the Hewlett-Packard Company, working with the group that established the successful dealer distribution channel for HP printers and personal computers. A baseball historian and SABR member, Bob has been a contributor to various publications, can be seen prominently on the YES Network's "Yankeeography – Casey Stengel," and is the author of *No Minor Accomplishment: The Revival of New Jersey Professional Baseball* (Rivergate Books / Rutgers University Press, 2008).

Margaret M. "Peggy" Gripshover is a Professor of Geography at Western Kentucky University. She earned her Ph.D. in Geography at the University of Tennessee and her M.S. and B.S. degrees in Geography from Marshall University. She has been a SABR member since 2006 and combines her love of baseball with her geographic research on race, ethnicity, urbanization, horse racing, and cultural landscapes. Peggy has published articles in the *Baseball Research Journal*, contributed a chapter to *Northsiders: Essays on the History and Culture of the Chicago Cubs*, edited by Gerald R. Wood and Andy Hazucha (McFarland, 2008), and a chapter in *Bittersweet Goodbye: The Black Barons, the Grays, and the 1948 Negro League World Series*, edited by Frederick C. Bush and Bill Nowlin (SABR, 2017). She is a native of Cincinnati and lives in Bowling Green, Kentucky, with her husband Thomas L. Bell and their Australian Shepherd, Bella.

Leslie Heaphy, Associate Professor of History at Kent State University at Stark, has written and edited books and articles on the Negro Leagues, Women's baseball, and the New York Mets.

Bill Hickman was the long-serving Chair of SABR's Pictorial History Committee. He has developed the Negro Leagues Image Index, a spreadsheet to identify images of Negro Leagues players, managers, and executives. He currently maintains the "near major leaguers" data base on the SABR website. He is the team historian for the Bethesda Big Train club in the Cal Ripken Collegiate Baseball League. He has published numerous baseball articles; this is his second for a SABR book. He is a graduate of Northwestern University and the Harvard Business School. He has served on the faculty of the US Naval Academy.

Paul Hofmann, a SABR member since 2002, is the Associate Vice President for International Affairs at Sacramento State University and frequent contributor to SABR publications. Paul is a native of Detroit, Michigan and lifelong Detroit Tigers fan. He currently resides in Folsom, California.

Dr. Lawrence Hogan is Professor Emeritus, Union County County, Cranford, New Jersey. Among other publications, he is the author of *The Forgotten History of African American Baseball,* and producer of the documentary *Before You Can Say Jackie Robinson: Black Baseball in America in the Era of the Color Line.*

Jay Hurd is a librarian, retired from Harvard University where he worked as the Preservation Review Librarian for Widener Library. He is also a museum educator and interpreter. A longtime member of the Society for American Baseball Research (SABR), he contributes to the SABR Baseball Biography Project, and presents on baseball related topics including the Negro Leagues, baseball literature for children and young adults, women in baseball, and baseball and the Blue Laws. Currently, he is studying baseball in Rhode Island. A longtime fan of the Boston Red Sox, Jay relocated from Medford, Massachusetts to Bristol, Rhode Island in 2016.

William H. (Bill) Johnson and his wife Chris live in central Georgia. He retired from the US Navy in 2006 after a 24-year career in naval aviation, has written a full-length biography, *Hal Trosky: A Baseball Biography* (McFarland & Co., 2017), along with over two dozen essays for the SABR BioProject. He is now working on a biography of Negro League star Art "Superman" Pennington.

Thomas E. Kern was born and raised in Southwest Pennsylvania. Listening to the mellifluous voices of Bob Prince and Jim Woods in his youth, how could one not become a lifelong Pirates fan? He contributed to SABR's 1979 Book on the 1979 Pittsburgh Pirates with a bio of Don Robinson. He now lives in Washington, DC, and sees the Nationals and Orioles as often as possible. He is a SABR member dating back to the mid-1980s. With a love and appreciation for Negro League Baseball, in addition to his bio of Leon Day (having met him at a baseball card show in the early 1990s), he has written a biography of John Henry Lloyd and a short history of the Homestead Grays, all published by SABR. Tom's day job is in the field of transportation technology.

Bob LeMoine grew up in Maine and joined SABR in 2013. He rarely finds a SABR book project he doesn't like. Recent interests include 19th Century baseball and forgotten games from the Negro Leagues. He co-edited (with Bill Nowlin) *Boston's First Nine: the 1871-75 Boston Red Stockings*. A future project will explore the Boston Beaneaters of the 1890s. Bob lives in New Hampshire and works as a librarian.

Len Levin, a retired newspaper editor, is the grammarian and copyeditor for the Rhode Island Supreme Court. He has been the copyeditor for most of SABR's recent books. He, his wife, and their cat live in Providence, Rhode Island.

Mike Mattsey lives in Sacramento with his wife Maia and his son Otis. He is a long-time fan of the 2016 World Series champion Chicago Cubs and is an avid collector of prewar baseball cards and sports memorabilia related to the team. His favorite baseball moment was managing his son's Little League team to the 2018 championship. He graduated from Indiana University and holds a Master of Arts degree from Indiana State University where he successfully defended a paper examining the role of minor-league baseball in the Progressive Era South. He has written for SABR's BioProject and contributed to three SABR books.

John McMurray chairs both the Deadball Era Committee and the Oral History Committee for SABR. He is a past chair of SABR's Ritter Award subcommittee, which recognizes the best book on Deadball Era baseball published during the year prior.

Skip Nipper is author of *Baseball in Nashville* (2007, Arcadia Publishing), serves as secretary of the Nashville Old Timers Baseball Association, is a member of SABR (Society of American Baseball Research), and SABR's Grantland Rice-Fred Russell (Nashville) chapter. He and his wife Sheila reside in Mt. Juliet, Tennessee with their dog, Ellie, and cat, Stell. Together they have seven children and 17 grandchildren. They all love baseball.

Bill Nowlin was one of the founders of Rounder Records back in the year 1970. As his time with Rounder wound down, his activity writing about baseball wound up. He has written or co-written, edited or co-edited, several dozen books, mostly about baseball with about half of them as a volunteer for SABR. He lives in Cambridge, Massachusetts.

Richard J. Puerzer is an associate professor and chairperson of the Department of Engineering at Hofstra University. He has contributed to several SABR Books, including *Mustaches and Mayhem: The Oakland Athletics: 1972-1974* (2015), *When Pops Led the Family: The 1979 Pittsburgh Pirates* (2016), and *Bittersweet Goodbye: The Black Barons, The Grays, and the 1948 Negro League World Series* (2017). His writings on baseball have also appeared in: *Nine: A Journal of Baseball History and Culture, Black Ball, The National Pastime, The Cooperstown Symposium on Baseball and American Culture* proceedings, *Zisk*, and *Spitball*.

Chris Rainey is a retired teacher and baseball coach who now lives in Oxford, Ohio. He happily occupies his time now by researching and writing for SABR's BioProject. He has an odd fascination with obscure players and bringing their stories to SABR.

Curt Smith grew up near Rochester, New York, whose Red Wings often visited Ruppert Stadium. He enjoys recalling their rivalry with the Newark Bears—and learning about the wonder of the Newark Eagles. Smith's 17th book was released in 2018, *The Presidents and the Pastime: The History of Baseball and the White House*, the first book to chronicle in-depth the tie between two American institutions. Smith's prior books include *Voices of The Game, The Voice,* and *Pull Up a Chair: The Vin Scully Story.* From 1989-93, he wrote more speeches than anyone else for President George H.W. Bush. Smith is Senior Lecturer of English at the University of Rochester and a GateHouse Media columnist who has hosted or keynoted the Great Fenway Writers Series, numerous Smithsonian Institution series, and the Cooperstown Symposium on Baseball and American culture. The former *The Saturday Evening Post* senior editor has written ESPN TV's *Voices of The Game* series, created the Franklin Roosevelt Award in Communication at the National Radio Hall of Fame, and been named to the Judson Welliver Society of former Presidential speechwriters.

Bill Staples, Jr. has a passion for researching and telling the untold stories of the "international pastime." His areas of expertise include Japanese American and Negro Leagues baseball history as a context for exploring the themes of civil rights, cross-cultural relations, and globalization. He is a board member of the Nisei Baseball Research Project, member of the Japanese American Citizens League, and chairman of the SABR Asian Baseball Committee. He is the author of *Kenichi Zenimura, Japanese American Baseball Pioneer* (McFarland, 2011), winner of the 2012 SABR Baseball Research Award, and coauthor of *Gentle Black Giants: A History of Negro Leaguers in Japan* (NBRP Press, 2019). Bill lives in Chandler, Arizona, with his wife and two children and is an active community volunteer and youth coach.

As a longtime fan of the Negro League baseball ever since he read *Only the Ball Was White* by Robert Peterson and a fan of the New York Yankees for more than forty years, **Mark S. Sternman** wishes that the 1946 Newark Eagles could have taken on the 1946 Boston Red Sox. Sternman would have rooted ardently for the Eagles.

Bryan Steverson is a lifelong baseball fan and a founding member of the East Tennessee Chapter of SABR. He is a HOF sustaining and NLBM member. As a researcher and writer, he has taught and given presentations at numerous local and national venues. Bryan is the author of three books on baseball, *Amazing Baseball Heroes, Inspirational Negro League Stories* (2011), *Baseball, A Special Gift from God* (2014), and the recently published, *Baseball's Brotherhood Team* (2018). In 2014 he was named the recipient of the Norman "Tweed" Webb Award for Lifetime Achievement by the Negro Leagues Committee of SABR. Originally from Portsmouth, Virginia, Bryan is a 1964 graduate of Virginia Tech. He is a veteran with an additional degree from the Univ. of Minnesota and further post graduate work at Cal. Poly in Pomona. In 2005, he retired from Alcoa, Inc as Chief Metallurgist of the Rigid Packing Division. He and his wife, Barbara, have five children and nine grandchildren. They are currently in the process of relocating from Maryville, Tennessee to Venice, Florida.

Jeb Stewart is a lawyer in Birmingham, Alabama, who enjoys taking his sons (Nolan and Ryan) and his wife Stephanie to the Rickwood Classic each year. He has been a SABR member since 2012, and is a Board Member of the Friends of Rickwood Field. He is a regular contributor to the *Rickwood Times* newspaper and has presented at the annual Southern Association Baseball Conference on several occasions. He spent most of his youth pitching a tennis ball against his front porch steps, hoping a Yankees scout would happen by and discover him. Although he remains undiscovered, he still has a passion for baseball.

Tim Tassler joined SABR in 2014 and is currently the chair of the Kekionga Chapter in Fort Wayne, Indiana. He has spent the last five years researching black baseball in northeast Indiana and is also a board member of the Northeast Indiana Baseball Association (NEIBA) – Fort Wayne Baseball Hall of Fame.

David Wilkie is an Upper Elementary teacher at the Montessori School of the Mahoning Valley in Youngstown, Ohio. He grew up in Western Canada idolizing the San Francisco Giants and Willie McCovey. This is his second SABR biography, the first being on Negro League legend Sam Bankhead for the book, *Bittersweet Goodbye*. He lives with his wife and three kids and plans to continue writing biographies on forgotten Negro League players.

Made in the USA
Coppell, TX
05 November 2020